Conclusion

Calvinism was the most dynamic and disruptive religious force of the later sixteenth century. Its emergence on the international scene shattered the precarious equilibrium established in the first generation of the Reformation, and precipitated three generations of religious warfare. This new 39 collection of original essays probes different aspects of this complex phenomenon at a local level. Contributors present the results of their detailed work on societies as diverse as France, Germany, Highland Scotland and Hungary. Among wider themes approached are the impact of Calvin's writings, Calvinism in higher education, the contrasting fates of Reformed preachers in town and country, Calvinist discipline and apocalyptic thought, and the shadowy affinity of merchants and scholars who formed a critical part of the 'Calvinist International'.

Calvinism in Europe, 1540–1620

Calvinism in Europe, 1540–1620

Edited by

Andrew Pettegree
University of St Andrews

Alastair Duke
University of Southampton

and

Gillian Lewis
University of Oxford

CAMBRIDGE
UNIVERSITY PRESS

Published by the Press Syndicate of the University of Cambridge
The Pitt Building, Trumpington Street, Cambridge CB2 1RP
40 West 20th Street, New York, NY 10011-4211, USA
10 Stamford Road, Oakleigh, Melbourne 3166, Australia

First published 1994
Reprinted 1996
First paperback edition published 1996

Printed in Great Britain at the University Press, Cambridge

A catalogue record for this book is available from the British Library

Library of Congress cataloguing in publication data

Calvinism in Europe, 1540–1620 / edited by Andrew Pettegree,
Alastair Duke, and Gillian Lewis.
   p.   cm.
Papers originally presented at a conference held at
St Anne's College, Oxford, Sept. 1–4, 1993.
Includes bibliographical references.
ISBN 0 521 43269 3
1. Calvinism – Europe – History – Congresses. I. Pettegree, Andrew.
II. Duke, A. C. III. Lewis, Gillian.
BX9422.5.C35   1994
284'.24'0903 – dc20   93-37383   CIP

ISBN 0 521 43269 3 hardback
ISBN 0 521 57452 8 paperback

SE

Contents

Figures

Notes on contributors

ALASTAIR DUKE is Reader in History at the University of Southampton.

GILLIAN LEWIS is Fellow and Tutor in Modern History at St Anne's College, Oxford.

ANDREW PETTEGREE is Director of the St Andrews Reformation Studies Institute and Lecturer in Modern History at St Andrews University.

ROBERT M. KINGDON is Hilldale Professor in the Institute for Research in the Humanities, University of Wisconsin-Madison.

BRUCE GORDON is Lecturer in Modern History at St Andrews University.

FRANCIS HIGMAN is Director of the Institut d'Histoire de la Réformation, Geneva.

PENNY ROBERTS is Lecturer in History at the University of Warwick.

MARK GREENGRASS is Senior Lecturer in History at the University of Sheffield.

GUIDO MARNEF is Lecturer in History at the University of Antwerp.

BODO NISCHAN is Professor of History at East Carolina University, Greenville, North Carolina.

DAVID P. DANIEL is Executive Director of the Slovak Academic Information Agency in Bratislava.

JANE DAWSON is the John Laing Lecturer in the History and Theology of the Reformation at New College, Edinburgh.

OLE PETER GRELL is a Research Fellow of the Wellcome Institute for the History of Medicine, Cambridge University.

Preface

The papers collected in this volume were originally delivered at a conference on European Calvinism at St Anne's College, Oxford, 1–4 September 1992. The editors and contributors gratefully acknowledge the part played by those who attended this conference, whose questions and contributions in discussion are reflected in the revised versions published here. In addition, the assistance of Julian Crowe of the St Andrews University Computing Laboratory has been invaluable in rendering computer discs into a compatible form.

Abbreviations

AHR	*American Historical Review*
ARG	*Archiv für Reformationsgeschichte*
Bèze, *Correspondance*	*Correspondance de Théodore de Bèze*, ed. Hippolyte Aubert, Henri Meylan *et al.* (Geneva, 1960–)
BCRH	*Bulletin de la Commission Royale d'Histoire*
BHR	*Bibliothèque d'Humanisme et Renaissance*
BN	Bibliothèque Nationale, Biblioteca Nacional
BSHPF	*Bulletin de la Société de l'Histoire du Protestantisme Français*
CH	*Church History*
CO	*Calvini Opera*
CR	*Corpus Reformatorum*
EHR	*English Historical Review*
HJ	*Historical Journal*
JEH	*Journal of Ecclesiastical History*
NAK	*Nederlands Archief voor Kerkgeschiedenis*
P & P	*Past and Present*
RCP	*Registre de la Compagnie des Pasteurs de Genève*, ed. R.M. Kingdon, J.-F. Bergier *et al.* (Geneva, 1964–)
RGP	Rijks Geschiedkundige Publicatiën
RHPR	*Revue d'Histoire et Philosophie Religieuses*
RV	*Acta der provinciale en particuliere synoden gehouden in de noordelijke Nederlanden gedurende de jaren 1572–1620*, ed. J. Reitsma and S.D. van Veen (8 vols., Groningen, 1892–9)
SCH	Studies in Church History
SCJ	*Sixteenth Century Journal*
TRE	*Theologische Realenzyklopädie*
WMV	*Werken der Marnix-Vereeniging*

1   Perspectives on international Calvinism

Alastair Duke

With the notable exception of Scandinavia, Lutheran churches were confined to the German lands, to the German-speaking minorities in the Slav countries and to foreign merchants who traded with the cities of the Empire. By contrast Reformed Protestant communities were scattered, more or less thickly, right across late sixteenth-century Europe, from Transylvania to the Western Isles of Scotland: Italy, the Iberian peninsula and the Nordic countries alone proved unreceptive. Reformed Protestant churches not only flourished, or at least cohabited with other confessions, in several cultures, they exhibited a marked sense of confessional solidarity. For that reason the moderate English Puritan William Bradshaw declined to speak of 'those Churches being all the same household of faith that we are' as 'Forreyners ... because they are all citizens of heaven and we all make one family.'[1]

True, their Catholic and Lutheran enemies sometimes took needless alarm at the bellicose fraternal rhetoric in which Reformed theologians and statesmen indulged. Pulpit invective against the forces of the Antichrist did not necessarily translate into effective military support as the Elector Palatine found to his cost in 1620. Yet we cannot therefore dismiss the notion of a Calvinist international as a figment of Catholic imagination. Through their collections and their fast days Reformed communities not only inculcated the habit of lending material and spiritual help to their 'distressed' coreligionists in France and the Palatinate, they became participants in an unfolding apocalyptic drama whose stage was Europe.[2] In the 'language of Canaan' so natural to ministers of the Word, they were engaged as the 'children of God' in a spiritual warfare with the 'children of the world'.

To a marked degree Calvin was himself the architect of this cosmopolitan

---

[1] P. Collinson, 'England and International Calvinism, 1558–1640' in M. Prestwich (ed.), *International Calvinism 1541–1715* (Oxford, 1985), p. 213.
[2] For a detailed investigation of the collections initiated by the London Dutch consistory chiefly for 'the poor exiled Ministers of the Palatinate' during the Thirty Years War, see O. Grell, *Dutch Calvinists in Early Stuart London. The Dutch Church in Austin Friars, 1603–1642* (Leiden, 1989), ch. 5.

character. His reverence for the catholicity of the church and his lifelong dedication to 'the common defence of the gospel'[3] prevented the French-born reformer from devoting himself for long exclusively to ecclesiastical matters in Geneva. The visible church comprised, in his opinion, the 'whole multitude of men spread over the earth who profess to worship one God and Christ'.[4] This church also contained 'individual churches, disposed in towns and villages according to human need, so that each rightly has the name and authority of the church'.[5] Calvin did not expect such 'individual churches' to achieve 'perfect conformity in ceremonies',[6] and he warned that 'we must not thoughtlessly forsake the church because of any petty dissensions'.[7] In 1553 the French-speaking Reformed congregation at Wesel in Cleves was pressed to follow the Lutheran eucharistic rites and to use candles and hosts. Conscience-stricken, the strangers sought the advice of the Genevan ministers, only to be told bluntly to conform 'in all those ceremonies, which do not have a decisive influence on our faith so that the unity of the church is not disturbed either by our excessive severity or timidity'.[8]

The divisions within Christendom as a result of the Reformation made the definition of the true church an urgent matter. Luther invariably made the preaching of the Word the first requirement, 'for God's people cannot be without God's Word', to which he usually added the sacraments and sometimes other signs, including discipline. The Anabaptists hedged their exclusive notion of the Christian congregation about with several more signs, six in the case of Menno Simons and no fewer than twelve according to Dirk Philips. Calvin however considered the indispensable characteristics of this visible church to be the pure preaching of the Word and the administration of the sacraments 'according to Christ's institution'. He also believed discipline to be essential to the 'well-being' of the church and he praised the revised Ecclesiastical Ordinances of 1561 'as a light [for] all the churches instructed in the Christian reformation'. Yet if he deliberately stopped short, at least in principle, of making discipline a mark of the church, it is less clear quite how preaching and the sacraments could in practice be detached from discipline. Indeed the very care Calvin lavished

[3] W. Nijenhuis, *Calvinus oecumenicus. Calvijn en de eenheid der kerk in het licht van zijn briefwisseling* (The Hague, 1959), pp. 143–4.

[4] *Institutes of the Christian Religion*, Bk. IV, i, 7.

[5] *Institutes*, Bk. IV, i, 9. The Dutch statesman and lay Calvinist theologian Philippe de Marnix faithfully expressed this notion of the universal church when he reminded a coreligionist in 1585 'that the Church of God is not tied down to particular places or seats: it is Catholic, that is to say Universal, not Alexandrian, nor Roman, nor Belgic'. *Philips van Marnix van St. Aldegonde. Godsdienstige en kerkelijke geschriften*, ed. J.J. van Toorenen-bergen (4 vols., The Hague, 1878), IV, p. 66.

[6] W.J. Bouwsma, *John Calvin. A Sixteenth Century Portrait* (New York–Oxford, 1988), p. 224.   [7] *Institutes*, Bk. IV, i, 12.   [8] Nijenhuis, *Calvinus oecumenicus*, 84–5.

on the consistory at Geneva warns us that within his comprehensive view of the visible church there lurked a sectarian streak which was, as we shall see shortly, to have momentous consequences for the further development of Reformed ecclesiology. Significantly, several Reformed churches elevated discipline to the third *nota ecclesiae* even in Calvin's own lifetime.[9]

Nevertheless, since Calvin's discussion of the church had been remarkably free from confessionalism and his attitude to church order (to a degree) pragmatic, his influence extended well beyond the synodal-presbyterian churches emerging in the late 1550s. Indeed the Genevan reformer initially owed his authoritative position in the theology of the English Elizabethan church to his flexibility in the matter of church order and of discipline. As a result both the 'zealous Gospellers' and their opponents in the English Elizabethan church could appeal to 'that learned and godly minister of Christ Maister Calvin'.

Calvin's ecumenical instincts also appeared in his sincere concern for friendly relations with other reformers. He especially deplored the conflicts between the Swiss and the German Protestants because these played into the hands of the enemies of the gospel, and he therefore worked for a *rapprochement* between Zurich and Wittenberg. Calvin concealed neither his distaste for the Lutheran liturgy nor his dismay at the deficient discipline in the German evangelical churches, yet he always held Luther in the highest regard and took an evident delight when the older reformer commended one of his works.[10] The outbreak of the second sacramentarian controversy in 1552, into which the gnesio-Lutheran Joachim Westphal dragged Calvin, first undermined this policy of reconciliation and then wrecked it in 1557. Though Calvin lamented this outcome, the debate about the real presence extended his reputation in Germany among non-Lutheran Protestants and from that time the stranger churches there tended to look to Geneva, rather than to Zurich, for advice.[11]

Swiss mistrust of the Lutheran theologians certainly contributed to the breakdown, but this only spurred Calvin on to seek an agreement with Bullinger. These efforts were crowned in 1549 when they concluded the Consensus Tigurinus, an agreed statement on the eucharist. This achievement brought Genevan Protestantism two important benefits. Locally, it

---

[9] J. Plomp, *De kerkelijke tucht bij Calvijn* (Kampen, 1969), 125–8, 208 n.355. The Scots, Belgic and Hungarian Confessions, composed between 1560–2, went beyond Calvin when they added discipline to the *notae ecclesiae*, though it is a moot point whether in this respect they went against the Genevan reformer.

[10] Nijenhuis, *Calvinus oecumenicus*, 131–41; R.D. Linder, 'The Early Calvinists and Martin Luther: A Study in Evangelical Solidarity', in J. Friedman (ed.), *Regnum, religio et ratio. Essays Presented to Robert M. Kingdon* (Sixteenth Century Essays and Studies, VIII, 1987), 103–16.

[11] A. Pettegree, 'The London Exile Community and the Second Sacramentarian Controversy, 1553–1560', *ARG*, 78 (1987), 223–52.

brought recognition from Zurich for Calvin and, though more grudgingly, for his church order so that when Calvin's theological and political opponents there appealed to Zurich for support, Bullinger was prepared to thwart their manoeuvres. In the context of the Reformation as a whole the agreement between the two leading Swiss theologians heralded a form of Protestantism which is more aptly described as 'Reformed' rather than 'Calvinist'.[12] The church order of Marten Micron, intended for use in the Dutch stranger church in London in Edward VI's reign, is a product of this hybrid churchmanship. For all Micron's regard for Calvin, he called the Zurichers 'our fathers, teachers and guides in the reformation of the churches' and he therefore adopted certain practices, among which the prophesyings, from the church at Zurich. These Ordinances might have lacked official sanction, yet they helped to shape the orders of other Dutch stranger churches as well as the church at Emden and, consequently, contributed to the earliest orders of the Reformed churches in the Dutch-speaking Low Countries.[13] The greater warmth of the relationship between the churches of Geneva and Zurich may also have persuaded Hungarian evangelicals, who at first looked to Bullinger, subsequently to extend their horizons to include Geneva.[14]

Ironically the actions of Catholic rulers also contributed to the formation of a Calvinist, or more properly Reformed, international. The repressive policies of Charles V and Philip II in the Low Countries, of Mary Tudor, of Francis I and Henry II in France and of the Holy Office in Spain and the Roman Inquisition in Italy not only created martyrs; they also drove many dissidents abroad, into the arms of the Reformed stranger churches. Though persecution compelled the religious dissidents to flee, the leading reformers added to their anguish: they declared the mass to be an abomination in which evangelicals could not in conscience partake. In the 1540s Calvin wrote scathingly of those 'protonataires delicatz' who heard the gospel yet did nothing, alleging in defence of their inaction the example of Nicodemus. Other reformers, including Pierre Viret and à Lasco, also joined the attack on those whom they called 'trimmers' or 'temporisers' because they continued to attend mass. 'Christians', they insisted, should

---

[12] The term 'Calvinist' as a pejorative description of a follower of Calvin first circulated in 1553 among evangelicals at Basel who deplored the execution of Servetus earlier that year. Calvin's rise to prominence is reflected in the rapid spread of this epithet, Pettegree, 'The London Exile Community', 251.

[13] A. Pettegree, *Emden and the Dutch Revolt. Exile and the Development of Reformed Protestantism* (Oxford, 1992), pp. 22–4; M. Micron, *De Christelicke Ordinancien der Nederlantscher Ghemeinten Christi te Londen (1554)* ed. W.F. Dankbaar (The Hague, 1956), pp. 23–30. Bullinger's theology may have also left its imprint on the Heidelberg Catechism (1563). It would, however, be a mistake to suppose that the agreement between Bullinger and Calvin settled the substantial differences between Zurich and Geneva on ecclesiastical discipline.   [14] See below David Daniel, ch. 11.

withdraw from the 'execrable blasphemies' of the Roman church, even at the risk of persecution or they should depart for some place where they might freely follow the gospel.[15]

Although assorted dissidents from France and the Low Countries had made their way to Germany since the early 1520s,[16] the first major diaspora of the magisterial Reformation began in the early 1540s. It coincided with the onset of the Counter Reformation and of confessionalisation, and continued until the outbreak of the wars in France and the Low Countries in the 1560s.[17] After 1542 a trickle of evangelicals began leaving the Veneto and the towns of northern Italy for Zurich and Geneva. At about the same time larger groups of merchants and skilled artisans emigrated from the Low Countries; Walloons headed for Wesel and Flemings, Brabanders and Hollanders went first to London and subsequently to Emden and the Lower Rhine. Meanwhile Walloon and French evangelicals, particularly from the lower Rhône valley, no longer as welcome at Strasburg after the Lutheran party gained the ascendancy there, made their way to Geneva. It is impossible to calculate the total number of emigrants, not least because the exiles were forever on the move. They could be the victims of a change in the religious régime of the host community or they might choose to leave to take advantage of commercial opportunities elsewhere. Some 800 English Protestants left for the Continent in Mary's reign while more than 5,000 refugees registered as *habitants* at Geneva in the decade 1549–60.[18] Aside from Geneva the chief cities of refuge in this first exodus were London and Frankfurt, each of which counted between 1 and 3,000 church members. At Emden where the Netherlanders (unlike the Walloons and the English Protestants) joined the town church the population of the town swelled by approximately one-third between 1555 and 1562.[19] In addition substantial communities of Netherlanders settled in the towns of the Lower Rhine as well as at Sandwich and Norwich.

In this period the experience of exile confirmed the Reformed character of the *emigrés*. Few of the dissidents would ever have encountered confessional Calvinism before they left their native cities. 'Églises dressées',

[15] E. Droz, 'Calvin et les nicodémites', in *Chemins de l'hérésie* (4 vols., Geneva, 1970–6), I, pp. 131–71.
[16] Already in 1524 Capito claimed that religious exiles from every country were finding asylum at Strasburg, P. Denis, *Les Églises d'étrangers en pays rhénans (1538–1564)* (Paris, 1984), p. 63. Anabaptists also sought refuge abroad but apart from Moravia they were no safe havens for them.
[17] The first 'stranger church' emerged at Strasburg in 1538 for the 'welsche', that is the French-speaking, fugitives and Calvin, then in exile from Geneva, served as its pastor.
[18] E.W. Monter, *Calvin's Geneva* (New York, 1967), pp. 165–7.
[19] H. Schilling, *Niederländische Exulanten im 16. Jahrhundert. Ihre Stellung im Sozialgefüge und im religiösen Leben deutscher und englischer Städte* (Gütersloh, 1972), pp. 175–9; Pettegree, *Emden and the Dutch Revolt*, p. 41.

congregations with consistories, only emerged around 1555, and though several hundred quickly sprang up in France, their first pastors were often autodidacts, hedge-preachers and ex-monks with scant knowledge of the Calvinist ministry. Most dissidents fled because they had fallen foul of the anti-heresy legislation, though some Flemings may have left for England in search of employment, rather than out of religious conviction. But whatever the reasons for their going, they gravitated out of choice or necessity towards the stranger congregations. Often aliens could only stay if they became members of the stranger churches, which stood surety for their good conduct. The churches were also charged with the relief of their own poor and recent arrivals might find employment within the congregation.[20] In other words, many of those who fled only became Calvinists after they had gone into exile. Except in the case of Emden for Dutch speakers and Geneva for francophones, differences of language and of confession not only set, but kept, the members of these stranger churches apart from the native populations and the consistories, which had political as well as religious responsibilities, did little to assist the process of integration.[21] Instead the Reformed leadership fostered the *esprit de corps* among the local strangers as well as a sense of belonging to a wider Calvinist fraternity. Informal networks not only linked the 'Églises du refuge' together but also extended to the 'churches under the cross'. French, Dutch and Walloon ministers met in the London *coetus*, the Walloon community at Antwerp kept in touch with the brethren at Wesel and Frankfurt and their Dutch-speaking colleagues received advice, ministers and books from Emden; Calvinists in foreign parts corresponded with family and friends left behind, Reformed merchants criss-crossed Europe on business and the immature congregations in France despatched their promising young men to Geneva to train for the ministry.

The development of the Calvinist international entered a new phase with the outbreak of civil war in France in 1562 and of the 'Troubles' in the Low Countries in 1566. Alva's repressive régime, the massacre of St Bartholomew and Parma's reconquest of Flanders and Brabant in the early 1580s reduced the once powerful and influential Protestant communities of Tournai, Paris, Rouen, Lyons, Ghent and Antwerp, to a pale shadow of their former selves. In Germany the succession of a Lutheran elector in the

---

[20] There was, however, less need to belong to a stranger church in a cosmopolitan city like Tudor London with its several alien communities than in the smaller English towns.

[21] Though contacts between natives and strangers were harder to police in London, the consistories of the Dutch and French churches in the capital still censured those members who married in the parish churches, A. Pettegree, *Foreign Protestant Communities in Sixteenth-Century London* (Oxford, 1986), pp. 186, 302–5. Work in progress on the foreign Protestants at Sandwich and Southampton suggests that few took English spouses in Elizabeth's reign.

Palatinate in 1576 precipitated an exodus of Calvinist ministers, some of whom subsequently served in the Reformed churches of the Low Countries. Since the existing stranger churches could not absorb these influxes, new Calvinist communities sprang up in south-east England and Germany as towns vied with one another to attract these industrious *emigrés*. The urban infrastructure of Holland and Zeeland profited hugely from the influx of Flemings and Brabanders during the first generation of the Dutch Republic's existence. These revived the cloth industry of Leiden, provided capital and commercial expertise for the Amsterdam market, expanded the printing industry, set up schools and bolstered the Reformed ministry. The culture too of the Dutch Golden Age is inconceivable without the literary and artistic contribution of these southern Netherlanders.[22]

In this period previously freestanding clandestine congregations in France slowly found niches in a presbyterian system with its pyramidal structure of consistories, colloquies and synods. The Calvinist churches in the Low Countries followed the French example. The national synod of Emden in 1571 prepared an ambitious blue-print for the organisation of the Netherlands churches 'scattered through Germany and East Friesland' as well as the 'churches under the cross'. The greater ecclesiastical convergence of the Calvinist world found expression in the mutual recognition of church orders, the widespread use of the Genevan and Heidelberg catechisms and increasingly the adoption of a presbyterian polity. Whereas Calvin had taken a rather relaxed view of church government, Beza showed himself to be increasingly intolerant of episcopacy. In his view the principle of the parity of ministers, enunciated at the first national synod of French Reformed churches in 1559 and reiterated at Emden in 1571, was alone in being in full accord with Scripture. Though the association of presbyterianism with Calvinism certainly gave the Reformed churches a sharper focus, it was at a price. In the ensuing debate about church order in England the proponents of episcopacy also claimed that the office of bishop was 'apostolical and divine'.[23] After the defeat of the English Presbyterians in

[22] It has been tentatively estimated that between 1540 and 1630 as many as 60,000 left the southern Netherlands for England and Germany, most of whom emigrated before 1585. Roughly 150,000 southerners may have settled in the United Provinces, mainly after 1584, of whom perhaps 35,000 reached the north from England or Germany. In all 175,000 southerners may have migrated, see J. Briels, *De Zuidnederlandse immigratie 1572–1630* (Haarlem, 1978) pp. 9–22 and his *Zuid-Nederlanders in de Republiek 1572–1630. Een demografische en cultuurhistorische studie* (St Niklaas, 1985), pp. 213–21. The scale of the migration from the southern Netherlands in the late sixteenth century bears comparison with the better known exodus of French Protestants under Louis XIV, calculated at 200,000 by P. Joutard, 'The Revocation of the Edict of Nantes: End or Renewal of French Protestantism?' in Prestwich (ed.), *International Calvinism*, pp. 346–7.

[23] W. Nijenhuis, 'Beza's Treatise "De triplici episcopatu"', in his *Ecclesia reformata. Studies on the Reformation* (Leiden, 1972), pp. 138–39.

the 1580s, it proved hard to disentangle the theology of Calvin from the offensive ecclesiology of Beza, and the discredit into which the latter fell with the late Elizabethan episcopate gradually dimmed 'the great reputation and renowne' of the Genevan reformer in England.

The conflicts in France and the Low Countries hastened the politicisation of Reformed Protestantism. A new vocabulary reflected this dilution of the purely religious agenda. Alongside such specifically confessional labels as 'Calvinist' and 'the Religion', contemporaries now also employed a party political terminology. They spoke of 'Huguenots', 'Beggars' and 'Patriots' and distinguished between 'gueux de religion et des Gueux d'estat'.[24] Their enemies claimed, with some justice, that the Protestant 'Cause' in France and 'the common Cause' in the Low Countries camouflaged outright rebellion. Some strict Calvinists too deplored the meshing of political and religious programmes. Perhaps this explains the conspicuous failure of the Reformed synod, meeting at Emden in 1571, to endorse William of Orange's enterprise for the 'restoration of the Netherlands'.[25] Yet despite such fastidiousness the politicisation proved irresistible. The freedom of worship granted to the Protestant *seigneurs hauts justiciers* since the edict of Amboise (1563) and the authority of the Huguenot political assemblies merely reflected the growing importance of the Protestant nobility in the French Calvinist movement. Likewise, the presence of Jeanne d'Albret and her son Henri of Navarre with Coligny and Orange's younger brother Louis of Nassau at the synod of La Rochelle in 1571 exposed the inseparability of political faction and religion as well as the interconnected character of the conflicts in France and the Low Countries.

The interventions of the Palatinate and Christian of Anhalt on behalf of the Huguenots, and of John Casimir and John VI of Nassau-Dillenburg in the Dutch Revolt brought small benefit to either cause. They did, however, demonstrate that Reformed Protestantism, only represented in the Empire before the conversion of the Elector Palatine in 1561 in the Calvinist stranger churches, now had the aggressive support of an influential minority of the German princes. The courts of the Electors Palatine (after 1561), and those of John VI of Nassau-Dillenburg (after 1577) and John I of Zweibrücken (after 1588) and Christian of Anhalt (after 1596) became the magnets for a talented, if restless, array of Reformed theologians, academics, learned counsellors and pastors. Few of these were native-born and

---

[24] *Correspondance du Cardinal de Granvelle, 1565–1586*, ed. E. Poullet (12 vols., Brussels, 1877–96), I, p. 341.

[25] J.J. Woltjer, 'De politieke betekenis van de Emdense synode', in D. Nauta *et al.* (eds.), *De synode van Emden oktober 1571* (Kampen, 1971), pp. 45–8. In 1571 a Protestant supporter of William of Orange lost patience with 'those heretics who loudly proclaim that the clattering of arms does not accord with the Gospel', *Texts Concerning the Revolt of the Netherlands*, ed. E.H. Kossmann and A.F. Mellink (Cambridge, 1974), p. 91.

several indeed came from France and the Low Countries. Their remarkable mobility between the German centres of Reformed Protestantism has been attributed to the general dearth of administrators with the legal qualifications necessary to consolidate the prince's authority in the territories.[26] This may be so, yet their turbulent diplomatic and political careers reinforced the cohesion of the Calvinist cause in the Empire. The Reformed Protestants in Germany also had connections with the wider Calvinist world, in particular with the Low Countries.[27] Before the outbreak of the Thirty Years War students with Calvinist credentials might matriculate at several of the best Reformed academies, which included Heidelberg, Herborn, Geneva, Saumur and Leiden. Their peregrinations and *alba amicorum* testify to the existence of a cosmopolitan, yet far from exclusive, Calvinist fraternity.

If Calvin is commonly perceived as the stern schoolmaster of the Reformation, and Geneva as the 'school of Christ', then the Reformed churches might be regarded as being preternaturally preoccupied with what a Scots kirk session called 'the maneris of the pepill'. Though this mistakes the form for the substance, the original Calvinist rationale for discipline was readily susceptible to subversion. Calvin's insistence on discipline sprang from his doctrine of the visible church and, above all, from his concern to prevent the 'profanation' or 'pollution' of the Lord's Supper. The church contained both 'the saints presently living' and 'hypocrites who have nothing of Christ but the name and outward appearance'.[28] Christ had therefore given the 'power of the keys', to his church to ensure 'that the Supper of our Lord may not be polluted by people of scandalous lives',[29] to avoid the corruption of the good and to shame sinners into repentance. The community that sat at the Lord's Table should aspire to become the body of Christ.[30]

---

[26] H. Schilling, 'Confessionalization in the Empire: Religious and Societal Change in Germany between 1555 and 1620', in his *Religion, Political Culture and the Emergence of Early Modern Society. Essays in German and Dutch History* (Leiden, 1992), pp. 215–16.

[27] For example, the Reformed churches of the Wetterau counties adopted in 1586 the Dutch church order of Middelburg (1581).   [28] *Institutes*, Bk. IV, i, 7.

[29] Cited in J. Calvin, *Institutes of the Christian Religion*, ed. J.T. McNeill (2 vols., London, 1961), II, p. 1232 n. 8.

[30] A. Th. van Deursen, *Bavianen en slijkgeuzen. Kerk en kerkvolk ten tijde van Maurits en Oldenbarnevelt* (Assen, 1974), p. 198. Arguably the precautions taken to preserve the purity of the eucharistic community thwarted the realisation in the Reformed tradition of Calvin's ambition that the 'Sacred Supper' be 'set before the church . . . at least once a week' in most Reformed congregations, *Institutes*, Bk. IV, xvii, 43. Quarterly communions became the pattern in Geneva. In the Dutch Reformed churches the synods enjoined bi-monthly celebrations, though such frequency was rarely achieved. In the stranger churches and at Emden monthly communions were common. In Scotland 'Sacrament Sunday' occurred infrequently, sometimes only once a year in the seventeenth century, and was preceded by a

In his doctrine of the church Calvin always insisted that God alone knew who belonged to the church of saints, while the church on earth, though holy, 'is not yet perfect'. Geneva was a *corpus christianum* and its church a *Volkskirche* in the sense that it included all the inhabitants. He rejected the gathered fellowships of the Anabaptists which sought through their exclusivity and moral rigorism to close the gap between the visible and invisible churches. Yet Calvin's loathing of 'pigs and dogs among the children of God',[31] and his foreboding that the elect made up only 'a small and contemptible number' always threatened to disturb the delicate balance he tried to strike between his comprehensive vision of the church and the need for ecclesiastical discipline to 'restrain and tame those who rage against the doctrine of Christ'.[32] The latent sectarianism in the master's thought became more pronounced among some of the early Calvinist ministers, chiefly concerned to draw their flocks away from 'papist superstitions'.[33]

The Genevan consistory in its original form was a compromise between Calvin and the magistrates. Calvin therefore described the Ecclesiastical Ordinances of 1541 as 'tolerable given the infirmity of the age'. The *Messieurs de Genève* conceived of the consistory at first as an arm of the Council. After all the elders serving in the consistory were chosen from among the three councils and they exercised a delegated authority. For that reason the elders were originally also designated as 'commis pour la seigneurie'.[34] The magistrates of Geneva wanted a body to take the place of the defunct consistorial court of the bishop, with a competence similar to the new courts of morals, which the magistrates of Zurich and Berne had established after the Reformation to deal with matrimonial causes, suppress popery and, generally, to impose stricter codes of conduct.[35] At first too the Council tried to reserve the power of excommunication to itself, though from the outset Calvin fiercely contested any such claim.[36]

thorough examination of parishioners' scriptural knowledge and the reconciliation of quarrels, procedures which might take several weeks, D.B. Thoms, *The Kirk of Brechin in the Seventeenth Century* (Society of Friends of Brechin Cathedral, 1972) pp. 75–7. In the larger town congregations in seventeenth-century Holland the Reformed church abandoned regular visitations. Communicants were urged instead to search their consciences and attend the preparatory service on the preceding Saturday, van Deursen, *Bavianen en slijkgeuzen* pp. 197–9.   [31] *Institutes*, Bk. IV, i, 15.   [32] *Institutes*, Bk. IV, xii, 1.

[33] See below Mark Greengrass, on Pierre Viret, ch. 7, and Guido Marnef, on Gaspar van der Heyden, ch. 8.

[34] *RCP*, I, p. 1; this designation was omitted in the revised ordinances of 1561, cf. Plomp, *Kerkelijke tucht*, pp. 180, 191.

[35] The Bernese *Chorgericht*, established in 1528, and its subordinate 'consistoires' had the authority to fine and even to banish offenders. The Bernese had introduced these 'tribuneaux des moeurs' into the Pays de Vaud under their control, H. Vuilleumier, *Histoire de l'Église Réformée du Pays de Vaud sous le régime bernois* (4 vols., Lausanne, 1927–33), I, p. 254–6, 299–305.   [36] Plomp, *Kerkelijke tucht*, p. 203.

If the Genevan consistory had simply remained 'a committee of the municipal government',[37] its significance would have been no greater than that of the *Ehegericht* of Zurich or the *Chorgericht* of Berne. At Calvin's insistence, however, it evolved, not without difficulty, into a 'tribunal of the church' which punished open sins 'according to the Lord's Word' with spiritual penalties, suspension and excommunication.[38] Bullinger always felt uneasy about the Genevan discipline precisely because of its independence from the magistracy and its 'excessive sharpness'. Excommunication should not be used to maintain the purity of the eucharistic community, but to punish those whose crimes threatened the godly commonwealth.[39] But, as Kingdon explains below, the Genevan consistory was not simply a Reformed ecclesiastical court; it also served as a forum for religious instruction and for the reconciliation of conflicts. It was, however, the autonomy of the consistory from the magistrates which allowed Calvinist ecclesiastical discipline to develop outside Geneva.

The 'privy kirks' organised in France, the Low Countries and Scotland in the late 1550s appointed ministers and elders without, of course, reference to the magistrates. Nevertheless these consistories served, as in Calvin's Geneva, to maintain discipline, without which the Lord's Supper could not be properly administered. The consistory provided the means to ensure, as the synod of Poitiers put it in 1561, 'that all may not be received higgeldy-piggeldy without distinction to the Lord's Table'.[40]

Calvinist ecclesiastical discipline proved remarkably versatile. It could accommodate the circumstances of Calvinist congregations which survived as persecuted minorities or coexisted with other confessions; equally, the consistory could, in the case of Calvinist territorial churches, work hand in glove with the civil power. Naturally the composition of that consistory, the extent of its activity in the community, the type of offences under consideration and even the penalties prescribed varied according to the position, legal or otherwise, of the Reformed church. Besides, the ministers and elders were themselves men from the local community, whose preoccupations and prejudices were coloured by their sympathy with, or perhaps their desire to reform, local customs and codes of conduct.

Calvinist congregations 'under the cross', the stranger churches scattered through England and Germany, and the French Reformed churches

---

[37] R.M. Kingdon, 'Calvin and the Establishment of Consistory Discipline in Geneva: the Institution and the Men who Directed it', *NAK*, 70 (1990), 162.

[38] *Institutes*, Bk. IV, xii, 1.

[39] See below, Bruce Gordon, ch. 4. Also J. Wayne Baker, 'Christian Discipline and the Early Reformed Tradition: Bullinger and Calvin', in R.V. Schnucker (ed.), *Calviniana. Ideas and Influence of John Calvin* (Sixteenth Century Essays and Studies, X, 1988), 107–19.

[40] Quoted in A. Duke, G. Lewis and A. Pettegree (eds.), *Calvinism in Europe 1540–1610. A Collection of Documents* (Manchester, 1992) p. 77.

existed in a multi-confessional situation. The writ of their consistories therefore ran only as far as the church members, who had voluntarily submitted themselves to 'the yoke of Christ', and no further. The competence of the consistories was similarly restricted to the membership of the Reformed churches in the United Provinces. The Reformed churches there took the place of the Catholic church in many respects and their ministers baptised, married and buried whoever called on their services. But at the heart of this comprehensive 'public' church, there lay the eucharistic community, the 'congregation of Christ'. Only the members of this inner group, who had placed themselves under the discipline of the consistory, were admitted to the Lord's Table. As a result of this distinction, seemingly peculiar to early Dutch Calvinism, contemporaries referred to those who came to Reformed services without becoming members as 'liefhebbers', or 'favourers'.[41]

Vogler and Estèbe described the typical French Calvinist congregation in sixteenth-century Languedoc as 'une église composée surtout de professants'.[42] This characterisation might usefully be extended to include all those Calvinist churches which did not possess (or at least in the case of the Dutch, not fully) the legal standing of established churches. Here the consistories retained their autonomy *vis-à-vis* the civil magistrates, even where, as in cities like Nîmes and Montauban these supported the Reformed faith. In the towns of Holland the social gap between the consistories and the magistrates lessened when regents became elders and deacons.[43] Yet the religious pluriformity of the United Provinces prevented the town corporations from meeting the criteria of godly magistrates to the satisfaction of the more zealous ministers who expected these 'to uproot blasphemy and false religion'.[44] On the other hand the Dutch Calvinists' refusal to open the Lord's Table to all comers disappointed those regents who wanted 'the evangelical net' to be cast widely in order to draw as many as possible into the Reformed religion. Though the relationship between the reformed churches and the regents in the towns could be quite cordial, the Calvinist churches always kept a measure of local autonomy, but by the same token they forfeited some of their influence on the affairs of state.

The consistories of these churches followed the Genevan pattern in only having powers to impose spiritual penalties – admonition, *amende honorable*, suspension and excommunication. They seem, however, to have

---

[41] Other terms include 'toehoorders' (auditors), 'goetgunners' (favourers), 'goetwilligen' (well-wishers), 'den ommestandt des gantschen volcx' (bystanders from the common people).

[42] B. Vogler and J. Estèbe, 'La Genèse d'une société protestante: étude comparée de quelques registres consistoriaux languedociens et palatins vers 1600', *Annales. Économies, Sociétés, Civilisations*, 31 (1976), 385.   [43] Van Deursen, *Bavianen en slijkgeuzen*, 83–6.

[44] Art. 36 of Belgic Confession in J.N. Bakhuizen van den Brink, *De nederlandse belijdenisgeschriften in authentieke teksten*, 2nd edn(Amsterdam, 1976), p. 141.

employed the ultimate sanction with a restraint not always evident in Geneva.[45] Indeed as one reads the deliberations of some Dutch consistories, one is struck by their patience and pastoral care as well as their extreme reluctance to cast anyone out of 'Christ's congregation'.

The consistories of Languedoc, like their counterparts in Holland and Emden, employed the Reformed discipline for three purposes. The greatest part of the business recorded in the consistorial act books concerned the composition of disputes and quarrels, in the household, at work, on the street and in the taverns.[46] In this way the consistories played an important peace-making role in early modern European society. That however was incidental to their purpose: the consistories intended to realise the 'peace, love and harmony' which should prevail in the eucharistic community. Secondly, the ministers and elders watched jealously over the good name of the church. Church members who publicly broke the codes of conduct expected of Calvinists and, for example, danced at weddings, gambled at cards or took part in the carnival festivities would be called to account. For the same reason the consistories rebuked those suspected of breaches against public morality and the law of the land. It comes, however, somewhat of a surprise to discover that the sins of the flesh, though never glossed over, made up even in Geneva, only a small proportion of consistorial business during the late sixteenth century. Finally, the consistories were concerned, especially in the early years, to warn the Calvinist community against the siren voices calling members into apostasy. They therefore treated those who attended mass, gave way to superstitious practices or, in the case of Holland and Emden, sought fellowship with the Mennonites with exemplary severity.[47]

---

[45] Only 55 of 1,624 cases to come before the consistory at Nîmes between 1561–3 and 1578–83 resulted in excommunication, R.A. Mentzer, '*Disciplina nervus ecclesiae*: The Calvinist Reform of Morals at Nîmes', *SCJ*, 18 (1987), 112–13. For excommunication among the Dutch Calvinists see below, Andrew Pettegree, ch. 9, and at Emden, Pettegree, *Emden and the Dutch Revolt*, p. 49. For the greater severity of the Genevan consistory in this respect see E.W. Monter, 'The Consistory of Geneva, 1559–1569', *BHR*, 38 (1976), 471–84.

[46] The same holds good for Geneva if one adds together the cases concerning domestic quarrels, 'quarrels with others' and 'quarrels with kin', see Monter, 'Consistory of Geneva', 479.

[47] Mentzer, '*Disciplina nervus ecclesiae*', 109; Vogler and Estèbe, 'La Genèse d'une société protestante', 362–88. For Holland and Emden see H. Roodenburg, *Onder censuur. De kerkelijke tucht in de gereformeerde gemeente van Amsterdam, 1578–1700* (Hilversum, 1990); H. Schilling, 'Calvinism and the Making of the Modern Mind: Ecclesiastical Discipline of Public and Private Sin from the Sixteenth to the Nineteenth Century', in his *Civic Calvinism in Northwestern Germany and the Netherlands: Sixteenth to Nineteenth Centuries* (Sixteenth Century Essay and Studies, XVII, 1991), pp. 41–68; F. Wieringa 'Tucht en ontucht. Een onderzoek naar zonde en verzoening in de gereformeerde gemeente van Enkhuizen, 1572–1593' (unpub. *scriptie*, Amsterdam, 1980). There were, of course, also significant differences of emphasis between the Calvinists of Languedoc and those of Holland. Dancing seems to have worried the French consistories far more than their northern brethren. After disputes, drink seems to have been the besetting sin of Dutch Calvinists.

Where the Reformed churches found themselves in a confessionally competitive or religiously pluriform society, ecclesiastical discipline was directed inwards and served to reinforce the separate character of these Calvinist communities. As a result their outreach into the wider society was limited, most obviously in the stranger churches and in France. But where, as in Scotland, Béarn and in the Palatinate the doctrine and polity of the established or territorial church was broadly speaking Reformed, Calvinist discipline developed quite differently. In the first place the consistory or kirk session exercised spiritual jurisdiction over, as the Scots' *First Book of Discipline* declared, 'all the estates within this Realm . . . as well the Rulers, as they that are ruled'.[48] The Dutch distinction between church members, who submitted to the authority of the consistory, and the rest of the parishioners, who were exempt, was unknown. Secondly, though the jurisdiction of the church remained separate from that of the state, kirk sessions and bailies (magistrates) usually cooperated closely. The sessions might call on the assistance of the bailies to bring the recalcitrant to book and they delated offenders to the burgh courts for 'correctioun civilie'.[49] Sometimes the bailies attended the kirk session so that fornicators received both spiritual and civil punishment at the same time, their sentences being recorded in the consistorial act book.[50] The 'interlock of church and state' in Scotland tightened where a rural kirk session obtained a commission from the privy council to impose both spiritual and civil penalties.[51] As a result the church courts in Scotland could put fornicators in the 'jougs', scolds in the 'branks' and fine those who breached the sabbath.[52] Since bailies frequently attended kirk sessions either in their capacity as elders or as municipal office-holders, the distinction between the ecclesiastical and civil jurisdictions or indeed between sins and crimes became blurred almost to vanishing point.

The discipline of the kirk session contributed in the view of Geoffrey Parker, to 'the taming of Scotland'. His analysis of the kirk session records for St Andrews suggests that the kirk could, at least temporally, change sexual mores within the locality.[53] Furthermore, the Scots Parliament

---

[48] *The First Book of Discipline*, ed. J.K. Cameron (Edinburgh, 1972), p. 173.

[49] J. Kirk, 'Minister and Magistrate', in his *Patterns of Reform. Continuity and Change in the Reformation Kirk* (Edinburgh, 1989), pp. 272–5; for the Palatinate, Vogler and Estèbe, 'La Genèse d'une société protestante', 365.

[50] Numerous examples in *The Buik of the Kirk of the Canagait 1564–1567*, ed. A.B. Calderwood (Scottish Record Society, Edinburgh, 1961).

[51] On commissions see W.R. Foster, *The Church before the Covenants: the Church of Scotland 1596–1638* (Edinburgh–London, 1975), p. 79; for the phrase see G. Parker, 'The "Kirk by Law Established" and the Origins of the "The Taming of Scotland": St Andrews 1559–1600', in *Perspectives in Scottish Social History* (Aberdeen, 1988), 5.

[52] Parker, 'The "Kirk by Law Established"', 13–14; also Thoms, *The Kirk of Brechin in the Seventeenth Century*, pp. 22–6.

[53] Parker, 'The "Kirk by Law Established"', 17–18. T.C. Smout, *A History of the Scottish People, 1560–1830* (London, 1969), p. 82 also subscribes to the view that the Kirk's

endorsed, up to a point, the demands of the kirk for rigorous penalties against adultery, fornication, blasphemy and the profanation of the Lord's Day. It presumably did so because it saw that the means of achieving a godly congregation could also become the instrument of bringing about the reformation of manners for which the elites wished so devoutly.

In the Palatinate, as in Scotland, ecclesiastical discipline could promote social discipline. For the Calvinist Elector Frederick III the 'reformatio doctrinae' evidently complemented the 'reformatio vitae'. In 1563 he set out the reasons for his conversion to Reformed Protestantism. Among other matters, he mentioned his princely duty 'to maintain a disciplined, upright, and virtuous life . . . among [his] subjects . . . and especially, to instruct them . . . [in] the righteous knowledge and fear of the Almighty . . . as the only basis of all virtues and obedience, and also . . . to help them gain eternal and transient wellbeing'.[54] In this process Christian education played a crucial strategic role. Because education imparted obedience, discipline and a sense of duty, Frederick IV considered schools, with the churches, as 'the basis of all temporal and heavenly welfare'.[55] In this sense schools were the 'seminaries of the republic'.

The demand for a reformation of manners was not, of course, limited to the Calvinist territorial states; the pressures were no less strong in the Lutheran and Catholics states of Germany. But there is a considerable irony that the consistory which Calvin transformed with such difficulty into an ecclesiastical body employing only spiritual sanctions reverted in Scotland and in the Palatinate, arguably the most successful Calvinist régimes, into an instrument of the state. Where, however, the Calvinist reformation received only partial or no support from the civil authority, as in the United Provinces or France, the Reformed churches remained more faithful, whether from choice or necessity, to the Genevan reformer's ideal of ecclesiastical discipline. Nevertheless, we may suppose that their sectarian ecclesiology would have come as a grave disappointment.

The systematic analysis of ecclesiastical visitations and consistorial act books has transformed perceptions of the Reformation. These unimpeachable Lutheran and Calvinist sources have given the lie to the assumption that the triumph of Protestantism was achieved easily, even in the imperial cities. On the evidence of these records a significant proportion of the laity in the Protestant lands of early modern Europe embraced neither the doctrines of the Reformation nor its puritanical morality with any enthu-

sustained crusade against sexual promiscuity left its mark on the morality of the Scottish middle classes.

[54] R. Po-Chia Hsia, *Social Discipline in the Reformation: Central Europe 1550–1650* (London–New York, 1989), pp. 34–5.

[55] H. Cohn, 'The Territorial Princes in Germany's Second Reformation, 1559–1622', in Prestwich (ed.), *International Calvinism*, p. 151.

siasm; many indeed remained 'obstinately devoted', like the young Calvin, 'to the superstitions of popery', and resisted the pressures to conform.[56]

The Oxford Conference on Calvinism in Europe included several case studies of the local Reformation: in a particular town (Troyes and Antwerp), region (Gaelic-speaking Scotland) or in a small state (Béarn and Holland). Explanations for the 'success and failure' of the Calvinist Reformation in the local context vary according to the timescale under consideration. In France the opening decade of the civil wars decided the destiny of Calvinism. On the eve of the wars French Protestantism had experienced several years of 'disorderly growth' as men and women everywhere appeared ready to discard the religion of their fathers. Yet soon after the massacre of St Bartholomew, if not even before, it became clear that the tide had turned: Calvinism in France was doomed to become, except in cities like La Rochelle and Nîmes, the faith of a small (and diminishing) minority.

The early successes of the Calvinists in France (as also in the Low Countries) were contingent on a constellation of local circumstances. These included the depth of feeling against the local Catholic clergy, socio-economic tensions and political rivalries in certain towns,[57] the local reputation of those who endorsed the new religion and the charisma of the earliest preachers. Certainly the size of the crowds who flocked to hear the Calvinist preachers revealed widespread disenchantment with the old religion. For many townspeople devotion to Catholicism had apparently been so weakened that they felt no inhibitions about mocking the clergy, singing Marot's psalms and going to the heretical services.

Yet only a small proportion of those who flocked to hear the *prêches* in the French towns in the early 1560s and in the Low Countries in 1566 apparently became convinced Calvinists. The wholesale apostasy of Catholics in both countries dreaded failed to materialise. Many of those who then entered the Calvinist congregations, and even took communion and had their children baptised by the pastor, did not persevere in the new faith. At Troyes where 8,000–9,000 reportedly participated in the Calvinist communion in 1562, the same source complained that a month after the massacre of St Bartholomew scarcely twenty Protestants 'had kept themselves pure'.[58] Mass defections from the Calvinist ranks also occurred at Paris and Rouen after the massacre.[59]

[56] For the most wide-ranging contribution to the debate see G. Parker, 'Success and Failure during the First Century of the Reformation', *P & P*, 136 (1992), 43–82.

[57] In the case of the Low Countries, the magistrates' reluctance at Antwerp to enforce the anti-heresy edicts lest these damage commerce contributed to a climate which was more tolerant of religious dissent.   [58] See below, Penny Roberts, ch. 6.

[59] D. Richet, 'Aspects socio-culturels des conflits religieux à Paris dans la seconde moitié du xvie siècle', *Annales. Économies, Sociétés, Civilisations*, 32 (1977), 777.

The outbreak of the wars in France evidently checked the gathering momentum of the Reformed movement there. Moderates recoiled before the evidence of Calvinist iconoclastic destruction and Huguenot sedition while militant Catholics, who matched Protestant *chanteries* with provocative processions, did not hesitate to resort to violence. At the same time the lay confraternities and the *pénitents* reinvigorated Catholic piety. For all the confidence of the Huguenots during 1561–2, the contest into which they had become drawn was unequal. The Calvinist churches, numerous as they had become, were creations of the last few years while only a handful of their ministers had ever received a training in Geneva. It was therefore difficult to provide the discipline and religious instruction to convert the raw enthusiasm of those who went to the *prêches* into confessional commitment. Consequently when Catholic preachers inveighed against the pastors and the sporadic killings of known Calvinists began, many who had flirted with heresy could be persuaded to return to the Catholic fold.

Besides, the massacre of St Bartholomew demonstrated, in the most forceful way imaginable, that, as a former Protestant merchant in Paris told two of his Huguenot clients in Albi, the king intended to permit only 'une foy, une loy ung Dieu et ung roy' in France. He therefore begged his correspondents to give up their wishful thinking and make speedy profession of the Catholic religion, if they wanted to save their lives and their property.[60] The Calvinist minister Hugues Sureau, who also briefly abjured his Protestant faith at this time, initially saw the massacres as proof that God had 'condemned the profession and exercise of our Religion'.[61] To Reformed Protestants accustomed to see the hand of God in contemporary events, such an interpretation must have been hard to resist. They could, of course, return to the uncomfortable 'theology of martyrdom', but that was better suited to a religious elite than to a church of the masses.

In the Low Countries the hedge-preachings and the iconoclastic violence of 1566 did not, as one might have expected, provoke a Catholic backlash.[62] Though the sacking of the churches appalled many devout Catholics and certainly contributed to the isolation of the Calvinists by the winter of 1566, the image-breakers rarely encountered militant Catholic opposition. Perhaps the prolonged and widespread campaign against the antiheresy legislation, in which Catholic magistrates and nobles had participated, obstructed the creation of a Catholic counter-offensive of the

---

[60] Richet, 'Aspects socio-culturels des conflits religieux', 777–8.
[61] R.M. Kingdon, *Geneva and the French Protestant Movement 1564–1572* (Geneva, 1967), p. 117 n. 4. The Scottish General Assembly saw in the massacre divine punishment for 'our sins' and therefore ordered 'a public humiliation of them that fear God', *Calvinism in Europe*, p. 206.
[62] It is however notable that Reformed Protestantism, which had been strongly entrenched in the Walloon towns of Valenciennes and Tournai during 1566–7, never recovered.

extreme sort characteristic of France. Yet there is no reason to suppose that the crowds in the Low Countries who went to hear the new preachers became staunch Calvinists. At Antwerp as many as 20,000–25,000 allegedly attended the hedge-preachings during the summer of 1566. Yet more than 14,000 townspeople scrambled to make their peace with the Catholic church in 1570 while the relatively large Calvinist congregation there only counted between 3,000 and 4,000 members in 1578.[63]

No thorough-going reformation in the Calvinist sense could take place without substantial support from the civil authorities. They alone could endow the new church, guarantee it control of the means of indoctrination and give effect to anti-Catholic measures. Another prerequisite for a successful reformation was an adequate supply of competently trained pastors, preferably recruited from the region in which they ministered. Even with these advantages, success was neither guaranteed nor achieved quickly or easily. Between 1569 and 1599 the practice of Catholicism was forbidden in Béarn, yet even such an extended 'window of opportunity' proved too brief to win over the inhabitants to the new religion.[64] In the United Provinces, where the public celebration of the mass had been forbidden since at least 1581, around two-fifths of the inhabitants still belonged to the Catholic church in the mid-seventeenth century.[65]

Reformed Protestantism made only modest progress in the United Provinces and met with hostility or indifference on the part of predominantly Catholic Béarnais and of the Lutheran subjects of John Sigismund, the elector of Brandenburg. Many reasons can be offered for this state of affairs, including in the case of the United Provinces the refusal of the Reformed churches there to admit everyone to sit at the Lord's Table and, of course, the missionary activity of the Catholic church in Protestant lands after the Council of Trent. Yet we should perhaps give greater weight to the radical nature of Calvinism, a radicalism that expressed itself less in its advocacy of political resistance – after all, in Germany certain princes promoted the Reformed religion because they believed Calvinism would strengthen princely authority – than in its repudiation of all forms of 'superstition'. If this aspect of Calvinism appealed to intellectuals and humanist reformers in Germany and in Hungary, it also deterred many

[63] See below, Marnef, ch. 8.   [64] See below, Greengrass, ch. 7.
[65] S. Groenveld en H.L.Ph. Leeuwenberg, *De bruid in de schuit. De consolidatie van de Republiek, 1609–1650* (Zutphen, 1985), pp. 23–31. It does not, of course, follow that the other three-fifths were members of the Reformed churches. Besides the Remonstrants, Lutherans and Mennonites, many refused to commit themselves. It is difficult to determine what proportion of the population had no explicit confessional loyalties, though half the inhabitants of Haarlem around 1620 may have been 'neutrals' and 'undecided', J. Spaans, *Haarlem na de Reformatie: Stedelijke cultuur en kerkelijk leven, 1577–1620* (Leiden, 1989), p. 104.

ordinary Christians, who instinctively preferred the immanent theology of popular Catholicism.

The radical nature of Calvinism was proclaimed in its liturgy, which overturned the form of the mass, in its abolition of the church year, in its preference for expository preaching and for unaccompanied metrical psalms, the last being rather less to the taste of at least Dutch parishioners than legend would suppose. The church-building too was intended to be 'a house for the Word'[66] dominated by the pulpit and sparsely furnished with pews, communion table, boards inscribed with the Ten Commandments and the escutcheons of the local gentry. Calvinist ecclesiastical architecture, which repudiated the cruciform church in favour of a round or rectangular building has found few admirers. One critic described the great Dutch churches as 'vast warehouses of devotion and utter failures as works of art' and French Catholics ridiculed the *temples* as 'barns' and, presumably by association of ideas, 'rats' nests'.[67]

The Calvinist attack on 'papist superstition' began, as they said in sixteenth-century Scotland with the 'casting down' of the churches. Wherever Reformed Protestantism spread, it was accompanied by the orderly removal or more often the violent destruction of statues, altars, fonts, roods, pyxes, liturgical books, vestments, organs, paintings and stained glass windows. Outside the churches crucifixes, wayside shrines and calvaries were destroyed. Senior Calvinist ministers frequently deplored these unauthorised acts of the iconoclasts, but they had little control over preachers who, by comparing the images with the idols of Baal, left their auditors in no doubt where their duty lay.

The Calvinists' hostility to images and all other forms of superstition may be traced to their conviction that God was spirit and should therefore only be worshipped in spirit. The notion that the divine, the Creator, could in any way be contained in an object, in particular the host, made by the creature struck them as blasphemous. The German Calvinists' repugnance of the Lutheran doctrine of ubiquitarianism stemmed from the fear that this, in effect, revived the 'miracle of the mass'.[68]

Late medieval Catholics had sought to ward off thunderstorms by ringing the church bells and they had found comfort and consolation when sick from the administration of the last rites. Women in child-bed wore amulets with scriptural texts and farmers brought talismans to be blessed

---

[66] The phrase is borrowed from the C.A. van Swigchem, T. Brouwer and W. van Os, *Een huis voor het Woord. Het protestantse kerkinterieur in Nederland tot 1900* (The Hague, 1984).

[67] Cited in G.L. Burke, *The Making of Dutch Towns. A Study of Urban Development from the Tenth to the Seventeenth Centuries* (London, 1956), p. 157; J. Pannier, *L'Eglise réformée de Paris sous Henri IV* (Paris, 1911), pp. 459–60.

[68] See below, Bodo Nischan, ch. 10.

by the priest to ensure the fertility of their crops and their cattle. The Reformed churches would have none of this. They tended to confound the paraliturgical rites and 'church magic' with divination, witchcraft and necromancy and to condemn all such practices as superstitions associated with 'popery'. Instead the Reformed ministers advised their troubled parishioners to place their trust in God's providence. To all but the saints that must have seemed an unconvincing substitute for the miracles of the medieval church and the tangible benefits the priest had provided.

The Reformed synods demand for the 'root and branch' abolition of superstition and the concern of Reformed régimes for social discipline did nothing to assist the advance of the Calvinist reformation, especially in the countryside. It is therefore tempting to concur with the observation of the American historian R. Po-Chia Hsia who, when writing about the resistance of the inhabitants of the Palatinate to Reformed Protestantism in the late sixteenth century remarked that, 'Calvinism proved in the long run to be an abstract, intellectual religion of the elite.'[69] And yet the Genevan Reformation did sometimes succeed in winning support from rural populations in the sixteenth century. After all it put down roots in the backwoods of the Cévennes and also, as Jane Dawson has demonstrated,[70] in the Gaelic-speaking parts of Scotland. Here the kirk succeeded in transmitting the Protestant gospel by working with, rather than as happened in Béarn, against the grain of the local culture.

[69] Po-Chia Hsia, *Social Discipline*, p. 154.   [70] See below, Jane Dawson, ch. 12.

2 The Geneva Consistory in the time of Calvin

Robert M. Kingdon

This paper is a progress report upon a research project in which I have been involved since 1987. It is a project designed to make possible a full study of the Consistory established in Geneva by John Calvin in 1541, as a part of the bargain that brought him back from Strasburg to take over general direction of Geneva's newly Reformed church. It is one of a number of projects currently under way that are designed to describe with more precision than ever before what early Calvinists meant by discipline. Even a cursory examination of early Calvinist creeds indicates how seriously their authors took discipline. Most of them, indeed, made it one of three *notae* or marks that are necessary to define an institution as the true church. In this they deliberately went beyond their Lutheran brethren, indeed went beyond Calvin himself, who defined the true church by only two marks, the preaching of the Word of God, and the proper administration of the sacraments.

But what did discipline mean to early Calvinists? I would like to suggest that it meant two things: (1) It meant, first of all, a type of ecclesiastical organisation, an ecclesiastical constitution if you will, that had its roots in the apostolic church as described in the New Testament. A discipline in this sense could be written down, cherished, and carefully revised to adapt it to changing circumstances. Each national Calvinist church crafted its own discipline. The French discipline, to which Calvin himself made some contributions, is only now being studied with the intensity it deserves. Bernard Roussel of the Ecole Pratique des Hautes Etudes in Paris has assembled a team of scholars to prepare the first true critical edition of this discipline, using all the bewilderingly various manuscript copies of it that survive. A preliminary report on some of their discoveries can be found in a Ph.D. dissertation presented to the History Department of the University of Wisconsin-Madison in 1992 by a member of this team of editors who is also a former student of mine, Glenn Sunshine.[1] It distinguishes with fresh

---

[1] Glenn S. Sunshine, 'From French Protestantism to the French Reformed Churches: The Development of Huguenot Ecclesiastical Institutions, 1559–1598' (unpublished Ph.D. dissertation, University of Wisconsin-Madison, 1992).

precision the elements in the French discipline that were shaped by Calvin and the model he created in Geneva and the elements that were independently worked out by religious leaders who remained in France.

(2) But discipline also meant something else to early Calvinists. It meant a serious attempt to control human behaviour in all its variety. It meant that the church had a responsibility not only to present true Christian doctrine but also to shape true Christian behaviour. And this responsibility, Calvinists believed, could not be left to individuals or to governments. It had to be assumed, to as great a degree as possible, by the church. This conviction led to the creation of the Consistory in Geneva and of other institutions like it in other communities. It is to an understanding of discipline in this second sense that the project upon which I report hopes to contribute.

What did the Consistory as Calvin established it in 1541 actually do? It is clear that it became a remarkably intrusive institution, penetrating every aspect of Genevan life, summoning to its meetings in later years, after it was fully accepted and entrenched, as much as a fifteenth of the entire adult population of the city in a single year.[2] It is an astonishing fact, however, that we do not really know much of what happened at those weekly meetings, that our ideas of what the Consistory did are incomplete, imperfect and distorted. This is not because it did not leave substantial records. A secretary was hired at the very beginning to keep a record of its Thursday meetings, meetings that came to last from three to four hours every week.[3] Most of the resulting registers were carefully saved and can now be found in the Geneva State Archives. There are only a few relatively short lacunae, mostly at times between regular secretaries, when records were not carefully kept. There are microfilm copies of these registers available in a number of additional research centres. But no modern scholar to my knowledge has ever read these registers all the way through. They were written in considerable haste in very bad handwriting. They require some skill in sixteenth-century French paleography to decipher.

Back in 1853, a local Genevan antiquarian named Cramer prepared a transcript of selections from these registers which he distributed in a primitive sort of photocopy. Practically all serious scholarly work on the Consistory has used this transcript instead of the originals. That would include the work of scholars of such signal importance to Calvin studies as

---

[2] This is the estimate for 1569 of E. William Monter, 'The Consistory of Geneva, 1559–1569', *BHR*, 38 (1976), 484.

[3] This of course meant that the lay elders, who with the pastors constituted the Consistory, had to devote a considerable amount of their time to this public service. Most of them seem to have been elderly merchants and professional men, in a position to leave to sons or other relatives the daily management of their businesses. In later years at least one, the marquis Galeazzo Caracciolo, was an immigrant noble.

the editors of the *Calvini Opera*, the biographer Emile Doumergue and the great German church historian Walther Köhler.[4] A close inspection of the Cramer transcripts, however, reveals that they are entirely inadequate. They include only about 5 per cent of the total cases. When Cramer got stuck on a passage that was hard to read, he simply omitted it. He was not an expert paleographer and often made small errors. And, worst of all, he concentrated on the lurid and spectacular cases, the ones that involved prominent people and that took up a lot of time. He simply ignored most of the routine cases. The result is that almost all previous work on the Geneva Consistory is distorted, sometimes seriously.

It was to remedy this problem that in 1987 I assembled a team to prepare a complete transcript of the twenty-one volumes of the Registers of the Geneva Consistory for the period of Calvin's ministry, from 1542, the date of the earliest surviving registers, to 1564, the date of Calvin's death. Our work in the beginning was based on microfilm copies of these registers kept in the H. H. Meeter Center for Calvin Studies at Calvin College and Seminary in Grand Rapids, Michigan. It was supported financially by grants from the Meeter Center and the University of Wisconsin-Madison. I am happy now to report that the first stage in this project is finished. We have completed a full transcript of the twenty-one volumes, and deposited electronic copies of all or most of this material in several research institutions, including the Meeter Center, the Princeton Theological Seminary Library, the University of St Andrews in Scotland, and the University of Wisconsin-Madison. This transcript is still very rough, with many dubious readings and probable errors. It must be used with caution. But it is at least available.

Our second step will be to begin preparing this material for publication. Two of my assistants who worked on the transcription, Isabella Watt and Thomas Lambert, have carefully rechecked and corrected copy for the first volume of these registers and are now assembling the footnotes that are often needed to authenticate readings of the manuscripts, particularly of proper names, and that are also needed to make the fullest possible sense of these texts. Much of this work must be done in the Geneva State Archives.

We have also begun work on a computerised data bank of the material contained in these registers. That work is only beginning, and still faces some technical problems. It should ultimately prove to be very useful, however, since it will make it possible to prepare a rough statistical analysis of the types of cases heard by the Consistory and of how they varied over

[4] See *Annales calviniani* in *CO*, XXI, cols. 292 and ff.; Emile Doumergue, *Jean Calvin, les hommes et les choses de son temps*, V, pp. 189 and ff.; Walther Köhler, *Zürcher Ehegericht und Genfer Konsistorium*, II, pp. 580 and ff. NB p. 614, n. 544, in Köhler, for statistics that are meaningless, because they are based on Cramer's samples.

the decades. Some sort of statistical analysis is absolutely necessary before we can rectify past stereotypes about the Consistory and reach a full appreciation of what it actually did and of what kind of behaviour it tried to influence. But that remains for the future. All that I can give you now is a rough impression of what the Consistory tried to do, based on my own readings of only a part of this total record.

It is my current impression that the Geneva Consistory had three basic functions: it served as an educational institution, as a compulsory counselling service, and as a kind of court. Only the last of these functions is well known. So let me dwell on the other two.

Educational institution

The Consistory served as an educational institution in that it assumed some responsibility for making sure that everyone in Geneva had an elementary understanding of what the Christian religion as reformed by John Calvin and his associates really meant. Particularly at the beginning, considerable numbers of people were summoned before the Consistory to be examined on their knowledge of Christian belief. Even those summoned for other reasons were often interrogated as well on their religious beliefs. A clear majority of people questioned on these matters were women.[5] Many of them were elderly. Some of them were illiterate. These registers thus serve as an unusual and precious record of what ordinary people actually believed, of what they made of the Reformation as it was being installed for the first time in their community. In general the Consistory expected only two things of these people. It insisted that everyone be able to recite from memory, in the maternal language, the Lord's Prayer and the Apostles' Creed. The Consistory frequently examined people who had learned to pray in Latin, and who had no notion of the meaning of the Latin texts they had learned to recite. Most of these people said that they had learned these Latin texts from their parents. One gets the impression of a network for religious instruction in the home before the Reformation that in some ways was rather effective. But this instruction was necessarily rather superficial in a population most of whom understood no Latin and many of whom were completely illiterate. The prayers and creeds they repeated were simple feats of rote memory. Many of them had no idea of what they meant. Their use of these Latin prayers and creeds illustrates neatly the very real cultic value of using formulae one makes no attempt to understand intellectually. This was a value, however, which members of the Consistory could not perceive. They insisted that all of these people learn to pray in a language they could

[5] This is demonstrated with precision by Jeffrey Watt, 'Women and the Consistory in Calvin's Geneva', *SCJ*, 24 (1993).

understand, their maternal language, the local dialect of French, and ordered them to keep returning until they could do so.

The Consistory also frequently encountered people who offered as one of their stock prayers the 'Hail Mary', again in Latin. This is testimony to the depths of Marian piety in Geneva and the surrounding area. These people would be told routinely that it did no good to pray to the saints or the Virgin Mary, that only prayers directed to God alone were of any utility. Most people got the point of the ban on prayers to the saints, although Saint Claude and others had been widely venerated in pre-Reformation Geneva. But many had difficulty in understanding the ban on prayers to the Virgin. They might protest, would not God listen to his own mother?

For people who had difficulty in accomplishing these simple tasks, the Consistory offered a variety of methods to assist learning. Most frequently it urged people to attend 'sermons', the generic term for religious services, including communal recitation of the Lord's Prayer and the Creed. During a single week there were as many as twenty to thirty different 'sermons' in the parish churches of Geneva. They were held every day, at several different times of the day. If attendance at only one service did not suffice, a person was urged to attend more – perhaps in addition to Sunday services, services on Wednesday (generally a half-holiday), perhaps services every day of the week. Obligations of work or household responsibilities were not accepted as excuses. The round of services had been designed to provide times that would fit into any schedule.

An additional possibility was to attend catechism sessions. These met every Sunday in each parish church after the services, and were intended primarily for children. But adults were encouraged to attend them as well. Those who could read were encouraged to obtain books, most probably some version of the local catechism first prepared by Calvin in 1537, and teach themselves at home. Yet another possibility was to obtain a private tutor. The Consistory was willing to help people who decided to take this route to find someone appropriate, sometimes starting with a bright child.[6]

The Consistory could be quite rough with some of these people, particularly if it suspected that they continued to harbour Catholic sympathies. Many were called back again and again, subjected to repeated scoldings, and barred from receiving communion until they got their prayers right. But the Consistory could also be surprisingly gentle. Consider the case of the evidently elderly widow Myaz Richardet. She could barely read, she had learned to pray in Latin, and she was obviously having trouble adjusting to the new religious forms. In September 1542, she was asked by the Consistory to memorise the Lord's Prayer and the Creed,

---

[6] For an example of a similar practice in Reformed Scotland, see below Jane Dawson, ch. 11.

and to report back in two weeks.[7] She duly appeared and was able to say the Lord's Prayer but only with the help of a slip of paper she carried with her. She had been unable to memorise anything. She was ordered to attend more 'sermons' and go to catechism.[8] She appeared once more before the Christmas communion, was now able to repeat the Lord's Prayer and the Creed by memory, and was judged not to have any 'scruples' about abandoning, when asked, Catholic beliefs. The Consistory decided that given her good will, even though she was not well informed, she would be permitted to receive communion, but with the stipulation that she attend 'sermons' even more frequently. It was felt that, no doubt due to her evident efforts, she was providing a good example to others.[9] A little over a year later the Consistory summoned her back to see how she was doing. She reported that she attended 'sermons' regularly, more regularly than most of her neighbours, that she joined in the prayers that everyone said during these services, that she was careful to avoid celebrating saints' days, and that she had forgotten the other superstitions of former times.[10]

It may not seem particularly revolutionary that the Calvinist church required that its members all memorise the Lord's Prayer and the Creed. Catholic priests had been urging their parishioners to do the same thing for centuries, if in Latin rather than the vernacular. What was different about Reformed practice in Geneva was the additional pressure it was able to generate through the Consistory to be sure that people complied. The Consistory did not limit itself to pious exhortations. It checked on individuals, repeatedly, until its members were sure each one had things right.

Counselling service

The Consistory served as a counselling service by establishing a mechanism to resolve disputes between family members, neighbours, and business partners. They would be summoned before the Consistory and given an opportunity to talk their problems out. Sometimes the problem would be worked out at that session. At other times, the Consistory would organise a later public service of reconciliation, most commonly in a parish church, after one of the 'sermons'. These attempts at reconciliation occurred most frequently shortly before quarterly communion services. People were not encouraged to receive communion if they were involved in a notorious public quarrel. After every communion service, the Consistory would summon before it a number of people who were identified as not having

---

[7] Archives d'Etat de Genève, Registres du Consistoire, I, fol. 61, 21 September 1542.
[8] *Ibid.*, fol. 64v., 12 October 1542.   [9] *Ibid.*, fol. 75v., 19 December 1542.
[10] *Ibid.*, fol. 160v., 24 January 1544.

participated. Some of them were obviously Catholics, who had scruples about participating in a Protestant sacrament. Indeed one can find examples of people who deliberately left Geneva on every Sunday communion was offered, and who sometimes even went to one of the many neighbouring villages that remained Catholic in order to receive mass. But many abstained from communion for other reasons. A frequent explanation for failure to participate was that one had 'hate in one's heart' for someone else, and thus felt unprepared and unworthy to receive the sacrament. This reflects a clear recognition of the undoubted fact that communion, after all, is a sacrament intended to strengthen the bonds that bring people together in a real community of christians.

Let me provide some examples of how these reconciliations were arranged, drawn from the earliest of the Consistory registers. In March of 1543, as plans were being made for the Easter communion service a few days later, the brothers Jean and Claude Curtet were summoned before the Consistory because of their 'debate and animosity'. Jean replied that he bore no ill will for his brother, but simply wanted what was rightfully his. Claude reported at more length on a joint business transaction that had gone sour about a year earlier and had led to a suit. The governing Council of the city, acting as the city's main court, had urged the brothers to resolve the dispute themselves and receive communion together. Jean said that he was willing to do anything that 'gens de bien', people of standing and property, would do. Claude said that he would leave vengeance to God. They were then treated to the 'admonitions' or ritual scoldings, involving invocations of pertinent passages from Scripture, that were a standard part of Consistory proceedings, and were urged to pardon each other. They dutifully agreed to pardon each other. As a sign of their agreement, they touched each other, 'in sign of peace'.[11]

A few months later, as plans for the next quarterly communion service were being drawn up, more people were summoned by the Consistory for reconciliations. This time they were summoned not to a regular session of the Consistory but rather to a special ceremony of reconciliation held in the parish church of the Madeleine, and supervised by John Calvin and Antoine Chicand, the 'syndic' or magistrate assigned to preside over the Consistory for that year. A first group of people included as one party Ypolite Revit, accompanied by his brothers, and as the other party the Noble Bartholomie, widow of Richardet and currently wife of Noble Jean Achard. The Noble Bartholomie had hurt Ypolite's feelings by calling him a traitor and wicked, among other insults. He offered to produce witnesses to these insults. Bartholomie replied that she had never called Ypolite a

[11] *Ibid.*, fol. 101v., 22 March 1543.

traitor, but confessed that she had indeed complained of his wickedness for losing some money her deceased former husband had entrusted to him. We may be witness here to some interclass conflict. Bartholomie was clearly of a higher social station than Ypolite and might have been scolding him as an unreliable former servant. The Consistory urged them to forgive each other, to receive communion together, and henceforth to live in peace and 'good charity' with each other. Ypolite asked for a written attestation of this reconciliation. Bartholomie agreed to regard Ypolite as a 'homme de bien', and promised to stop insulting him.

At that same session, the sisters Claudaz and Jane, both daughters of Claude Dentant and now married, were summoned for reconciliation. Their problem stemmed from insults Claudaz had hurled at Jane in retort to Jane's complaints about the price of some grain she had purchased, presumably from her sister. They quickly agreed to be reconciled, and to pardon each other for the exchange of insults and reproaches.[12]

Later that year, the Consistory uncovered yet another family it judged in need of reconciliation. This was the family of Pierre Tissot, a distinguished and prosperous patrician, then treasurer of the republic. For a long time he served as a leader in the government of Geneva, although probably not in the faction supporting Calvin. He had been elected to Geneva's governing Small Council in 1538, the year Calvin with Farel were dismissed from their positions in the Reformed church, but was no longer a member in 1541, when Calvin was recalled to take over sole responsibility for directing that church. Instead Tissot had in that year been named state treasurer, and was re-elected to that position for three terms. This was the position he held at the time of this family quarrel. The following year he rejoined the Small Council and was elected one of the reigning 'syndics' of the city. He was to serve again as syndic in two later terms. He was also to become 'lieutenant', or chief judicial officer of the republic, in 1553, and in that capacity would have had to supervise the burning of Servetus.[13] He was obviously a hardworking and highly regarded member of Geneva's governing elite.

Pierre Tissot had also married well. His wife was of the family of François Favre and he had thus acquired as a sister-in-law the wife of Ami Perrin, leader of the 'libertine' party that resisted the influence of Calvin and his fellow immigrants from France until it was finally crushed in 1555.

The Tissot case began when the widowed mother of Pierre, Françoise, was summoned before the Consistory. She apparently thought she had

---

[12] *Ibid.*, fols. 128v.–129, 31 August 1543.

[13] I have pieced together Pierre Tissot's political career from Amédée Roget, *Histoire du peuple de Genève depuis la Réforme jusqu'à l'Escalade* (7 vols., Geneva, 1870–83). At the end of every volume is a list of all the officers elected by the Genevan government in the years covered in that volume.

been summoned because of her religious practice, for she began by assuring its members that she attended 'sermons' every morning. But then she launched into a series of complaints about her ungrateful family. She was particularly critical of her illustrious son Pierre and his wife for neglecting her. The Consistory decided to summon Pierre Tissot, as well as his brother Jean, for a public reconciliation ceremony after a 'sermon'.[14] The very next day Françoise dutifully appeared at the parish church of the Madeleine, along with John Calvin and the syndic Chicand, who were to preside over the usual ceremony. But the rest of the Tissot family did not appear. Calvin and Chicand then arranged for a summons to a regular Consistory session of Pierre Tissot, his wife Loyse, and his brother Jean, to talk out their family problems.[15]

At the next regular meeting of the Consistory, Françoise, Pierre and Loyse, duly appeared. Tissot was informed that his mother was upset with him. He insisted that he held her in the high honour which God commands any man to hold for his mother, and greeted her with a polite 'bon jour'. She snapped back he could keep his 'bon jours' to himself and the devil. Tissot then informed the Consistory that he had done his best to care for his mother. He paid her a pension more generous than the financial support she had formerly received from her husband. He provided her with grain from his own supply for her bread, or with additional money if she preferred to buy her own grain. He provided her with the best wine from his own supply and had sent his servant with additional money. He had paid the apothecary for medicine during her recent illness and had sent his wife with some soup, which his mother, however, had not wanted to eat. He added that he had done his best to make his brother Jean behave, and felt that he really should not be held responsible for his debauchery.

Françoise was then asked to respond, and immediately launched into a tirade against her patrician son. She said that he had not paid her a pension for the previous year and that he had sent her a barrel of wine that was undrinkable. She said that she had got angry at the beginning of the session that day because her son had greeted her simply by saying 'bon jour', rather than 'bon jour, ma mère'. She insisted that his wife had never brought her soup during her illness. She blamed Pierre for the debauchery of his brother Jean. And she again insisted that the wine he sent her was undrinkable. Pierre replied that the wine had been good on delivery, and that if it had spoiled she must have put it into unsuitable containers. Françoise then blamed her son for the death of his two sisters from the plague two months ago and once more complained about her wine supply. When Pierre then addressed her as 'Mother' she cried she was no mother of his. Obviously

[14] Archives d'Etat de Genève, Registres du Consistoire, I, fols. 134–134v., 25 October 1543.
[15] *Ibid.*, fol. 135v., 26 October 1543.

Françoise had worked herself up into quite a state. This ceremony of reconciliation had degenerated into a flaming family quarrel.

Pierre's wife Loyse testified next. She did not feel in any way responsible for the tensions in her husband's family. She had done her best to care for her mother-in-law, visiting her during her recent illness, and bringing with her a number of things, as the neighbours could testify. But the old woman simply did not like these things and furthermore had made it very clear that she also did not like her daughter-in-law.

The Consistory tried to calm the Tissots down with its usual 'admonitions and remonstrances', urging them to abandon all past hate and rancour and in the future to live together in peace and friendship as a mother and son should. Pierre readily agreed to do all that he could to take care of his mother, and begged her forgiveness for any slips he might have made. She did not want to be reconciled. The Consistory gave her some time to think it over and told her to keep attending 'sermons'. She finally simmered down and agreed somewhat grudgingly to pardon her son and his wife for all their faults, 'for the love of God and of the government'. If we can trust this account, the Consistory had indeed arranged a reconciliation of sorts between Françoise Tissot and her distinguished son.[16]

A week later Jean Tissot, Pierre's brother, appeared before the Consistory in response to its summons and was asked to explain why he spent most of his time in taverns and gaming parties. It would seem that Pierre was an elder brother, that Jean was probably a minor at the time of their father's death, and that Pierre had thus had to assume some paternal responsibility for Jean. Jean acknowledged that his brother had been managing his property for him, presumably part of an inheritance, but blamed Pierre for not helping him get started in a decent career. He said he did not do anything because he had not been trained to do anything. The Consistory does not seem to have known what to do about this problem. It administered to Jean its usual 'admonitions and remonstrances', and told him to attend 'sermons' more often.[17]

It is a little hard on reading these accounts not to feel sorry for Pierre Tissot. He was probably so busy because of all his public responsibilities that he simply did not have much time for his relatives. His cantakerous old mother, whose memory seems to have been failing, and his undisciplined younger brother both blamed him for everything that went wrong in their lives. In future years, Pierre Tissot continued to have trouble with other family members for whom he felt responsible. In 1547, he appeared before the Consistory to apologise for the misbehaviour of his sister-in-law, Mme. Perrin, who had scandalized its members by roundly insulting them for

---

[16] *Ibid.*, fols. 136–7, 1 November 1543.   [17] *Ibid.*, fol. 138, 8 November 1543.

their harsh treatment of her old rogue of a father.[18] Later that same year, Tissot had appeared before the Consistory with his father-in-law, in an attempt to act as counsel for that irascible old man.[19] The Consistory permitted him to stay at the session but would not let him speak. We also find from later Consistory records that Jean Tissot continued to live a life of drunkenness and debauchery.[20]

The continuing misbehaviour of Pierre Tissot's relatives finally drove him out of power altogether. In 1555, his sister-in-law's husband, Ami Perrin, led the revolt of the 'libertine' party against the power of Calvin and his supporters that was crushed with violence, marking the definitive victory of the Calvinists in Geneva. In the following annual elections a number of office-holders deemed to be too close to the revolting 'libertines' were purged from the city government. One of them was Pierre Tissot.

If the Consistory found it difficult to resolve quarrels between siblings and between parents and children, it often found it even more difficult to reconcile quarrelling spouses. But this was a duty imposed upon the Consistory by the city government. In a sense the Consistory was in part a successor institution to the pre-Reformation bishop's court, and in that capacity was expected to handle any kind of marital problem requiring community adjudication. Unlike its predecessor it was willing to entertain petitions for divorce, on grounds either of adultery or wilful desertion, with permission for both parties to marry again. Calvin in particular was quite explicit in his support of petitions for divorce.

In handling divorce petitions, the Consistory went well beyond acting as a conciliation service. It also acted as a court of the first instance, or hearings court. As a court, it had no power on its own authority to issue a final divorce decree or to levy any kind of associated secular punishment. But it did have the power to recommend divorce decrees and punishments to the city government, and that power became considerable, given the fact that the Consistory had often collected much of the information upon which final judgements would be based. And punishments levied by the city government could be really severe, including on not infrequent occasions the death penalty. One of the crimes for which the government became willing to consider the death penalty was adultery of a notorious and public type. The possibility of these harsh sanctions must have influenced participants in divorce proceedings. The city government, however, remained reluctant to permit divorce, partly for economic reasons. It often suspected petitioners, particularly if they were men, of ulterior motives, of seeking to gain full control of the dowry property they had received with their wives as a part of their marriage settlements. So the governing Small Council of the

[18] *Ibid.*, III, fol. 104, 14 July 1547.   [19] *Ibid.*, fols. 146–7, 6 October 1547.
[20] *Ibid.*, fols. 200–4, 18 January–2 February 1548.

city would often turn back a petition for divorce with an order to the Consistory to arrange for a reconciliation. Thus conciliation attempts became a frequent part of the process.

We find this combination of attempts at conciliation and threats of punishment in the very first fully documented divorce case, that brought by Pierre Ameaux against his wife Benoite late in 1543, on grounds that she believed in adultery, an accusation she then proceeded to confirm before the Consistory in a barely coherent defence of the proposition that one should take literally the Bible's injunctions to love one's neighbours. The Consistory immediately referred the case to the city government which then imprisoned Benoite and subjected her to a full trial, forced her to retract her weird ideas, and finally returned her to the Consistory for a reconciliation. Pierre did not want to take her back, and was quite upset by the court order to treat her 'sweetly and aimably'. He suggested she was playing the hypocrite. He was finally persuaded, however, to accept the judgement of the church. In a ceremony of reconciliation, Calvin, on behalf of the Consistory, delivered first to the couple and then to Benoite alone, 'beautiful admonitions taken from Holy Scriptures'. She dutifully promised to obey her husband. She also promised to avoid seeing any person he did not want her to see. They were then dismissed to live together once more as a man and wife should.[21] This reconciliation did not last very long. Within a few months, Pierre Ameaux had thrown his wife out of their house, now charging that she not only believed in adultery, she had committed it. Eventually, after several months of further negotiations culminating in another trial that ended in Benoite's conviction and imprisonment for adultery, Pierre got his divorce, and married again.[22]

Similarly when John Calvin's own brother, Antoine, sued his wife Anne Le Fert for divorce, on grounds that she had committed adultery with a young man from a patrician family named Jean Chautemps, the city government refused the Consistory's recommendation for a divorce. Once again they imprisoned the accused adulteress, and this time her suspected lover as well, and extracted from them confessions that they had behaved with great imprudence. In particular they admitted that Chautemps had broken into the Calvin family house one night at three in the morning, and had made his way into Anne's bedroom, in the admitted hope of seducing her. But they both insisted that she had resisted his overtures. The Council accepted this explanation, released Anne from prison and ordered the Consistory to reconcile her with her husband. This time the Consistory's

---

[21] *Ibid.*, I, fols. 157–157v., 17 January 1544.
[22] For additional information on this case, see Archives d'Etat de Genève, Procés criminels, 1ère série, no. 385.

spokesman was William Farel, the grand old man of the Reformation in all of French-speaking Switzerland, who was then serving in Neuchâtel but happened to be visiting Geneva at that time. He first administered the expected admonitions to Anne Le Fert, telling her that she was a hypocrite and had brought great shame upon her household. Her husband was then led in. Anne fell to her knees and begged forgiveness from both her husband and her brother-in-law. They both received her apologies in good faith and forgave her.[23] This reconciliation, too, in the end failed, but only nine years later, when Anne was accused of adultery with an entirely different man, a hunchbacked household servant named Pierre Daguet who had abruptly left Geneva when he discovered he was under suspicion. Anne again denied all the accusations of adultery, even under torture, but was found guilty in a formal trial and banished from the city.[24] Antoine Calvin got his divorce. Both Antoine and Anne were married again in a few years.

Although these forced reconciliations of married couples did not always succeed, they also did not always collapse in a way that led to divorce. Shortly after the Antoine Calvin divorce, Jean Bietrix sought to get rid of his wife, Marie de la Maisonneuve, on similar grounds – of very imprudent behaviour with a household servant, without any solid proof of adultery. Marie was tried, found guilty of disobedience and adultery, and sentenced to life imprisonment.[25] But then her father, the politically powerful patrician Claude de la Maisonneuve, directed a successful petition for her pardon to the Genevan Council of the Two Hundred, an institution that had the right to forgive and release convicted prisoners. When Jean then tried to secure a divorce anyway, the government ordered a reconciliation attempt before the Consistory. After a great deal of pressure was brought upon Jean, he reluctantly agreed to take back his wife providing that she apologise to him and confess her adultery in public. She appeared before the Consistory, duly displayed 'a great and marvellous sign of repentance', fell to her knees, and begged her husband for forgiveness. But she flatly refused to confess to adultery, insisting that it had never occurred. He was so offended at her denial, that he refused to take her back, in spite of renewed pressure from the Consistory.[26] After trying a second time a week later to arrange a reconciliation between Jean and Marie, the Consistory finally gave up and decided to 'leave them both in liberty since one can think of nothing else to do'.[27] We do not know whether they later resumed living together. We can be quite sure that Jean did not get his divorce and never married again.

[23] Registres du Consistoire, IV, fol. 66v., 18 October 1548.
[24] Archives d'Etat de Genève, Procès criminels, 1ère série, no. 610.   [25] Ibid., no. 679.
[26] Registres du Consistoire, XV, fol. 63v., 13 April 1559.
[27] Ibid., fols. 69–69v., 20 April 1559.

Conclusion

The argument presented here is admittedly rather impressionistic, depending on a somewhat random collection of anecdotes. A more methodical and documented statement of this case will have to wait for the completion of our project. But I hope that I have nevertheless persuaded you of the plausibility of my tentative conclusion that the Consistory as John Calvin constructed it in Geneva during his ministry was indeed more than an integral part of a savage judicial system, that it did indeed try to act as an educational institution and as a counselling service. Discipline to these early Genevans meant more than social control. It also meant social help. This Consistory was no doubt a remarkably instrusive institution, leaving Genevans with none of the privacy that so many people in the western world today value so highly. But it was also a genuinely caring institution. It really tried to assist everyone in its city-state to live the kind of life it thought God intended people to live. Nobody in Calvin's Geneva could complain of the kind of 'anomie', or complete and hopeless anonymity, that is such a curse in so many big cities in today's world. In Calvin's Geneva there was always someone available to help.

3   The Geneva Academy

Gillian Lewis

In the late summer of 1572 events in France took a sharp turn for the worse. The St Bartholomew massacre in Paris was followed by further massacres in other parts of the kingdom. Why did these killings take place? How had hatred and mistrust of the followers of the Reformed religion reached such a pitch?

The jurist Pierre Charpentier, himself an advocate of religious reform, had no doubt where to lay the blame. In a vitriolic pamphlet written late in 1572 he declared that although most of the evangelicals were loyal and law-abiding subjects of the Crown of France, a few were highly dangerous, and fully deserved their reputation for active bigotry and for sedition.[1] Based in a city he did not name, but which was recognisable as Geneva, the members of this unrepresentative minority were up to their necks in international plots and intrigue. It was not surprising, he suggested, that their activities had aroused hostility and suspicion in high places, nor that rumours about their intentions had provoked fear and had brought upon the heads of devout and harmless Christians the terrible massacres of recent days.

Charpentier claimed that his testimony was expert. He knew these people well. He had lived among them. As Professor of Law in the Academy of Geneva, he had observed their dangerous game. His pamphlet was presented as an open letter to Francesco Portus, Professor of Greek in that same Academy. Charpentier claimed merely to lament divisions within the ranks of the Reformed. Transparently, however, his intention was to discredit the Geneva-based Huguenots and thus to represent as defensive and defensible the recent actions of the Crown. Charpentier's allegations about Beza and the pastors in Geneva were clearly hostile and tendentious. But were they also true? It has to be admitted that the picture, although in some respects dramatised and over-simplified, did have a grain of truth. Beza and the Geneva Company of Pastors did help place pastors and

---

[1] *Lettre de Pierre Charpentier, Jurisconsulte, addressée à Francois Portes, Candiois, par laquelle il monstre que les persecutions des Eglises de France sont advenues, non par la faulte de ceux qui faisoient profession de la Religion, mais de ceux qui nourrissoient les factions & conspirations qu'on appelle la Cause* (1572); *Registres de la Compagnie des Pasteurs de Genève*, ed. H. and F. Aubert *et al.*, (10– vols., Geneva, 1960–), III, 16 and n. 1.

professors in key places, they did help organise the French churches into synods,and they did intrigue openly with French noblemen and foreign rulers about money and military support.[2]

The pamphlet was greeted in Geneva with dismay and outrage. Pierre Charpentier was now seen there as a traitor, his evangelical sincerity totally discredited. But Francesco Portus in his reply made no attempt to deny the underlying charge of activism, confining himself to invective against its author and to asserting once more the evangelical reformers' loyalty to the Crown.[3] For although Charpentier's prose may have been vituperative and his allegations tendentious, no-one could deny that Beza and his followers were convinced that they had a providential calling, special to that time and place. They held that throughout history God had entrusted to certain of his servants an especial charge of vigilance against false doctrine, and responsibility for the welfare of his church. And right at the heart of these responsibilities, in Geneva, lay the institution of the Academy. If Charpentier's allegations were just, then the School between 1559 and 1572 must have been responsible, in part, for the indoctrination of bigots so unworldly as to be indifferent to the bloody consequences of their acts of faith. Does the evidence, dispassionately regarded, bear this out? Was the mentality he indicted one which was self-consciously, or otherwise, promoted by the Academy of Geneva?

The earliest aspirations of Calvin for educational provision in the city were very different from this. In the Ecclesiastical Ordinances of 1541 his preoccupation had been with the superstitious and ignorant state of the local population, now bereft of the ministrations of even a papist clergy. If the church was not to remain 'desolate' pastors must be trained and elders instructed. 'We need to found a college for the instruction of those young people who are to be prepared for the ministry and for civil government' declared the Ordinances, and ' with the Lord's help we hope to accomplish this quite soon.'[4]

This turned out to be optimistic. Genevan politics did not allow the project to be completed in its entirety for another eighteen years. During

---

[2] *Correspondance de Théodore de Bèze*, ed. H. and F. Aubert, *et al.* (15– vols., Geneva, 1960–), *passim*. For example III, pp. 7–10, 34–8, 63, 67–70, 86–9, 121–7, 132–45, 151–3, 161–72, 177–86, 194–207, 213–15, 225–9, 231–8, 259–63, IV, pp. 17–23, 25–7, 30–4, 42–6, 52–9, 67–9, 71–81, 87, 96, 104–7, 113–27, 130–43, 201–2, 254–8, 259–65.

[3] *P. Carpentarii J.C. Epistola ad F. Portum cretensem ... et ad Petri Carpentarii causidici virulenta in epistolam Responsio Francisci Porti Cretensis pro causariorum, quod vocat, innocentia* (np[Geneva?],1573); *Response de Francois Portus, Candiot, aux lettres diffamatoires de Pierre Carpentier, advocat. Traduite nouvellement du Latin en Francois* (np [Geneva?],1574).

[4] Emile Rivoire and Victor van Berchem, *Les Sources du droit du Canton de Genève* (Aarau, 1927–35), II, no. 794, p. 381; *CO*, X, I, 21; *RCP*, I, 1–13.

this time the city authorities did employ a few schoolmasters. Some good teaching in Latin, in Ciceronian eloquence and dialectic, and in Greek was available for a few boys in Geneva, under Castellio, among others, at the Collège de Rive. Private lessons in Hebrew could occasionally be found. The local pastors had charge of religious teaching, from catechising to offering lessons in advanced Bible study to candidates for the ministry of the Word. Calvin's own part in this was prominent, and central. In addition to his correspondence, his preparation of new editions of the Institutes, and the manifold duties of his pastorate, he took on the heavy responsibilities of the learned doctor's role, preaching and teaching indefatigably several times each week, his sermons and his lectures both taking the form, one way or another, of *ad lib* commentary upon a scriptural text, linguistic, heuristic, exhortatory, moralising. In this way he worked his way through much of the Bible book by book, chapter by chapter, passage by passage, word by word.

When these improvised arrangements are compared with the more institutionalised setting of teaching which came about later in Geneva, and which we call the 'Academy', they may seem to have been no more than the weakest of beginnings. Perhaps, however, this is to miss the point of the kind of institution which Calvin envisaged. For although he would not rest until he had secured formal backing from the city for a school in which teachers would be selected and put forward by the ministers, and recognised and paid by the magistrates, his real aim, as always, was to bring about a community-wide transformation of values. The institution of a school, as such, was to be only one means among many whereby ministers and magistrates could work together to make the city a single school of Christ. In the achievement of this extraordinary aim his preaching and his teaching and his creation of a sort of fraternal solidarity among the company of the pastors had in fact made a serious start.

During the 1550s two important series of events took place: one was a change in the balance of dominance within Genevan family politics, the other was a change in the scale and in the character of the immigration of French-speaking religious refugees. Both strengthened Calvin's hand. More and more often municipal elections produced a majority of town councillors favourably disposed towards cooperation with the largely French-dominated Genevan church, and incidentally towards the admission to *bourgeois* status of wealthy immigrants like the jurist Germain Colladon, the wholesale book distributor Laurent de Normandie and the leading printer and publisher Robert Estienne, all of them Calvin's friends. Detailed plans were now drawn up for the long-projected college, and moves were made to find a site for a building. Confident now in the backing of the city authorities, Calvin began to write around in search of learned and experienced teachers, to come and work in the School.[5] He was particularly anxious to find a competent Hebraist and a dependable Hellenist, since it was central to the whole enterprise to establish an authentic reading of the text of Scripture, and to teach the students to recognise how this was done.

A notably successful model for the kind of school he intended for Geneva had flourished for several years in Lausanne.[6] Its director Pierre Viret held views similar to Calvin's own. Its teachers were distinguished, its role in educating potential pastors similar to that envisaged for the Geneva School. Fortuitously (others said providentially) the Lausanne Academy in 1558 became involved in a bitter quarrel with its civil superiors, the sovereign rulers of the city of Berne. The upshot of the quarrel was the wholesale dismissal of many of the pastors in the French-speaking Pays de Vaud, including the entire teaching staff of the Lausanne Academy.

Recruitment of schoolmasters and professors for the projected Geneva School became, quite suddenly, much easier, and it was even possible to envisage utilising the talents of these uprooted pastors to meet the urgent supplications for shepherds of Reformed congregations springing up all over France. The professor of Greek from the Lausanne Academy, the brilliant and personable young Théodore de Bèze, had seen which way the wind was blowing in 1558. He had left Lausanne before the quarrel reached its peak, presenting himself in Geneva where recognition of his talents and of his potential usefulness had ensured him the promise of employment, and of eventual admission to the pastors' brotherhood. In 1559 he was made the new Academy's first Rector.

It is instructive to notice what propriety and decorum were observed in the opening ceremony of the new Academy on 5 June 1559.[7] The presence

[5] It proved especially difficult to fill the chair of Hebrew. With the authorisation of the Council Calvin opened negotiations with Jean Mercier at the Collège Royale in Paris: *CO*, XVII, 94, 97, 116, 163, 210, 213. These were unsuccessful. An offer was then made to Emmanuele Tremellio, who accepted, but was denied permission by his patron the Duke of Zweibrücken to leave the new academy at Hornbach where he had just been appointed rector. Calvin then approached François le Gay de Boisnormand a Hebraist then in Albret service at Nérac; *CO* XVII, 477; Charles Borgeaud, *Histoire de L'Université de Genève* (2 vols., Geneva, 1900–), I, *L'Académie de Calvin* p. 37, n. 2, 3. In the end Tremellio's son-in-law Antoine Chevalier was appointed; he immediately published in Geneva his *Rudimenta hebraicae linguae*, and remained in the Academy until 1566, despite repeated requests from the Reformed congregation in his native town of Caen that he should return and serve them as pastor. When he did leave, it was for the Regius Chair of Hebrew in Cambridge.

[6] Henri Vuilleumier, *Histoire de l'Église réformée du Pays de Vaud sous le régime bernois* (4 vols., Lausanne, 1927–33), I, pp. 671–739. Also *L'Académie de Lausanne au XVIe. siècle. Leges Scholae Lausannensis 1547. Lettres et Documents Inédits*, ed. Louis Junod and Henri Meylan (Lausanne, 1947).

[7] *L'Ordre estably en l'Escole de Geneve par noz Magnifiques et tres honnorez Seigneurs Syndiques et Conseil de ceste cité de Geneve, veu et passé en Conseil le Lundy Vingt Neufz de*

there of syndics and councillors, ministers and doctors, and the first batch of students, all duly seated, symbolised neatly the dovetailing of responsibility built in to the whole scheme. God's Providence, not human planning, was given the chief credit, deference was paid to the Seigneurie, whose authority was visibly present, but the talking was done by Calvin and by Beza, for it was the ministers and the Rector who were to take responsibility for the running of the School. Jean Calvin, as doyen of the ministers, opened and closed the proceedings with prayer.

The main speech was given by the Rector. Beza addressed the gathering thus:

Since God has endowed us, as members of the human race, with intelligence, we are in duty bound to use this gift. We are intended to think things out, and to make orderly sense of what we see, and to understand that everything can be accommodated within a single comprehensive philosophy. But we cannot do this properly without training and hard work. In our *respublica scholastica*, where doctors and students work together, it will be possible to acquire an education in good letters and in rational disciplines, so that, as they used to say in antiquity, men of reason and intelligence will be metamorphosed out of wild and savage beasts. Wisdom came down to us from Moses, but also from the Egyptians, passing from them to the Greeks. Solomon and Daniel were learned in all those arts wrongly referred to by some people as "profane", but which have the backing of Almighty God himself, and in which nothing appears which is not holy and right. In the same way, wisdom beyond that of ordinary men was imparted to the Prophets, wisdom which is also needed for the study of religion. Among the *profana gentes*, especially among the Greeks, there was, by the grace of God, light in the darkness. Because of that we should regard ourselves as at one with the academies of antiquity. Even in the Dark Ages the flame was kept alight, by Charlemagne and other Emperors, who founded in Europe academies which still flourish. These are the examples which have been heeded by the Senate of this city.

He continued:

Now I turn to you, *scholastici*, and I remind you of that famous saying of Plato which Cicero rendered thus: *Scientia quae est remota a iustitia, calliditas potius quam sapientia est appellanda*, 'that kind of knowledge which is remote from justice better deserves the name of ingenuity than of wisdom.' Yes – let us agree that the point of all philosophy is to pursue virtue, but let us also be careful to identify virtue correctly, and not to set up some vain simulacrum, some superstition, in its place. Virtue is that which is subordinated to the will of Almighty God. To this you must be obedient, and in that obedience, diligent in your studies. To be idle and negligent

May 1559. The Latin and French texts as transcribed into the *Livre du Recteur*, ff. 7–18, 23–30 and 36–43v are reprinted, together with the confession of faith required of entrants, in *Le Livre du Recteur de l'Académie de Genève 1559–1878*, ed. Suzanne and Sven Stelling-Michaud (6 vols., Geneva, 1964–80), I, pp. 61–4 and 67–77, and in *CO* XVII, col. 543–546, and X, part I, col. 68–9. Robert Estienne's printing of the French text as *Ordre de l'Ecole de la cite de Genève* (Geneva,[1559]), and of the Latin as *Promulgatio legum Academiae Genevensis* (Geneva,[1559])were reprinted in facsimile, ed. Charles Le Fort (Geneva, 1859).

is a perfidious rejection of the gift of God. You are not here to take part in frivolous games, but in order that you may become imbued with true religion and equipped with all good arts, the better to amplify God's glory and to be a credit to your native land. Never forget that you have enrolled under the sacred military discipline of the great Commander himself.

Beza's speech was a manifesto, a declaration of an evangelical position. He does not subscribe to the view that the study of pagan authors is blasphemous for Christians, nor even that it is a waste of time. On the contrary, such study is justified, not merely as a prolegomenon to Scriptural philology, but, more liberally, in terms of the wisdom it may provide. We are permitted to search in the writings of antiquity, although we would be well advised to confine our attention to those authors whose message is in conformity with the teaching of Holy Writ. His oration contains some warning notes, characteristic of the ethos selected by the founders of the Geneva School, although not unique to it. First, *calliditas*, ingenuity or artificiality: it was characteristic of Beza, as it was of Calvin also, to put special emphasis on the old Christian view that frivolity and 'curiosity' were besetting sins and that pride in one's own intellectual inventiveness was a danger against which all able men must guard. Secondly, industriousness: God requires us to serve him actively, and continually to monitor our activity so that it is in accordance with his will. Thirdly, Providence: the students are reminded to regard their obligations in the light of God's revealed purposes and never to forget that they are soldiers in an historic cause.

This urgent sense of history was entirely characteristic of Beza. He makes the point again, in the speech, when he describes the circumstances which led up to the inauguration of the School. He sets these events in a local and a European context of struggle and victory – indeed in a Providential context with God and Satan as actors on the stage. A whole sense of time, of topicality, of past, present and future, of human history and of eternity is here involved. Later, in his letters, and in the Registers of the Company of Pastors, there is constant reference to war and international politics, to bad news of persecutions and of martyrdoms; there are echoes of anxiety about money and morale. All these matters affected directly the fortunes of the School. One can see these concerns as practical, but, like everything else which was viewed through the *camera obscura* of the evangelical faith, they were also, in the eyes of the protagonists, aspects of revelation, part of a dimly discernible historic scheme.

In the *Ordre de l'Ecole* the organisation of the lower and upper schools, the *schola privata* and the *schola publica*, is set out in detail. Wednesdays, Saturdays and Sundays all begin with attendance at the public sermons in the *temple*, the younger boys having been marched there in four crocodiles from the four quarters of the town, each under the eye of a schoolmaster. On Sunday afternoons they return to church, similarly dragooned, for the second sermon and the catechism class. Roll-call is taken to take account of absentees so that no-one may be 'nonchalant about listening to the Word of God'. Mondays, Tuesdays, Thursdays and Fridays are classroom days. In the lower school the first lesson starts with the special school prayer (published with the Catechism), which each boy in turn must recite. After lessons for an hour and a half, breakfast is taken in school 'without noise and accompanied by prayers'. More morning lessons follow, and then each boy in his class recites aloud the Lord's Prayer 'with some brief prayers of thanks'. They then go home for dinner. On their return they spend a full hour in assembly singing psalms. More lessons follow, interspersed with play-time (again starting with prayer) and further lessons; the school day ends with assembly. Here, row by row, the pupils recite in French the Lord's Prayer, the Confession of Faith and the Ten Commandments. The Principal gives the Blessing, and they all disperse.

It is striking how much written work and indeed homework they were given in the lower school. On Wednesdays after the sermon they 'do their questions' in the groups of ten into which they have been streamed in relation to their scholastic prowess and industry. Every other Wednesday afternoon they assemble to listen to speeches on set themes prepared and delivered by pupils from the top class. On the other Wednesday afternoons each one of them (except the youngest) must sit down and write an essay. The masters mark these overnight and hand them back in class on Thursdays. On Saturdays after the sermon each pupil has to make and listen to a report on his week's work; in the afternoon he must listen to the older students engaging in debate, and then he must himself recite the part of the Catechism which is to be dealt with on the coming Sunday, and hear an explanation of it from his teacher. Sunday is to be spent listening to sermons, taking notes upon them, and copying them out. In the lowest class, the boys are taught to read and write in French and Latin, using the bilingual Catechism – three birds killed with one stone. In the next class, they begin Latin grammar 'comparing always the Latin with the French'. In the next class, they start Latin syntax and make their first efforts at writing in Latin for themselves. In class four, they do more advanced Latin, reading and analysing the simplest of the *Letters* of Cicero, and they are given an introduction to verse, with the *Elegies* of Ovid. And – a real moment – they begin now to learn Greek. In class three they concentrate intensively upon Greek. Latin authors here come in in greater numbers: Cicero, *De Amicitia* and *De Senectute*, Virgil's *Aeneid*, Caesar's *Commentaries*. In Greek, they read the *Orations* of Isocrates. In the second class there is provision for history, using Livy, Xenophon, Herodian or Polybius, for poetry, using

Homer, and for dialectic. Propositions and arguments are to be explained to them, using the authors they have already read, above all, the *Paradoxes* of Cicero or his shortest speeches. But (the *Ordre* adds austerely) 'they are not to amuse themselves at all with the artifice of Rhetoric'. On Saturday afternoons from three to four the Gospel of Saint Luke in Greek is read aloud to them. By the time the final class is reached, the students are almost ready for the upper school. 'To the rudiments of Dialectic are now added what the science teaches about predicates and categories, topics and elencha; and for this some textbook well-illustrated with examples should be used.' They should now be introduced to rhetoric, especially to those devices which show how to use language stylishly and to good effect; for this they should use the more polished of Cicero's *Orations*, his *Philippics* and the speeches of Demosthenes; for poetic diction, Homer and Virgil. They are to do this by taking the passages apart, and analysing the ornament employed, comparing the practice with the precepts. To polish their own style, students are to deliver speeches twice a month, on Wednesdays after dinner. On Saturday afternoons one of the Epistles of Paul is read to them in Greek.

There is an examination season, too. Every year in April, three weeks before the 1 May, all the pupils in the lower school assemble in the hall where one of the professors sets them a topic for an essay in French; they write it then and there; after that they all disperse to their classes, where they translate their own French essay into Latin, each pupil by himself, and without help. The essays are to be handed in and during the next few days each pupil's essays are corrected and awarded marks. In the light of this performance and of the form-master's report the Regent and the professors of the upper school decide which of the pupils can go up into a higher class.

On the first day of May each year the ceremony of 'promotion' is held in the *temple* of Saint Pierre. This is a solemn public occasion attended by the lord syndics and councillors of the city, the ministers and professors, the principal and regents. Prizes, awarded by the government, go to the best pupils, and the Rector makes a speech praising these pupils, to encourage them and so that the others will be incited by this good example to study well. The assembly closes with prayers.

The *Ordre de l'Ecole* now sets out the duties of the public professors of the upper school. There are to be professors of Hebrew, and of Greek and someone to teach the arts. This last provision had been absent in the scheme Calvin had presented to the Council in 1558. Its inclusion here may suggest that a slight broadening had occurred in the conception of the school since the arrival in Geneva of Beza, but it may merely have been prompted by the availability of a good philosophy lecturer, Jean Tagault, another refugee from Lausanne. Apart from their teaching duties it is incumbent upon the professors to attend the Friday 'congregations' (where elders, deacons and lay people gather) and after that the 'Colloque des Ministres'.

The professor of Hebrew is expected on classroom mornings to expound some book of the Old Testament. He is publicly to teach the language in the afternoon.

Interestingly, the professor of Greek does not follow precisely the same pattern; he does not expound the Greek New Testament, this being left to those designated by the Company to expound the Scriptures; instead he comments upon 'some book of Philosophy which has to do with morals, whether Aristotle, Plato or Plutarch, or some Christian philosopher'. In the afternoon he is to read from some Greek poet, or some orator, or historiographer 'choosing the most pure'.

The professor of arts shall read 'some book of Physics' (that is of natural philosophy) in the mornings, but only for half an hour. After dinner he is 'learnedly to expound the *Rhetoric* of Aristotle, the most famous of the *Orations* of Cicero, or the *De Oratore*.'

Although the *Ordre* does not go into great detail about the teaching in the upper school, its outlines are deducible from the weekly timetable. For example, the student will need, eventually, to be able to read in Hebrew, as well as in Greek and Latin, in order to catch and understand the nuances in the language of a Scriptural text. He will devote several hours each week to all three languages, with this aim in mind.

Dialectic will enable the student to question definitions and to break down problems into their constituent parts. This skill will equip him to spot unacceptable implications in propositions put forward by those who offer to the faithful erroneous and perverted readings of the Word.

The student will learn how to frame definitions and divisions in the approved Aristotelian–Ciceronian manner, probably using some recent well-illustrated textbook such as that of Neobar or Sturm.[8] He will then embark upon the figures of rhetoric, not for idle pleasure but so that he will be better able to persuade others of the Gospel message and to convince them that what he has to offer is the true reading of God's Word.

A little room is allowed in the syllabus for poetry, despite the fact that – dangerously – poetry awakens the imagination, and more dangerously still, uses vivid fictions to this end. Such stimulation is permissible provided that it is utilised scrupulously to enhance one's reading of the Word.

The function assigned to history, more sober than that of poetry, is to arouse awareness in the student of God's providential purposes in the

---

[8] Irena Backus, 'L'Enseignement de la Logique à l'Académie de Genève entre 1559 et 1565', *Revue de Théologie et de Philosophie*, 3 (1979), 153–63.

history of mankind. Physics, which is given only a small place in the timetable of the upper school, is presumably intended to serve the same purpose with regard to creation as a whole.

Ethics is self-evidently a study which enables one to analyse right behaviour. Profane authors can make a useful contribution, but the values they advocate must be tested, once again, against a faithful reading of the Word.

The Holy Scriptures are to be expounded on Mondays, Tuesdays and Wednesdays in the afternoon, by the two persons designated as instructors in theology by the Company of Pastors. They are to take turns in this duty in alternate weeks. Even in the upper school *bonae literae* are not cold-shouldered. Biblical scholarship directly accounts for only about half the ordinary student's time.

However, the directly Scriptural component is higher for those students 'qui se vouldront exercer es Sainctes escriptures', that is to say those who think they may have a calling to become ministers of the Word. On Saturday afternoons they are to take a passage from the Bible and expound it publicly in the presence of some of the ministers. The minister presiding will then comment upon and criticise this interpretation, after which everyone present may join in, so long as he speaks up modestly and in the fear of the Lord. In addition, such students are to draw up and defend every month a certain number of theses or 'positions' which are not to be 'curieuse, sophistiques, ni contenantes faulse doctrine.' They are to hand these in in good time to the professor of theology, and then 'they are to sustain them in public disputation with anyone who is prepared to argue a case'. Everyone present is permitted to speak. All 'sophisterie, curiosité impudente et audace de corrompre la parolle de Dieu' is forbidden, as is all 'mauvaise contention et opiniastreté.' Points of doctrine are to be treated 'simply and religiously by the disputants on both sides'. 'The professor of theology, who will preside over the disputation, will conduct everything according to his own discretion and in the case of queries handed in in advance will resolve the difficulties in accordance with the Word of God.'[9]

The classicism of the upper school is in some ways surprising, as is the relative liberty afforded to the regents and professors to adopt a style of exposition and of teaching all their own. Surprising, because Calvin believed that in the formation and perpetuation of a Christian community, right teaching had so central a role to play. Surprising also, because, like his old friend Viret, he had strong views upon the difference between a profane

---

[9] That something like this actually did occur is attested by surviving student notes: Pierre Fraenkel and Luc Perrotet, 'Cours sur les Épitres aux Romains et aux Hébreux 1564–66, d'après les notes de Marcus Widler. Thèses disputées à l'Académie de Genève 1564–67', *Cahiers de la Revue de Théologie et de Philosophie*, 13 (1988).

and a 'Christian' attitude to learning. This 'Christian' attitude is not always, in the hands of Calvin, what one might expect. Where salvation was concerned, there was no significant difference of opinion among Protestant intellectuals about whether or not the insights furnished by the Scriptures alone were sufficient; all agreed that they were. But some reformers went further, claiming that the Scriptures offered a total compendium of guidance on all aspects of human knowledge, and that therefore recourse to pagan writers was unnecessary, or even blasphemous. This standpoint did not meet with any sympathy from the architects of the Geneva School, who were perfectly content to see philosophical issues discussed in the light of the pagan writings of classical antiquity, provided that discretion had been exercised in the choice of authors, and provided that the whole debate was subordinated to the authority of the Word of God.

In this last sentence however, the dogmatism lies concealed. Take natural philosophy as a case in point. There is room for it – a little room – in the syllabus of the lower school. But how was it to be taught? The *Ordre de l'Ecole* does not specify. If the model of Calvin's own teaching, in his sermons and his biblical commentaries were to be followed, or if the matter was to be *traitée Chrestiennement* in the way Pierre Viret recommended in another context, it would not be taught in the usual way of the universities.[10] Instead, the subject-matter would be utilised primarily in a spirit of devotion, as a vehicle for directing the student's attention to the power and the glory of God.

This approach, if it had been followed rigorously by the God-fearing professors, as Calvin must surely have intended, would have had far-reaching implications for the entire range of studies, and would have revealed a chasm between the humanist intellectual priorities assumed in other schools and universities and those adopted in the Geneva School. But did the Geneva professors prove able or willing to subordinate, in this strict sense, all their teaching to the Word? Their published writings suggest that they did not.

There was another inhibition latent in Calvin's approach. This was his refusal to waste time teaching students, even those preparing for the ministry, the customary terms of school divinity, in the use of which he himself had had no training, and for which he affected a fine scorn. This policy was followed by Beza and the other pastors who took their turn as teachers of theology, so that in Geneva scholastic philosophical categories grew rusty with disuse. There was a danger that in debates with Catholics

---

[10] Pierre Viret, *Instruction Chrestienne en la doctrine de la loy et de l'Evangile; et en la vraie philosophie et theologie tant naturelle que supernaturelle des Chrestiens; et en la contemplation du temple et des images et oeuvres de la providence de Dieu en tout l'univers; et en l'histoire de la creation et cheute et reparation du genre humain* (2 vols., Geneva, 1564).

and Lutherans innocence (or ignorance) of the technical terms of theological debate would make Geneva-educated protagonists into prophets unarmed. Relying instead upon linguistically based textual scholarship the pastors and professors of Geneva did bring to completion the monumental enterprise known to posterity as the Geneva Bible, but in technical controversies with rival theologians they found that Platonist rhapsodies, non-Thomist readings of Aristotle and borrowing from Cicero were of little use as substitute weapons, and that they had to adapt or to buy in talent educated elsewhere.[11]

There were other risks in the strategy adopted in the framing of the Schools. What if it proved difficult to find professors whose evangelical credentials were as good as their linguistic ones, or vice versa? In the former case the pupils might be led astray into a world where the pagan authors would prove impossible to tame; in the latter case the teaching they were offered might be noticeably mediocre or weak.

If the architects of the Geneva School were aware of such dangers in 1559, they seem resolutely to have put their fears aside. The most important decision of principle which had been taken was to regard pagan authors not only as permissible, but indeed as indispensable in the early education of godly gentlemen and citizens and of future ministers of the Word. The Academy was not intended, after all, as a school for everyone. There were no plough-lads here, no butcher's boys, no shoemakers, no girls. An education appropriate to the Christian labourer or artisan or woman could readily have been defined. But such problems were not the immediate concern of the framers of these Geneva Schools; they confined their attention to the best way to educate future leaders of society, and learned ministers of the Word. The exacting linguistic and critical studies to be followed in the upper school could not be undertaken unless a firm groundwork had been laid. There is a continuum in the studies, from the beginners' work done by the little boys, right through the seven classes of the *schola privata* to the advanced studies in the *schola publica*.

A distinction was drawn between the *escholiers publics* in general and 'ceulx qui se vouldroient exercer les Sainctes escriptures' in particular; while all students were supposed to attend the theological lectures, the *proposants* or would-be pastors were expected in addition to try their hand (on Saturdays) at publicly pronounced exercises in Biblical exposition. However, specific training for pastoral duties formed no part of the curriculum.

---

[11] On adaptation, see below. On buying in of talent, see the case of Simone Simoni, an accomplished Aristotelian trained in Italy, professor of philosophy and lecturer in medicine in the Academy, 1565–67, who was employed by Beza in the task of bringing technical philosophy to bear in the important published controversy with the Ubiquitarian Lutherans over 'substance' in the Eucharist. Beza to Bullinger, 14 December 1565: Bèze, *Correspondance*, VI, pp. 220–1; *RCP*, III, 2, n. 1.; III, 15 and n. 3.

Future ministers of the Reformed faith were not given formal tuition in the Geneva Academy in how to deal with the problems they would face in dealing with their flock; they learned, if at all, later, and by first-hand experience.[12]

The Geneva Academy did not, then, set out to be mainly, or solely, a seminary. However, it did not set out to be a university either, at least not in the legislation of 1559. Young Protestant noblemen, touring with their tutors from one non-Catholic university to another in the 1590s, might well have supposed that the School they encountered at Geneva was a Protestant university of a kind. This was an optical illusion, even if it was one which the Genevan authorities, secular and ecclesiastical alike, were, by that time, in no hurry to dispel. For obvious reasons Protestant noblemen and princelings from Germany and Poland, Scandinavia and Bohemia, Scotland and England, were among the choicest of their prey.

Despite appearances, the School of Geneva was not, in institutional terms, a university at all. Unlike the ancient schools of Bologna, Padua, Paris, Oxford and Salamanca, and unlike most of the princely foundations, Catholic and Protestant, of the period 1520–90, it had no corporations of students, no 'faculties' of masters in arts, law, medicine or divinity, no chancellor, no dean and no proctors. It charged no fees (until 1584) and it awarded 'testimonia' instead of licences or degrees.[13]

The founding statutes demand of the schoolmasters and professors as well as of all students of the upper or 'public' school a written statement that they had read, assented to and bound themselves to the contents of a highly detailed confession of faith designed to exclude Roman Catholics and Anabaptists, anti-Trinitarians and sceptics, but which, if interpreted strictly, would also have excluded Lutherans, and even some Protestants of the Swiss Reform.

This confession begins with an affirmation to follow the teaching

---

[12] Charles Perrot wrote a memorandum of advice to his successor in the rural parish of Genthod: *Archives d'Etat*, Geneva: *Archives Communales, Etat Civil*, Genthod; *Calvinism in Europe,1540–1610. A Collection of Documents*, ed. Alastair Duke, Gillian Lewis and Andrew Pettegree (Manchester, 1992), pp. 73–83.

[13] The *Ordre* specifies that students who have studied theology in the School may, if they satisfy a rigorous oral examination, be awarded a *testimonium vitae et doctrinae* in one of two grades, 'mediocre' or 'honourable'. Among the testimonials which survive are the following: testimonial for Thomas van Til, on his departure in May 1572, *RCP*, III, 73; testimonial for Andrew Melville on his departure for Scotland in 1574, Ms.fr.408, *Bibliothèque Publique et Universitaire*, Geneva; testimonial for Antoine de La Faye on his departure for Italy to study medicine,1574, *RCP*, III, 143. In the last two decades of the century Geneva students found that other institutions increasingly demanded evidence of a degree, or at least of the completion of a conventional course of study. Students in theology more and more often had printed copies made of the theses they had defended. Henri Heyer, *Catalogue des Thèses de Théologie soutenues à l'Académie de Genève pendant les XVIe., XVIIe., et XVIIIe. siècles* (Geneva, 1898).

contained in the Geneva Catechism, to subject oneself to the church discipline there by law established, and not to adhere to or consent to any sects which might disturb the peace. It demands assent to sola-fideism, to the practice of infant baptism, and to the doctrine of predestination. It demands rejection of the errors of the Manicheans, the Nestorians, the Anabaptists and the Papists, expressly condemning the 'alleged' five sacraments and the 'abomination' of the mass. It has a powerful rhetorical rhythm, using repetition of the formula 'Je confesse. . . . ainsi je déteste . . .' It is categorical, almost ceremonial. Anyone made to read this document out loud in the presence of the Rector and to put his hand to it when he signed the Rector's book could have been in no doubt of the seriousness of the engagement he had made. The Geneva School, as the confession implies, was in its aims dogmatic and evangelical. Its starting-point was credal, and it had the Gospel as its *raison d'être*. The intention of its promotors was profoundly ideological, their aim being, as the Ordinances of 1541 had declared, to 'indoctrinate' as well as to 'instruct'. The School, in its early days, was intended to be a citadel, a theatre of edification for those who studied there and who were, as they had testified, already committed to the Word.

In 1559 publicity was given to the existence of the new Academy by Robert Estienne. With his habitual elegance he printed the School's Statutes as *Promulgatio Legum Academiae* for an international scholarly audience, and as *L'Ordre du Collège* for French-speaking circles and for the Genevans themselves. Interestingly, the two texts are not identical. The Latin version prints the Rector's oration, and includes a reference to the 'tempestates et congiuriae' which God's servants had suffered in Geneva before the fruition of the scheme. Michel Roset, Secretary to the Council, who wrote the French version, tactfully made no mention of these events. Roset at one point referred, a little hyperbolically, to 'l'université', whereas Beza spoke throughout of 'scholae'. Under the legislation passed in 1559 the Schools were placed under the joint direction of the City Council and of the Company of Pastors, the former to appoint and to pay the regents and professors, the latter to oversee the teaching. All agreed that the Schools were a dual dependency of magistrates and ministers. The congruity of their perceptions was intended to be complete. In fact, however, these tiny discrepancies in the presentation of the project to two different audiences reveal a slight difference in perspective which was later to increase. On the one hand there was the (largely French immigrant) pastors' vision of a godly school for future leaders of the wider church; on the other there was the councillors' determination that the Schools must prove themselves to be an investment useful to the interests of the city. Some councillors, no doubt, at this stage envisaged little more than efficient local schools; others, as

Roset's text implies, already could imagine the advantages a full-scale university might bring to the town.

If salaries were to be paid to professors of Hebrew and of Greek, why not also to professors of law and medicine? Other cities had found profit and prestige in celebrated schools of medicine and of law. However, once a school admitted law students, it might as well resign itself to becoming little more than a school of law, since the law students would soon outnumber the rest. In the sketchy project for the Geneva Schools presented by Calvin to the Council in May 1558, and again in the detailed specification agreed in May 1559 no mention was made of any intention to appoint professors of law, or indeed of medicine. Surprisingly, however, when the Latin text of the *Ordre* was printed, a significant sentence appeared at the end. It read: 'If God in his goodness will allow us, as we hope that he will, we intend to complete that which is unfinished, by adding professors in jurisprudence and in medicine.' Whose were the hopes here expressed? It is unlikely that they were Calvin's own. The statement reveals a view of the purpose of the Schools at odds with the one which had just been so solemnly approved. Calvin must surely have known that some voices were arguing for the inclusion of these studies, and he must surely have been aware of the publication of this statement, if only after the event. It looks as if he decided, in the interest of the main project, to make no formal protest, despite any qualms he may have felt about such wavering from the prime, and godly, purpose of the Schools. It now remains to be considered how the 1559 plan for the Schools worked out in practice over the next half-century, and to examine the question of how faithful the professors, and the city councillors proved to Calvin's vision for an educational establishment devoted, above all, to the promulgation of the Word.

During their first five years the Schools were a resounding success. The buildings were completed, and classes were established according to plan. Schoolmasters were engaged for all seven classes of the lower school, and professors of Greek, Hebrew and philosophy appointed in the upper school. Printers in the city made the first steps in what was to prove a long and cooperative association by publishing textbooks, works of reference and treatises needed by the students, and writings by some of the professors.[14] Students enrolled in gratifyingly large numbers, although only 3 out of 160 recorded in the first four years came from Geneva itself, and only another 10 from the rest of the Swiss Confederation; 13 came from Italy,

---

[14] Paul Chaix, *Recherches sur l'Imprimerie à Genève de 1550 à 1564. Étude bibliographique, économique et littéraire* (Genève,1978), pp. 92–117; P. Chaix, A. Dufour, G. Moeckli, *Les Livres imprimés à Genève de 1550 à 1600*, new edn, revised G. Moeckli, (Geneva, 1966), *passim*; Jean-François Gilmont, *Bibliographie des Éditions de Jean Crespin 1550–1572* (2 vols., Verviers,1981), nos. 51/15, 54/10, 60/4, 61/7, 61/8, 62/4, 65/4, 66/4, 66/6, 68/4, 69/1, 70/7.

mostly from Piedmont, 10 from Germany and 10 from the Netherlands. No less than 114 came from the Kingdom of France;[15] 66 of the 116 are known to have become pastors, many of these later playing a leading role at *colloques* and synods of the French Reformed church; 5 were martyred. The students who enrolled in these early years included Antoine Olevianus, son of Gaspard (professor of theology at Heidelberg and framer of the Heidelberg Confession), Jakob Ulrich, later professor of Latin and logic in Zürich, Claude Textor, who later taught French at Wittenberg, Simon Girard and Michel Hortin, who became professors of Greek and of Hebrew at Lausanne, Philippe Birgan, who taught Hebrew at Cambridge and at Saumur, Jean-François Salvard, architect in the 1580s of the Harmony of Reformed Confessions, Jean de Serres, later historiographer of the Reform and director of the Academy at Nîmes, Philippe Marnix de Sainte-Aldegonde, subsequently counsellor to William of Orange, Peter Young, later tutor to James VI of Scotland, and Florent Chrestien, later tutor to Henry of Navarre. Among those whose names do not appear in the Rector's Book, but who certainly studied in the Schools, were François du Jon (Junius), and Lambert Daneau, distinguished contributors to Calvinist thought, each of whom in turn was professor of theology at Leiden, Thomas Bodley, later founder of the Bodleian Library at Oxford, and Charles Perrot, who was to remain a member of the Geneva Company for the rest of his life, and to contribute notably to the teaching in the School. Lambert Daneau was later to recall:

In 1560 I came, my heart filled with enthusiasm, to your Academy, not because it was situated at the very gates of France, for this was true of other places also, but because it was your Academy which offered me the purest well-spring of the celestial teaching which had been that of my master, the jurist and martyr Anne Du Bourg. I have no need to describe the masters whom I encountered there. Praise is to be heard on every hand of those who are still alive, as well as of those who are now dead. I will always say, frankly and without holding back for fear of arousing jealousy among our contemporaries, that I saw in that city so much light on the world, so many men of the greatest possible merit and of the greatest renown in all branches of learning, that the place seemed to me to be one of the most rich of all the market-places of the literary commerce of mankind.[16]

Charles Perrot in a letter to his brother Daniel dated 25 February 1564, described his studies in Geneva thus:

Things are going very well for me here, both as regards the town and the School. I have embarked seriously upon Hebrew, and if the Lord is willing, will persevere in it

[15] Stelling-Michaud, *Livre du Recteur*, I, 81–4; Robert M. Kingdon, *Geneva and the Coming of the Wars of Religion in France 1555–1563* (Geneva, 1956), p.10.
[16] Lambert Daneau, *D. Aurelii Augustini Hipponensis Episcopi liber de haeresibus* ... (Geneva, 1576), Letter of dedication to the Syndics and Council of Geneva; Borgeaud, *Académie*, p. 52.

with great pleasure. I am working at Theology, both in the School and on my own. Our good master and our common father [Calvin] is giving us lessons on the Book of Ezekiel, which he has in hand, according to this year's programme, on the first three days of the week, in alternate weeks. In the other week it is our Théodore [Beza] who explains the Catechism in Greek, also on the first three days of the week, because they each have the other three days off. We derive great profit from the lessons of the latter [Beza], in part because of the way the Catechism is treated, and partly because he is always there. The former [Calvin] can scarcely manage to take his turn regularly because of illness, especially in the winter; in the summer he is a little better. This means that Theodore carries almost all the weight of the School, which is testimony to his resilience: the more fields there are to be cultivated, the more the plough-ox shows his strength.

The audience is large, about two hundred. It consists of the most brilliant students in the entire school. The others, less advanced in their studies, work away on Greek, Hebrew and Philosophy with Portus, Chevallier and Scrymgeour, as is appropriate at their age. The Gymnasium is also very full, although I don't know this at first hand; they reckon that it contains more than four hundred boys, most of them from this region, the others mostly French, with a few Italians ... Chevallier is engaged upon a revision of the Alcalá edition of the Bible – the Polyglot – but as far as I can see it will take him ten years. The New Testament will follow, with the annotations of Theodore.[17]

These were also the great years of the Academy's contribution to the missionary effort, which had been in full swing since 1556, and which had accelerated when the quarrels in Lausanne released for the French churches a supply of pastors from the Pays de Vaud. The Geneva Company of Pastors was deeply involved in the enterprise, into which the new School was soon swept up. The pattern of demand – and supply – reached an early peak in 1561 and declined sharply thereafter. The number scarcely recovered during the following decade. Well-founded rumours of insecurity and of epidemics in the Geneva area deterred student recruitment, which may have declined also because competition had set in from other Reformed educational establishments set up in France, notably the Academies at Orleans and at Nîmes.[18] More significantly the civil disorders ensured that fewer and fewer French churches were in a position to seek pastors far afield. Activity withered away every time military disturbance increased, and recovered only feebly every time there was an interval of peace. In the 1570s, 1580s and 1590s demand had fallen off spectacularly, and, even then

[17] MS 141 *Burgerbibliothek*, Berne, printed (in French translation) by Henri Meylan, 'Professeurs et étudiants: Questions d'horaires et de leçons', *La Réforme et l'Éducation: Actes du IIIe. Colloque tenu par le Centre d'Histoire de la Réforme et du Protestantisme de l'Université Paul Valéry, Montpellier, 1973*, sous la direction de Jean Boisset (Toulouse, 1974), p. 20.
[18] Neither Beza in his letters nor the Company of Pastors in their registers give any indication that they were aware of competition for students from other schools, but in 1572 and again in 1575 there is reference to the depopulating effect on the schools of the epidemics which had visited Geneva almost every year since 1567: *RCP*, III, 77, 82, IV, 17.

the Academy was supplying only a minority of the much smaller number of pastors still sought by churches in France. Despite this, the contribution of the Geneva School to the ethos of the French Huguenot movement before 1580 may well have been disproportionately high: of the thirty-one men sent out from Geneva as pastors between 1563 and 1572 fourteen had been students at the Academy, several of them having been sent specially by their local church to train, seven had been pastors in Geneva itself, two had been schoolmasters in the lower school, and five had been professors.[19] In later quarrels over church discipline among the French Reformed, Beza and most of the Company put their weight behind synodical organisation and the principle of ministerial dominance over congregations. In synods and in colloques they could rely, almost always, on the backing of ministers who had passed through the rigours of the Geneva Company or School. This caused some resentment among the wider constituency of Huguenots, and created some ambivalence towards the Genevan School.

Beza was absent from Geneva for much of the period of his rectorate of the School, June 1559–May 1563, heading the Genevan delegation at the Colloquy of Poissy, and attending upon Condé in Orleans. His correspondence reveals the extent of his political preoccupation during these years, and lends some colour to Charpentier's accusation that much of the energies of the leaders of the refugees was being put at this time into planning and intrigue.[20]

When Calvin died in the summer of 1564, there were dark clouds enough for the Cause, but the Schools at least seemed to be working more or less as he had hoped. However, a certain conflict of priorities was becoming apparent. From 1560 on, and repeatedly thereafter, professors were called away to be pastors or counsellors of princes, or persuaded to take their learning and their services to another school. Some of these departures were delayed by reluctance on the part of town or church to release the professor concerned; but others were hastened by personal animosities or by ambition, or by the inability or unwillingness of the Genevan seigneurie to pay at the going rate. The Company was genuinely concerned about the needs of the Academy, but at the same time it was subjected to all kinds of pressures to oblige it to try to cater for every urgent pastoral need. Educated and experienced pastors were always in short supply, and the Geneva schools were bled to supply them.[21]

[19] Robert M. Kingdon, *Geneva and the Consolidation of the French Protestant Movement 1564–1572. A Contribution to the History of Congregationalism, Presbyterianism and Calvinist Resistance Theory* (Geneva, 1967), p. 35; Stelling-Michaud, *Livre du Recteur*, Biographical material, vols. 2–6, *passim*

[20] Bèze, *Correspondance*, III, IV, V, *passim*; examples in note 2, above.

[21] The Registers of the Company of Pastors supply innumerable examples of such pressures and of the Company's ambivalent response to them. For instance: 1562: Jean Ribit, who

No sooner was Calvin dead than his successors showed the first significant weakening of resolve. Rector after rector neglected to insist that students declare in writing their subscription to the full version of the confession of faith which seems quietly to have fallen into desuetude.[22] The intention, at the outset, had been to deny entry to the unsound in doctrine lest they pollute the School with their presence, just as unregenerate offenders must be denied access to the Supper of the Lord. But this was to prove impractical. The length and technicality of the Geneva document became an embarrassment from the start. In June 1576, the Company commissioned the ex-Rector Charles Perrot to look into the whole question. He put in his report promptly. On his advice, the Company took the remarkable decision to substitute for Calvin's detailed confession of faith a mere 'Sommaire de la doctrine chrétienne, laquelle est enseigné à Genève.' In doing so they made the important statement of principle that 'il ne semble raisonnable de presser ainsy une conscience qui n'est résolue de signer ce qu'elle n'entend pas ancores'.[23] The only members of the Academy required to subscribe to the full confession from now on were the schoolmasters and the professors. The Company had officially conceded the impossibility of upholding the 1559 demand. This did not mean that the Company was happy with a situation in which entrants no longer made a religious statement of any kind. In 1584 they laid down that candidates should state that they had 'abjuré toutes les superstitions papales de même que toutes les hérésies condamnées et manifestes.'[24] It was important that the Company should assert itself at this point, for between 1581 and 1584 the city had shown signs of wanting to intrude to an unprecedented extent in the supervision of the Schools. Two new civic officials, the 'scholarchs' had been established with the duty of overseeing the financial management of the Academy.[25] The Council seems to have been worried about the rising costs of the Schools and about unaccounted-for persons crowding out the city. After 1584 all non-local students had on arrival to register, to take an

taught in the lower school, and François Bérauld, professor of Greek, called away to serve in the newly opened school at Orleans, where Condé was establishing his headquarters: *RCP*, II, 96; March 1563: Jacques des Bordes, lecturer in philosophy, seconded to pastoral duties and Henry Scrimgeour put in to teach philosophy in his place: II, 101; August 1563: the Company sends a negative response to the church in Bordeaux which claimed the services of Bordes, whom they had sent to study in Geneva precisely so that he should return as their pastor; March 1565: similar negative response by Company and city to claims of church in Caen on Antoine Chevalier, professor of Hebrew: III, 1 and n. 2; April–June 1566: resistance to requests from Lyon for Le Gaigneux who was needed to help teach theology: III, 7–9; October 1566: Antoine Chauve, principal of the *schola privata*, called away to the ministry: III,12 and n. 7; June 1567: Louis Enoch leaves for France and Simone Simoni leaves under a cloud: III, 15 and n.1.

[22] Stelling-Michaud, *Livre du Recteur*, I, 14.   [23] *Ibid.*, 14–15.
[24] Archives d'Etat, Geneva, *Registres du Conseil* 79, ff. 160v.–161; Stelling-Michaud, *Livre du Recteur*, I, 15.   [25] Stelling-Michaud, *Livre du Recteur*, I, 15.

oath to obey the law of the city and the rules of the School and to pay a matriculation fee. The fee receipts were to go towards the cost of one more minister in the city and to endow a third chair in law, the first two having been set up soon after the arrival of Hotman and Bonnefoy at the end of 1572. The new post was intended specifically to provide for adequate lectures on the Institutes of Justinian, for which there was student demand.[26] However this flurry of efforts to raise funds was ineffective. The worst moment came in 1586, when despite the protests of Beza, all the professors were laid off, and the Schools closed down. There was simply no money to pay them, because the funds supplied by pious benefactors had not been kept separate from the city coffers, as they should have been, but instead had been swallowed up in the bottomless expenses of an ongoing war.[27] After only a few months classes started up once more, everyone available being drafted in to teach. It was not a bad haul; the talented minister of the Italian congregation, Jean-Baptiste Rotan, was seconded with his flock's permission to help teach theology, and the youthful Isaac Casaubon was elevated to the chair of Greek.[28] But some former professors, including the veteran Corneille Bertram, had been lost for ever. After 1587 students came and went, classes were held, theses were disputed and received. But to veteran observers Charles Perrot and Simon Goulart the *élan* had departed and the Schools were 'cold', poorer and less spiritual than once they had been.[29] Meanwhile, the question of the confession did not go away. Some rectors made efforts to reintroduce a watered-down version. On the other hand, in 1593 Beza himself argued for leniency, on the grounds that 'les étudiants allemands font difficulté de faire foy de leur confession'. He asked that they should be allowed merely to swear to 'vivre selon les ordonnances de la ville'.[30]

By this time the Schools were dependent on the admission of German students for their very survival. The whole pattern and scale of recruitment seems to have changed in the course of the period 1560–90.[31] Unfortunately, the best single source of information about student numbers and origins, the *Livre du Recteur*, has been shown to have many imperfections.

---

[26] Introduction of a fee: *Archives d'Etat*, Geneva, *Registres du Conseil* 79 fol. 161: Arrêt of 9 October 1584; Borgeaud, *Académie*, I, 148. Establishment of a third chair in law: *Archives d'Etat*, Geneva, *Registres du Conseil* 79 fol. 135; Rivoire and van Berchem, *Droit*, 3, document 1238.

[27] The names of some hundreds of donors are recorded. Some left money in their wills, but many took out covenants and paid over a stated sum at regular intervals over several years. *Archives d'Etat*, Geneva, *MSS Historiques* 73: *L'Argent recu en l'an 1559 de legatz et donations faites pour la fondation du Collège*; *Archives d'Etat*, Geneva, *Instruction publique*, A 1.   [28] Borgeaud, *Académie*, I, pp. 237–8.

[29] *Ibid.*, p. 262; J.E. Cellerier, 'Charles Perrot, pasteur genevois au seizième siècle. Notice biographique', *Mémoires et Documents publiés par la Société d'Histoire et d'Archéologie de Genève*, 11 (1859), 25–6.   [30] Stelling-Michaud, *Livre du Recteur*, I, 16.

From the very beginning some students were allowed to attend classes without having entered their names in the Rector's Book. Germans, in particular, may be underrepresented in its pages for the early years. Their names appear there in large numbers once the constraint of having to subscribe to the confession has formally been relaxed. French students continued to come when they could, but the wars hampered travel. Evidence from the city's *Livre des Habitants* suggests that desperation caused a sudden jump in the numbers of French refugees immediately after St Bartholomew.[32] If this influx also caused a bulge in recruitment to the Schools, the fact is hidden from us, because during the rectorates of Le Gaigneux, Perrot and Pineau (1568–76) the practice of signing in the Rector's Book seems virtually to have died out. The practice was revived by Rectors Chauve and La Faye (1576–84), no less than 343 names being recorded for these eight years alone.[33] The pace (of recording, at least) keeps up; 262 names were registered between June 1584 and May 1592 (despite the complete closure of the Schools for several months in 1586–87), 58 between June 1592 and May 1596, and 245 between June 1596 and May 1600. The most striking change in the period was the (sustained) increase in the numbers registering as 'student of jurisprudence' or 'student of law', a process which had begun because of the presence of the celebrated lawyers Hotman and Doneau in the city in the 1570s.[34] The city council welcomed this development, but the Company had mixed feelings. In March 1573 Beza and Perrot registered their anxiety on three counts: that law students would prove disruptive, since they were often from families of rank and might well be reluctant to submit obediently to church discipline, that more than one law professor would be needed, at a higher salary than the professors already in post, and that the expense of this would make it difficult for the city to help the School in its more urgent need for a second teacher of theology.[35] The most disappointing feature, in terms of the original aim of the Academy, was the persistent failure of theology to attract more than a handful of candidates at any one time. Disappointing also was the fact that fewer and fewer students, as time went on, came to the city as schoolboys and underwent the full *cursus* of the Geneva Schools. By the 1580s most of them when they arrived had already studied in Heidel-

[31] *Ibid.*, 101–29.
[32] *Livre des Habitants de Genève*, ed. Paul-F.Geisendorf (2 vols., Geneva, 1957–63), II, pp. viii–ix, 1–108; Albert Perrenoud, 'La Population de Genève du seizième au dix-neuvième siècle. Étude démographique', *Mémoires et documents publiés par la Société d'Histoire et d'Archéologie de Genève*, 47 (1979), 41–4; Robert Mandrou, 'Les Protestants français refugiés à Genève après la Saint-Barthélemy', *Revue suisse d'histoire*, 16 (1966), 243–9.
[33] Stelling-Michaud, *Livre du Recteur*, I, 101–15   [34] *Ibid.*, 102–32.
[35] *Archives d'Etat*, Geneva, *Registres du Conseil*, 2 March 1573: P. de Felice, *Lambert Daneau, pasteur et professeur en théologie, 1530–1595. Sa vie, ses ouvrages, ses lettres inédites* (Paris, 1882), p. 72.

berg, or Cambridge, or Leiden, or Basle. The stay of many of these in
Geneva was short, even perfunctory, little more than a tourist's visit, a mere
matter of form. Some silences and absences are striking: as early as the mid-
1560s we hear little of students from the universities of the kingdom of
France, with the single exception of the medical university of Montpellier,
unmolested by ecclesiastical authority, and for much of the century a
hotbed of the Reformed faith.

The teaching of theology was guarded with some watchfulness by Beza
throughout his active life. He who had started as a *suppléant* or fill-in
teacher for Calvin, taking over the scripture lessons in alternate weeks when
Calvin was overworked and ill, came to monopolise the official role of
theology teacher for the next thirty years, himself utilising *suppléants* and –
significantly – being slow to put his weight behind the creation of a second
theology chair. In 1587 he acquiesced in a scheme to divide the responsibility between three teachers, one for Old Testament studies, one for New,
and one for 'commonplaces' or theology taught by topic.[36] It proved
difficult, in the event, to carry this scheme out, so acute was the shortage in
Geneva of suitable candidates for these tasks. In any case, one cannot,
strictly, speak of second and third 'chairs' in theology in Geneva, since the
first, Beza's own, had never really so been designated. Technically, it was
not on the same footing as the created chairs in Hebrew, Greek and arts, or
even as the law chairs set up for Hotman and Doneau. It was merely the
recognised responsibility Beza had inherited from Calvin. This odd situation, which would have been a startling institutional anomaly if the School
had been a university, looks much less odd when one recalls the evolution
and the ecclesiastical matrix of the Geneva School. Even so, the situation
caused uneasiness among his closest colleagues. It was all very well for the
Company to extend to Jerome Zanchi or to Thomas Cartwright the chance
to give some lectures when they were briefly passing through.[37] It was a
godsend to Lambert Daneau in flight after St Bartholomew to be given the
opportunity once more to resume his studies in a serious way, just as it was a
godsend to the School in the 1570s to have him there in a teaching role. But
it was awkward and unsatisfactory that Daneau was not made a proper
professor. When the Company, at his request relieved him of the pastoral
responsibilities which his frail health found too much to combine with his
theology teaching, he was so badly paid by the city for the theology teaching
alone that he now accepted a long-standing invitation to go to a proper
theology chair in Leiden.[38] His departure was a real loss to the Geneva
School.

[36] Duke, Lewis and Pettegree, *Calvinism*, pp. 347–8.
[37] Zanchi's visit, March–April 1567: *RCP*, III, 14; Cartwright's visit, June 1571–January
1572: *RCP*, III, 43,49.
[38] *RCP*, III, 90, 93, 138, 139, 140. Olivier Fatio, *Méthode et Théologie. Lambert Daneau et les
débuts de la scolastique réformée* (Geneva, 1976), pp.14–19.

There were other departures of professors, rather too frequent for comfort. Joseph-Juste Scaliger made use of Geneva as a temporary refuge, and they made use of him. He was snapped up as philosophy lecturer on his arrival in 1572 and served them with distinction, although also with some cynicism, spending a good deal of his time in Basle before finding pressing family reasons for pleading for release. He was tempted by an offer from Leiden of a paid post without teaching duties. Restlessness and ambition seem to explain his departure; there is nothing to indicate unmistakably – though it is possible – that his was a flight from unwelcome ideological pressure or from an atmosphere of mediocrity.[39]

Isaac Casaubon was another distinguished professor, this time a home-grown product, an alumnus of the School, who left it in circumstances which have led posterity to believe, as perhaps posterity has wanted to, that bigotry and intolerance drove this complex man away. Contempt for mediocrity and for narrow-mindedness he certainly expressed. He told Daniel Heinsius that he regarded as stupid those theologians 'qui se putant solos sapere, solos intelligere Sanctam Scripturam, solos esse Ecclesiam Dei'.[40] ['Who suppose that they alone are wise, they alone understand the holy scriptures and that they alone make up the church of God.'] However it is not clear whether or not he left because he had become disillusioned with the church and the Academy. He may well have been pulled away simply by concern for his career and reputation, and by his thirst for the neglected classical manuscripts which he spent his life editing and restoring to the learned world.

Despite all these difficulties and temptations there was, after all, a considerable measure of continuity – and of distinction – among the Geneva professors. The record of the Geneva School was much the same as that of other establishments all over Protestant Europe. Sometimes it succeeded in securing – and keeping – the services of the God-fearing *érudits* whom it approached, sometimes it failed. The same few names were in demand everywhere, and so great was the discrepancy between the demand for expert scholars and the supply, that Geneva was by no means unusual in living from hand to mouth. Even Heidelberg and Leiden, Geneva's main competitors, experienced difficulties, and could not be sure of retaining the services of those they employed. On the other hand all these institutions had some professors, including some famous teachers, who stayed put and were not tempted away. In Geneva such valuable continuity was provided by the presence there of the Greek Professor Portus and the Hebraist Corneille Bertram, both of whom were celebrated instructors of the young, and solid scholars in their own right. Bertram in particular made

[39] *RCP*, III, 91–4, 107–8, 143, 144, 153, 302.
[40] Matteo Campagnolo, *Isaac Casaubon e Ginevra 1578–1610: Ricerche sulle relazioni con Théodore de Bèze e Jacques Lect* (Venice, 1980), p. 87.

an important contribution to the great Geneva Bible at last published in 1588.[41]

Meanwhile, how well had the city kept its side of the bargain? There had always been determination to get value for money out of the professors. There had often been apprehension lest the city be dragged as a result of immigrant intrigues into the civil wars of neighbouring France or damaged in its fragile relationship with Berne, or threatened by renewed aggression from Savoy. On the other hand, in later decades, there was sympathy with the wider aims of the Academy among younger members of leading local families, themselves products of the School, some of whom had also attended Protestant universities elsewhere.

The appointment of the scholarchs was not a threat to the Academy's autonomy, for in practice such autonomy had never really existed. The School's institutional identity disintegrates, on scrutiny, into episodes and problems which have left their traces not exclusively in the Register of the Company of Pastors, or in the correspondence of Beza, but also, almost invariably, and contemporaneously, in the deliberations of the ruling councils of the town. Individual professors had to deal individually with all these bodies, which would then consult with each other and provide a resolution with which the professor, short of abandoning ship, had to be satisfied. The registers reveal that in School matters, even in Calvin's day, the Company proposed, and the Council disposed. When the Pastors wanted to send an experienced emissary to the court of Condé at short notice, or to release a professor from his lectures to go to take charge of some key congregation, or to go and serve in his own native locality, or to start up a branch of Christian study in another school, they could not legally do so without permission from the city.

The initiative did not always come from the Company; individual professors approached the Council all the time, seeking permission for leave of absence or claiming to be overworked or underpaid. No instance has come to light of the professors acting collectively; they may have been a happy few but they do not seem to have been a band of brothers. Some of the learned men who taught in the Geneva School were mercilessly exploited by their brethren in the Company, others with little scruple exploited the Geneva School in turn.

A distinct impression emerges from these documents that, funding apart, the School, as a school, was safer in the hands of lay councillors like Amblard Corne and Michel Roset and Jean Mailliet and Paul Chevalier who did regard it as a sort of crypto-university, than in the hands of Beza and of the Company of Pastors, who certainly believed in principle that classroom tuition of students was important, but who could not resist using

[41] *RCP*, V, p. 331; Duke, Lewis and Pettegree, *Calvinism*, pp. 335–6.

a good man for something else. The School was not always their first priority; clearly Beza saw it as one part only of a vast continuum of Christian activity, in which quick and hard decisions had to be taken about competing duties, in response to the most pressing urgency of any given time. Just as pastors stood in, if asked to, for professors, so professors might be called upon to take up their pen in polemic or in propaganda, or to journey to some princely court, or to serve the Lord in some remote parish, or to wrestle with opponents in synod or *colloque*.

The Academy in the sixteenth century was repeatedly hampered by public anxieties about money and about the very survival of Geneva as an independent state. It was affected also, on occasion, by friction over the boundaries of authority between magistrates and church.

On the other hand, it is striking how rare, in the Company's records, are conflicts over the actual content of the teaching in the School. What is the explanation for this apparent measure of agreement? Were the professors so well-chosen that they were in effect self-policing? Did most of them teach in the same way as each other because of their common membership – inside the wider world of Protestantism and of letters – of a tiny (if international) coterie of like-minded friends? There is some truth in all of this. It was the case also that one could survive in a public position in Geneva only on this coterie's terms. There was no room for overt dissenters in the Genevan church. The relative infrequency there of open intellectual discord was the result not of official flexibility, let alone of tolerance, but of the departure of some independent spirits and, presumably, of the discretion shown by those who had qualms but wished to stay.

There were, of course, some rows, perhaps the most celebrated being the double rebuff administered to Ramus, in May 1570 and again in December of that year. When Ramus arrived in Geneva he was already a controversial celebrity who had spent the two years since his expulsion from his post as Principal of the Paris College de Presles moving from one Protestant university to another. Everywhere his reception had been spectacular, with large and enthusiastic audiences of students, and a welcome from some professors; everywhere, however, it had turned sour. He had encountered bitter hostility from other philosophers and theologians, who regarded as dangerous and unacceptable his affectation of contempt for Aristotle ánd his proselytising for his own rhetorical brand of dialectic. Neither in Basle nor in Heidelberg had the university offered him a post. All this was known in Geneva. Despite this, rather surprisingly, on 8 May 1570 the Company of Pastors informed the city council that they had invited Ramus to give some lectures.[42]

Soon after the lectures began, alarm bells began to ring. Within a week or so, the Register of the Company of Pastors records that

[42] Kingdon, *Consolidation*, p. 101, n. 5.

M.de Bèze and the Rector have spoken to M. Ramus, to get him to change the way he sets about teaching and giving lessons in the public auditorium. It was thought that he did not take kindly to this, believing that he knew as well as anybody else the way that he should teach. Since he could no longer go on lecturing, he would stop his other lessons too. Some students were angered by all this, and posted up certain verses in honour of M. Ramus, criticizing those whom they thought responsible for forbidding him to continue with his lessons.[43]

A compromise was reached: prohibited from giving his celebrated lectures on dialectic, he was allowed nevertheless, in deference to his learning, to lecture on Cicero's *In Catilinam*. Within the School, feelings were mixed. As was later recalled by Francesco Portus, then professor of Greek:

Everyone knows in what esteem this School held the learning and the piety of Petrus Ramus, since he was received here with such *humanitas*, and given permission to lecture in public, despite the fact that we in no way approved of many things in his logic, and in his manner of teaching.[44]

It is possible that some of the pastors and professors would have been happy for him to stay, but the issue was resolved in any case by a bad outbreak of plague which temporarily closed the School. Ramus departed for Lausanne. From here he put out feelers about the possibility of a post in the Geneva Schools. Beza's response, dated 1 December 1570, is uncompromising and only formally polite:

I would have preferred to hear from you yourself, rather than from our common friends, your plans in favour of our School. It is not that I have the ambitious desire to see myself in receipt of supplications, from you, or from anyone else, but because this indirect approach makes me think that you have doubts about my good will towards you ... I respect you, although we disagree on some matters concerning studies. I would like to help you while at the same time serving the interests of this Academy. But I cannot. I regret to inform you that we have no vacant chair, and no money to establish a new one. In any case, we really could not have you here in a post, because of our statutory resolution to follow the Aristotelian approach, without deviating from a single line of it, as much in the teaching of logic as in the rest of our studies. You will, however, always be welcome in Geneva, where you have left behind many friends and followers.[45]

Beza's intemperate outburst to Bullinger reveals more clearly not only his exasperation but his defensive attitude towards the studies in the School:

Ten years ago I told you, when I heard that Ramus had joined our cause, that this would cause trouble and that a quarrelsome spirit would enter our French Churches

[43] *RCP*, III, 25; Borgeaud, *Académie*, I, 112.
[44] *Response de Francois Portus*; Borgeaud, *Académie*, I, 12–113.
[45] Bèze, *Correspondance*, XI, p. 295; Borgeaud, *Académie*, I, 113–14.

with that man ... how could we possibly have endured as a colleague someone who regards Aristotle as a sophist, who believes Cicero to be no good at teaching rhetoric, who thinks Quintilian is ignorant, and that Galen and Euclid are devoid of method![46]

Beza had been somewhat disingenuous in his earlier letter to Ramus in claiming that Geneva professors were bound by anything as formal as a statutory prohibition from even the smallest deviation from Aristotle's own handling of logic. Neither he nor Ramus, familiar as they were with the ways in which logic was in fact taught, can have taken literally so over-simplified a view. Even so, a genuine point of principle was at issue. Ramus's combative style of teaching was feared because of its deliberate flouting of academic decorum, and its seductive promise of a short-cut to learning, but also because it undermined the solidarity of the republic of letters, fomenting animosity and creating cliques. For Beza, in earnest and dogged pursuit of a calling to protect the Word, this mercurial irreverence and stubborn dissent looked like irresponsibility. His brushes with Ramus over these matters and over church discipline were uncomfortable and inconclusive, and ended only with the death of Ramus in 1572.

The stresses which were experienced inside the School of Geneva after Calvin's death cannot be summed up tidily as conflicts between open-minded classicists and obscurantist biblicists, nor as clashes between dogmatists and dissenters, although such frictions did occasionally show themselves among the pastors. The strains which developed in the Academy arose from the fact that some of the professors were incomparably more lucid and learned scholars than their colleagues, and that they made their contempt for mediocrity clear. But there was another, and deeper cause: Beza never relinquished his self-imposed burden of responsibility for the welfare of the Schools, and for a generation fussed over the professors and virtually dominated the teaching of theology. It mattered, therefore, that he had early become entangled in European religious polemic, expending his energies on the ultimately futile task of defending intellectually the spiritual and non-intellectual values of the Reformed religious cause. Theological teaching became more and more technical, a training for controversialists, where once it had been an induction for fledgling pastors and future elders into a lifetime of teaching and living by the Word.[47]

There had always been a few among the Geneva doctors who had been uneasy with the crabbed and carping way Reformed theological debate was developing, and with the distracting effect of Beza's repeated interventions in the polemics raging in the Lutheran world. Polemic was an unwelcome if

---

[46] Bèze, *Correspondance*, XIII, p. 31.
[47] Pierre Fraenkel, 'De l'Écriture à la Dispute: le cas de l'Académie de Genève sous Théodore de Beze', *Cahiers de la Revue de Théologie et de Philosophie*, 1 (1977).

unavoidable call upon their time. The gap which yawned between Matthieu Béroald and Joseph Scaliger over the Biblical element in the study of chronology was an intellectual one.[48] But it was differences in temperament and above all in religious priorities which caused coolness between the sensitive and reclusive Charles Perrot and more workaday figures busy in Academy and city, like Antoine La Faye and the magistrate Jacques Lect.[49] And if time hardened some positions, it made others open to doubt.

Throughout its first half-century, the Academy had been a hard-working school, a place of effective technical instruction in the disciplines necessary for sound interpretation of the Word. Many of those whose substantial studies had been in Geneva later showed some recognisably godly outlook and values when they went on, in one capacity or another, to lead the Reformed cause in other parts of the European world. In the Schools, pastors and professors cooperated, as Calvin had hoped they would, in the same evangelising effort, their teaching and their writing complementing their preaching and their work upon the Bible text. The theology teaching, entrusted as it always was, to one of the Company, exemplified this overlap between the spheres most clearly of all. Even more decisively the fruits of long years of such collaboration are apparent in the great Geneva Bible, which is introduced, appropriately, in the name of 'the Pastors and Professors of Geneva'. In the early years of the seventeenth century the Academy continued to attract students, but more and more of these were birds of passage from England, Scotland, Holland, Germany, passing briefly through Geneva on their way elsewhere. Fewer Frenchmen now came, and in Geneva itself the long strains of war and of uncertain peace began to tell. The fortunes of the Reformed religion in France had passed through many changes between 1572 and the final promulgation of the Edict of Nantes. At national synods of the religion it had not proved possible for Beza to maintain the ascendancy he had once possessed. The Genevan church, still held in high regard for its symbolic significance, no longer carried much weight in the theological controversies of the day. By the late 1570s its School was eclipsed in celebrity by Heidelberg where 'even rich Genevans send their sons to study the arts and theology ... the unanimous admission of the Genevan ministers [being] (as they often tell us) that the Genevan School was more fertile and productive in times past than it is now'.[50] It would be easy to conclude, from the way in which the

[48] Anthony Grafton, *Defenders of the Text. The Traditions of Scholarship in an Age of Science,1450–1800* (Cambridge, MA, 1991), p. 137.

[49] J.-E. Cellérier, 'Charles Perrot, pasteur genevois au seizième siécles', *Mémoires et documents publiés par la Sociéte d'histoire et d'archéologie de Genève* XI (1859); Borgeaud, *Académie*, pp. 264–6 on La Faye; Campagnolo, Casaubon, de Bèze et Lect, *passim.*; Grafton, *Defenders of the Text*, pp. 144–77.

[50] Daniel De Dieu to Godfried Wingius, 17 April 1579: Duke, Lewis and Pettegree, *Calvinism*, pp. 344–6.

early Academy became absorbed in the great project for supplying pastors for the churches of France, and from the way in which Hotman's presence briefly swamped the School with young hopefuls avid to learn a little law, that its fortunes rose and fell in response to events in France. And so they did, but not entirely. When the surviving evidence is taken as a whole, what emerges is a clear sense of the professional competence and faithfulness of its professors in performing the tasks of education and its remarkable and continuing share in a diminishing if still international clientele.

Pierre Charpentier, writing with bitterness in the political crisis of late 1572 had taken too narrow and too mean a view. Even in the earlier years, when the sense of providential mission was at its height, with students flocking to the School, new churches being established, and princely houses showing sympathy towards the Cause, the teaching provided by the professors in Geneva was not the education in fanaticism appropriate to the conspiratorial world he describes. It was, however, consistent in its expectation that education received would be paid for in service given. It was also uncompromising in its opposition to Papist superstition, anti-Trinitarian heresy and Lutheran error. Where its spokesmen advocated flexibility and tolerance, they were concerned not so much with the long-term aim of promoting concord and reconciliation between Protestants and Catholics as with the more immediate, less visionary, tasks of educating men in godliness and of bringing about a more complete harmony of Confessions among the Reformed.

4   Calvin and the Swiss Reformed churches

Bruce Gordon

At the synod of Dordrecht in 1618 the head of the Zurich church, Johann Jakob Breitinger, was forced to defend the orthodoxy of Heinrich Bullinger by demonstrating the concurrence of opinion between Zwingli's successor and John Calvin on double predestination.[1] Apart from being an act of theological creativity, the occasion was a painful reminder of unresolved tensions within the Reformed churches. These tensions went back to the very beginning of the Swiss Reformation, long before Calvin arrived in Geneva as a young refugee. In Geneva, Calvin depended upon the support of the Swiss churches, and his was not a position of strength; indeed for much of his career he appeared as supplicant before the more established leaders of the Swiss German churches. A study of Calvin's relations with the Swiss thus acts as a useful corrective to the traditional picture of the all powerful and independent Genevan reformer.[2]

With the exception of the Strasburg years, Calvin lived from 1536 until his death within the Swiss sphere of influence. Geneva was not a member of the Confederation, the city was bound to Berne by an alliance which guaranteed its semi-independence as a republic and provided protection against the ambitions of Savoy and France.[3] The Bernese, as protectors of Geneva, were anxious that the city's dependence on their military support should be extended to uniformity in doctrine and religious practices. Berne formed with Basle, Schaffhausen and Zürich, as full members of the Swiss Confederation, the four principal Reformed churches; a loose alliance based on the principle of fraternal consultation.[4] When Calvin arrived in Basle in 1535 there were, however, few signs of unity among the Swiss churches. Humiliated by the Kappel War of 1531, each of the states was

I wish to thank Professor Fritz Büsser in Zurich and Chris Brown in Mainz for their suggestions in the preparation of this paper.

[1] R. Pfister, *Kirchengeschichte der Schweiz* (3 vols., Zurich, 1974), II, pp. 417–18.
[2] An exception to this trend is W. Nijenhuis, *Calvinus oecumenicus. Calvijn en de eenheid der kerk in het licht van zijn briefwisseling* (The Hague, 1959). Nijenhuis provides an English summary of the Dutch text.
[3] On the background to Geneva and Berne, see R. Feller, *Geschichte Berns* (4 vols., rpt. Berne and Frankfurt, 1974), II, pp. 394–96.
[4] For an overview of the Swiss Reformation, see B. Gordon, 'Switzerland', in A. Pettegree (ed.), *The Early Reformation in Europe* (Cambridge, 1992), pp. 70–93.

consumed with its own affairs.[5] Zurich was particularly quiet, disinterestedly observing events in Germany, France and in the Pays de Vaud. Basle was more drawn to Imperial than Swiss affairs, often not sending representatives to the Swiss Diet in Baden, fuelling rumours that it would soon leave the Confederation. Berne alone took up Zwingli's ideal of the forceful expansion of the Reformation, and by 1536, having conquered the Pays de Vaud and liberated Geneva, it began the imposition of the Reformation in its French-speaking lands.[6]

Calvin ceaselessly cultivated contacts with churchmen, politicians and refugees within the Confederation in order to secure the position of the church in Geneva. To Calvin's inner circle, however, belonged two men: Guillaume Farel in Neuchâtel and Pierre Viret in Lausanne.[7] Farel and Viret were privy to the hopes, frustrations and plans which Calvin concealed from others. As Calvin was increasingly reviled in Berne, Farel and Viret became his voice within the French-speaking church. Outside Zurich, Calvin had few allies in the German-speaking churches; notable supporters were Vadianus in St Gall,[8] Ambrosius Blarer in Constance and Nicholas Zurkinden in Berne.[9] It was, however, with Heinrich Bullinger, the 'bishop' of the Swiss Reformed churches, that Calvin came to enjoy the closest relationship.[10]

The development of Calvin's relations with the Swiss was not merely about personalities. The whole movement of the Swiss Reformation after 1531 was a coming to terms with Zwingli's ambiguous legacy. In each of the Reformed cities the consequences of the Zwinglian Reformation were everywhere apparent. For the Swiss, the power of the Zwinglian Reformation lay in its unshackling of the bonds of foreign domination. The connection between the freedom of the Gospel and political freedom was underscored in the refusals of Zurich and Berne to enmesh themselves in German and French affairs. Everywhere that Calvin looked, from Lausanne to St Gall, he saw Zwingli's spectre; Calvin's own process of 'Turning Swiss' was less an acceptance of this tradition than an accommodation.

Huldrych Zwingli was one of Calvin's least favourite topics.[11] Such was the emotive nature of the subject for the Swiss that Calvin would have

---

[5] On the situation in the Confederation after Kappel, see H. Meyer, *Der Zweite Kappeler Krieg* (Zurich, 1976), pp. 301–14. On the rebuilding of the church in Zurich, B. Gordon, *Clerical Discipline and the Rural Reformation. The Synod in Zurich 1532–1580* (Berne, 1992). [6] K. Guggisberg, *Bernische Kirchengeschichte* (Berne, 1958), pp. 191–5.

[7] R. Pfister, 'Pierre Viret, 1511–1571', *Zwingliana*, 11 (1959), 321–34.

[8] E.G. Rüsch, 'Die Beziehungen der St Galler Reformatoren zu Calvin', *Zwingliana*, 11 (1959), 106–16.

[9] E. Bähler, *Nikolaus Zurkinden von Bern 1506–1588. Vertreter der Toleranz im Jahrhundert der Reformation* (Berne, 1912), pp. 28–58.

[10] See particularly F. Büsser, 'Calvin und Bullinger', in W.H. Neuser (ed.), *Calvinus Servus Christi* (Budapest, 1988), pp. 107–26.

[11] F. Blanke, 'Calvins Urteile über Zwingli', *Zwingliana*, 11 (1959), 66–92.

gladly passed his time in Geneva without ever having to mention his name. In a letter to André Zébédée in 1539, Calvin claimed to have found Zwingli's sacramental theology 'wrong and pernicious' before his arrival in Basle.[12] Calvin credited Zwingli for his courage in opposing Rome and the Emperor, and granted that Zwingli's sharp distinction between the material and the spiritual was a necessary correction, even if it was taken too far. But, in the end, Calvin remained adamant that Zwingli delivered an empty doctrine of the sacraments which stripped them of all divine presence.[13] When Viret optimistically wrote in 1542 that he had found a greater flexibility in Zwingli's later writings, Calvin replied dismissively: 'Concerning Zwingli's writings, you can, as far as I'm concerned, think what you will. I have not read everything. It is possible that at the end of his life he took back and improved what he had earlier too rashly arrived at. But I remember all too well how profane his early writings on the sacraments are.'[14]

For Calvin, Zwingli's name was for ever linked with the sacramentarian quarrel with the Lutherans, the great stumbling block to theological agreement.[15] Because they were ultimately irreconcilable, Calvin believed that neither Luther nor Zwingli's theology was an adequate starting point for a unified Protestant doctrine. Calvin defended Bucer's attempts to mediate, but rejected the idea that the two polar opposite positions could be unified. 'I admit', writes Calvin to Zébédée, 'that Bucer made a mistake in endeavouring to soften the ideas of Oecolampadius and Zwingli, for in so doing he almost makes them agree with Luther.'[16] But while Bucer erred in his zealous pursuit of unity, Calvin refused to condemn his efforts, choosing rather to contrast the Strasburger's flexibility with the obduracy of the Zurichers, who 'flame up into a rage if one dares to prefer Luther to Zwingli, just as if the Gospel were to perish if anything is yielded by Zwingli'.[17]

For our purposes, there are three distinct phases in the development of Calvin's relations with the Swiss: from 1535 until his return from Strasburg in 1541; the period leading up to the *Consensus Tigurinus* in 1549; and, finally, the period ending with his death in 1564.

---

[12] Calvin to Zébédée, 19 May 1539. The letter is printed in Rudolf Schwarz, *Johannes Calvins Lebenswerk in seinen Briefen. Eine Auswahl von Briefen Calvins in deutscher Übersetzung* (2 vols., Tübingen, 1909), I, p. 71.

[13] For Calvin's criticism of Zwingli, see Calvin, *Institutes of the Christian Religion* (2 vols., trans. F.L. Battles, Philadelphia, 1960), II, 4.14.17 p. 1293.

[14] 11 September. *CR* 39: 438.

[15] Although Calvin clearly preferred Luther to Zwingli, B.A. Gerrish's treatment of Calvin's relationship to Luther overstates the case and disregards the complexities of the Swiss dimension. B.A. Gerrish, *The Old Protestantism and the New. Essays on the Reformation Heritage* (Edinburgh, 1982), pp. 27–48.   [16] 19 May 1539. *CR* 38: 346

[17] 28 February 1539. Cited from Jules Bonnet, *Letters of John Calvin* (English edn, 4 vols., Edinburgh and Philadelphia, 1855–8), I, p. 85.

1535–1541. The fruits of Calvin's first visit to Basle in 1535 are well known: the time of concentrated study, the development of exegetical methods with Simon Grynaeus and the renowned Hebraist Sebastian Münster, the contacts with publishers and the publication of the *Institutes* in 1536.[18] It was, however, his contacts with the French refugee community in Basle which convinced Calvin that the Swiss could play a role in the reformation of his native land. Basle was, however, a humanist haven, and it was not until Calvin left the city and travelled west into the newly conquered territories that he was introduced to the complexities of the Swiss Reformation.

Three events proved decisive in establishing Calvin's place on the Swiss scene: the conquest in 1536 of the Pays de Vaud by Berne, the Caroli affair in 1537 and the battle between the Zwinglian and Lutheran parties in Berne. Despite the preparatory work by Farel, the Reformation in the French-speaking lands was imposed by Berne.[19] The Synod of Lausanne in 1536 was intended to implement the Zwinglian theology and ecclesiology as practiced in Berne and enshrined in the acts of the 1528 Disputation and the 1532 Synod.[20] In Lausanne, Calvin made his first appearance with an intervention on the question of how the glorified Christ is present in the Eucharist.[21] The successful outcome of the synod convinced Calvin that true religion was taking root, and he returned to Geneva determined to carry out the practical reforms of the faith. The Bernese were not prepared to give the French reformers a free hand, and the ordinances of 1537 for the French lands gave no expression to Calvin's desires for frequent communion and an independent ecclesiastical discipline. Following Kappel the mood in Berne was distinctly xenophobic and anticlerical, and there was little enthusiasm for a Frenchman with new ideas about church polity.

The controversy surrounding Pierre Caroli's attack on Farel, Viret and Calvin brought into sharp relief what had only been hinted at in Lausanne: that Calvin had a theological position distinct from the Zwinglian line.[22] The importance of the conflict lay in the fact that in early 1537 the churches

---

[18] On the Basle years, see A. Ganoczy, *The Young Calvin* (1966, trans. D. Foxgrover and W. Provo, Edinburgh, 1987), pp. 91–102.

[19] Charles Gilliard, *La Conquête du Pays de Vaud per les Bernois* (Berne, 1935), Henri Naef, *Les Origines de la Réforme à Genève* (Geneva, 1936). The classic work on the reformation of the French-speaking lands remains Karl Hundeshagen, *Die Conflikte des Zwinglianismus, Lutherums und Calvinismus in der bernischen Landeskirche 1532–1558* (Zurich, 1842).

[20] E. Junod, 'De la conquête du Pays de Vaud à la Dispute de Lausanne', in E. Junod (ed.), *La Dispute de Lausanne (1536)* (Lausanne, 1988), pp. 13–22.

[21] Ganoczy, *Young Calvin*, pp. 109–10. Emile-Michel Braekman, 'Les Interventions de Calvin', in E. Junod (ed.), *La Dispute de Lausanne (1536)* (Lausanne, 1988), pp. 170–8.

[22] On the dispute with Caroli, see E. Bähler, 'Petrus Caroli und Johannes Calvin. Ein Beitrag zur Geschichte und Kultur der Reformationszeit', *Jahrbuch für Schweizerisches Geschichte*, 29 (1904), 39–168.

of Berne, Basle and Zurich believed that there was a strong heretical element among the French clergy. Calvin, forced on the defensive, even had to write to Grynaeus in Basle to defend himself.[23] He believed the matter to be a theological question for the church in Berne to resolve, and wrote to Caspar Megander, the leading theologian, asking him to settle the debate: 'But, in truth, my honourable brother, you can do the most in this affair yourself, and ought, in virtue of the power which belongs to your place, above all other persons, to strive for it in the extreme.'[24] Calvin's refusal to acknowledge the role of the council as final arbitrator proved damaging to his relations with the Bernese magistrates. Also, the Caroli affair was tied to the bitter fight between the Zwinglian Megander and the Lutheran party in Berne (Peter Kunz, Sebastian Meyer and Simon Sulzer). On account of Megander's support, Calvin and his supporters were vindicated by two synods and the other Swiss churches were assured of their orthodoxy.[25]

It was following his banishment from Geneva on 28 April 1538, that Calvin realised the strength of the opposition arrayed against him in Berne. Calvin and Farel immediately sought the support of the other churches, who were meeting in Zurich to consider a response to Luther's letter to the Swiss on the sacraments. Bullinger received Calvin warmly, and was deeply troubled by events, but admonished the Genevans for their haste and 'excessive sharpness' in implementing church discipline. Calvin returned to Berne hoping that the positive response by the other Swiss churches, who requested that the ministers be supported, would move the council.[26] The hope was in vain: the Genevans were attacked for using leavened bread and not adopting the Bernese rites for the Eucharist. According to Calvin, Kunz, in the course of the interview became so exasperated, 'that he would not listen to any reasoning, but continued to storm about until the others interrupted him with the reading of the next article. Not content with screaming, he rushed from his desk and threw his body into so many contortions, that his colleagues were hard pressed to pin him down and keep him quiet.'[27]

In Strasburg, Calvin kept abreast of Swiss affairs, but what he saw left him with a sinking heart. Bucer and Simon Sulzer worked to negotiate conditions for a possible return to Geneva, but Calvin could not share their optimism. 'Should we endeavour', wrote Calvin to Farel shortly after his arrival in Strasburg, 'to calm the others as if we were the authors of the

---

[23] 15 May 1538. *CO* 10: 106–9.
[24] Calvin to Megander, February 1537, cited from Bonnet, *Letters of Calvin*, I, p. 25.
[25] Megander to Bullinger, 26 June 1537, *CO* 10: 111.
[26] The meeting in Zurich was intended to consider the Wittenberg Concord. It was on account of Calvin's intervention that the matter in Geneva was addressed. The letter is from the convent to the Genevan council; 28 April 1538, *CO* 10: 192–3. The articles drawn up by Calvin for the meeting, *CO* 10: 190–2.   [27] *Ibid.*,

quarrels? . . . My opinion is, at least, that one can neither improve the past nor properly take care of the future.'[28]

Farel and Viret pursued every avenue to bring Calvin back to Geneva. Viret even wrote to Calvin suggesting that a stay in Geneva might improve his health. The letter received the laconic reply: 'I read the passage in your letter, certainly not without a smile, in which you show so much concern for my health, and recommend Geneva on that ground . . . it would be far preferable to perish for eternity than be tormented in that place of torture. If you wish me well, my dear Viret, don't mention the subject!'[29] Calvin's reluctance was only overcome in the spring of 1541 when he heard that the Zurich church had written to the Strasburg council petitioning them to allow Calvin's return to Geneva.[30] In desperation Farel and the Genevan magistrates enlisted Bullinger's aid in the hope of succeeding where they had failed.[31] Calvin, clearly surprised and moved by Zurich's intervention, was persuaded by the Zurichers' promise of support and their apparent openness to an agreement with Strasburg.[32]

In his reply to the ministers of Zurich, Calvin admits that the letters from the Genevan council had not convinced him to return to the city, for he feared that little had changed.[33] Through their intervention Zurich had shown 'that it will henceforth take a direct interest in Genevan affairs' and 'that you are earnestly concerned for the welfare of the church in Geneva, whose administration, as a sacred charge, has been entrusted to me'.[34] Calvin concludes the letter with the implicit understanding that Zurich has opened the door to a theological agreement: 'I rejoice that you have come to an opinion of me, that with regard to yourselves [Zurich ministers] there is scarcely anything you may not promise yourselves. You may certainly do so, for I will not disappoint your expectations.'[35] The timely intervention of Zurich and the letters of recommendation from Strasburg and Basle gave Calvin the hope that the theological wounds could be healed.

1541–1549. During the 1540s Calvin's dealings with the Swiss centred on three principal points: the establishment of peace with Berne, theological unity and the winning of the Swiss to an alliance with France. The three questions were naturally inexorably linked, with the unifying theme being that all roads led to Zurich.

---

[28] *CO* 10: 246.   [29] Calvin to Viret, 19 May 1540. *CO* 11:36
[30] The Geneva council to the council in Zurich, 25 May 1541. *CO* 11: 221–3 (Latin), 223–6 (German).
[31] Letter from the Zurich council to Strasburg. *CO* 11: 233–4. The answer of Strasburg to Zurich *CO* 11: 239–40. The Basle council also wrote on Calvin's behalf, *CO* 11: 236–7.
[32] 4 May 1541. *CO* 11: 213–14. Calvin seems to have known of the contacts before the letters were sent. His response to Farel predates the official correspondence between the Swiss and Strasburg.   [33] 31 May 1541. *CO* 11: 229–33.   [34] *Ibid.*, 229.   [35] *Ibid.*, 233.

The return to Geneva did not lead to a warming of relations with his opponents. Already in 1542 the uneasy peace between the Zwinglian and Lutheran parties in Berne was shattered by a renewal of the quarrel over the Eucharist.[36] On 27 August the deans of the Bernese church were to present themselves in the city to ratify the council's decision on the question. Calvin immediately wrote to Viret advising him to instruct the dean of Lausanne to argue against any reaffirmation of Zwingli's symbolic language.[37] There was another issue which alarmed Calvin:

> Concerning the second question, that is the way in which this matter is being handled, he (the dean) must consider what an example the brethren might give, if they should recognise the council as an arbiter of dogma, that one must accept as an oracle whatever they should decide. What an important and monstrous precedent for the future that would be![38]

To Calvin's horror, not only did the deans acquiesce to the council but Viret himself was prepared to accept the decision.[39] Viret had argued that the new statement on the sacraments was tolerable because it was to be attached to the documents of the 1528 Berne Disputation and the First Helvetic Confession of 1536. Calvin retorted that neither of these texts were sufficient, and, further:

> nobody can make me believe that these two hundred magistrates, who have decided on this doctrine, have a proper idea of the matter. For who proclaims a law has the right to interpret it. Those who teach anything other than what the judges understand will be condemned as perjurers. There is also the danger that they will forbid the discussion of any new liturgies and ceremonies. And who knows whether they might include under this (term) innovations excommunication, the frequent celebration of the Eucharist and many other things which we want to implement.[40]

Calvin believed that the inattention of the council in Berne to the content of theological debates had led to a dangerous confusion of externals with essentials.

In Berne the winds of theological change were blowing strong. By 1544 the pendulum began to swing back towards the Zwinglians, who, under the leadership of Jodocus Kilchmeyer, were becoming more vociferous.[41] Decisive was the shift in Berne's foreign policy during the 1540s. Following the Kappel War Berne had distanced itself from Zurich and had looked to Strasburg and the German states for support against the Habsburg Duke of Savoy. The success of Charles V against Francis I caused the Bernese to fear that the emperor and king might strike a deal to restore the Savoyan lands

---

[36] Guggisberg, *Bernische Kirchengeschichte*, p. 208.
[37] 23 August 1542. *CO* 11: 430–2.   [38] *Ibid.*, 432
[39] 3 September 1542. *CO* 11: 436–9.   [40] *Ibid.*, 438.
[41] On the decline of Lutheranism in Berne, see Guggisberg, *Bernische Kirchengeschichte*, pp. 208–12.

to the duke, with whom Berne was still officially at war.[42] Following the defeat of the Schmalkaldic League at Mühlberg in April of 1547, the Bernese Bürgermeister Nägeli, at a session of the Swiss Diet in Baden, voiced the fear of the Reformed states when he warned that the emperor would not stop at the border of the Confederation.[43] The expectation of an attack by the Imperial forces brought Berne and Zurich together again. Simon Sulzer, the remaining leader of the Lutherans in Berne, was increasingly isolated.

As Sulzer's position in Berne began to crumble, Calvin took up the role of mediator between the rival Zwinglians and Lutherans, outlining in a letter the disputed points: the nature of the office of the minister and the efficacy of the sacraments. Calvin's efforts were scuttled by the Zwinglians, who held him to be a Lutheran and cursed him and Sulzer in the same breath. In 1548 the focus of the strife shifted to Lausanne, where the majority of the clergy supported Calvin's teachings. Berne objected to Geneva's influence on the church in Lausanne, especially when rumours began to circulate that Calvin's *Institutes* were being taught in the academy. Calvin told Viret that the only way of mollifying the Zwinglian attacks on the church in Lausanne was by securing Bullinger's intervention. In the end, the feared split erupted when Viret held a disputation of 95 theses in support of Geneva. Sulzer's support of these theses led to his dismissal from Berne.[44]

The weakening of the Protestant cause in Germany in the 1540s forced Zurich to reconsider its policy of neutrality.[45] Temptations abounded on every side as the diplomatic missions of the emperor, king and pope jostled with one another for Swiss support. Despite Zurich's aloofness from the Schmalkadic League, and Bullinger's abandonment of any hope of reconciliation with the ageing Luther, the magistrates and churchmen kept a watchful eye on events in Germany. Of particular interest was the rumoured split between Luther and Melanchthon and the suggestions that the latter was looking to leave Wittenberg.[46] Unbeknown to Calvin, Bullinger wrote to Melanchthon inviting him to come to Zurich, 'where all the houses are open to you'.[47] Melanchthon did not reply and this incident seems to have ended Bullinger's fading interest in an alliance with the Lutherans.

---

[42] Feller, *Geschichte Berns*, p. 393. On Charles and Francis, see R.J. Knecht, *Francis I* (Cambridge, 1982), p. 298.   [43] *Ibid.*, 392.

[44] E. Bähler, 'Der Kampf zwischen Theocratie und Staatskirchentum in der welschbernische Kirche im 16. Jahrhundert', *Zeitschrift für schweizerische Geschichte* 5 (1925),' pp. 5–6.

[45] On Zurich internal politics after Kappel, see R. Hauswirth, 'Zur politischen Ethik der Generation nach Zwingli', *Zwingliana*, 13 (1971), 305–42.

[46] W.H. Neuser, 'Die Versuche Bullingers, Calvins und der Strassburger, Melanchthon zum Fortgang von Wittenberg zu bewegen', in U. Gäbler and E. Herkenrath (eds.), *Heinrich Bullinger 1504–1575. Gesammelte Aufsätze zum 400. Todestag* (2 vols., Zurich, 1975), II, pp. 35–55.

[47] Bullinger to Melanchthon, 3 December 1544, cited by Neuser, 'Versuche Bullingers', 41–2.

The publication in 1545 of the *Warhaffte Bekanntnus*, Zurich's response to Luther's renewed assault on Zwingli and his theology, dashed any further hopes for unification. Calvin regretted the appearance of this polemical defence of Zwingli, for he regarded the insistence on the sanctity of Zwingli as a serious impediment to negotiations.[48] This decisive split between Zurich and Wittenberg did, however, clarify Calvin's options. The first step had to be a theological agreement among the Swiss churches which avoided Zwingli's wording of the sacraments.

The negotiations between Bullinger and Calvin began with the latter's first visit to Zurich in January 1547, when he received a copy of Bullinger's unpublished work 'De sacramentis'.[49] This work, as Paul Rorem has shown, is not the work of the public defender of Zwingli, rather of an independent thinker more open to agreement.[50] In giving the work to Calvin for his comments Bullinger insisted that their differences be discussed in private. Calvin continued to remind Bullinger that this bond of trust allowed them to be open with one another on their theological differences. It was not easy, and Calvin quickly discovered how sensitive Bullinger could be to criticism. During 1547–8 Calvin repeatedly wrote to a reluctant Bullinger begging him to keep the lines of communication open and protesting that an agreement on the Lord's Supper was possible. The first fruit of this collaboration was their written reply on behalf of the Swiss churches to Rome's call for a council.[51]

There is some irony in the fact that Calvin's greatest achievement with the Swiss, the agreement with Bullinger on the sacraments, only served to alienate Berne and Basle. Calvin's letters to Bullinger reveal his extraordinary patience and perseverance in proving to Bullinger that his language on the presence of Christ in the sacraments did not echo Luther. The meeting of the two men in Zurich was a triumph for both Calvin's refusal to be put off by Bullinger's reticence and for his own theological acumen. As Rorem has shown, Calvin maintained a discreet silence at crucial moments to allay Bullinger's concerns, and in so doing he won an agreement by adopting the word 'testimonies' instead of 'instruments' to describe the efficacy of the sacraments. The agreement aroused deep suspicion in Berne, Basle and Germany. In Berne there were many, including Haller, who believed that Calvin was attempting a flanking manoeuvre by allying Geneva with Zurich. The general feeling was that Calvin was dragging the Swiss towards France. In Germany, conversely,

---

[48] Gerrish, *Old Protestantism*, pp. 35–36.
[49] On the Consensus Tigurinus, see Paul Rorem, *Calvin and Bullinger on the Lord's Supper* (Nottingham, 1989).   [50] *Ibid.*, 21.
[51] Bullinger and Calvin led the Reformed Swiss response to the Councils in 1546–7 and after 1551 in Trent. See Julia Gauss, 'Etappen zur Ablösung der reformierten Schweiz vom Reich', *Zwingliana*, 18 (1990), 239–41.

Calvin's agreement with the Zwinglians was seen as a betrayal of the Lutherans.[52]

Dependent on Calvin's efforts for theological agreement was his hope for the renewal of the Swiss alliance with the France. Following Mühlberg, Calvin reminded Bullinger of what the Swiss knew all too well: that having occupied Strasburg the Emperor was poised to attack the Confederation. 'For when you remain inactive', Calvin wrote to Bullinger in September 1547, 'are you not stretching your neck out to the executioner? ... There are many reasons, quite rightly, which frighten you away from an alliance with the French. Although it would not be prudent to agree to too much with France, I do not understand why every connection should be avoided.'[53] Bullinger continued to preach and write against the alliance, but in Zurich itself the mood was divided. The issue was forced in November by Henry II's invitation to the Swiss to act as supporters at the baptism of his daughter Claudia.[54] The invitation was a public acknowledgement of the active courting of Zurich by the French, and the political leadership in Zurich viewed the invitation as a chance to re-establish the city's presence on the European stage.

Calvin used all his powers of persuasion, so effective in the discussions on the sacraments, together with an exegetical grounding, to move Bullinger to change his mind on the French alliance.[55] Such was Bullinger's influence in the Confederation that Calvin found himself allied with the ambassadors of the French court, who came to Zurich to lobby the eminent churchman.[56] 'Quite rightly', Calvin writes,

I admit, pious people are deterred by the example of Josophat, who led his empire to disaster through an alliance with a godless empire. But as I interpret it, he was not punished because he concluded an alliance with the King of Israel, but rather because he took upon himself an unrighteous matter merely to please the desires of his allies.... This example is not for me definite proof that every alliance with the godless is prohibited. I see that no religious consideration hindered Abraham from forming a friendship with Abimelech (Gen. 21: 22ff). I see the same from Isaac, David and others without reprimand or punishment. Certainly, I am convinced that alliances of this sort are not always worth striving after, for there is always a danger present. But when we have good reason, or are actually compelled, I do not understand why one must abhor it.[57]

Bullinger held firm, insisting that convenient political alliances were an anathema to true religion and that religious wars were to be avoided.

---

[52] *Ibid.*, 241.   [53] 19 September 1547. CR 40: 590–1.
[54] Hauswirth, 'Politischen Ethik', 316–17.   [55] 7 May 1549. *CO* 13: 266–9.
[56] On Bullinger's extensive relations with the French ambassadors, see above all the unjustly neglected André Bouvier, *Henri Bullinger. Réformateur et conseiller oecuménique. Le successeur de Zwingli* (Zurich, 1940), pp. 191–278. Bouvier bases his study on a thorough use of Bullinger's correspondence.   [57] *Ibid.*, 267.

Following a plebiscite, Zurich and Berne refused to join the other Swiss states in renewing the alliance with France in October 1549.

The arrival of Johannes Haller and, later, Wolfgang Musculus in Berne in 1548 restored Zurich's influence in the Bernese church. Bullinger pressed Haller to cultivate relations with Calvin and Viret in order to end the split between the German and French-speaking churches. Calvin was optimistic that by using Zurich as leverage he could exert influence in Berne to secure the independence of the Genevan church, introduce Genevan-style reforms in the Pays de Vaud and suppress the growing anti-Genevan polemic of the ultra-Zwinglian ministers in Berne's rural territories. Haller, however, had no intention of being Calvin's agent in Berne. He had inherited a church riven by fifteen years of theological rancour, and his only recourse was to mediation. Haller complained to Bullinger of how the propensity of Calvin and his supporters to debate theology openly was pouring oil on old fires. Nor did Haller sympathise with the extreme Zwinglians, under the leadership of Kilchmeyer and Zébédée. Haller shared with the Bernese magistrates the objective of peace.

1549–1564. The five years following the conclusion of the *Consensus Tigurinus* were fraught with dangers for Calvin and his Swiss colleagues. Relations between Geneva and Berne sank to their nadir, leaving Calvin with virtually no supporters in Berne.[58] The tact which Calvin had shown in finding an agreement with Bullinger could not mask theological differences between the two men. Nevertheless, the major events of this period: the Bolsec affair, the trial of Servetus, the debate over excommunication in Geneva and the defence of the Consensus against Westphal indicated a new order in the Confederation. Calvin was no longer merely the dangerous outsider: while the Swiss might not agree with him and might find his presence disquieting, there was no disputing that he now belonged to the family of churches.

Between 1549 and 1552 Calvin's hopes for an improvement in relations with Berne were battered by one crisis after another as the council in Berne moved to extend its control over the church and establish peace in the rural areas. The first victim of this policy were the local meetings of ministers, known as colloquies, which were intended as occasions for instruction, study and the discussion of local problems.[59] The council, with the support of Haller and Musculus, abolished these meetings in August 1549 because they were too often marred by disputes and debauchery. Johannes Haller noted in his diary that: 'One reason for the abolition of colloquies was that in many places the people were more interested in dipping into the cup than

[58] Bähler, 'Der Kampf', pp. 29–30.   [59] *Ibid.*, p. 25.

the Scriptures.'[60] Calvin and the ministers in Lausanne regarded the abolition as an unacceptable infringement on the liberties of the church. Calvin wrote to Musculus defending the colloquies as the best way of preserving the unity of teaching and guarding against innovations.[61] The policy in Berne was not implicitly aimed against Calvin but at containing the factional politics which continued to split the church. Calvin assumed that Haller understood that the Genevans stood for a true Christian polity; it was, therefore, all the more wounding when Haller spoke of Calvin as the leader of a faction. The attack on the 'innovations' of the Genevans reached its zenith when Calvin was forced to write to Bullinger and deny that he had abolished Sunday. Calvin thanked Bullinger for putting no stock in the rumours and then provided an account of the ordering of feast days in Geneva. Against the charges that he caused the disruption by introducing innovations, Calvin argued that he had wanted to show good will towards Berne by adopting its practices, but the people of Geneva themselves had voted for the abolition of all feast days.[62]

All of these disputes paled in comparison to the trouble unleashed by the arrest of Jerome Bolsec in Geneva in October 1551. Calvin called on the other Swiss churches to provide opinions on the heterodox nature of Bolsec's attack on Calvin's doctrine of predestination. In Berne, Haller, whose method of reconciling the warring parties involved the eschewing of precise doctrinal statements, decided to assent to whatever Zurich wrote.[63] Oswald Myconius, leader of the church in Basle, was eager to support Calvin and he penned a defence of predestination that proved so incomprehensible that Calvin could only sigh.[64] Worse, the answer from Zurich was positively depressing. Bullinger made it clear that there was room for doubt on the question and he did not conceal his distrust of Calvin's teaching on predestination. Angry with the poor show of support, Calvin wrote to Farel:

I have recently complained about Basle, but in comparison to Zurich they deserve to be praised. Dear Farel, I can hardly say how much this problem has irritated me. Must there really be less fraternal unity among us than among the animals of the forest? It does not hurt us when we might have enemies around us. But when three or four churches are bound closely together and do not accept one another, that is unbelievable.[65]

[60] E. Bähler (ed.), 'Das Tagebuch Johann Hallers aus den Jahren 1548–1561'. *Archiv des Historischen Vereins des Kantons Bern*, 23 (1917), 255.

[61] 22 October 1549. *CO* 13: 433–4.

[62] 23 April 1551. *CO* 14: 104–6.   [63] Bähler, 'Der Kampf', p. 30.

[64] M. Geiger, *Basel im Zeitalter der Orthodoxie* (Basle, 1958), p. 10. On Myconius as leader of the Basle church, W. Brändly, 'Oswald Myconius in Basel', *Zwingliana*, 11 (1959), 183–92.

[65] 8 December 1551. *CO* 14: 218.

To Calvin's dismay, Bolsec was warmly received in Zurich and Berne after his expulsion from Geneva. Far from recanting his views, Bolsec settled in the Bernese countryside and became one of Calvin's most vociferous critics. Bolsec employed the successful tactic of portraying Calvin as the dangerous outsider by emphasising the differences between Geneva and Zurich; in so doing he brought into the open the most serious unresolved doctrinal difference. Bullinger prudently avoided public comment on the well-known disagreements.

In contrast to the Bolsec case, the much celebrated trial and execution of Servetus in 1553 considerably shored up Calvin's position in Geneva. All of the churches supported the trial of a heretic, though there was little enthusiasm for an execution. The only serious opposition was in Basle, where the Italian refugee community, led by Castellio and Curione, made the case the centre of their opposition to Calvin.[66] The councils of the Reformed states and the leading churchmen fell into line. 'The Baslers', wrote Calvin to Farel, 'are courageous, but the Zurichers are the most passionate of all. They emphasise emphatically the dreadfulness of his godlessness and they admonish our council to strength. Schaffhausen supports this judgement. With the letter from Berne is appended a document from their council which has encouraged our magistrates.'[67]

Shortly after Servetus' execution Calvin became embroiled in a quarrel with the Genevan council after refusing to accept its decision on excommunication. The day of reckoning was at hand, and Calvin needed the support of the other churches if he was to succeed in finally securing the implementation of this pillar of his polity. On 26 November he wrote to the ministers in Zurich asking them to petition the Zurich council for a statement of support.[68] Bullinger moved quickly, despite their obvious differences on the question, and by late December the favourable letter from Zurich was in Geneva.[69] In Basle a similar debate between the church and council over excommunication was likewise smouldering.[70] Once again the attempt by the Basle church to show support misfired. Sulzer sent a copy of the disciplinary statutes in Basle with a letter explaining how they were stronger than what was proposed in Geneva.[71] Not only was this not true but Sulzer failed to answer the question which Calvin had put; whether the use of excommunication is in accordance with the Gospel. Zurich and Schaffhausen clearly supported Calvin, while Basle's answer was judged to be of little use. Berne refused to reply.

[66] U. Plath, *Calvin und Basel in den Jahren 1552–1556* (Zurich, 1974), pp. 54–67.
[67] 26 October 1553. *CO* 14: 657.
[68] The Geneva council wrote to Zurich on 30 November. *CO* 14: 685–6.
[69] The Zurich council to Geneva, 23 December 1553. *CO* 14: 711–13.
[70] Plath, *Calvin*, pp. 98–102.
[71] Sulzer to the Genevan council, 13 December 1553. *CO* 14: 699–70.

Despite the opposition to Calvin in both Berne and Basle, he profited from the refusal of the councils in the cities to tolerate an open debate on his theology. When Zébédée and Bolsec renewed their attacks on Calvin in 1554, denouncing the Genevan as a heretic, Bullinger leaned on Haller to resolve the dispute. Calvin himself travelled several times to Berne demanding satisfaction from the council and defending his teaching on the sacraments and predestination.[72] Calvin feared that the union with Zurich could be scuttled by Zébédée and Bolsec, who were intentionally emphasising the differences between Calvin and Zwingli. Zébédée produced Calvin's letter from 1539, in which he had condemned Zwingli, as evidence for his case. Calvin was in dangerous waters; for while he rejected the claim that he had condemned Zwingli, his main defence was that the Zurich church had not taken offence.[73] In truth, Bullinger once again rescued Calvin by remaining silent.[74] In Berne, the Council simply banned all preaching on predestination and forbade those living in its territory from attending the Eucharist in Geneva.[75] The solution pleased no one, but it did have the effect of preventing an open split in the church. In Basle the Council, with Sulzer's support, likewise proscribed an open debate on predestination and through the book censors prevented Castellio and Curione from publishing their polemics against Calvin.[76]

Early in 1554 Bullinger informed Calvin that Joachim Westphal in Hamburg had published a tract against the *Consensus Tigurinus*. Bullinger wanted Calvin to answer on behalf of the Swiss churches, a task which Calvin accepted without delay. By October of the same year Calvin's *Defensio* was ready and he sent the text to Zurich for their approval. On 1 November Calvin wrote to Farel:

It pleases me greatly that the defence of our Consensus meets with your approval. If only the Zurichers will judge it in a similar manner! By the way, I see that they have become so mild that I have an almost certain hope that they will not delay with their signature nor make any difficulties. I do not trust the Bernese, they will likely provide the usual excuse that their council will not allow them to sign.... The Baslers will follow Sulzer's pliable art ...[77]

In fact, neither Berne nor Basle received a copy of the text and had no knowledge of its contents until the final draft was published. The defence of the *Consensus* was purely a matter between Calvin and Bullinger. When Calvin received the corrections from Zurich, concerning the wording of the

---

[72] Bähler, 'Der Kampf', p. 43.
[73] Geneva to Berne, April 1555. The letter is printed in Schwarz, *Johannes Calvins Briefen*, II, pp. 76–7.
[74] Calvin explains to Bullinger his statements on Zwingli and expresses his gratitude for Bullinger's discreet handling of the sensitive issue, 20 April 1555. *CO* 15: 572–3.
[75] The judgement of the Bernese council on whether Calvin contradicted Zwingli's theology: *CO* 15: 542–6.   [76] Plath, *Calvin* p. 168.   [77] *CO* 15: 297.

sacraments and with a request that Westphal not be named directly, he moved quickly to incorporate the changes.[78] It was Bullinger who suggested that Calvin not send the text to Berne and Basle as that would only cause delay and risk the outbreak of further opposition and undermine the appearance of unity among the Swiss churches.[79] The partnership between Calvin and Bullinger reached its zenith with their cooperation against Westphal. Calvin wrote the text and Bullinger was given the task of securing the agreement of the other churches.

In Germany the growing split between the Gnesio-Lutherans and the Philippists provided, Calvin hoped, the chance for reconciliation between the moderate Lutherans and the Swiss. The problem was to get around Johannes Brenz, the reformer of Württemberg, who had attacked Bullinger's theology.[80] Calvin wanted an agreement in order to facilitate an alliance of German Protestant princes to help the Huguenots. Calvin began by trying to persuade Bullinger that the only way forward was to establish contact with Melanchthon. Once again there were rumours that Melanchthon would have to abandon Wittenberg on account of his views on the sacraments.[81] Calvin believed that an indication of support might win the moderate Lutherans to their side. Zurich, clearly thinking of its earlier efforts, repeatedly expressed its doubts that anything could be expected from Melanchthon. Further, Calvin's method of dealing with Westphal had made the Zurichers uneasy; in his defence Calvin contrasted Westphal's writings with Luther's to demonstrate their inaccuracy. This use of Luther worried Bullinger that Calvin would abandon the Swiss for the Germans if he could reach an agreement. Indeed Calvin himself confided to Farel that he was prepared to meet with the Lutherans, even if it meant damaging his relations with the Zurichers. 'I have decided that I must not obey them.'[82] Although the Swiss, by supporting Calvin on excommunication, had facilitated the victory over the Perrinists in 1555, Calvin believed that the triumph marked a watershed in the relationship: no longer would he be the supplicant.

Throughout 1556 and 1557 Calvin continued to press Bullinger to show a willingness to negotiate with the Lutherans. In a reversal of the events leading to the *Consensus*, Calvin invited Bullinger to come to Geneva in order that they might agree to terms for a possible religious conference.

You write that Peter Martyr and Rudolf Gwalther will come to Geneva, but that

---

[78] The text of the recommended changes *CO* 15: 272–90. Calvin's reply to Zurich on 13 November, *CO* 15: 303–7.

[79] Bullinger to Calvin, 15 December 1554. *CO* 15: 349; Plath, *Calvin*, p. 184.

[80] On Brenz and the situation in Württemberg, see Martin Brecht and Hermann Ehmer, *Südwestdeutsche Reformationsgeschichte* (Stuttgart, 1984), pp. 427–8.

[81] Neuser, 'Versuche Bullingers', 46–8.   [82] 18 May 1556. *CO* 16: 147.

you are hindered by poor health. A private religious discussion, you believe, has little hope of success, because Brenz, a obstinate man who is too much taken with his own madness, will play a leading role. Although I have more than once testified that I understand the dangers of such meetings, I do not want to evade (the opportunity) so that our opponents are able to triumph because we have not dared.[83]

In April 1557 Beza and Farel travelled to Germany to drum up support for the Waldensians and the Huguenots. So desperate were the Genevans for German support for the French cause that when they met Melanchthon at the Worms Colloquy they agreed to a theological formula. Beza rashly promised that with the exception of the articles on the Lord's Supper the Swiss Reformed churches could accept the *Confessio Augustana*. Beza drew up an agreement which both parties, unknown to Geneva and Zurich, signed.[84] Further, Melanchthon agreed to the formulation at Worms which reaffirmed the exclusion of the Zwinglians and damned Zwingli.

For the Swiss, Beza and Farel had betrayed the Reformed churches by presuming to sign a text which was unacceptable. It is no overstatement to say that the Zwinglians hated the *Confessio Augustana*, and Bullinger, despite Calvin's arguments to the contrary, continued to attribute its authorship to Luther. The events in Worms confirmed Zurich's suspicions that Melanchthon was no better than Luther and that the Genevans could not be trusted. Calvin, clearly distraught by Beza's *faux pas*, tried to repair the damage by arguing that Geneva was not abandoning Zurich, but that the pressure on Beza to indicate good will required him to act alone.[85] Concerning Melanchthon, Calvin wrote to Bullinger that he too was hurt by this betrayal and suggested that it can only be explained by Melanchthon's weakness.[86] The damnation of the Reformed churches at Worms precluded the possibility of further negotiations and fatally damaged the possibility for a Protestant alliance to aid the French churches. Calvin's last letter on the subject is full of disappointment and a certain bitterness towards Zurich. The unhappy conclusion of the Worms colloquy, Calvin says, has divided the parties more than ever. The blame for this, however, lay partially with the Swiss churches on account of their refusal to negotiate. Calvin says that they have been blind in their opposition to the *Confessio Augustana*; the German churches were bound by its proscriptions, but had never demanded that the Swiss ascribe to it as a condition for agreement. The refusal of the Zurichers had only led the Lutherans to take a harder line. Although he personally despaired of further discussions,

[83] 30 May 1557. *CO* 16: 501.
[84] See 'Wormser Religionsgespräche', in *Realencyklopädie für protestantische Theologie und Kirche*, XXI (Leipzig, 1908), 492–6. The text of Beza's formulation of the Lord's Supper is found in *CO* 16: 469–72.   [85] Calvin to Peter Martyr, 20 July 1557. *CO* 16: 544–5.
[86] 23 February 1558. *CO* 17: 60–2.

Calvin informed Bullinger that should he receive another invitation he would accept it, not to abandon Zurich but to break the impasse. At the end of the letter Calvin pointedly reminds Bullinger that his commitment to the unity of the Swiss churches did not preclude the freedom to act as his conscience led him.[87]

In the final years of his life Calvin was consumed with events in France. From the Swiss churches there was little more to be expected. Although Berne and Geneva, under pressure from the other Confederates, had renewed their alliance in 1558, the animosity between the two continued unabated.[88] Calvin's opponents claimed that he was opposed to the alliance, but, in truth, he fully appreciated, however regrettable, Geneva's dependence on Berne.[89] To secure its renewal, Calvin implored his contacts in Basle, the traditional adjudicator of disputes between Geneva and Berne, to promote Geneva's case. Berne, however, harboured Calvin's opponents, who railed against the 'Calvinism' of Geneva. As ever, rumour poisoned the air between the two cities, and many believed that Calvin was torturing and executing his political and religious opponents. The two cities also suspected one another of secretly negotiating with Savoy, to the detriment of the other. In Basle, Sulzer had also become superintendent of the Lutheran church in Baden and had signed the *Confessio Augustana*, thus breaking the theological unity of the Swiss churches.[90] Although Calvin continued to correspond with Sulzer on French matters, the Westphal affair had effectively ended their working relationship. It was, however, Zurich which caused the greatest pain. Calvin, in a letter dated 2 December 1559, told Bullinger that the conditions demanded by Zurich left the Genevans with little room to manoeuvre and that the errors of men like Beza had arisen on account of frustration with Swiss irresolution.[91] Calvin never explicitly blamed Bullinger for the collapse of the German talks, which, in his view, robbed the French Protestants of a much needed alliance, but the message was clear. Calvin was also offended by Bullinger's continued suspicion of his 'Lutheran' teachings on the sacraments. Bullinger had complained that the confession for the Academy in Geneva returned to the language of 'substance', and thus contradicted the *Consensus*.[92]

[87] 22 May 1558. *CO* 17: 173–5.   [88] Feller, *Geschichte Berns*, p. 396.

[89] Calvin had voiced his opposition to the use of Swiss symbols in Geneva. Those who wore the Swiss cross were identified as Eidgenots, a movement identified with Swiss nationalism. A. Roget, *Histoire de Genève* (8 vols., Geneva, 1890–1900), III, pp. 56–59. I am grateful to Dr Bill Naphy of St Andrews for this reference.

[90] On the quarrel of the Swiss churches with Basle and Sulzer, see Amy Nelson Burnett, 'Simon Sulzer and the Consequences of the 1563 Strasbourg Consensus in Switzerland', *ARG*, 83 (1992), 154–79.   [91] 2 December 1559. *CO* 17: 687–91.

[92] Calvin's defence of the term *substancia*. *Ibid.*, 690.

With the outbreak of the wars of religion in France, Calvin, increasingly ill, attempted to convince the Swiss to send soldiers. Following the negotiations with the German princes and Swiss cities there was a plan that an army should be raised and sent to France. Zurich refused to send any troops but Calvin was hopeful that Berne, on account of her war with Savoy, could be persuaded. Calvin entreated Bullinger to use any influence he had in Berne to ensure that the commitment of forces to recovering the Burgundian cities was fulfilled.[93] In return, Calvin gave Bullinger his word that the Lutherans would not be allowed to get a toe-hold in France. Calvin had told Sulzer that he would rather die than agree to the presence of Lutheran theologians at the colloquy of Poissy in 1561. In December 1563, Calvin, in his last letter to Bullinger, assured him that the *Confessio Augustana* would not be introduced in France. He had not, however, lost his dream of a united Protestant front to support the beleaguered churches in France. 'The best way, believe me, to check the evil (of Lutheranism) would be that the confession written by me in the name of the Prince of Condé and the other nobles should be published, by which Condé would pledge his good faith and reputation, and endeavour to draw over the German princes.'[94]

The foregoing events, so close to the end of Calvin's life, demonstrate how Calvin's foreign French ministry continued to depend on the stability of Swiss relations; thus he devoted immense time to them. The traditional picture has emphasised Calvin's westward orientation towards France, and without impugning this argument, this survey has argued that Calvin's work as a reformer was only possible because of the support given by the Swiss churches. He had, in fact, to look both ways. In the early years Calvin was the supplicant, only emerging later as a more equal partner, and events such as the excommunication crisis demonstrate the degree of dependence until quite late. Calvin found this reliance frustrating, and it explains his bitter, and frequently unfair remarks about contemporaries in letters. Seen from the Zurich side, Bullinger treated Calvin with an indulgence and generosity which covered real disagreements over doctrine and ecclesiology. It shows that both men appreciated the importance of a united front in presenting the Swiss Reformation to outsiders. This, and not just Calvin's work, laid the basis for the dominance of Calvinism in the second half of the sixteenth century.

[93] Calvin to Bullinger, 15 August 1562. *CO* 19: 498–500.
[94] December 1563. *CO* 20.

5   Calvin's works in translation

Francis Higman

In this chapter I should like to explore the role of translations of Calvin's works into modern languages up to 1600. This is, of course, to leave aside the most important line of communication to specialist theologians, namely publications in Latin. Just one illustration will show how vast this exception is: in Dr Leedham-Green's study of book inventories in Cambridge thirty-five copies of Calvin's *Institutio* are listed in Latin, and only seven in English.[1] However, the broader extension of knowledge of Calvin in the public at large is significant enough to warrant attention. What I have to say falls into two sections: a survey of all known translations into European languages in the sixteenth century; and a more detailed look at the special case of translations into English.

1   Some facts and figures

What works by Calvin were translated, into which languages, when, where and by whom? That makes five questions. I shall try to answer all of them later in the case of England; for our general survey of the picture in Europe a full answer is not possible, since for example the identity of the translators is not usually given.[2]

A preliminary note is needed on the languages of Calvin's originals. While works in Latin were already 'international' in nature, and accessible to any properly educated person as a base for translation, writings in French had either to pass through an intermediate stage of translation into Latin, or to have the good fortune to find that relatively *rara avis* in the sixteenth century, someone bilingual in modern languages. The *Institution*, the biblical commentaries, and many theological treatises (for example the

---

[1] E.S. Leedham-Green, *Books in Cambridge Inventories. Book-Lists from Vice-Chancellor's Court Probate Inventories in the Tudor and Stuart Periods* (2 vols., Cambridge, 1986), II, pp. 178–9.

[2] It is a pleasure to acknowledge my immense debt to Jean-François Gilmont, who provided me with a 'short-title catalogue' of editions of Calvin up to 1600. It is on this STC that most of the information in my general survey is based.

writings on the Trinity, on predestination and on the eucharist in the 1550s) were originally published in Latin, so could circulate freely. On the other hand the popular polemical tracts, Calvin's 'ecclesiastical' writings (catechism, liturgy, ecclesiastical ordinances) and his sermons appeared first in French. For the most part the sermons were never translated into Latin, and therefore depended on a writer versed in French as well as in the target language. Most of the polemical treatises were fairly rapidly translated into Latin, or at the latest appeared in one of the editions of Calvin's collected *Opuscula* (1552, 1563). They sometimes suffered delay in transmission (for example the major Nicodemite treatises of 1543–4 did not appear in Latin until 1549 in *De vitandis superstitionibus*), but no serious obstacle.

A survey of translations into European languages

We shall take the list in ascending order, beginning with those countries with the fewest known translations.

Scandinavia No translations at all of Calvin are known in Norway, Sweden or Denmark – or for that matter into Irish or Welsh.

Hungary Only one translation into Hungarian is known, a *Catechism* published without address or date. There may be others concealed among the numerous anonymous Reformation tracts which appeared in the period, but which have never been properly studied.[3]

Poland Calvin's contacts with the Polish Reformation were almost entirely in Latin, by letters or by treatises. The only known translation into Polish consists of extracts from the *Institutio*, published in Cracow in 1599.

'Czechoslovakia' Only two translations into Czech are known, both dating from 1546: the *Duae Epistolae* (1537) on how the faithful should behave in 'Papist' territory, and the *Supplex Exhortatio* to the Emperor (of 1543), both translated from Latin and published at Nuremberg.

Scotland As emerges from Dr Dawson's paper in the present volume, adaptations of Calvin's liturgy and of his catechism appeared in Scots Gaelic in 1567.

---

[3] See Gedeon Borsa, *Régi Magyarországi Nyomtatványok 1473–1600 (Res litteraria Hungariae vetus operum impressorum 1473–1600)* (Budapest, 1971).

Spain Four translations are attested: extracts from the *Institutio* (of 1536) translated probably by Francisco de Enzinas and printed in Antwerp in 1540 (one of the earliest of all Calvin translations into a foreign language), and the complete *Institutio* (of 1559), printed in London in 1597; the *Catéchisme* and *Forme des prières* were printed by J. Crespin in Geneva in 1559.

So far there is nothing to get excited about, except to note that Calvin's role in Hungary and in Poland was far more significant than is suggested by translations of his works into the vernaculars. His contacts with church leaders in these countries do not seem to have carried over into direct access by the faithful.

The Netherlands Here we move into more fruitful territory. A chronological list of all known translations totals eighteen editions:

Petit Traité monstrant que doit faire un homme fidele quand il est entre les Papistes; *Excuse aux Nicodemites* (originals 1543 and 1544, Latin translation 1549), printed (probably) in Emden in 1554.[4]

Institutio (1559), translated in 1560 in Emden, followed by six further editions.

In omnes Pauli epistolas atque etiam in epistolam ad Hebraeos commentaria (1551), Emden 1566 (one further edition).

Confession de foi (1559, French), printed in Norwich in 1568.

Sermons sur le cantique du roi Ezechias (French 1562), Antwerp, 1581.

Commentarii in epistolas canonicas (1551), Amsterdam, 1582.

Harmonia ex tribus evangelistis composita, In evangelium secundum Johannem commentarius, Commentariorum in Acta Apostolorum libri duo (series completed in 1555), Antwerp, 1582.

Traité des Reliques (1543), Antwerp, 1583.

Plusieurs sermons touchant la divinité, humanité et nativité de nostre Seigneur Jésus Christ (1558), Delft, 1598.

De Scandalis (1550), Amsterdam, 1598 (again in 1599).

This list deserves some comments. Translation of Calvin into Dutch begins remarkably late (1554) and slowly. It must be remembered that in the early Reformation Luther was much prized in Dutch (forty-one translations of Luther have been counted before 1542);[5] he was displaced in the

---

[4] See Andrew Pettegree, *Emden and the Dutch Revolt. Exile and the Development of Reformed Protestantism* (Oxford, 1992), p. 92.

[5] See C.C.G. Visser, *Luther's geschriften in de Nederlanden tot 1546* (Assen, 1969).

second half of the century not only by Calvin but also by Bullinger (translated as frequently as Calvin).[6] The Calvin translations include a high proportion of 'heavy' works (*Institutio*, commentaries), while the popular treatise on relics only appears once, and late (1583).

Italy Here we meet with two surprises: more translations into Italian have been identified than into Dutch – nineteen in all; and Calvin's ideas were circulating in Italy remarkably early. However, a distinction must immediately be introduced: these Italian translations come from various sources, and those produced in Italy itself are heavily disguised and adapted to conceal their origins. A chronological list gives the following:[7]

> Extracts from the *Institutio* (of 1536) incorporated into Antonio Brucioli's *Pia espositione* (Venice, 1542, two further editions).
>
> *Catéchisme* (1542), printed in 1545, it is not known where (with three further editions).
>
> Adaptation of the *Petit Traité de la sainte Cène* (French 1541, Latin 1545), printed under the title *Operetta utile* . . . in Venice in 1549.
>
> *Petit Traité monstrant* . . . and *Excuse aux Nicodemites* (1543 and 1544), Florence, 1549 (further editions from Basle and Geneva).
>
> *Forme des prières* (French, 1542), Geneva, 1551 (one further edition).
>
> *Quatre Sermons* (French 1552, Latin 1553), Geneva, 1553.
>
> *Epistre . . . que Christ est la fin de la loi* (1535), Geneva 1555 (one further edition).
>
> *Institutio* (1553 edition in Latin?), Geneva, 1557 (one further edition).
>
> *Petit Traité de la sainte Cène*, full text, Geneva, 1561.
>
> *Interim adultero-germanum* (Latin, 1549), Geneva, 1561.
>
> *Confession de la foi* (French, 1559), Geneva, 1561.
>
> *Commentarii in epistolam Pauli ad Romanos, ad Galatas, in epistolam ad Hebraeos* (1540, 1548 and 1549 respectively), Lyons, 1565.

There is a clear contrast between those works produced in Italy, heavily disguising the origins of the text, and those produced in Geneva in mid-century (when there was a flourishing Italian community, with their own printers). Most characteristic of the former group, perhaps, is the adap-

---

[6] See J. Staedtke, 'Die niederländischen Ausgaben der Werke Heinrich Bullingers', *Zwingliana*, 13 (1969–73), 407–19; and his *Heinrich Bullinger Bibliographie* (Zurich, 1972).

[7] See Ugo Rozzo and Silvana Seidel Menchi, 'Livre et réforme en Italie', in *La Réforme et le livre: l'Europe de l'imprimé (1517–c.1570)*, ed. J.-F. Gilmont (Paris, 1990), pp. 327–74, in particular pp. 355–60 which give a list of all translations into Italian from Reformation writers up to 1566.

tation of the *Petit traité de la sainte Cène*, which presents the positive aspects of Calvin's eucharistic theology, but omits the attacks on the mass as sacrifice, on transubstantiation, and on the practice of communion in one kind only.[8] The Calvin represented within Italy gives a religious and spiritual message, but not a challenge to the Church of Rome. Thus in Italy (in contrast to Holland) there are few 'heavy' works translated (only the *Institutio* and one group of commentaries): and these represent the group of translations produced by the exile community, in Geneva or Lyons.

It may be added at this stage that Calvin's writings on coexistence with the Papists attract attention in almost every country: while his is by no means the only voice to be heard in the debate, clearly his strongly defined doctrine of no compromise was taken very seriously.

Germany The total number of translations, thirty-two, seems more impressive. But here we are in Lutheran territory initially, and the impact of Calvin is slow in coming:

> One of the *Duae Epistolae* (1537), Basle, 1540. Then a gap until
> *Consensus Tigurinus* (1549), Zurich 1551.[9]
> *Catéchisme* (French 1542), printed in Basle, 1556 (one further edition).
> *Traité des reliques* (French 1543), Wittenberg, 1557 (the *only* case of Calvin published in Luther's city); seven further editions.
> *Duae Epistolae* (1537), Neuburg, 1557.
> *Forme des prières* (1542), Heidelberg, 1563.
> *Confession de foi* (1559), Heidelberg, 1563 (reprinted once).
> *Commentariorum in Acta Apostolorum libri duo* (1552/4), Heidelberg, 1571 (reprinted once).
> *Institutio* (1559), Heidelberg, 1572 (also extracts the same year; thereafter two editions of the whole, and four editions of extracts).
> *65 sermons sur l'harmonie ou concordance des trois evangélistes, Sermons sur le ... Deuteronome* (French, 1562 and 1567), Herborn, 1586.
> *Petit Traité monstrant ...* (1543), Herborn, 1588 (reprinted once).
> *Harmonia ex tribus evangelistis composita, adiuncto seorsum Iohanne* (1555), Heidelberg, 1590.
> Extracts from *Sermons sur le livre de Job* (1563), Herborn, 1592.

If one leaves aside the particular cases of Heidelberg and Herborn, the list

---

8   See R. Peter and J.-F. Gilmont, *Bibliotheca Calviniana. Les oeuvres de Jean Calvin publiées au XVIe siècle* (3 vols., Geneva, 1991–), I, pp. 325–7.

9   Apart from this text (which belongs as much to Zurich as to Geneva), the Zwinglian Reformation seems to have taken no interest at all in propagating the ideas of Calvin in the vernacular.

is remarkably light, consisting mainly of short and accessible texts (the treatise on relics was more successful in Germany than anywhere else); the writings on coexistence with the Papists again feature (but without the *Excuse aux Nicodemites*). It would seem that Calvin interested most Germans more for his anti-Papist polemics rather than for his theological thought. The pattern is however revolutionised if we include Heidelberg, where from 1560 the Elector Frederick III resolved to adopt the Calvinist Reformation: alongside the liturgy and the confession of faith we find the first translation of the *Institutio* and of some of the 'heavyweight' commentaries resulting from this situation. After the death of Frederick III (1576) Lutheranism was reimposed in Heidelberg; some of the Calvinist leaders expelled as a result settled in Herborn – hence the appearance of translations published there from 1586 on.

The total of editions of Calvin translations to date is eighty-six, spread among eight languages. One final stage of our survey remains.

England We move into a different world: the ninety-one known editions of Calvin translations into English constitute a higher total than all the other languages put together! It would be fastidious to give a detailed list. Let us summarise by reigns:

Henry VIII (to 1547): a letter (otherwise unknown) on the question of coexistence with the Papists, Antwerp, 1544 (one further edition).

Edward VI (1547–53): a shower of short, but serious, texts (*Petit Traité de la sainte Cène, Petit Traité monstrant ...*, *Forme des prières, Catéchisme, Contre les Anabaptistes*), printed mainly in London. These texts reflect the preoccupations of the English Reformers at the time: questions of liturgy and organization, and (a rarity?) the translation of Calvin's treatise against the Anabaptists (cf. also the publication of several tracts by Bullinger on the same subject).[10] One chapter of the *Institutio* (the last) was printed in 1550, and the translator, Thomas Broke, said in his preface that he had translated more of the work; but nothing more is known to have been published at the time.

Mary Tudor (1553–8): only two reprints, both from Geneva: the *Forme des prières* and the *Catéchisme*.[11]

Elizabeth I (1558–1603): at first a series of reprints of short texts like the *Catéchisme*, plus some new translations (*Contre l'astrologie judiciaire, Traité des reliques*, both 1561; neither was

---

[10] Cf. Staedtke, *Bullinger Bibliographie*, nos. 30–2.
[11] See E.J. Baskerville, *A Chronological Bibliography of Propaganda and Polemic Published Between 1553 and 1558* (Philadelphia, 1979).

reprinted in the sixteenth century); above all, the *Institutio* (of 1559) printed in 1561. Then from 1570 to 1580 we have the following series: *Praelectiones in librum prophetiarum Danielis, In librum psalmorum Commentarius, Sermons sur l'épître aux Galates, Sermons sur le livre de Job, In omnes Pauli epistolas atque etiam in epistolam ad Hebraeos commentarii, Sermons sur l'épître aux Ephésiens, In librum Josue brevis commentarius, In primum Mosis librum commentarius, In Jonam praelectiones, Sermons sur les deux épîtres à Timothée et sur l'épître à Tite, Sermons sur les dix Commandements.* All of these are long to very long texts. Further large translations follow in the next decade; and throughout this period there is an uninterrupted flow of reprints of the *Forme des prières, Catéchisme,* and of the *Institutio* either complete or in abridged form.

The quite exceptional place occupied by Calvin translations in England in the sixteenth century invites us to look more closely at the phenomenon.

2   The translations into English

How do we explain the difference not only in number, but also in nature, between the English translations and the rest? And why should there be a particular peak in the production of large-scale, properly theological works, in the 1570s? Finally, what can be known about the intended readership of these translations? Let us look first at the translators (this task is facilitated by the fact that a good number of translations into English are signed, unlike most translations into other languages); we shall then turn to the dedications of the translations. After a brief note on the intended readership we shall attempt a conclusion.

(a)   The translators

I had rather assumed that a major input into the translation effort in England, and particularly in the increasing number of texts translated directly from French into English (most of the sermons mentioned above) came from the Marian exiles, the community of English people who settled in Geneva between 1556 and 1559, returning home on the accession of Queen Elizabeth.[12] In a direct sense it turns out I was quite wrong: few of the named translators seem ever to have been to Geneva.

---

[12] Information about the Marian exiles in Geneva is based on *'Le Livre des Anglois', or Register of the English Church at Geneva under the Pastoral Care of Knox and Goodman, 1555–1559*, ed. by A.F. Mitchell, no place, no date (c. 1889); C.H. Garrett, *The Marian Exiles* (Cambridge, 1938); Charles Martin, *Les Protestants anglais réfugiés à Genève au temps de Calvin, 1555–1560, leur église, leurs écrits* (Geneva, 1915); reference is also made to the *Dictionary of National Biography*, referred to henceforth as *DNB*.

Miles Coverdale (1488–1568) Miles Coverdale is known to have been in Geneva in 1557 and 1558. But his only known Calvin translation, of the *Petit traité de la sainte Cène*, was printed in 1549; after his stay in Geneva no further translation is known from his pen.

Anthony Gilby (d. 1585) One of the first pastors of the English church in Geneva, appointed to replace John Knox during the latter's absence in 1555; on Knox's return in 1556 Gilby became an Elder, or 'Senior'. Gilby was a graduate of Christ's College, Cambridge in the 1530s, went into exile in 1553, and while in Geneva worked on the Geneva *Bible* and on the *Form of Common Order* (translated with modifications from Calvin's *Forme des prières*). He returned to England in 1559, became vicar of Ashby de la Zouche (Leicestershire), 'where he laboured with much zeal and lived in high honour, though for a time suspended for his persistent non-conformity' (Mitchell). The *DNB* describes Gilby as 'one of the most acrimonious and illiberal writers [of the Reformation], and a "dear disciple of Calvin"'; J. Strype calls him 'obnoxious'.[13] Both evaluations emanate from middle to high church Anglicans. Gilby is believed to have translated Calvin's *Commentaries upon the prophet Daniell* (London, John Day, 1570) (though the initials A.G. may stand for 'Arthur Golding', to whom we shall come shortly).

Goddred Gilby Son of Anthony Gilby, he accompanied his father to Geneva. He translated Calvin's *Contre l'astrologie judiciaire* in 1561, but does not seem to have translated anything else, and little else is known about him.

Anne Lock The wife of a London merchant, Henry Lock, Anne Lock went to Geneva, on the invitation of John Knox, in 1557; a week later her daughter died, and was buried in Geneva. After returning to London, she published four *Sermons on the song that Ezechias made after he had been sick* (London, John Day, 1560), sermons concerning the sufferings of the righteous and the consolation of faith, which she herself could have heard, since Calvin preached them in November 1557. Anne Lock was later clearly associated with the forward Protestants of Elizabeth's reign: her second husband was Edward Dering, one of the most eloquent preachers of the period. She did one further translation from French, thirty years later: Jean Taffin's *Of the marks of the children of God, and of their comfort in afflictions* (1590).[14]

---

[13] John Strype, *The Life and Acts of Matthew Parker* (London, 1711), p. 326.
[14] Patrick Collinson, 'The Role of Women in the English Reformation Illustrated by the Life and Friendships of Anne Lock', in *Studies in Church History*, II, ed. G.J. Cuming (London, 1965), pp. 258–72.

Stephen Wythers Arrived in Geneva in 1556; his brother Francis was a Deacon of the English church in 1557. After returning to England Stephen published a translation of the *Traité des reliques* (London, Rowland Hall, 1561). He also translated J. Sleidan, *The Foure principall Empyres* (1563).

This is a singularly thin list of translations stemming directly from the Marian exiles. We could add one other name, but on slender justification:

Robert Horne (1519?–80) Educated at St John's College Cambridge in the 1530s and 1540s, Horne was appointed (despite the hostility of the Chapter) dean of Durham in 1551, and chaplain to Edward VI. Obliged to emigrate on Mary's accession, he went to Strasburg, Zurich, Frankfurt (where he became chief minister, and deeply involved in the quarrels of the Frankfurt community), Strasburg again, Basle, and finally a brief visit to Geneva in the winter of 1558–9, before returning to England. He later became bishop of Winchester. The *DNB* mentions his 'puritanical fanaticism' and blames on him the destruction of paintings and ornaments in St John's College, Cambridge, and New College, Oxford. But his only contribution to the translation of Calvin's works was *Certain Homilies containing admonition for this time* (Wesel?, J. Lambrecht?, 1553), before his voyage abroad.

There is no evidence that any of the other translators ever set foot in Geneva. Of these, some are obscure figures about whom little is known apart from their name on the title page of their translations (John Harmar, William Becket, for example); others have left traces elsewhere. First, three notable laymen:

Thomas Broke (fl. c. 1550) Broke was an alderman of Calais and MP for that town; he was twice imprisoned under Henry VIII for speaking out against the 'Romanising' tendencies at the end of the king's reign. In 1549 he was Paymaster of Dover when he published (London, John Day and William Seres) *Of the life and conversation of a Christian man*, a translation from the Latin of the final chapter of Calvin's *Institutio* (1539 version). Broke did other translations besides this; in the prologue to his book he writes: 'I have, good reader, translated a good part more of the *Institution of a Christian man* written by this noble clerk, which I cannot now put in print, partly through my own busyness, as well at Dover as at Calais, and partly by reason the printer hath presently no leisure for the same.'

It may be that this is the same person as the 'Brooke' who translated *Two*

Epistles [of Bullinger and Calvin] whether it be lawful for a christian man to be partaker of the mass of the papists in 1544, printed at Antwerp by Matthew Crom.

Thomas Norton (1532–84) Norton was a lawyer, poet and MP (for Gatton, then Berwick, finally the City of London); he wrote at least twice to Calvin in the 1550s, expressing his great admiration for the Reformer. He was tutor to the earl of Hertford. He married the daughter of archbishop Cranmer in 1555; his wife's step-father was Edward Whitchurch, 'a Calvinistic printer' (*DNB*). At the request of two printers, Reginald Wolffe and Whitchurch, Norton translated the 1559 *Institutio* into English (first edition London, Reyner Wolffe and Richard Harrison, 1561). In the preface to the third edition (1574) he says of Whitchurch: 'a man well known of upright heart and dealing, an ancient zealous Gospeller, as plain and true a friend as ever I knew living, and as desirous to do any thing to the common good, specially by the advancement of true religion'. Norton was one of the MPs who introduced two bills in Parliament in 1572 on behalf of the Puritan party. The *DNB* adds that Norton later 'showed much zeal in torturing Catholics'.

Norton's translation of the *Institutio* is remarkably faithful. He comments in his introduction (to the third edition, 1574) on Calvin's well-known brevity, which he says leads to a great 'hardness' in the original, 'insomuch that it sufficeth not to read him once, unless you can be content to read in vain'; he resolved in his translation to 'follow the words so near as the phrase of the English tongue would suffer me', even though this leads to even more 'hardness' in the translation than in the Latin. One characteristic of Norton's translation (as of several other translators) is their preference for brief, Anglo-Saxon words rather than Latinate forms: *acceperunt* becomes 'took', *claritatem* is translated 'brightness', *subrogarentur* becomes 'put'.

Thomas Stocker I know little about Stocker's biography; but he describes himself on the title page of one of his publications as 'Gent'. He came to my attention first by a so-called translation of Pierre Viret's *Cauteles et canon de la messe* (1584), in which Stocker gives a very free translation of Viret's knockabout humour. The *STC* notes (no. 2029) a 'translation' by Stocker from Théodore de Bèze, *The Pope's canon ...*, but adds: 'not a translation of any known de Bèze text, but rather loosely based on some of his ideas'. How does he treat Calvin? His *Two and twenty sermons on the hundredth and nineteenth Psalm* (London, Thomas Dawson for John Harrison and Thomas Man, 1580) handle the Genevan leader with much more respect; but he has a tendency to underline or reinforce the sense, either by an insistent use of doublets where the original has few or none ('the most ignorant shall easily acknowledge *and confess* that I mean nothing else but to make open *and plain* the simple *and pure* substance of the text'), or by adding to the violence of the original:

ils vivent en ce monde comme bestes, n'ayans ne sens ne raison.	we are blind, and do live in the world as savage and wild beasts, utterly void of sense and reason.

It will be noticed that Stocker also changes Calvin's third-person form ('les hommes') systematically into the first person plural: '*we* are blind'. There is no real deformation of Calvin's thought; but there is a constant effort to ram it home.

The rest of the translators are clergymen; and all of them are what the *DNB* labels 'Puritan divines'. Many of those we know something of were in trouble with the authorities in one way or another.

William Fulke (1538–89) Fellow of St John's College, Cambridge (in 1564), closely associated with Thomas Cartwright, the Puritan leader in Cambridge. In the serious conflicts between the church leaders and the Puritan centre in St John's, Fulke lost his Fellowship, but was later reinstated. He translated Calvin's *Commentary on Joshua* (London, Thomas Dawson for George Bishop, 1578), as well as composing 'many treatises in defence of extreme Protestant principles' which were 'learned and effective, though their language was often coarse and virulent' (*Oxford Dictionary of the Christian Church*).

Eusebius Pagit (1551?–1617) After studies at Christ Church, Oxford, he became a rector in 1572 at the latest. He was in trouble for arguing against the *Thirty-Nine Articles* and for non-conformity.[15] He translated Calvin's *Commentary on the concordance of three evangelists* (London, Thomas Dawson for George Bishop, 1584).

Arthur Golding (1536?–1605?) The most active of all Calvin's translators into English (or indeed into any language). He studied at Queens' College, Cambridge, and was a most industrious translator. Apart from his translations of Calvin, he provided English versions of Ovid's *Metamorphoses* (in the 1560s), Bèze's *Abraham sacrifiant*, the *Mémoires de Coligny*, and the *Beneficio di Cristo*. From Calvin he translated: *De Scandalis* (London, Henry Wykes? for William Seres, 1567); *Commentary on the Psalms* (London, Thomas East and Henry Middleton for Lucas Harrison and George Bishop, 1571; this was from the Latin); *Sermons on*

---

[15] See Patrick Collinson, *The Elizabethan Puritan Movement* (Oxford, 1967), in particular pp. 143, 151 and 193 for further details.

the book of Job (London, Henry Bynneman for Lucas Harrison and George Bishop, 1574; translated from French); *Sermons on Ephesians* (London, Thomas Dawson for Lucas Harrison and George Bishop, 1577; translated from French); *Sermons on Deuteronomy* (London, Henry Middleton for George Bishop, 1583; from the French). The *DNB* adds: 'in London he moved in good society, although he showed strong puritan predilections'. (We shall return shortly to this 'good society'.)

Golding's translations, whether from Latin or from French, are of high quality. Time and again in his prefaces he stresses the 'plainness' of his translations: 'rather endeavouring to lay forth things plainly (yea and sometimes also homely and grossly) to the understanding of many, than to indite things curiously to the pleasing of a few' (*Commentary on the Psalms*, 1571).

Golding's manner of writing 'plainly, homely, grossly' is particularly seen in his handling of some of Calvin's more colourful expressions (examples taken from the *Sermons on Job*):

quand le diable nous vient mettre en phantasie	when the devil comes to put a toy in our head
Dieu lasche la bride à Sathan	Yet doth God let Satan run so far upon the bridle
Job se jette ici hors des gonds	Job rangeth here out of his bounds
matiere caducque	brittle stuff
sans y ajouster en façon que ce soit	without adding of some trick of our own

To give a more extensive example of Golding's manner of translating, a final example from the *Commentary on the Psalms*:

videmus tamen quam secure sibi indulgeant in peccatis: imo ut quisque pro sua libidine a justitia longissime recessit, quia votorum suorum compos est, beatus censetur. Contra vero hic propheta docet, neminem ad Dei timorem et cultum, legisque studium rite posse animari, donec statuerit, miseros esse omnes impios, et eodem implicitos fore exitio qui non procul ab eorum consortio discesserint.	Yet do we see how carelessly they *cocker themselves* in their sins: yea, the further that every of them hath ranged from righteousness after his own *lust*, because he obtaineth his heart's desire, he is counted blessed. But *clean* contrarywise the Prophet teacheth here that no man can be rightly minded to the fear and worshipping of God and to the study of his law, until he be fully persuaded that all ungodly men are wretched, and that all those shall be *wrapped* in the same mischief that depart not a great way from their company.

John Field Field translated *Thirteen Sermons ... entreating of the free election of God in Jacob, and of reprobation in Esau* (1562), published in 1579 (London, Thomas Dawson for Thomas Man and Tobie Cooke). Field is generally held responsible (with Thomas Wilcox) for the anonymous *Admonition to the Parliament* of 1572, the most comprehensive attack on the incomplete reformation of the Church of England in the period; he and Wilcox were imprisoned in Newgate for their pains, but appear to have escaped a threatened banishment.[16] We shall return in our conclusion to Field's translation; suffice for the moment to note that his version is more adventurous than most. He adds to Calvin's original an allusion to Ariadne's thread:

Nous avons beau travailler, appliquons-y tous noz sens et toutes noz estudes: où est-ce que nous parviendrons? Ce sera nous fourrer toujours tant plus avant au labyrinthe, sinon que nous aions la conduite de Dieu pour nous esclairer.	We shall have *spun a fair thread* if we apply all our senses and all our studies thereto: whither is it that we shall come? This shall be always to *enwrap* us so much the more in a labyrinth and maze, unless we have the direction of God to *show us the way*.

Field also provides the best schoolboy howler I have encountered in these translations:

[Dieu] vint là comme la main armée.	God had come with a main army.

(b)   The dedications

Most of these translations carry an 'Epistle dedicatory'. In some cases (Thomas Norton's *Institution* (1561), Laurence Tomson's *Sermons on the Epistles to Timothy and Titus* (1579) these are simply to 'The Reader'. Sometimes the dedication is an expression of gratitude for past generosity: Christopher Fetherstone to Lady Judith Pelham (abridged version of the *Institution*, 1585), Robert Vaux to several clergymen who were instrumental in getting him appointed to his parish (*Commentary on Colossians*, 1581?).

Edmund Grindal, archbishop of Canterbury from 1575, received dedications in 1577 from Arthur Golding (*Sermons on Ephesians*) and Thomas Tymme (*Commentary on Corinthians*). It was in June 1577 that Grindal was suspended from his functions for his sympathy towards the 'forward Protestants'. (I know of no dedication to Grindal's less radical predecessor Matthew Parker!)

Most of the dedications are to eminent noblemen – but, it would seem,

[16] Field is one of the leading figures in Collinson's *Elizabethan Puritan Movement*.

not just on the grounds of their nobility. Sir William Cecil, Lord Burghley, the most powerful of Elizabeth's ministers, receives a dedication from Arthur Golding in 1574 (*Sermons on Galatians*); Sir Thomas Bromley, lord chancellor (and *protégé* of Cecil's) from the same Arthur Golding in 1583 (*Sermons on Deuteronomy*). Arthur Golding also dedicates the *Commentary on the Psalms* (1571) to the earl of Oxford, son-in-law of Cecil and one-time pupil of Golding. And here one discovers Golding's connections with 'good society': he was uncle (on the maternal side) to the earl of Oxford. In 1581 Thomas Stocker dedicated the *Divers sermons concerning the divinity, humanity and nativity of Christ* to the same earl. It must be added that these particular dedications were more in pious hope than for any realistic reason: the earl of Oxford was a spendthrift who ruined the family fortunes, abandoned his wife, and lived extravagantly abroad.

So we find one group of dedications around William Cecil, the principal architect of the Elizabethan settlement. Another group centres on none other than Robert Dudley, earl of Leicester, Queen Elizabeth's favourite at the time, well known for his outspoken support of forward Protestantism (he was a good friend of Thomas Cartwright, the leading Cambridge reformer). The earl received dedications from Arthur Golding (*Sermons on Job*, 1573), John Harmar (*Sermons on the Ten Commandments*, 1581; Leicester had got him his scholarship to New College, Oxford), Christopher Fetherstone (*Commentary on John*, 1584). His brother Ambrose, earl of Warwick, who had been exiled to Geneva during Mary's reign, received the *Commentary on Genesis* from Thomas Tymme (1578). Warwick's father-in-law by his third marriage was the earl of Bedford, dedicatee of *Thirteen Sermons entreating of the free election of God* (John Field, 1579), and the *Harmony on Matthew, Mark and Luke* (Eusebius Pagit, 1584). Catherine, sister of Leicester and Warwick, was the wife of the earl of Huntingdon, who received dedications from J. Field (*Four Sermons*, 1579) and Christopher Fetherstone (*Commentary on Acts*, 1585). Also related by marriage (via the family of Lady Jane Grey) was the earl of Hertford (once tutored by Thomas Norton), to whom Christopher Rosdell dedicated the *Commentary on Romans* in 1583. Finally, Sir Francis Walsingham, eminent public servant, zealous Protestant, and consistently supported by Leicester, received dedications from Nathaniel Baxter (*Lectures on Jonah*, 1578) and William Becket (*Commentary on Philippians*, 1584).

We have effectively done the rounds of the major noble protectors of the 'godly' party. In one case, that of Arthur Golding, we find one of the 'Puritan divines' actually related to the family of William Cecil; and in another, that of Thomas Norton, we find a tutor to one of Leicester's clan. These dedications provide fascinating evidence of the ramifications, and family coherence, of the forward Protestant movement.

Apart from these demonstrations of solidarity with the great, however, these texts were published, and clearly intended for a wider audience than the nobility. Let us turn to the question of readership.

(c)   The readership

The drive to translate Calvin into English needs first to be set in context. Strype says of the 1570s:

It was usual nowadays to translate the Latin works and labours of good Protestant authors into English, for the better instruction of the honest people of the nation in sound religion, and knowledge of the Scriptures; and especially the clergy, who then were none of the best scholars, and scarce half of them understood Latin.[17]

The particular translation Strype is talking about is not from Calvin, but Augustin Marlorat's *Commentary on Matthew*. The bishops were encouraged to make their clergy purchase a copy; and the Bishop of London added that, if clergymen were guilty of some offence, 'it were a good part of penance for them to buy the said book, either for their private use, or else to be laid in the church for the common use'.

So education of the clergy, and of the 'honest people of the nation', is on the agenda in the 1570s. The prefaces of our Calvin translations make several allusions to intended readership; but they concentrate not on the clergy but on the common people. Thus, Arthur Golding regularly links his 'plainness' of style to the need to communicate to the 'simple reader'; 'in this and such other works the rude and ignorant have more interest than the learned and skilful' (*Commentary on the Psalms*); in his dedication of the *Sermons on Job* to the earl of Leicester, he urges his lordship to set a good example: 'the well-liking of such noble men and magistrates as God hath moreover ennobled with the knowledge of his Gospel is a great furtherance to the good acceptance of both of them [the scriptures and commentaries on them] among all inferior degrees'. Thus, while our translators frequently dedicate their works to eminent noblemen, their aim is much wider.

Thomas Norton has another approach in his third edition of the *Institution*: 'the volume being smaller [than the first two editions], with a letter fair and legible, it is of more easy price, that it may be of more common use, and so to more large communicating of so great a treasure to those that desire Christian knowledge'.

In none of the prefaces and dedications do I find any mention of the clergy as an intended readership. It looks as if our translators were doing exactly what Calvin had done before them: seeking to spread the Protestant message as widely as possible to the lay population, bypassing the church

---

[17] Strype, *Life of Parker*, p. 333. Cf. similar comments relating to Bullinger's *Decades* in Strype's account of 1577, in *Annals of the Reformation*, II, ii, pp. 144–6.

hierarchy. Just as Calvin wrote for 'les simples et rudes', so our translators have in mind the 'rude and ignorant'.

Conclusion

It is clear, from our list of translators, that the massive importation of Calvin into English is the work of the 'forward Protestants' in the Elizabethan church and period. The movement was particularly strong during the 1570s,[18] and some of the more radical leaders threatened to shatter the unity of the Church of England, already under threat from the 'Papists'. It is precisely at the period around 1570 that the name 'Puritan' was coined; the history of the period is peppered with arrests, trials, exclusions from office and threats of banishment. The wave of translations from Calvin's works is evidently not simply based on a desire to make available Calvin's message, but to provide ammunition in a quite violent confrontation.

Ammunition, in fact, for various parties to the battle. On the one hand many of the translators – Golding, Norton most notably – while promoting the spread of solid Calvin teaching, remained firmly within the Church of England. Their translations – the *Institution*, the New Testament commentaries – offered good, mainstream Calvin to the Reformed Church of England. It may be recalled that in the 1570s there was a considerable development, encouraged by many bishops, of Bible study and theological discussion in the 'prophesyings' or 'exercises' of the godly ministers;[19] even when the queen attempted to ban the meetings (in 1577) they were stoutly defended, notably by archbishop Grindal of Canterbury (who was suspended as a result). Many of these Calvin translations square exactly with this movement within the church.

The ostensible centre of controversy in the period was not doctrinal matters such as would emerge from the works of Calvin, but vestments, ordinary bread or wafers at Communion, the liturgy of the *Book of Common Prayer*. Calvin and Beza, it seems, did not regard these matters as being of sufficient importance to disturb the unity of the church (though they themselves would not have chosen the Anglican practices). It would appear that at least some of our translators, godly but non-Genevan, were acting as 'back-room boys', working hard to reinforce within the church the basic doctrinal teachings of which the vestments quarrel and the rest formed the superficial crust. Representative of this group is Thomas Norton, who raises on high the status of Calvin as religious leader:

Though many great learned men have written books of common places of our religion, as Melanchthon, Sarcerius and others, whose works are very good and

---

[18] See Collinson, *Elizabethan Puritan Movement*.   [19] *Ibid.*, pp. 168–76.

profitable to the Church of God, yet by the consenting judgement of those that understand the same, there is none to be compared to this work of Calvin, both for his substantial sufficiency of doctrine, the sound declaration of truth in articles of our religion, the large and learned confirmation of the same, and the most deep and strong confutation of all old and new heresies: so much that (the holy scriptures excepted) this is one of the most profitable books for all students of Christian divinity.[20]

But Calvin was also invoked by the more radical leaders who were willing to contemplate schism in order to achieve a 'full' reformation. It is symptomatic that Strype associates this tendency with Geneva:

Many of them withdrew from the national Church and the religious communion of the rest of Christians, and set up separate assemblies, where, casting away wholly the book appointed for the public and common service of God, they served Him according to ways and platforms of their own, and used prayers and preaching, and administering of the sacraments by themselves. . . . The book they used in these their private meetings was, for the most part, the Book of Service made and used by the English at Geneva. Which was mostwhat taken out of the French book of Calvin.[21]

One of the most ebullient of the 'radicals' was John Field, whose praise of Calvin is even more lavish than that of Norton. For Field, Calvin is 'one of the rarest instruments whom God hath raised up in these last times to give light amidst our great ignorance, and to draw many to that blessed knowledge . . .'. He acknowledges that 'some unthankful wretches, puffed up with pride and a vain opinion of themselves, will hardly endure that I should speak thus either of the work, or of this singular instrument of God . . . Being behind others in gifts, they pout and swell against them whose shoe latchets they are not worthy to loose . . .'!

Field's choice of Calvin texts for translation is significant. On the one hand he retranslates the *Quatre sermons* of 1552 on the need to refuse compromise with the Papists (1579); on the other he selects Calvin's sermons on the election of Jacob and the rejection of Esau. In his epistle dedicatory, together with much invective against 'open Papists, counterfeit professors or manifest heretics', he says of his subject that 'the everlasting predestination and election of God [is] the most comfortable doctrine that can be, being the foundation of all the rest, where it is wisely taught according to the Word'. Now this assertion of the centrality of predestination is something that Calvin did not teach; it is rather the consequence of

---

[20] Light is shed from another angle on the place of Calvin in theological debate in the period by E. Leedham-Green's study of Cambridge book inventories (see note 1). A rough indication of relative 'popularity ratings' emerges from her table of authors (in vol. II): Calvin occupies seven pages, Melanchthon six, and Bèze, Brenz, Bucer, Bullinger, Luther, Peter Martyr three pages each, approximately. Only Erasmus (seventeen pages) rates higher. These lists involve works in all languages; the proportion of translations is higher in the case of Calvin than in any other.   [21] Strype, *Life of Parker*, p. 241.

his central doctrines. One sees here the evolution of Calvinism, under the tension of the debates within the Church of England, towards that stress on predestination as central which characterised Presbyterianism for centuries.

What emerges from this overview seems to be a twofold conclusion. On the one hand there is an immense interest in Calvin in the formative years of the Elizabethan church, and firmly within that church. On the other hand, a part of that interest, by the 'radicals', involves that move towards the image of Calvin the legalistic predestinarian which has persisted ever since.

I end with a delightful quotation from a nineteenth-century Anglican divine, given not so much for its historical accuracy as to exemplify a certain perception of Calvin:

The divines of the latter days of Elizabeth were still much under the influence of the bold speculations of Calvin. The great foreign theologians, and especially Calvin, were men of a more powerful cast of mind than the English fathers of the Reformation; and hence the spell of their genius exercised a fascination, which sober judgements ought to have better resisted and withstood. Meaner teachers of antinomianism would have been summarily suppressed, but Calvin, who, with a bolder flight, ventured even to impeach the righteousness of the Most High, was accepted with a trembling acquiescence. His system, complete and perfect as it appeared in all its parts; accounting, as it did, for all difficulties by a daring dogmatizing on matters lying far out of the province of the human understanding, challenged and obtained a profound and deferential homage.[22]

The author adds that the seventeenth century saw the waning of this foreign influence in the face of a 'broad scriptural view'; and he concludes: 'At the beginning of the reign of James it is probable that the tenets of Calvin as to the absolute decrees of God were the popular theology, though not heartily acquiesced in by some of the more learned divines.'

So it seems our godly translators had some success in their popular appeal via translations of the works of Calvin.

[22] George G. Perry, *The History of the Church of England from the death of Elizabeth to the present time* (3 vols., London, 1861), I, p. 20.

6   Calvinists in Troyes 1562–1572: the legacy of Vassy and the background to Saint Bartholomew

Penny Roberts

Nicolas Pithou, elder and chronicler of the Reformed church at Troyes in Champagne, reported that at the Lord's Supper held at Pentecost 1562, 'There was one of the finest companies ever seen, for those present numbered eight to nine thousand people, come from all parts, most of whom received communion which was continued the next day because of the great throng of communicants.'[1] By September 1572, Pithou noted with dismay, 'that out of so many people who had previously received communion and made open profession of the religion, there remained in the city at that time only twenty who kept themselves pure and unpolluted by the abominations of the papacy'.[2]

The contrast between the size and confidence of the Reformed church in Troyes in 1562 and its position in 1572, could be made for other Huguenot congregations torn apart by the events of the first decade of the Wars of Religion. On the eve of the conflict Calvinism looked poised to succeed in many French cities, and, although their rate of increase was checked, Huguenot communities continued to flourish into the late 1560s. The massacres of 1572, and subsequent emigration and abjuration, dealt a serious blow to the numbers and morale of the French Reformed church. Thereafter, the Huguenots' sphere of influence was largely confined to the south-west, to the Midi, whilst in the north the churches had become a shadow of their former selves.

This north/south disparity, so decisive for the future of French Calvinism, was in no way a foregone conclusion in the Huguenot 'wonder year' of 1561–2. Indeed, the confidence of the Reformers at this time is as striking as the resignation and fatalism of later years. How are we, then, to explain the dramatic demise of the Reformed churches in the north? Generalisations may be made about the repercussions of national events and royal policy, but it is also important to determine the influence of local factors on the fate of individual churches. Troyes was a city both favourably and ill-placed to receive the Reform; and this double-edged position can help to

All translations are the author's own.
[1] BN Dupuy, MS 698, Nicolas Pithou, 'Histoire ecclésiastique de l'église réformée de la ville de Troyes' (hereafter Pithou), fols. 215v–16r.   [2] *Ibid.*, fol. 392v.

explain the swift rise and steady diminution of its Huguenot congregation. Troyes' location ensured that it was susceptible to the flow of new religious ideas, through its local commerce with Meaux, 'the Cradle of the French Reform', and its situation on a major route between Paris and Geneva. However, its proximity to the capital and, more importantly, to the estates of the Guises, made it equally vulnerable to Catholic backlash and persecution.

The establishment of the Huguenot community at Troyes was in many ways typical of those other large northern cities, such as Paris and Rouen, where Calvinism was destined to remain a minority religion.[3] The Reformed church began in the 1550s as a clandestine congregation, with small groups meeting in private houses for readings and prayers. From 1561 services began to be held in public, and three ministers were required to serve the rapidly increasing congregation. Yet whilst other churches, such as Caen in Normandy and Amiens in Picardy, experienced a continuing growth, despite the troubles, into the late 1560s, in Troyes (as, indeed, in Paris) decline after 1562 was gradual but unrelenting.[4] In order to examine the reasons for this deterioration in Calvinist fortunes, this chapter will deal with three crucial developments in turn. Firstly, the events of 1562, which marked a watershed for the future of the Reformed church at Troyes; secondly, the problems faced by the Huguenots in maintaining their faith between 1562 and 1572; and finally, how the events of this decade had a direct bearing on the reaction of the authorities in Troyes to the news of the Saint Bartholomew's Massacre in Paris.

What, then, was the position of the Reformed church at Troyes on the eve of the civil wars? The Huguenots entered the year 1562 in buoyant mood, and indeed it appears that they had every cause to view the future with optimism. Writing excitedly to his former training centre of Neuchâtel in October 1561, Jacques Sorel claimed that he and his fellow ministers had 'good reason to thank God for the growth and prosperity which He gives to His church here ... We hold assemblies day and night, and at least four to five hundred attend. There would be more than a thousand people, if we had the bells to summon them.'[5] This prediction was no exaggeration, for by Easter 1562, there were said to be several thousand attending services in the fields outside the city walls.[6] The confidence of the church was further

---

[3] On Paris, see Barbara B. Diefendorf, *Beneath the Cross: Catholics and Huguenots in Sixteenth-Century Paris* (Oxford, 1991); and Rouen, Philip Benedict, *Rouen during the Wars of Religion* (Cambridge, 1981).

[4] On Caen, M.S. Lamet, 'French Protestants in a Position of Strength: The Early Years of the Reformation in Caen, 1558–1568', *SCJ*, 9 (1978), 35–55; and Amiens, D.L. Rosenberg, 'Social Experience and Religious Choice: A Case Study, the Protestant Weavers and Woolcombers of Amiens in the Sixteenth Century' (Yale University Ph.D. thesis, 1978).

[5] 'Le Protestantisme en Champagne, 1561', *BSHPF*, 12 (1863), 352.

[6] *Histoire ecclésiastique des églises réformées au royaume de France*, eds. G. Baum, E. Cunitz and R. Reuss (3 vols., Paris, 1883–9) (hereafter *Hist. ecc.*), II, p. 461.

boosted by the support for their cause of the provincial governor, the duke of Nevers, nephew of the prince of Condé, and of the controversial bishop of Troyes, Antonio Caracciolo, who was accepted into the Reformed ministry at the end of 1561.[7] However, Huguenot hopes were soon to be dashed. Within a few months the bishop had resigned from his see, having conducted only one service in the Reformed faith at Lent 1562, and the governor had defected to the Catholic side. The sudden removal of such influential pillars of support seriously undermined both the political strength and the morale of the Reformed church. Furthermore, the massacres of Huguenot congregations at Vassy and at Sens, which sparked off the first religious war, occurred only a day's ride from Troyes. These attacks on their near-neighbours and coreligionists formed the immediate context for subsequent events in the city.

The massacre of Huguenots attending a service at Vassy by the duke of Guise's men, on Sunday 1 March, had particular resonance in Troyes.[8] For, as the city's Reformed church had flourished, it had come to play an important role in a provincial network of Huguenot communities, encompassing congregations not only at Vassy, but also at Meaux, Châlons-sur-Marne, Vitry-Le-François and Sens. The Reformers at Troyes were thus shocked at the assault on a church which they had helped to establish, and fearful that they might be the next target of those responsible. Consequently, they began to arm themselves, as congregations were to do elsewhere, so as to be better prepared for an attack than had been their coreligionists at Vassy.[9] Mutual suspicion was reinforced when Catholics became aware that Protestants were carrying weapons to services, and because of the increasingly sinister behaviour of the local Catholic officials. In particular, the annual election of aldermen to the municipal council was postponed for a week, allegedly in an effort by the authorities to prevent the nomination of Huguenots to the posts. This situation may be contrasted with that of another city in Champagne, Châlons-sur-Marne, where a similar purge was conducted and the pacific role of the city council was decisive in preventing the sectarian violence experienced elsewhere.[10] In Troyes, it was believed that Catholic councillors were secretly requesting the presence of a Guise representative to ensure that no Huguenots were elected.

The influence of the Guises in the events of 1562 in Troyes, though not

---

[7] For a detailed study of the bishop, see the biography by J. Roserot de Melin, *Antonio Caracciolo, évêque de Troyes, 1515?–1570* (Paris, 1923). On his appointment and the controversy surrounding it, see Pithou, fols. 178–81, 184–5 and 187.

[8] On events in Troyes in 1562, see Pithou, fols. 192–264; *Hist. ecc.*, II, pp. 461–78.

[9] Cf. the reaction to the news in Rouen, Benedict, *Rouen during the Wars*, p. 96; and in Paris, Diefendorf, *Beneath the Cross*, pp. 63 and 123.

[10] Mark Konnert, 'Urban Values versus Religious Passion: Châlons-sur-Marne during the Wars of Religion', *SCJ*, 20 (1989), 393–4.

insignificant, should not be overrated. The duke himself only participated indirectly in town affairs, and only after his support was actively and repeatedly sought by the municipal authorities. It was local officials who were responsible for the measures taken against Huguenot citizens; Guise authority was simply used as a source of legitimacy for their actions when the attitude of governor Nevers proved unreliable and inconsistent. More-over, the Guise representative, the seigneur d'Esclavolles, who arrived in Troyes on 6 April, by no means commanded the universal obedience or respect of the city council. Some of his grievances reveal that he had been excluded from much of the important decision-making, and that his requests and proposals were largely ignored.[11] Likewise, the vacillating nature of royal religious policy encouraged the local administration to seize the initiative in dealing with the Huguenots under their jurisdiction. Thus, royal ordinances could be flouted when they did not fit in with the preferred policy of local officials, whilst being loudly publicised when they did so.

The beginning of the first civil war involved the attempted seizure of cities throughout France by their Huguenot citizens, following the example set by the prince of Condé at Orleans.[12] In Troyes, the circumstances surrounding the capture of two gates by the Huguenots in April 1562 remain obscure. Nevertheless, the significance of these few days for the future of the city's Reformed church requires as full a reconstruction of events as the sources will allow. The coup was apparently motivated by self-protection, in order to provide the Reformers with an opportunity to negotiate with the Catholic authorities on equal terms. Esclavolles' presence, and their exclusion from office and from guard duty, persuaded the Huguenots to act to pre-empt any plot against them, and they were assisted by their allies from neighbouring towns who had infiltrated the city. The seizure of the gates took place on 12 April, the day of the massacre at nearby Sens, news of which must have confirmed the timeliness of the Huguenots' actions.

Nicolas Pithou describes the takeover as unplanned and achieved without force; the Catholic guards at the gates had simply melted away when they became aware of the Protestant military presence.[13] Catholic accounts, on the other hand, refer to a number of deaths and acts of vandalism.[14] Even so, the affair seems to have passed off with relatively little bloodshed when compared with events elsewhere, such as at Toulouse

[11] Esclavolles' complaints are recorded in the city council deliberations, Bibliothèque Municipale de Troyes (hereafter BM Troyes), Boutiot A 13, 15 April 1562; and in BB 14 i. no. 12.

[12] For instance Lyons, *Hist. ecc.*, III, pp. 254–7; Rouen, Benedict, *Rouen during the Wars*, pp. 96–7; and Toulouse, Mark Greengrass, 'The Anatomy of a Religious Riot in Toulouse in May 1562', *JEH*, 34 (1983), 375.   [13] Pithou, fol. 203.

[14] BM Troyes Boutiot A 13, 15 April 1562. 'Chanoines et Huguenots à Troyes en 1562', letters copied by Ch. Desguerrois, *Annuaire de l'Aube*, (1887), 100–1.

and, later, at Bar-sur-Seine.[15] Esclavolles complained that he had been threatened since his arrival and his letters intercepted, the Huguenots justifying this by claiming that he 'was sent by a butcher (Guise) who wished to carry out such carnage in this town as that he had committed at Vassy'.[16] He was further aggrieved that, following the coup, the municipal council and royal officials had sought a parley with nine principals of the Reformed church, which had resulted in an agreement for joint guard of the gates and equal rights for Huguenot inhabitants.[17] However, neither side really trusted the other, believing the negotiations were simply a ruse to stall for time until their opponents could secure further outside support.

For the first time the leadership of the Reformed church had come out into the open and challenged the dominance of the Catholic majority, and their stance would be remembered and resented. The nine Huguenot representatives included members of the city council and royal officials, posing a direct challenge to their municipal colleagues, a challenge that would lead to their removal from office and label them as troublemakers. A further source of provocation, and measure of Huguenot distrust, was the Reformers' continuing refusal to lower their arms before the arrival of governor Nevers on 20 April. The duke appears to have retained a residual affection for his former coreligionists, as was indicated by his rather ambivalent actions and promises of continuing protection. It was these, the Huguenots believed, which fatally persuaded them to maintain their trust in the duke's ultimate goodwill, and prevented them from taking decisive action when the opportunity arose.[18] However, it is unlikely that Huguenot numbers were sufficient to have secured ascendancy in the city in 1562, even if this was their intention.

The following months saw a period of uneasy coexistence between the faiths under the vigilance of Nevers. However, by the beginning of August, with the seigneur Des Bordes, the governor's deputy and a staunch Catholic, in command, and the raising of a company of 300 Catholic militia, the Catholic authorities had gained the upper hand. Troops were assembled to search for suspects; they barricaded the streets in which most Huguenots were known to reside, and set about a round of pillage and destruction, assaults and arrests.[19] It was decreed that only Catholics were to serve as guards or to bear arms, that no Huguenots were to sit on the council until further notice, and all officials were to take oaths and sign a declaration of Catholicism or be replaced.[20] Furthermore, representation

[15] On Toulouse, see Greengrass, 'Anatomy of a Religious Riot', where an estimated 4,000 died as a result of the disturbances.

[16] BM Troyes Boutiot A 13, 15 April 1562.   [17] Pithou, fol. 204r; *Hist. ecc.*, II, p. 463.

[18] Pithou, fols. 204v, 210v–11r and 217; 'Chanoines et Huguenots à Troyes en 1562', 101.

[19] Pithou, fols. 219v–20 and 223–9r; *Hist. ecc.*, II, pp. 465–9.

[20] BM Troyes Boutiot A 13, 13 August; BB 14 i. no. 19. Pithou, fols. 224v–5r; *Hist. ecc.*, II, p. 467.

was made to the Paris Parlement concerning charges against Huguenots currently holding office. An investigation was undertaken, and Pithou states that most of the accusations were false and trumped-up charges were made against those who were not even of the religion.[21] This may suggest the existence of rivalries within the local administration beyond the purely religious issues, and conflict between militant and moderate elements on the council. Later the Parlement would order the arrest and trial of about sixty Troyen suspects, many of whom had already taken a wisely timed absence.[22] Among these nearly half were officials in some capacity or another, a far greater proportion than their representation in the movement as a whole.

Additional measures were taken in August 1562 to force the Protestants to compromise their faith, following a royal decree which stipulated a return to Catholic observances. Huguenots, through coercion or choice, participated in processions, were remarried in the Catholic tradition, or had their children rebaptised and renamed.[23] Catholic baptismal registers reveal hurried rebaptisms at this time of crisis and following the massacre of September 1572, when there was another rush for the Catholic baptism of Huguenot children.[24]

It was not only the spiritual anguish of rebaptism and remarriage, or the more tangible loss of office or threat of arrest which persuaded some that their interests would be better served by a temporary exile. Back in Troyes, murders had been committed, houses seized and their pillaged contents sold, their owners terrorised, ransomed, or forced to make 'loans' which would never be repaid. The Huguenots were convinced that the authorities had connived with the soldiers against them, and many left the town, abandoning their possessions in order to seek refuge in the villages around Troyes.[25] From here many of the exiles transferred to the town of Bar-sur-Seine, just up the river, after its takeover by their coreligionists. However, they were not to be left in peace. The military in Troyes, offended by the Protestant stronghold which was doubtless felt to be too close for comfort, resolved to take Bar. On 24 August, Saint Bartholomew's day (which was thus to be a tragic date for the Huguenots of Troyes a decade before the infamous massacre in Paris), Bar was besieged. A brutal massacre of more

---

[21] Pithou, fols. 234–6; *Hist. ecc.*, II, pp. 469–70. *Ordonnance contre les Protestants, 1562* (contemporary copy in BN; Troyes, 1562); and BM Troyes Boutiot A 13, 17 September.

[22] Archives Nationales (hereafter AN) X 2a, criminal registers of the Parlement, reg. 130, fols. 233v and 242. Pithou, fols. 243–5.

[23] Pithou, fols. 232v–3r; *Hist. ecc.*, II, p. 469. Cf. enforced attendance at mass, remarriage and rebaptism in Meaux, II, pp. 445–7, and Autun, III. p. 489.

[24] BM Troyes Boutiot GG IV supplement, reg. 6 (1561–3), fols. 58–61; for 1572, reg. 10 (1572–6), fols. 20–6. Cf. rebaptisms in Rouen following the massacre, Benedict, *Rouen during the Wars*, pp. 120 and 135.

[25] Pithou, fols. 233–4r and 237v–8r. Also see Jacques-Auguste de Thou, *Histoire Universelle (1543–1607)* (12 vols., London, 1734), IV, p. 272.

than 140 Huguenots from Troyes, hunted down by Catholics from their native city, was said to have ensued.[26] The trials, executions and mutilations of about twelve prisoners followed in Troyes.[27]

The publication of the Peace of Amboise of March 1563, which brought the first civil war to an end, prompted the local authorities to deal with their remaining religious prisoners before the amnesty provided by the treaty became effective. A group of Catholic soldiers dispatched several Huguenots in the prisons, many of whom had been arrested at the time of the search conducted in the previous August; their bodies were thrown on a dung-heap.[28] This was to be a precursor of the action taken against Huguenot prisoners in September 1572. In 1563, Pithou ascribes direct supervision to the mayor, Claude Pinette; in 1572, other officials would be held responsible for the murders; on both occasions, although the authors were well known, no judicial action was taken. In April and May, refugees returning to Troyes trusting in the protection conferred by the edict of pacification, were nevertheless butchered by Catholic soldiers. Thus, despite the peace, the difficulties and dangers for the Huguenots of Troyes were hardly at an end. Although it would be some years before there was another massacre in the streets, isolated murders were not uncommon, and victimisation of Protestants continued.

The events of 1562–3 were decisive for the future of the Reformed church at Troyes. Although the struggle would continue until 1572, a pattern of decline had been established from which the Huguenots would not recover. The outcome of the seizure of the city gates was to prove crucial. The failure of the Huguenots to maintain their advantage was due partly to the overwhelming numerical odds, and more significantly the support of the Crown and the provincial governor for the local authorities' anti-Huguenot measures. Once deprived of political and judicial influence, the Reformed congregation was rendered helpless before a concerted policy of repression and prohibition.

Further difficulties confronted the Huguenots of Troyes between the first civil war and the Saint Bartholomew's massacre of 1572. Chief among these were the dilemmas involved in ensuring the continuation of Reformed worship: whether it was the choice between abjuration or exile, or the need to secure a more convenient site on which to conduct services.

In the face of persecution and growing disillusionment, many felt that they had to make a choice between renouncing their home or their faith. Eighteen Troyens and their families were registered in Strasburg in the last

---

[26] Pithou, fols. 237v–42r, printed in G. Hérelle (ed.), *La Réforme et la Ligue en Champagne: Documents* (2 vols., Paris, 1888–92), II, pp. 29–37. *Hist. ecc.*, II, pp. 476–8.
[27] Pithou, fols. 242r and 248v–53r; *Hist. ecc.*, II, pp. 470–1.   [28] Pithou, fol. 273–5r.

few months of 1562, five of whom – two royal officials, two merchants and a goldsmith – had been summoned to answer charges before the Paris Parlement.[29] Others sought temporary or permanent residence in Geneva, or preferred to stay in France under the protection of a sympathetic noble, such as the counts of Brienne and Sedan.[30] Many would return in more peaceful times, only to take off again at the first hint of trouble. Pithou was critical of his coreligionists for allowing their faith to be compromised rather than seeking refuge and liberty of conscience elsewhere. However, those who for better or worse decided to stay true to their faith and their native city, would be lucky to escape unscathed from subsequent waves of persecution.[31]

The second and third civil wars of 1567–70 initiated new acts of victimisation against Huguenots in cities where Catholics remained predominant. Similarly in Troyes: in December 1567, all Huguenot men were expelled, and women placed under house arrest and given strict instructions to reveal to governor Guise's representative any communications received from their husbands.[32] With the exclusion of known or suspected members of the Reformed church from official and judicial posts, hopes waned of bringing a successful conviction in the courts, and of seeing justice done for the crimes committed against the persons and property of Huguenots. Even Catholic magistrates who proceeded against the perpetrators of sectarian offences laid themselves open to threats against their lives, and were thus deterred from following a prosecution through to its conclusion.[33] Bereaved widows found that not only was it extremely difficult to ensure that those convicted of murdering Huguenots were duly punished, but that the woman who sought justice and compensation was likely to be taunted and hounded by her husband's killer.[34]

Those who stayed in Troyes might also be persuaded to return to Catholic devotions; some perhaps through conviction, but probably many more through fear. After the troubles of 1562, only six Troyen Huguenots, out of a former congregation of several thousand, were said to have remained steadfast in their faith 'without kneeling before Baal'. With the

[29] R. Zuber, 'Les Champenois réfugiés à Strasbourg et l'église réformée de Châlons: échanges intellectuels et vie religieuse (1560–90)', *Mémoires de la société d'agriculture, commerce, science et arts du département de la Marne* (1964), 50–4. AN X 2a, reg. 130, fols. 233v and 242.   [30] For examples, see Pithou, fols. 372 and 402.

[31] Extraordinary levies were one drawback of staying put: for example in 1562, Pithou, fols. 261v–2r; *Hist. ecc.*, II, p. 473, cf. Senlis, p. 428.

[32] BM Troyes Boutiot A 16, 1 and 3 December Cf. house arrests in Provins, *Mémoires de Claude Haton: le récit des événements accomplis de 1553 à 1582, principalement dans la Champagne et la Brie*, ed. F. Bourquelot (2 vols., Paris, 1857), II, p. 448; Paris, Diefendorf, *Beneath the Cross*, p. 83; Rouen, Benedict, *Rouen during the Wars*, pp. 118–19; and Dijon, J.R. Farr, *Hands of Honor: Artisans and Their World in Dijon, 1550–1650* (Ithaca and London, 1988), pp. 229–30.   [33] Pithou, fols. 291v–5r and 302v.

[34] *Ibid.*, fols. 123, 283r and 291v–4.

renewal of services in 1564 many threw off the pretence of Catholicism and returned to the Reformed church, although their numbers were much reduced and there appears little likelihood that many new converts could have been made in these troubled times. After the massacre in 1572, when Huguenots went in droves to the cathedral to recant, only twenty refused to conform, and this time there would be no joyful revival of worship to bring the others back into the fold.[35]

The second civil war had proved more damaging to Huguenot purses than to their lives, but the third was to prove more bloody.[36] The premise that Troyes emerged virtually unscathed from the sectarian conflict of the 1560s cannot therefore be sustained.[37] The years 1568–70 saw renewed persecution, largely in response to local rather than national events. The imprisonment in May 1568 of six Catholic soldiers for abducting and nearly raping the wife of a Huguenot blacksmith from Troyes, provoked an angry, but by now familiar response from the Catholic militia. Huguenot property was pillaged; Huguenots were dragged from their houses, murdered, and their bodies thrown in the Seine; and Huguenot prisoners were also victimised.[38] The following year, sixty-two Protestant soldiers seized at Condé's château of Noyers were brought to Troyes. The prisoners, chained together, were set upon by the mob as they proceeded through the streets on their way to prison, and forty-one of them were killed.[39] The pillage of Villeneuve-l'Archévêque by Protestant soldiers, in June 1570, prompted the further confinement of the Huguenots of Troyes, in the prisons or in their homes. Midwives were instructed to report the births of Huguenot children so as to ensure that they were baptised. At this time, the city of Troyes appeared as if it were a prison to its incarcerated Huguenot inhabitants.[40] Their ordeal was only to be relieved by the edict of pacification that August.

Following a further royal decree in February 1571, a discussion was held in the council chamber between the Catholic authorities and nineteen Huguenots who had recently been readmitted to office.[41] It seemed that at last the Huguenots might be able to negotiate for equal rights and freedom of worship. The edicts did indeed allow for liberty of conscience, although there were still many restrictions imposed. Nevertheless, Huguenot prisoners were to be released and their possessions returned, Huguenot children were not to be baptised as Catholics against the wishes of their

---

[35] *Ibid.*: on 1562, fol. 256v; on 1564, fols. 308–9; and on 1572, fol. 392v.
[36] Pithou, fol. 337v.
[37] Philip Benedict, 'The Saint Bartholomew's Massacres in the Provinces', *HJ*, 21 (1978), 222, that Troyes and some other cities were not 'especially troubled by confessional violence' in the decade 1562–72.   [38] Pithou, fols. 338v–41, Bèze, *Correspondance*, IX, p. 90.
[39] Pithou, fols. 350–3r; also *Mémoires de Claude Haton*, II, p. 452.
[40] Pithou, fols. 354–5 and 357r.
[41] BM Troyes Boutiot A 17, 8 March 1571; BB 14 ii. no. 35.

parents, and for the first time Huguenots were granted their own ceme-
tery.[42] But the peace only provided a brief respite before the return of
persecution in September 1572.

The mounting problems of the beleaguered Huguenot community were
exacerbated by divisions within its own ranks. Two of the issues which
caused tension between various groups within the church, were the innate
conservatism of those in the consistory, and the difficulties of regular
attendance at services held in far-flung corners of the province.[43] The
criticism levelled at the principals of the church for being overcautious in
sending ministers away in times of increased persecution, came not only
from the body of the congregation who resented being deprived of
instruction, but also from the ministers concerned.[44] A further difference
had emerged over the validity of iconoclasm as a source of protest and
rejection of Catholic beliefs. In Troyes there were only a few isolated
incidents involving the desecration of statues, but the main concern was
that the actions of a few would endanger the safety of the whole congregation and the Reformed cause in general.[45]

One of the consistory's functions was to discipline members for views or
conduct contrary to the standards laid down by the Calvinist church. The
rigour with which such discipline was applied by a select minority of twelve
elders over the rest of the congregation understandably caused friction,
whether in Geneva or in Troyes.[46] Even before the introduction of such a
system in 1561, the Reformed church at Troyes had been prepared to
ostracise some of its members. In 1557, a breakaway group of artisans was
meeting for worship in the fields near Troyes; they were said by Pithou to
have been excluded from the main services for 'some good reason'.[47] Their
devotion was not in doubt, and it is possible that these men had come into
conflict with church notables for criticism of their cautious attitudes, or
overzealous provocation of Catholic hostility. Immoral and frivolous
behaviour were especially frowned upon by the consistory.[48] Such miscon-
duct had become a particular problem in Troyes by the mid-1560s, when the
provision of ministers was erratic and the allegiance of many was wavering
in the face of recent persecution. In 1564 (as recently recommended to the

---

[42] *Ibid.*, A 17, 8 and 22 March; BB 14 ii. no. 36. Pithou, fols. 360–4.
[43] Such tensions seem to have been commonplace among the churches in France, for example,
see D.N. Nicholls, 'The Origins of Protestantism in Normandy: A Social Study' (University of Birmingham Ph.D. thesis, 1977), 191.
[44] For examples, see Pithou, fols. 102 and 131.
[45] *Ibid.*, fos. 85v–6 and 106v–7r; BM Troyes Boutiot A 11, 9 September 1554.
[46] The structure of the church at Troyes was described in a letter by the minister, Jacques
Sorel, in October 1561: 'Le Protestantisme en Champagne, 1561', *BSHPF*, 12 (1863), 353.
[47] Pithou, fols. 97v–9r.
[48] Such behaviour was specified and explicitly condemned by the Genevan Company of
Pastors in 1546, *RCP*, I, pp. 17–18.

French Reformed church by Calvin), the elders began to distribute a special token or *méreau* which acted as a pass for admission to Holy Communion.[49] It was to be withheld from any unregenerates whose behaviour was thought to be bringing disrepute to the church. Such a policy must have served simply to exacerbate the existing antagonisms between the elders and the congregation. By this time, however, the consistory was experiencing difficulties in summoning the guilty to account.

In the summer of 1567, the authorities were alerted to the existence of a clandestine artisan group meeting for Sunday worship in private houses in Troyes.[50] There is little doubt that these gatherings were unofficial; no elders appear in the substantial list of those named as present, and their prominence would not have allowed them to be overlooked. At this time, official services were being held at Céant-en-Othe, some eighteen to twenty miles west of the city. The artisan assemblies surely represent a desire on behalf of these craftsmen to continue with communal worship, despite their absence from the official services, the inconvenient distance of which cost them time and trade. Indeed, the mass of the congregation may have thought it all very well for the wealthier members of the church to afford time off, and they were also concerned about the danger of transporting new-born babies so far in order to be baptised. The church elders were not unsympathetic to these grievances, demonstrated by the petition they presented to Charles IX during his visit in 1564.[51] They requested that the Huguenots be provided with a site for worship at a more convenient distance from Troyes, suggesting a church in the suburbs as nominated in the 1563 edict, or failing that the village of Isle, only five miles away and owned by the duke of Nevers. Nothing was to come of this approach in 1564; but by 1572, unofficial services were being held at Isle.

These setbacks and internal divisions demonstrate just how difficult it was to sustain a community in a hostile environment. The cumulative effect of such crises was to ensure an inexorable decline in the prosperity of the Troyen church. Confrontations between the faiths also served to shape relations as they stood at the time of the Saint Bartholomew's massacre in 1572. Barbara Diefendorf has recently shown how the violence in the streets of Paris cannot be viewed in isolation, but was the culmination of a number of long-established grievances.[52] The repetition of the massacre in the

---

[49] Pithou, fol. 308; this is an early reference to the use of *méreaux*. For descriptions of those distributed by other churches, see *BSHPF*, 37 (1888), 205–8 and 316–18. On its use in Nîmes, see R.A. Mentzer, '*Disciplina nervus ecclesiae*: the Calvinist Reform of Morals at Nîmes', *SCJ*, 18 (1987), 96.

[50] BM Troyes Boutiot BB 14 ii. nos. 13 and 14.   [51] Pithou, fols. 298–9r.

[52] Diefendorf, *Beneath the Cross*, pp. 76, 81, 83–6 and 177; also see her earlier article, 'Prologue to a Massacre: Popular Unrest in Paris, 1557–72', *American Historical Review*, 90 (1985), 1076–91.

provinces, although prompted by events in Paris, can also be shown (at least in the case of Troyes) to have roots deeply embedded in the confessional conflicts of the previous decade. The dispute over the location of Reformed services is a case in point.

The Peace of Amboise of 1563 granted the Huguenots permission to worship at one designated site in each *bailliage*. The location of the site nominated, its accessibility for its potential congregation, and if favourably situated, whether or not Huguenots were able to enforce their right to worship there, appear to have crucially affected the welfare of Reformed churches in northern France. In Caen the increase in the congregation after 1562 has been attributed to the moderate stance of the provincial governor, Bouillon, who allowed Reformed services to continue on the outskirts of the city; a situation in stark contrast to that prevailing in Troyes and in Dijon, where services in the suburbs were immediately and repeatedly obstructed by the Catholic authorities.[53] The sympathy of governor Guise and his entourage for strong-arm Catholic tactics doubtless also reinforced the policy of the city council in Troyes. In Paris the 1563 edict prohibited Protestant worship within the city or its *prévôté* in an attempt to reduce sectarian conflict in the capital. Moreover, Catherine de Medici sought to relegate Reformed preaching from large towns in the Paris region to small and obscure locations, a policy imitated by local authorities.[54] In such circumstances, the difficulty of attending services seems to have been a major contributor to the demoralisation of Huguenot congregations during the 1560s.

The initial nomination of a site for Reformed worship in the *bailliage* of Troyes was the suburbs of the city. However, their ministers having fled and their enemies having gained the upper hand, the Huguenots of Troyes were unable to implement this decision.[55] Meanwhile, the city council protested against the prospect of Reformed services in such uncomfortable proximity, and carried out a door-to-door survey of public opinion to reinforce their case.[56] Whilst the Huguenots sought and obtained confirmation of their position in May, the council's campaign continued unabated. Pithou

[53] On Caen, see M.S. Lamet, 'Reformation, War and Society in Caen, Lower Normandy: 1558–1610' (University of Massachusetts Ph.D. thesis, 1978), 157 ff. However, once an arch-Catholic was appointed to the governorship and with the renewal of the civil war in 1568, there was a sharp reversal in this upward trend, although a renewed increase during periods of peace suggests that the attitude of the governor was not the only significant factor. On Dijon, *Hist. ecc.*, III, pp. 477–8. Cf. Rouen, Benedict, *Rouen during the Wars*, p. 114, where although the Parlement and council opposed implementation of the edict which allowed for services in or near the city, they were overruled by the governor and the Crown.

[54] Diefendorf, *Beneath the Cross*, pp. 77 and 123–4, and on Parisian Huguenots travelling up to 30 kilometres to attend services and receive the sacraments.

[55] Pithou, fol. 281r. BM Troyes Boutiot A 14, 14 July 1563, refers to the Reformed church pursuing implementation of the edict; as did that in Dijon, *Hist. ecc.*, III, pp. 477–8.

[56] For the survey, see BM Troyes Boutiot BB 14 i. no. 24, 20–25 April; for instructions to deputies to execute it, Delion Lay 72, nos. 86–95.

comments, 'what they feared and dreaded most was the establishment of religious worship in the suburbs of the city, convinced that the increase of the faithful which, in the circumstances, would doubtless shortly ensue, would not be small'.[57] In December 1563 another royal decree left the decision up to the provincial governor. A compromise perhaps, but one that ensured victory to the Catholics, with the new governor Guise represented at this time by his uncle, the duke of Aumale. The Huguenots protested against the designation of Céant and the difficulties posed by its location, first to the duke and then to the king on his tour of the province, but their petition was unsuccessful. Finally, resigning themselves to make the best of a bad job for the moment, and not wishing to appear to be opposing the royal will, services began at Céant on 30 April 1564.[58] Nevertheless, the Reformed church continued to send representatives to plead with the king, directly or through Condé, to be provided with a more convenient site for carrying out their devotions.[59]

Frustrated by royal inaction on their behalf, at the beginning of August some Huguenots from Troyes attended a service and baptism at Dosches, only a few miles outside the city, at the house of Jacques Ménisson.[60] This was to be the first of a series of sites offered by the local nobility, who claimed freedom of worship on their estates, and thus evaded prosecution by the authorities. From 1566, there were complaints by royal officials in the locality, the clergy of Troyes, and even the king himself, against the exercise of the new religion at Saint-Pouange, under the protection of another member of the Ménisson family, Antoine. However, to the irritation of the local authorities, the repeated demands that he should curtail the services were ignored, for the same complaints were still being reiterated in November 1571.[61] In 1570, Odard Piedefer allowed services at Saint-Mards, twelve miles to the west of Troyes, following the disastrous designation of Villenaux, one of two official sites in the province, in the recent edict of pacification. Not only was Villenaux situated even further from the city than Céant, but its inhabitants, who were predominantly Catholic vinegrowers, were hostile to the Huguenots who gathered there to worship. After a number of clashes, the worshippers, who were drawn from churches in the south and west of Champagne, were driven away, and thereby deprived of any official site on which to hold their assemblies.[62]

By May 1572, the proximity of a further *prêche* at Isle, this time owned by Marie de Clèves, future wife of Condé, infuriated Catholic members of the

---

[57] Pithou, fol. 288r. On the council's continuing campaign to maintain Céant as the official site following the Peace of Longjumeau of March 1568, see BM Troyes Boutiot BB 14 ii. no. 19, 6 April, and A 16, 5 April.   [58] Pithou, fols. 289–91 and 297v–308.
[59] *Ibid.*, fols. 319v–23, Pithou himself was sent in 1565; and fols. 324–5 (1566).
[60] Pithou, fol. 317.   [61] BM Troyes Boutiot BB 14 ii. nos. 7–9, 11 and 39–40.
[62] *Mémoires de Claude Haton*, II, pp. 605–7; Pithou, fol. 357.

administration in Troyes. Several prominent Huguenot officials were prohibited by the council from going to Isle, and so from attending services.[63] On behalf of the Catholic citizens of Troyes, the duke of Guise approached the king, who in turn sought to persuade the marquise d'Isle of the disturbances that would ensue if she allowed these services 'so near to the city of Troyes'.[64] The marquise agreed in principle, but asserted her right, following the most recent edict, to provide for assemblies when she was present on her estates. Nevertheless, a royal decree of 31 July completely suppressed the exercise of Reformed worship at Isle; and on 10 August, the Catholics of Troyes took its enforcement into their own hands.[65] There had been attacks on Protestants returning from services through the city gates on previous occasions.[66] This time two separate incidents resulted in the killing of a newly baptised child and the injury of a joiner, revealing the tension already present in the city prior to the Saint Bartholomew's massacre in Paris.[67]

After the attack on their congregation returning from Isle, the Huguenots informed Condé of their case and requested that he bring the matter to the attention of the king. The Reformed church also sent its own representative to Paris, the councillor, Antoine Huyart. Catholic officials were not slow to forward their own version of events to their deputies, present at court since the beginning of August in a further attempt to prohibit the services at Isle.[68] Chief of these Catholic deputies was the former mayor, Pierre Belin, a man consistently hostile to the Reformers, who was to play a crucial role in the events leading up to the massacre in Troyes. However, the Reformed church continued to thrive as a result of the increased congregation attracted by the proximity of Isle, confirming the authorities' fears of a decade before.

On 30 August, a few days after news of the massacre in Paris had reached Troyes, about thirty-five Huguenots were rounded up and taken to the prisons. Five days later, on 4 September, they were murdered one by one in cold blood; seven Huguenots were also killed in the streets in the days before and after. Although the number killed in Troyes was small compared with those reported for other cities (only 36 in Crespin's martyrology as compared to 186 for Rouen and 141 for Lyons), it is one of the most reliable

---

63 BM Troyes Boutiot BB 14 ii. no. 41, 1 May. On the enforcement of a general prohibition see nos. 42 and 43, 13 and 29 May, and Pithou, fol. 366.

64 BM Troyes Boutiot BB 14 ii. no. 43, 29 May.

65 *Ibid.*, no. 45, 31 July. On 6 August the clergy were invited to do all they could to prevent the *prêche* at Isle.

66 For example, Pithou, fol. 308v, 1 May 1564; fol. 317, 1565. BN Dupuy, MS 333, fol. 67v, that stones had already been thrown at those returning from Isle.

67 Pithou, fol. 367; BN Dupuy 333, fols. 67v–8r. The joiner, Pantaléon Bours, was one of those whose child was rebaptised in 1562: BM Troyes Boutiot GG IV supplement, reg. 6, fol. 60v.   68 Pithou, fols. 366v–8; BN Dupuy 333, fol. 67v.

accounts as all the victims are named.[69] A contemporary narrative names forty-three victims, most of whom can be identified as leading members of the Troyes community.[70] Indeed, closer investigation into the identity of those who died suggests that the prisoners taken were not a random selection, but were chosen specifically as known Huguenots who had come to the attention of the authorities during earlier periods of tension.

Among their number were several prominent in the Reformed church, such as the merchant, Christophe Ludot, who had previously avoided such a fate by fleeing Troyes (as in 1562–3 when his house was pillaged), and who was one of those who had been banned from Isle on 1 May.[71] Also among those killed were Claude Gaulard and Thibaut de Meurs, who had represented the Huguenots at the talks with the Catholic authorities in 1562, and Jean Robert, who had represented them in 1571.[72] The massacre in 1572 thus paid off a number of old scores, some of them longstanding. Others the authorities might have targeted had taken the precaution of a well-timed absence, or were safely hidden, such as the doctor, Jacques Douynet, and Christophe de Vassan, both of whom had been prohibited from going to Isle.[73] One of the few survivors, both in 1563 as in 1572, was Antoine Huyart, who had narrowly escaped death in the prisons in 1563, and in 1572 avoided imprisonment as the Reformed church's representative in Paris.[74] Notable absentees included those who had represented the church at the talks in 1562, Nicolas Pithou and Jacques Duchat, who had been in exile for some years, and Jean Doré, who was registered in Geneva in September 1572.[75]

A significant proportion of those murdered in 1572 had relatives killed or accused in earlier conflicts, particularly in 1562, or who were registered as exiles. A few examples must suffice. The Chevry family were goldsmiths in Troyes: Guillaume was registered in Strasburg and listed as a suspect by the Parlement in 1562; Pierre was absent for the 1563 commission to ascertain public opinion about the holding of services in the suburbs, and represented the Huguenots in 1571; Henri was murdered in the prisons in 1572.[76] The

[69] Jean Crespin, *Histoire des martyrs persecutez et mis à mort pour la verité de l'évangile, depuis le temps des apostres jusques à présent*, ed. D. Benoît (3 vols., Toulouse, 1885–9), III, pp. 684–91; Benedict, 'The Saint Bartholomew's Massacres in the Provinces', 223, n. 51.

[70] BN Dupuy 333, fols. 66–75r; also on the massacre, see Pithou, fols. 371–82. Cf. *Mémoires de l'état de France sous Charles IX*, I, 'Relation du Massacre de la Saint-Barthélemy', in L. Cimber and F. Danjou (eds.) *Archives curieuses de l'histoire de France depuis Louis XI jusqu'à Louis XVIII*, VII (Paris, 1835), pp. 271–92.   [71] Pithou, fols. 253 and 265.

[72] BM Troyes Boutiot A 13, 12 April 1562, and A 17, 8 March 1571.

[73] Pithou: on Douynet, fol. 371r, and Vassan, fol. 392r. BM Troyes Boutiot BB 14 ii. no. 41, 1 May 1572.   [74] Pithou, fols. 267 and 275–6.

[75] Pithou, fol. 372. Duchat was registered in Strasburg in September 1562: Zuber, 'Les Champenois réfugiés à Strasbourg', 52. Doré in *Livre des habitants de Genève*, ed. P.-F. Geisendorf (2 vols., Geneva, 1957–63), II, p. 9, 8 September 1572.

[76] Guillaume: Zuber, 'Les Champenois réfugiés à Strasbourg', 51; AN X 2a, reg. 130, fo. 242. Pierre: BM Troyes Boutiot BB 14 i. no. 24, fol. 84; A 17, 8 March 1571.

Blampignons, also active Huguenots residing in the same district as the Chevrys, included painters Étienne, murdered in 1562, and Symon, registered in Montbéliard in January 1572, as well as the tinsmith, Pierre, who died in the street that September.[77] François and Jean Mauferé, who lived next door to each other, left their houses locked up at the time of the 1563 enquiry; Jean, a tinsmith, had recently had his house pillaged, and François was to be killed in the prisons in 1572.[78]

Some of the victims had themselves taken refuge in earlier years, such as the merchants and brothers, Denis and Étienne Marguin.[79] Such absences were doubtless marked and held in evidence against them. In the 1563 commission, it is notable that six of those recorded as absent were to lose their lives in 1572, and two out of those three later to be murdered who were present, were questioned on the first day, presumably before word could be relayed.[80] In addition, Jean Hanard, a merchant draper who died in 1572, had refused to conform with the commission in 1563. Others had been accused of attending illicit assemblies, such as the cobbler, Jean Niot, in 1557, and the draper, Nicolas Robinet, who was one of those accused of being seen leaving suspect services in 1567.[81] Occupational groups that were strongly represented in the Huguenot community in Troyes, such as joiners, painters and drapers, were also prevalent among the victims of 1572. In contrast, some of those killed in the street died as a result of personal vendetta.[82]

The Huguenot reaction to the massacre at Vassy in 1562 appears in stark contrast to their lack of resistance a decade later, although on both occasions they were in a relatively strong position prior to the troubles.[83] In Troyes in 1572, despite their recent resurgence, the Huguenots were a weakened group numerically and psychologically, as a result of recurring persecution. In contrast to 1562, there was less opportunity to flee, to arm themselves, or to seek assistance from neighbours or, indeed, a sympathetic bishop or governor. The Catholic authorities acted swiftly, seizing control of the city gates and rounding up Huguenot troublemakers. There was no question this time of a parley between the faiths; out of the nine Huguenot representatives of 1562, one had been executed following the siege at Bar in that year, at least three were in exile and two were killed in the prisons.

[77] Étienne, Pithou, fol. 264; Symon, C. Jouffroy, 'Les Peintres champenois et le refuge de Montbéliard au seizième siècle', *La Vie en Champagne*, 361 (1986), 5.
[78] BM Troyes Boutiot BB 14 i. no. 24, fo. 84; Jean Mauferé, Pithou, fol. 277r.
[79] Denis, *Livre des habitants*, I, p. 200; Étienne, Zuber, 'Les Champenois réfugiés à Strasbourg', 53; and his wife, Marie, in Lausanne, *BSHPF*, 21 (1872), 471.
[80] BM Troyes Boutiot BB 14 i. no. 24. Cf. Diefendorf, *Beneath the Cross*, p. 86, on Parisian Huguenots as marked men.
[81] Niot, Pithou, fol. 98v; Robinet, BM Troyes Boutiot BB 14 ii. no. 14.
[82] For examples, see BN Dupuy 333, fol. 71v, and Pithou, fol. 382r.
[83] Cf. N.Z. Davis, *Society and Culture in Early Modern France* (Stanford and London, 1975), p. 187 and n. 124; and Benedict, *Rouen during the Wars*, p. 97.

Not only the victims, but their opponents too – both members of the authorities and the murderers themselves – had been involved in the earlier troubles, and were thus well-rehearsed in their roles. The chief protagonists on the Catholic side were town councillor Pierre Belin, and royal *bailli* Anne de Vaudrey, as was the case with local officials in other cities.[84] As already noted, Belin headed the delegation to Paris sent by the council to secure an injunction against the services at Isle. It was he who relayed the supposed orders of the king, supported by governor Guise, to kill the Huguenots, although Belin must have been well aware of the royal will that the bloodshed should cease having been present in Paris when the king's declaration was announced.[85] Belin was thus the council's go-between with the duke of Guise, a role he had first adopted in 1562. Later he would be one of the main promoters of the Catholic League in Troyes.

Anne de Vaudrey, seigneur de Saint-Phal, had actively sought to prosecute Huguenots, and to disrupt their assemblies in the city and its district, since his appointment as *bailli* in 1559. The Huguenots believed that de Vaudrey had given the orders for the murders in the prisons, and that he was responsible for concealing the royal letters which declared that the Huguenots should be left in peace until after the massacre in Troyes, and only published them then because of their prohibition of Reformed services; thus, as Pithou puts it, 'administering the cure after the death'.[86] The *bailli* adopted the role played by mayor Pinette in the massacres of 1562–3: closely supervising the work of the soldiers under his command, and using a signal to indicate to his men whether or not a detainee was to be killed outright before reaching prison.[87] The mayor in 1572, Pierre Nevelet, does not appear to have played as active a role in the religious conflict as his predecessor, but had already shown himself hostile to his Huguenot neighbours. In August 1562, he declared that, 'those of the religion have gone too far, and we have endured too much from them, they are all worthless, and ought to be removed from the city'.[88] It is uncertain whether mayor Nevelet actually gave the go-ahead for the massacre in 1572, but such sentiments suggest that he would have done little to prevent it taking place.

The leaders of the 'murderous gang' who carried out the execution of the prisoners in 1572, Jean Perrenet and Jean Mergey, were involved in previous acts of sectarian violence.[89] Both men participated in the murder

---

[84] De Thou, *Histoire Universelle*, VI, p. 423. Cf. Benedict, 'The Saint Bartholomew's Massacres in the Provinces', 222.

[85] BM Troyes Boutiot BB 14 ii. no. 50; on the royal declaration see Pithou, fols. 376v–8r.

[86] Pithou, fol. 382v; Agrippa d'Aubigné, *Histoire Universelle*, ed. A. de Ruble (9 vols., Paris, 1886–97), III, p. 345. A copy of the king's declaration survives in BM Troyes Boutiot BB 14 ii. no. 48, 27 Aug.   [87] Pithou, fol. 374r.   [88] *Ibid.*, fols. 226v–7r.

[89] BN Dupuy 333, fol. 74r; Pithou, fols. 373v–4r. Cf. the previous experience of the militia in Paris, Diefendorf, *Beneath the Cross*, pp. 168–70.

of prisoners in 1563, and Mergey brought home the ears of one of his victims as a trophy following the massacre at Bar-sur-Seine in August 1562.[90] Some of those under their command were also no newcomers to shedding Huguenot blood. However, although in the past they may sometimes have acted on their own initiative, in 1572 as in 1563 they were acting under instruction from the authorities; in 1572 they received their orders from Anne de Vaudrey. Thus, the *bailli* knew his men, his men knew their job, and their victims were carefully chosen. The massacre at Troyes in 1572 was organised and systematic, the culmination of the sectarian tensions which had divided the citizenry irreparably since the spring of 1562.

Yet to what extent was the citizenry divided? The recurrence of the same individuals participating in the persecution of Huguenots begs an interesting but virtually unanswerable question, as to how far their actions were condoned by the remaining majority of Catholic inhabitants. The indications from the isolated glimpses we have of Catholics assisting and harbouring Huguenot relatives, neighbours or friends, and the evident anxiety caused by the divisive nature of the troubles revealed in the responses to the commission of 1563, suggest that there was a body of opinion which condemned the violence.[91] However, even these cases are not clear-cut, as some of the most hardened persecutors of the Reformed would make exceptions in the case of their relatives, whilst others seized the opportunity offered by the troubles to hand over relatives or neighbours to the authorities and almost certain death.[92] The decisive factor was the attitude of the authorities, who, in Troyes, unfortunately for the Huguenots, were bent on eradication of the new religion.

The struggle for survival of the Reformed church at Troyes was that of Huguenot congregations across northern France, although local circumstances varied, as did the difficulties confronted by individual churches. It is tempting to speculate that the legacy of Vassy was such that the fate of the Calvinist movement had already been decided by the events of 1562. The confessional tensions of that year had sown suspicion and hatred between the faiths, and grudges that would not soon be forgotten. Despite subsequent, and seemingly favourable edicts of pacification, the attitude of government at a provincial and local level was decisive for the welfare of the religious minority in many cities. The provincial governor in Caen and the municipal council in Châlons provided much needed protection for their

---

[90] Pithou, fols. 242r and 274r.
[91] See note 73, and BM Troyes Boutiot BB 14 i. no. 24. The responses to the 1563 commission are discussed in detail in my article, 'Religious Conflict and the Urban Setting: Troyes during the French Wars of Religion', *French History*, 6 (1992), 259–78.
[92] For example, Pithou, fols. 371r and 373–4; BN Dupuy 333, fol. 74r.

Huguenot citizens. Whereas, in Troyes, Dijon and Paris, the hostile policy of those in authority, and their relegation of Reformed worship to distant sites far from each city, placed an inexorable burden on the Huguenot community. Noble protection allowed for convenient worship on seigneurial estates, but only weak provision for safeguarding citizens in their homes. With a purged municipal administration and insufficient numerical strength, Huguenots were vulnerable to further intimidation and violence. Whatever the depth of conviction of the faithful, the need for political influence and the support it provided was overwhelming. Without it churches could not establish themselves on a secure enough basis to ensure regular provision of worship. Although on the eve of the Saint Bartholomew's massacre, it appeared that the Calvinist cause might regain its former strength, Huguenots were never again to enjoy the optimism and confidence of the early 1560s. By the close of 1572, the Calvinist struggle to establish its churches on a sure footing in northern France was all but over.

7 The Calvinist experiment in Béarn

Mark Greengrass

For two generations, the small sovereign Pyrenean principality of Béarn was the most southerly flank of state Protestantism in Europe. It was also the only substantial part of what is now France to experience a full Protestant Reformation. In addition, its experience of reformation is not merely of local interest. As the birth-place – and power-base – of Henri de Navarre, later the first Bourbon king of France, the consequences of Béarn's Reformation impinged upon French politics. So it provides an excellent basis for a case-study from which to view the French Reformation more generally.

Decrees issuing from the Béarn chancery proudly proclaimed that the principality was 'separate and distinct from the crown of France'.[1] The historical and legal case for its independence had been well-rehearsed in disagreements with the Parlement of Toulouse in the first years of the sixteenth century. It had its own language, laws, government and written customs or *fors*. It was by no means a feeble relic of the days of Gaston Febus, whose inheritance and royal title as king of Navarre had been half annexed by Ferdinand of Aragon in 1512. Indeed it is hard not to be impressed with the institutional renewal and strength of the Béarn state, particularly under Henri II d'Albret (1517–55).[2] Unlike the patchy administrative reforms of the Valois in France, the d'Albret had some solid achievements to their credit. Justice was reformed, law was unified and increasingly determined the life of ordinary people.[3] A professional body of

Some of the research for this paper was undertaken with the assistance of a Small Research Grant in the Humanities from the British Academy. I am grateful to Professor Christian Desplat of the University of Pau for his critical comments on this paper prior to publication.

[1] *La Principauté de Béarn* (eds.) P. Tucoo-Chala and C. Desplat (2 vols., Pau, 1980)) provides the best introduction. Vol. I, ch. 3 concerns the Reformation.

[2] C. Dartigue-Peyrou, *La Vicomté de Béarn sous le règne d'Henri d'Albret, 1517–55* (Paris, 1934).

[3] Béarn's first historian, Nicolas de Bordenave, reflected his Protestant enthusiasm for the kind of ordered state which Henri II d'Albret had set about trying to create: 'le païs estoit remply de querelles et bandes, d'ou procedoit une infinité de meutres, et les adultères y estoient fréquens, encores qu'ils soient punis de la peine de fouet, il érigea une chambre criminelle parlaquelle les maléfices furent, sinon du tout abolis, au moins de beaucoup amoindris'. *Histoire de Béarn et de Navarre*, ed. P. Raymond (Paris, 1873), p. 42. (Henceforth cited as Bordenave).

judges, the *Conselh Ordinary* or Sovereign Council, was constituted by an ordinance of 27 June 1519 as the court of last appeal in civil cases. Its authority was assured through the town and village councillors (*jurats*) and lesser officials of the court (*bayles*) whose activities it monitored. A separate criminal chamber followed in 1546, regulated definitively by an edict of the 29 June 1552.[4] The chamber of accounts which he also established in Pau in 1520 was complemented by a second chamber in Nérac to handle the vast patrimony of the d'Albret in France. With prudent financial management, the rulers of Béarn enjoyed relatively buoyant incomes.[5] In Béarn, domain revenues more than kept up with sixteenth-century inflation. Receipts for 1584–5 were five times what they had been in 1530–1 and at least twice the returns achieved on the eve of the wars of religion.[6] Extensive inventories (*dénombrements*) of various parts of the patrimony were undertaken and a variety of long-lapsed rights reclaimed. One satisfied agent reported in 1539 that 'the viscounty's domain increased by 2,000 écus without doing an injustice to anyone', a self-congratulatory, but not inaccurate, tribute to the loyalty and competence of its administrators.[7]

The chamber of accounts in Pau also supervised the production and quality of the principality's coinage, the 'bacquettes' or 'vaches de Béarn' which circulated widely in south-west France because it did not depreciate to the extent of the *livre tournois* with which, in 1515, it had been intended to have parity. A scheme for civil defence forces for the principality, raised through the financial subdivisions of the principality (the *parsans*) was put in place in the late 1530s and, unlike the equivalent in the kingdom of France, was still capable of being activated in the wars of religion. An impressive new fortification along the latest Italian lines was commissioned at Navarrenx. Constructed in the period 1538–46 by Italian engineers to costly specifications, the fortress more than matched any equivalent erected by the Valois.[8] The cornerstone of the renewal of the Béarn state was, however, the custom (the *For Renové*), instigated by Henri II d'Albret in collaboration with the estates, accepted by them on 27 November 1551 and published the following year.[9] The custom unambiguously proclaimed the elective origin of the principality's rulers which was reinforced by the oath of office of its princes, given orally before the assembled estates and

---

[4] M. Faget de Baure, *Essais historiques sur le Béarn* (Paris, 1878), pp. 40 etc.

[5] See the analysis in J. Russell Major, 'Noble income, inflation, and the wars of religion in France', *American Historical Review*, 86 (1981), 21–48, esp. 25–35.

[6] The custom of Béarn prevented any alienation of the domain; elsewhere there were, however, extensive alienations of the d'Albret patrimony to pay for the political ambitions of the house of Navarre, particularly in the second half of the sixteenth century.

[7] A. Elkrich, 'The Estates of the House of Navarre in the Sixteenth Century' (unpublished doctoral dissertation, Emory University, 1987), esp. ch. 1 (quotation cited p. 12).

[8] Bordenave, p. 44; 'cette ville ne doit aujourd'hui rien de fortification et de munitions de guerre à autre place forte'.

[9] C. Desplat, *Le For de Béarn d'Henri II d'Albret* (Pau, 1986).

enregistered in their minutes.[10] It also delineated the constitution of the state, reinforcing the authority of the Sovereign Council, exercised through the *jurats*.

Béarn was, of course, a tiny state. It had just over 450 parishes spread through four dioceses (Oloron, Lescar, Tarbes and a small fragment of the French diocese of Dax) and a population of 100–150,000 inhabitants. But this gave it coherence. Small states retained their viability in the sixteenth century and their vigour and ability to adapt to changing circumstances, especially in the context of the Reformation, is apparent.[11] In this respect, Béarn's Calvinist experiment bears comparison with the 'second Reformation' in German principalities.[12]

It was, however, the comparison between the French and the Béarn Reformations which was uppermost in the mind of Béarn's first Protestant historian, Nicolas de Bordenave.[13] Bordenave was an active and engaged first-generation Protestant pastor from Nay who had received a classical education at the collège de Guyenne in Bordeaux. He subsequently returned to his native town to be its pastor for over thirty years.[14] The synod encouraged him to begin collecting materials on the Béarn Reformation as early as 1563.[15] The invitation was renewed in 1569 and reinforced by Jeanne d'Albret.[16] Subsequently he received a pension as the royal historiographer to Henri de Navarre, playing a distinguished part in the provincial synods of the principality and attending the French National Synod at Nérac in 1578 on behalf of the Béarn churches. His history, completed after 1591, presented a Reformation which grew naturally out of, and thus reflected, the principality's culture and past.[17] Bordenave

---

[10] *Ibid.*, p. 83; 'Les habitants de la Seigneurie et Principauté de Béarn se gouvernaient à l'origine au moyen de Fors et Coutumes. Et pour se maintenir en liberté et dans le respect de celles-ci, ils élirent successivement plusieurs cheveliers comme seigneur ...' Cf. pp. 47–60 for the oath.

[11] M. Greengrass (ed.), *Conquest and Coalescence. The Shaping of the State in Early Modern Europe* (London, 1991), p. 4.

[12] The recent literature on this subject is amply cited in H. Schilling, 'Die Konfessionalieserung im Reich: Religiöser und Gesellschaftlicher Wandel in Deutschland zwischen 1555 und 1620', *Historische Zeitschrift*, 246 (1988), 1–45.

[13] Bordenave (editor's introduction) provides a brief and inadequate conspectus of his career. Cf. *Bibliothèque de la société du protestantisme français* (henceforth *Bib. prot.*) MS 548¹ p. 65 (Collection Auzière – notes on Béarn ministers).

[14] He was censured by the Synod of Nay in 1566 as a 'calomniateur de sa patrie & Contemteur du Magistrat' for his behaviour during a lawsuit involving a pregnant nurse in his household, a censure which was withdrawn at the following synod of April 1567 (*Bib. prot.* MS 433⁴ fol. 82 etc.).

[15] *Ibid.*, fol. 39v. 'Que M. Bordenabe aura la charge de coucher par escrit les Commencemens de lEglise en ce pays de bearn.' When he submitted his first written work to the Synod, a 'dialogue', it was rejected because of 'l'obscurité tant de language que du sujet' (*ibid.*, fols. 52v and 61).   [16] *Ibid.*, fol. 243.

[17] Cf. J. Garrisson, 'Le Protestantisme en Béarn', in *Arnaud de Salette et son temps – colloque* (Pau, 1984), p. 56 – 'Le nationalisme béarnais a trouvé dans le protestantisme une représentation religieuse.'

annually engaged his loyalty to the prince and the *pays* as well as the Confession of the church in the 'main d'association' at the Béarn synod. He would have known the legend, already current in the fifteenth century, that the Béarn people had originated in Switzerland, in Berne to be precise.[18] But the Béarnais had decided against being a republic. Instead they had agreed to accept the rule of a prince or princess (for no Salic law applied in Béarn and queens ruled as of right there, as Jeanne d'Albret once tactlessly reminded Catherine de Medici) under contingent loyalties which all, clergy and laity alike, had agreed to maintain. It was this constitutional arrangement, Bordenave implied, which ensured the success of the Protestant Reformation there. With the beneficent assistance of a Swiss reformer who had shaped the Reformation in Berne (Pierre Viret), the Béarn Reformation had proceeded, despite hostile interventions from without, especially France and Spain. By implication, France's Reformation had been perverted by capricious princes and their duplicitous consorts, abusing their absolute authority for their own ends and allowing an obstinate legal and clerical establishment to betray the truth. The analysis was not so far from that which the high priests of French resistance theory had openly espoused in the 1570s.

Superficially, too, Bordenave's presentation made some sense of events. The d'Albret did not set their face against Protestantism in the way that the Valois did. This perhaps had something to do with the alacrity with which the Papacy had accepted Ferdinand of Aragon's usurpation of the title of king of Navarre in 1512. It was even more the consequence of the decisions and determinations of its queens and princesses. The history of its Reformation is inextricably linked to the fortunes of the three *femmes fortes*, Marguerite de Navarre, her daughter Jeanne d'Albret and her grand-daughter Catherine de Bourbon. Between them, they were queens or regents of Béarn for over a quarter of a century. Of the three, Marguerite of Navarre did not have a political role to play in Béarn in the first half of the century and it would be hazardous to draw too close a link between her evangelism and the religious choice of her daughters. Yet, despite being surrounded by two powerful Catholic neighbours, Béarn's Reformation gradually took shape. Protestantism was officially tolerated in an uneasy *simultaneum* from 1561 to 1568. From 1569 to 1599 it was the only religion recognised and accepted in the principality. Then, for a generation after that, Protestantism continued to enjoy a privileged and advantageous position until the invasion of the principality and the union with the French regnum by Louis XIII in 1620.[19]

In another respect, too, Bordenave's analysis had some merit. The

---

[18] Desplat, *Le For de Béarn*, pp. 39–42.
[19] The standard history of the Protestant Reformation is M. Forissier, *Histoire de la Réforme en Béarn* (2 vols., Tarbes, 1953).

principality's custom only gave very limited jurisdiction to its officers to pursue heresy in respect of 'renégats et blasphémateurs'.[20] All other matters, such as the control of preaching, public disputation and illegal assembly for religious purposes, had to be left in the hands of episcopal authority.[21] But the bishoprics of Oloron and Lescar were in the patronage of the d'Albret.[22] The political preoccupations of Jacques de Foix, bishop of Lescar from 1534, and the notoriously easy-going disposition of his successor in 1555, Louis d'Albret, allowed reformed preachers a hearing and it was in their diocese that the earliest Protestant congregation appeared in the capital of the principality at Pau in around 1545.[23] Meanwhile in neighbouring Oloron, Gérard Roussel had been appointed bishop thanks to the influence of Marguerite of Navarre.[24] Of all the former reformers from Meaux, Roussel enjoyed Marguerite's confidence the most and he was in attendance on her during her later years of voluntary retirement on the d'Albret estates in Béarn and south-west France. According to Florimond de Raemond, Roussel turned Nérac into a Protestant enclave and Oloron into a second Meaux. Private masses were abolished, there was no elevation or adoration of the host, communion was under both kinds, all references to the Virgin and saints were eliminated, ordinary bread was used and clerical marriages were licensed.[25] He gave simple homilies in French from the altar 'afin d'attirer le simple peuple' and, because he seemed of upright life, he had 'beaucoup de créance parmi le peuple'. How much of this really went on in and around Oloron, and how much of it was merely part of the spiritual and learned table-talk with Marguerite that we know went on, is impossible to determine.[26] His catechism, the *Familière exposition du symbole, de la loy et oraison*

---

[20] Desplat, *Le For de Béarn*, p. 130.

[21] Compare the edict of 30 August 1546 against heresy with the letters patent against blasphemers of 30 July 1550 (both printed in V. Dubarat ed., *Documents et bibliographie sur la réforme en Béarn et au pays basque* (Pau, 1900), pp. 36–41).

[22] They were not bound by the terms of the French concordat of 1516 and thus fell into the jurisdiction known as the 'pays d'obédience' where appointments lay with the papacy. In reality, however, the patrimonial rights of the d'Albret were too powerful and immediate to be ignored (l'abbé Poeydavant, *Histoire des Troubles survenus en Béarn dans le 16e et la moitié du 17e siècles* (2 vols., Pau, 1819), I, pp. 55–6).

[23] The canons of Lescar petitioned the estates of Béarn 'suus lo feyt de la fee et religion christiane, contre Moss. de Lascar, fray Henric de Barran, et autres ...' on 29 September 1558 (printed in *ibid.*, pp. 47–9).

[24] On Roussel see, in general, C. Schmidt, *Gérard Roussel, prédicateur de la reine Marguerite de Navarre* (Strasbourg, 1845) and A. Degert, 'L'Evêque d'Oloron, Gérard Roussel et la curie romaine', *Revue de Gascogne*, 45 (1904). He had been Marguerite's confessor and almoner and had been provided with the abbeys of Uzerche and Clairac before being nominated to Oloron in 1536 (*Gallia Christiana* I, cols. 1277–8; II, cols. 592; 943).

[25] F. de Raemond, *Histoire de la naissance, progrez et décadence de l'hérésie de ce siècle ...* (2 vols., Paris, 1605), II, 154v etc.

[26] R. Ritter, *Les Solitudes de Marguerite de Navarre: 1527–49* (Paris, 1953); Pierre Jourda, *Marguerite d'Angoulême, duchesse d'Alençon, reine de Navarre (1492–1549)* (2 vols., Paris, 1930), I, pp. 294–5.

dominicale, and his distinctive visitation handbook, the *Somme de visite de diocese*, written a year or so before their condemnation by the Sorbonne in October 1550, provide evidence of Genevan influence on his thinking at a time when he was certainly in Oloron.[27] At the same time, these are blended into more general Augustinian tendencies within a context of reconciliation with various aspects of traditional doctrine. Raemond's statement that Calvin had written his treatise *Contre les Nicodemites* 'principalement' against Roussel's pollution of the Protestant faith is quite possible.[28] In the preface to these two treatises, Roussel claimed that he had required the Apostles' Creed, Ten Commandments and Lord's Prayer to be recited each Sunday throughout his diocese.[29] Whatever the truth or effect of Roussel's activities in his diocese, it was the case that, in comparison with France, the principality's constitution let heresy flourish.

Despite this, Béarn's Protestantism appeared relatively late and from the beginning it was a religion of the elite, albeit with some artisanal elements, concentrated particularly on the capital Pau. It was a religion of those in the principality who spoke French and whose horizons were broader than simply Béarn. The early Protestants in the principality stand out very clearly as students at Toulouse or the collège de Guyenne in Bordeaux, merchants with business contacts in the flourishing cities of the French Midi, and gentlemen and women in the radius of the Albret court.[30] The early Protestant wills are, in this respect, distinctive.[31] A typical example is the will of the merchant Jean de Gassion, drawn up in Pau on 19 March 1562. It opens with an unambiguously Protestant formula: 'Primo recommanda a diu nostre sr son anima lo preguan e requeran an nom e en faveur de Jesu Christ son filh lo donar lo salut eternel per lo meri de la mort e passion deud sr Jesuchrist moyenan loqual Ay si assureu de leffayt de sa promesse e par consequence de la vite eternalle.' He asked to be buried 'en lo temple de lade ville de Pau en loc honeste et digne lo melhor e plus

---

[27] *BN MS Fr* MS 419. See, for example, his definition of the church, cited in H. Heller, 'Marguerite of Navarre and the Reformers of Meaux', in *BHR*, 33 (1971), 303.

[28] F. Higman, *Three French Treatises* (London, 1969), pp. 23–6, drawing on R. Autin, *La Crise du nicodémisme 1535–1544* (Toulon, 1917).

[29] *BN MS Fr* MS 419 fol. 1v 'a voulu et ordonne que tous et chacune dimanches seroient par les Recteurs et vicaires Recitz a votre peuple en leur vulgaire ces troys briefs sommaires Affin que du grand Iusques au petit ung chacun Recongneust la volunte de dieu lobeissance quil Requiert de nous'. This was clearly recalled by Jeanne d'Albret two decades later in her letters patent of 13 July 1568. C-L. Frossard, *BSHPF*, 55 (1896), 309.

[30] 'Une grande partie des gentilhommes et officiers desdits Roy et Royne, ayant abjuré la religion romaine, feroient profession de cette religion et désireroient d'en avoir exercise à la suite de leur maistre et maistresse' (Bordenave, p. 53).

[31] The following two examples come from a larger study of testamentary evidence in sixteenth and early seventeenth-century Béarn. They emerged from the sample of 390 wills from the notarial registers of Pau taken over the period 1510–1640 and which will form the basis for a separate study.

honestement *que* far se poyra'.[32] This should, however, be counter-balanced against the equally Protestant sentiments of the *cordonnier* of Pau, Peyroton de Gabarden, drawn up on 15 May 1561.[33] 'Premierement recommande son anime a diu ly presentant ab son filh Jesus Christ desan mon diu je recommande mon anime enter tas mas ab asegurance Et Confidance que la haben purgade en la bade au sang de son fils Jesus crist Et la recevrere en la vita eternalle.' He asked to be buried in 'lo temple de la presente ville' with his family and that of his wife Germaine and one of the children, his burial to be 'fendans augune Idolatrie et superstition de serimonys contre la parole de diu'. The witnesses to these, and other early Protestant testaments in Pau, give an impression of the social nexus of its congregation; booksellers, physicians, councillors to the queen, lawyers, some artisans. It is not difficult to imagine that, for many of these individuals, France and its culture framed the horizon which shaped and organised their world for the future. After Beza's visit to Nérac in the summer of 1560 and Jeanne d'Albret's subsequent dramatic Christmas Day proclamation of Protestantism in Pau, Béarn's Reformation was an unambiguously Calvinist and an unashamedly official affair.[34]

No religious change in the sixteenth century, however, was ever directed with a free hand or dictated wholly from above. In addition to responding to pressures from the French court of which she was a member through her marriage to Antoine de Bourbon, Jeanne d'Albret also had to take account, given the constitution in Béarn, of the hostile response from below.[35] She found herself having to respect the wishes of a council of state which was by

---

[32] *AD Pyrenées Atlantiques* E 1997 fol. 294. The Gassion family are an excellent example of the middle-managers of the principality (see A. de Dufau de Maluguer, *Armorial de Béarn* (2 vols., Pau, 1893) I, p. 103 etc. Jean's uncle had assisted Henri II d'Albret in the payment of his ransom to the Spanish. His father, Peyroton de Gassion, was a merchant in Oloron and *fermier* and *receveur* for the abbey of Lucq. He himself became a merchant in Toulouse in association with Pierre Sirvent and his cousin Jean de Balanquier. He was proud of his fortune 'acquise de son labor & industrie' which included a half-share in a shop in Toulouse as well as a house there, the profits of his business partnership and a joint investment with his cousin in a consignment of woad. There was also some wool in the hands of another brother who was acting as a merchant in Saragossa. Some of his estate passed to his brother, 'Egregy' Jean Gassion 'avocat en lo conseil de la regine.' His brother invested the bequest in purchasing the farm of tithes from one of the queen's favourites. In 1566, he became a syndic of the estates, bought a house next to François de Tisnès, one of the great ruling families of Pau. In 1570 he became a councillor to the Sovereign Council, a commissioner to farm the ecclesiastical lands in the financial district (*parsan*) of Oloron and, in 1582, the third president to the Sovereign Council. The Protestant chronicler Olhagarry referred to him as the 'grand justicier'.

[33] *AD Pyrenées Atlantiques*, E 1998 fol. 71.

[34] According to Bordenave, the Reformation began with the arrival in Béarn of François le Gay, a preacher from Geneva: 'Il fut conduit au commencement en la maison du sieur de Masères les Pau, où il précha le dimanche prochain publiquement au temple au sortir de la messe parrochielle' – p. 54.

[35] Nancy Roelker, *Jeanne d'Albret* (Cambridge, MA., 1968), chs. 10–11.

no means entirely Protestant and which resisted any proposition which might breach the privileges of the *for*. The estates of Béarn also voiced the opposition to religious changes which came from various groups, particularly the senior clergy. Jeanne d'Albret resorted to the expedient of not summoning them to the estates of 1567 and 1568.[36] In their place, she invited the important group of 'abbots', in reality lay patrons of Catholic benefices,[37] largely in the hands of modest gentry families whose pensions on their benefices she promised to protect.[38] More important were the barons of Béarn, attached by ties of kinship and roots to the Catholic families of Navarre – with Gabriel de Béarn, baron de Gerderest at their head, son of the senechal of the principality. There was also a robust group of Catholic deputies among the *jurats* from the town communities. They protested at the abandonment of Corpus Christ day processions which left local inhabitants 'greatly scandalized'.[39] They voiced the fears of merchants whose trade necessarily involved them in contact with France and Spain.[40] Their concerns were not unjustified for there would be a steady stream of Béarnais presented before the Inquisition in Saragossa after 1560. They were joined by the Pyrenean valley communities whose syndics were agitated about the trading and agricultural links which again took Béarnais into Spain and involved locally agreed rights of passage across the mountains.[41] They were also disturbed by the disbandment of confraternities and objects of veneration which played an important part in the complex culture of these independent valley communities.[42]

Three sets of ecclesiastical ordinances provided the focus for opposition. In July 1561, Protestantism was legalised in the principality.[43] In September 1563 the synod convoked at Pau by the Genevan-trained pastor Merlin agreed a Discipline to be used throughout the churches. In July 1566, Jeanne d'Albret issued a set of ordinances, probably with the

---

[36] C. Dartigue Peyrou, *Jeanne d'Albret et le Béarn* (Mont-de-Marsan, 1934), pp. lvii–lxxxv.

[37] The local significance of the seigneurial and ecclesiastical rights of the lay abbots may be estimated from G. Tucat, *Dictionnaire des communautés de Béarn sous l'ancien régime et des fiefs y compris* (Tarbes, 1973). By my calculations, this detailed investigation of the sénéchaussée of Morlàas suggests that lay abbots exercised seigneurial jurisdiction in just over 60 of the 193 communities. In 51 parishes they had rights to presentment to the benefice either solely or in alternance with another patron. In a further 8 they shared the *ius patronatus* in a more elaborate way. In 46 communities the lay abbots enjoyed rights to tithe.   [38] Dartigue Peyrou, *Jeanne d'Albret*, p. 83 ff.

[39] Dubarat, *Documents* pp. 67–9 – 'grandement escandalisatz et admervulhatz'. Cf. the ordinance of Antoine de Gramont of 24 May 1564 preventing processions on Corpus Christ Day, pp. 89–91.   [40] *Ibid.*, p. 71.

[41] For the significance of the *traités de lies et passeries*, see D.A. Gómez-Ibáñez, *The Western Pyrenees* (Oxford, 1975), p. 45.

[42] Dubarat, pp. 87–8 (Requête de la vallée d'Ossau pour la restitution des calices, croix et autres ornements d'église et la restauration du culte – 18 February 1564).

[43] C-L. Frossard, 'La Réforme en Béarn. Nouveaux documents provenant du château de Salies', *BSHPF*, 44 (1895), 354–8.

assistance of Pierre Viret, the theologian sent her by Calvin in 1564 as a kind of unofficial superintendant to the religious changes.[44] These dismantled the material resources of the Catholic church and its public profile. All legacies and gifts to the Catholic church were forbidden. Its wealth, benefices and monastic establishments were transferred to the administration of a branch of the Sovereign Council known as the ecclesiastical council. On the basis of these confiscated domains, Jeanne d'Albret claimed the right to create new 'terres nobles' and thus to import a clientèle of Protestant nobles into the principality's estates. Catholic processions, preaching and images were all forbidden and monasteries disbanded.

The reaction to these changes was hostile. 'The more the queen tried to lead people towards the religion, the more they turned against her' admitted Bordenave.[45] From Toulouse, the cardinal d'Armagnac warned the queen forcibly that her experiment was doomed to failure. 'You are vainly expecting to transplant the new religion into your sovereign principality. The desires of the pastors accord in no way with those of your subjects. They will never agree to abandon their religion; They have already protested about it in the recent meeting of the Estates ...'[46] Protestant refugees had to be protected from popular hostility.[47] There were incidents of popular sedition against the commissioners sent by Jeanne d'Albret to establish Protestant church services in 1563.[48] There was continued resistance to pastors being required to be given hospitality at community expense.[49] The reaction to the 1566 ordinances was particularly acute. As Bordenave said, 'being brought to Béarn, they were found to be so astringent by many of the Reformed faith and all those of the roman faith that they said they would have to be angels rather than men to live according to these laws and they frustrated their implementation all they could'.[50] Even Jeanne d'Albret, whose personal commitment to a total reformation led to her fining herself 100 sols for failing to introduce a session of her council with prayers, admitted that the 'ignorence du peuple' was a force to be reckoned with.[51] The regulations of 1566 were only

---

[44] The published version of the ordinances of July 1566 is from a defective copy; M. Weiss, *BSHPF*, 40 (1891), 295–301.   [45] Bordenave, p.118.

[46] l'abbé Poeydavant, *Histoire des Troubles survenus en Béarn dans le 16e et la moitié du 17e siècles* (2 vols., Pau, 1819) I, p. 180. A different version, with similar sentiments, is provided in Faget de Baure p. 414.

[47] 'et y eussent esté fort mal traittez sans la présence de la Reyne' (*ibid.*, p. 111).

[48] *Ibid.*, p. 119. 'aussi par plusieur endroits du païs plusieurs tumultoient journellement avec telle audace qu'il estoit aisé de juger qu'ils ne cerchoient que l'occasion d'entrer ouvertement en sédition et quelques gentilshommes empeschoient ou troubloient les prédications des ministres en leurs villages'. Cf. P. de Salefranque, *Histoire de l'Hérésie de Béarn . . .*, ed. V. Dubarat (2 vols., Pau, 1920) I, ch. 7.

[49] Dubarat, *Histoire*, pp. 128–9 (Jeanne d'Albret's discharge of towns from this requirement, 13 July 1568). C-L. Frossard, *BSHPF*, 45 (1896), 265–73.

[50] Bordenave, p. 125.   [51] 'Lettres de Jeanne d'Albret', *BSHPF*, 76 (1927), 42–3.

registered in the council with her repeated insistence and the sessions of the estates of 1567 and 1568 turned out to be highly charged.[52] The commissioners sent out to inventory and, as appropriate, arrange for the sale of ecclesiastical wealth found themselves the target of popular hatred. Bordenave took comfort from his belief that his countrymen 'knew that they were allowed to oppose the will of the sovereign prince only by remonstrances and supplication and not by force' but an organised insurrection of uncertain dimensions was only averted at Pentecost 1567 by the treachery of one of its adherents.[53]

In the event, it was an invasion from France two years later which tried to reverse the Reformation and brought war to the principality. After considerable hesitation, Jeanne d'Albret had finally left the principality and travelled north to meet with the leaders of the French Protestants, Condé and Coligny, at La Rochelle on 29 September 1568. In so doing, she expressed her solidarity for them in their revolt against the French king, Charles IX. He replied by proclaiming the seizure of the lands of the House of Navarre in France and taking the principality of Béarn under his 'protection' during the 'captivity' of the queen in La Rochelle. This convenient legal fiction justified an invasion without declaring war on Béarn, thus offending regional sensibilities and opening up old quarrels about the status of the principality *vis à vis* the French crown. An army 'of protection' under the leadership of the baron de Terride, and strongly supported by the Catholics in the south-west of France, set about the conquest of Béarn from the north and east.

Resistance to Terride's 'army of protection' was organised by the Sovereign Council and the queen's lieutenant, but it was ineffective. Although the French troops were not generally welcomed in the principality, they received enough cooperation from the local population, thanks in part to the collaboration of some of the barons of the estates of Béarn, that they overran it in the space of two months and established a provisional government. But the d'Albret fortress at Navarrenx, with over fifty Protestant ministers and a good many others sheltering within its walls, withstood a long siege of seventy-seven days before it was relieved by the Protestant 'army of relief' led by the Huguenot commander Montgomery. Running the gauntlet of the royal armies in the south-west, Montgomery set out from Castres on 24 July and arrived before Navarrenx on 9 August. Blaise de Monluc much admired his sense of strategy.[54] With Montgomery's arrival, Terride's occupation collapsed. Viret returned to Pau and preached at a service of thanksgiving on the text: 'Our soul is

[52] Dartigue Peyrou, *Jeanne d'Albret*, pp. 83–106. Cf. Dubarat, *Histoire*, pp. 116–28.
[53] Bordenave, pp. 127–33.
[54] 'In all these wars there has not been a finer example of military strategy.'

escaped as a bird out of the snare of the fowlers: the snare is broken and we are escaped' (*Psalms* 124:7). The brief but destructive civil war in Béarn had been won by the Protestants. It left bitter memories but Jeanne d'Albret was once more queen of Béarn.

This victory, more than anything else, ensured the Protestant settlement in Béarn for the next generation. Prominent Béarn Catholics who had collaborated with the 'army of protection' sought exile in Navarre or France. Their property was confiscated. From Pau on 26 November 1571 Jeanne d'Albret issued the *Ordinances for the police of the Church in which God's Majesty shines forth* ... These were accepted, along with the Confession agreed by the French churches at La Rochelle earlier in the year, by the Sovereign Council and then by the estates whose submission to the Protestant ascendancy after 1570 is as marked as their reluctance had been in the 1560s.[55]

These ordinances deserve to be better known amongst Reformation historians. They are a thorough and uncompromising attempt to provide an ecclesiastical and moral reformation through the power of the state.[56] The long preamble justified the changes in the context of the recent failed rebellion:

to obey the Lord's commandment, to fulfil the obligation of a Christian, to respond to the vocation given us by God, to procure the salvation of our people and subjects, to preserve public peace and the unity of our administration, to follow diligently the example of all good princes and kings, to avoid the terrible wrath of God's judgment and to respond to the submission of the recent estates of Béarn. . . . who have of their own volition humbly begged us to banish all false religion, idolatry and superstition . . .[57]

There followed seventy-seven paragraphs which re-established the ecclesiastical council, regulated the education, training, appointment, payment and behaviour of ministers, introduced Protestant precepts into many aspects of public life in the principality and required their enforcement by the *jurats* and *baillis* under the overall supervision of the council of state. Many of its articles implemented parts of the Calvinist experiment which had been blocked by resistance in earlier years but which had now become politically possible. Although issued seven months after his death, their

[55] The ordinance is partially published in Dartigue Peyrou, *Jeanne d'Albret*, pp. 145–64 (clauses 34–69 are not reproduced; see *Bibliothèque Nationale* MS Brienne 217 fol. 145 etc for the full text).

[56] 'Nous ordonnons et commandons que le sainct ministère soict sans demeure et sans difficulté estably en toutes les villes, bourgs et villages ainsy que lieu de nostre pays, et que tous les ministres . . . soint bien examinés, esleu et approuvés tant en doctrine qu'en moeurs selon la règle de Saint-Paul, affin que paissans leur troupeau en piété et saincteté, ils attirent par leur exemple les ignorans et les infirmes à la cognoissance de Dieu' (p. 147).

[57] *Ibid.*, pp. 146–7 (and mainly following the English translation of the preamble by Roelker, *Jeanne d'Albret*, pp. 430–1).

overriding vision was that of Pierre Viret.[58] Since his arrival in the principality in 1564, he had developed the main lines of the Béarn state Reformation.[59] When Viret died in April 1571 Jeanne d'Albret wrote to the Council of Geneva that she counted 'the loss of M. Viret, whom God has called to Himself, as the greatest' and honoured him with burial in the crypt of her ancestors, the vicomtes de Béarn, with almost royal panoply.[60] Recent commentary has stressed those clauses in which moral reform and social discipline were uppermost.[61] Magic and sorcery, dancing, lewd singing, games of chance, usury, blasphemy as well as a wide range of sexual offences were all the subject of its disapproving gaze. But the cutting edge of their changes was the investment of ecclesiastical revenues in the hands of a revived ecclesiastical council in clause 15.[62] Nine individuals (two ministers and seven deacons), nominated annually by the Calvinist synods, were to be responsible for the ecclesiastical revenues which, in turn, would support the evangelical pastorate, schools and the relief of the poor envisaged in the ordinance. The Calvinist church in Béarn would be better endowed than any other in French-speaking Europe.

How effectively, however, were the ecclesiastical ordinances enforced? In a narrow sense, the Calvinist experiment in Béarn was a remarkable success. Some notes of the deliberations of the Ecclesiastical Council in its early years have survived in a nineteenth-century copy and they testify to its extraordinary zeal and energy.[63] The council's first treasurer (*premier diacre* or *receveur général*) was Bernard de Montaut. He pursued the arrears

---

[58] For Pierre Viret, see J. Barnaud, *Pierre Viret (1511–71)* (Nieuwkoop, 1973; reprint of 1911 edition) and the discussion of his theology in G. Bavaud, *Le Réformateur Pierre Viret (1511–1571)* (Geneva, 1986).

[59] He wrote several policy documents on various aspects of the Béarn Reformation. The Béarn synods mention those on church–state relations and mixed marriages although they have not survived. That on the application of ecclesiastical discipline was recorded as an appendix to the synod of 1571. *Bib. prot.* 433⁴ fols 263–75, reproduced with modernised orthography in H. Meylan, 'Un Texte inédit de Pierre Viret: le règlement de 1570 sur la discipline', *Revue de théologie et de philosophie*, 3 (1961), 209–21.

[60] Roelker, *Jeanne d'Albret*, pp. 274–5.

[61] J. Garrisson, *Les Protestants au XVIe siècle* (Paris, 1988) pp. 63–4, 67.

[62] 'le synod national de nostre pays de Béarn ... procédera soubs nostre authorité et relation d'un conseil qui sera composé et estably de neuf personnes bien zélées à la piété et remplies de l'esprit de Dieu, au nombre desquels la charge à offrir sera de fidellement rechercher tous les biens ecclésiastiques, les conserver et dispenser ...' (Dartigue Peyrou, pp. 153–4). In reality, the council had already been agreed and elected at the synod of 17 October 1571 in Pau and held its first meeting a week later, a month before the formal pronouncement of the ordinances in the estates the following month (*Bib. prot.* MS 433⁴ fols. 140–v. MS 432 p. 13).

[63] *Bib. prot.* MS 432. According to a note from Gustave Cadier dated 2 November 1933 inside the document, the copy was taken from an eighteenth-century copy of the deliberations which had been in the hands of M. le baron de Laussat at Bernadets. The spelling and grammar has been progressively modified in the copying.

on ecclesiastical revenues (estimated at 18,000 *livres* in early 1572).[64] He organised an inventory of all ecclesiastical wealth, which ran to four large volumes and which was completed by February 1572.[65] This was designed, at least in part, to ensure that the *jurats* and others did not expropriate ecclesiastical property to their own account.[66] The annual adjudication of farms was undertaken by the Council in early April each year.[67] The annual remuneration of all those within the new ecclesiastical establishment was established, from Viret's successor as first minister and quasi-'surintendant' (Des Gallars) (600 *livres*) through ministers (300 *livres* for married pastors), university lecturers and schoolmasters to catechists (60 *livres*).[68] The most intractable problem concerned those who held rights of patronage to benefices in the old church. The *Ordinances* had required them to be compensated, providing that they were Protestants, by means of a pension (clause 29). They had further required that all widows and infants of lay patrons should be given preferential treatment in the charitable and educational endeavour of the state (clause 27). This threatened to become an open-ended commitment and, at a meeting in the town hall in Pau on 2 February 1573, called by the lieutenant-général of the principality and attended by ministers, nobility and others, they finally agreed on a formula which, in effect, commuted the *ius patronatus* into a free educational place at the collège de Béarn for anyone nominated by them from the ages of 8 to 18.[69] This resolved a delicate political problem which touched on fundamental property rights and, at the same time, fostered an educational objective which was a necessary prerequisite to the longer-term success of the Calvinist experiment in Béarn.

To what extent did the Calvinist experiment transform the principality in the longer term? In the absence of consistory records in the principality before 1620, this is difficult to answer. But there is enough evidence to suggest that, as elsewhere in Europe, Protestantism found it hard to win the hearts and minds of the predominantly rural population of Béarn. Church services were commanded at particular times of day, depending on the season, but how much did people really understand of them?[70] There was the problem of language. The Confession was recited in Sunday morning services and ordered to be translated into Béarnais in May 1565; it was presumably distributed around the churches in manuscript because there is

---

[64] *Ibid.*, p. 12 (23 January 1572).   [65] *Ibid.*, p. 17 (6 February 1572).

[66] See, for example, the case of Orthez *jurats* – p. 18 (13 Feb 1572).

[67] *Ibid.*, p. 24 (16 April 1572).

[68] *Ibid.*, p. 15 (23 January 1572).   [69] *Ibid.*, pp. 75–7.

[70] For the timetable of services, determined by the *jurats* of Lagor in accordance with the queen's instructions in 1564, see Dubarat, *Documents*, pp. 92–3. Such timetables were generally determined locally and were not laid down by the synods or by the ordinances.

no evidence that it was printed.[71] The Ten Commandments were recited in the Sunday afternoon catechisms and this, along with the catechism (apparently based on the Genevan catechism) was published in 1564 at the behest of Ramon Merlin. But, although Jeanne d'Albret commissioned a translation of the Psalms from Arnaud de Salettes in 1568 which was completed in 1571, it remained unpublished until 1583 when it finally appeared from the press of the Academy of Orthez run by Louis Rabier, the first substantial literary work printed in Béarnais. This version of the Psalms was printed alongside a cycle of prayers as well as a further Béarn catechism.[72] But Béarnais was not the only language in use in the principality. There was also a Basque population which found French more inaccessible. The domains of the Béarn princes in Basse Navarre to the west of Béarn were Basque-speaking and the Reformation made little impression there. The New Testament was translated into Basque on Jeanne d'Albret's encouragement and published by the synod of Béarn in sufficient copies to distribute around each church.[73] Although efforts were made from the beginning to encourage pastors with a knowledge of Béarnais and Basque, it can hardly have been the case that all preaching was in the local language.[74] Synods reiterated that preachers should use what knowledge of the local language they had when preaching.

This presumes, however, that the Protestant clergy in Béarn were able and wanted to conduct an ambitious, self-appointed evangelisation to a predominantly rural population which had traditionally low levels of literacy in terms which they would understand.[75] The synods appeared to be more concerned to establish a morally upright and learned pastorate rather than one filled with missionary zeal. Periodically it urged pastors to preach 'les livres et matieres les plus faciles & propres pour la capacite du peuple'.[76] The *colloques* conducted annual visitations of churches and the 'Formulary' for such visits specified the qualities of a good preacher – simplicity, methodical development of the subject, learning and suitable

---

[71] *Bib. prot.* MS 433[4] fols. 61v–2.

[72] *Arnaud de Salettes et son temps* (Pau, 1984) and R. Darrigrand, 'Version béarnaise du catéchisme de Calvin par Arnaud de Salettes (1583)', in *Henri de Navarre et le royaume de France 1572–89* (Pau, 1984), pp. 149–70.

[73] *Bib. prot.* MS 433[4] fol. 157v; 50 écus towards the printing of Jean Lisserargues' translation; fol. 174v arrangements for the printing and collection of the copies; 421 fol. 89 (50 *sols* per copy).

[74] Bordenave, p. 116 refers to the pastors sent with Merlin in 1562 'et plusieurs autres savans personnages, la plus part de la langue gasconne et bearnoise pour prescher au peuple en son langage ...'. The children of Basque clergy were given added encouragement to attend the college at Orthez by the synod in 1574. The sons of the Basque-speaking ministers such as Tartas, Landecheverry and Tardetz were invited to spend a year in Basse Navarre 'pour apprendre le langage basque' (*Bib. prot.* MS 433[4] fol. 168).

[75] Only about twelve to thirteen communities had schoolmasters in the early sixteenth century.   [76] *Bib. prot.* MS 433[4] fol. 107 (1568).

demeanour.[77] Periodically the synods lamented the reluctance of the population to hear sermons and urged the *jurats* and *procureurs* of local communities to compel them to attend church services. That of the synod of Pau of 16 April 1577 was entirely typical:

> Car, depuis quelque temps les habitants de ce pays se sont tellement licenciez qu'ils ne tiennent [*pas*] conte des predications ne [*de la*] discipline Ecclesiastique & publiquement au mesprix de dieu et desdites ordonnances, vont faire Exercice de la Religion Romaine hors de cette souveraineté, & se desbourdent a toutes dissolutions, & scandalles, ce que le prince Chrestien ne doit permetre ny tollerer, veu qu'il est Constitué de Dieu gardien de l'une et de l'autre tables de ses Commandemens et a receu le glaive de luy aussi bien pour la punition et Extermination du mal, comme pour la protection et conservation du bien . . .[78]

One is reminded, however, of the attack by the erstwhile Protestant of Basque origins, Jean de Sponde, who certainly knew these parts intimately, on the standards of the Protestant clergy and their achievements. 'Je n'ay point remarqué que le peuple en soit devenue plus sçavant, si ce n'est comme on apprend une espèce de jargon à force de coutume'; and 'il ne faut que faire un Presche sur un lieu common, et une perpetuelle invective contre la Papauté, vous avez suffisamment servy Dieu et son Eglise . . .'.[79] The only observable 'missionary' endeavour of the Béarn churches was its annual preaching ministry at the spa at Eaux-Chaudes.[80] Underlying the Béarn Calvinist church establishment was a nervous and unresolved tension as to whether it was an 'inclusive' or 'exclusive' church. So long as it was a minority faith, the question did not arise. But having become the state religion in the aftermath of Terride's defeat the issue was more delicate. At the synod of Lescar in October 1569 it was debated and agreed that 'tous ceux qui voudront protester seront Receuz en lassamblee de lEglise moyennant qu'ilz ne soyent de vie scandaleuse'.[81] But then doubts began to emerge. Should not those who had notoriously 'blasphemé contre la doctrine de levangile' be excluded from the church, not to mention those who had openly criticised the queen on religious grounds? And 'les plus rudes du peuple' could scarcely be accepted as full confessional members without being 'Catechumes jusque a ce qu'ilz soyent bien Instruictz'. Viret was asked to produce 'un petit traité' on the question. It is amongst the

---

[77] *Ibid.*, fols. 291v–3 ('Formulaire de faire la visite des Eglises'; 'Sera diligement Enquis si le pasteur presche aux Jours & heures ordonnees en son Eglise, si en langage Intelligible, si en habit decent & avec la Robbe, ez lieux de sa residence pour le moins, si avec les Gestes Convenables a la Maiesté de la parole de dieu et sans Affection ou ostentation, sy la parole est preschee purement simplement & methodiquement – si elle est Appliquee aux usages Necessaires de l'instruction, exhortation, Reprehension, Consolation, & Refutation des Erreurs abus & superstitions . . .'. [78] *Bib. prot.*, MS 433⁴ fol. 178v.
[79] A. Boase, *Vie de Jean de Sponde* (Geneva, 1977), p. 122, 125.
[80] This took place generally in the two Spa seasons of May and August.
[81] *Bib. prot.* 433⁴ fol. 239.

blueprint treatises he prepared for the Béarn Reformation which have not survived. But his preference for an 'exclusive' church was clearly expressed in a document on the form and use of excommunication prepared in 1570;

il ne faut pas tant travailler à amasser grand nombre de gens pour avoir de grandes assemblees, qu'à travailler comme ceux qui sont receuz soyent bons et biens reiglez. Car il vaut trop mieux d'avoir un petit troupeau de brebis et d'aigneaux qu'un fort grand, auquel il y ait plus de loups, de chiens et de pourceaux que d'aigneaux et de brebis, veu que telles bestes ne peuvent porter que dommage au troupeau, et qu'il faut puis après avoir la peyne de les en chasser au grand scandalle de l'Eglise ...[82]

Since the *Ordinances* of 1571 did not require the population to swear individually to the Confession and the Discipline, the issue remained unresolved, or rather deflected into related areas, particularly the question of whether the church should bless mixed marriages. We are left with the impression of a Calvinist experiment whose experimenters were not prepared to carry it through to its logical conclusion.

Did Béarn have an adequate provision of properly trained Protestant clergy? There were about eighty 'gathered' churches in the principality. The total number of clergy represented at the general synod of the principality in Pau in 1571, arranged in six *colloques* was seventy-nine.[83] In 1578–9 there were seventy-one ministers in post and several pulpits vacant, perhaps temporarily.[84] By 1598 there were only fifty-nine in post and shortly after that Henri IV announced that he would only fund the salaries of sixty ministers from the revenues of the state. (See figure 1) There was, therefore, a more or less permanent shortage of well-trained ministers. In the 1560s and 1570s, considerable efforts were invested in attracting pastors from outside the principality, from Paris, La Rochelle, Bordeaux and, of course, Geneva.[85] A pastor was despatched to the Cévennes and the French national synod at Nîmes, for example, in 1572 to tempt ministers to Béarn.[86] The problem was far from being limited to the principality and their success in attracting good quality pastors to the Pyrenees was partly a consequence of its comparative security and tranquillity. Although the synods were disposed to lament that the vocation of pastor was unreward-

[82] Meylan, 'Texte inédit', 213.

[83] René Mieybegué, 'Note sur le protestantisme dans les Pyrénées Atlantiques' (unpublished typescript in *AD Pyrénées Atlantiques* 1J 1364); this is based on the payments to ministers made from the ecclesiastical council and recorded in B 2368 fols 310–19.

[84] *ADPA* B 2368 (payments to ministers in the year 1 October 1578–30 September 1579).

[85] In 1564, only twenty-six ministers attending the synod were able to swear to the discipline and loyalty to the *pays*. A further nine did so with the reservation that they were not natives of the principality and three refused to take the oath at all, presumably because they felt it conflicted with loyalties already entered into in the kingdom of France or elsewhere. (*Bib. prot*. MS 433[4] fol. 43).

[86] *Bib. prot*. MS 433[4] fol. 145v (October 1571); he returned with five ministers – MS 432 p. 23 (5 March 1572 – costs of journey, 150 *livres* and the hire of a horse) p. 28 (26 June 1572).

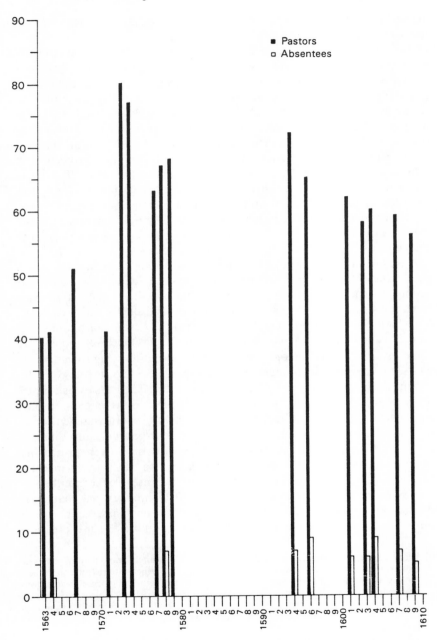

1 Pastors at the synods of Béarn, 1560–1620
Source: Bibliothèque de la Société du protestantisme français Ms 433[4]

ing and unattractive, the impression one has is that Béarn's pastorate was regularly and, in comparison with their coreligionists in France, well paid, with a range of fringe benefits. Even in the 1580s, there were still notables like Bernard Casenove from a small Béarn community writing to Beza in the enthusiastic 'langue de Canaan' to attract a pastor to their local church.[87] The decline in numbers of pastors was partly the result of restrictions on the use of the ecclesiastical revenues. Already in 1572, in the wake of the French massacres, the lieutenant-général of the principality temporarily suspended the operations of Bernard de Montaut, the first *diacre général*, because the revenue was needed for military protection.[88] This was exceptional in the 1570s but more common in the 1590s. But it was also a failure to recruit adequately for the next generation. As the synod recorded in 1601: 'D'autant qu'il y a plusieurs Eglises au pays qui sont totalement despourveus de pasteurs & qu'il n'y a grande esperance d'avoir moyen de les pourvoir de long temps a Cause que la plus part des enfants presentez par lEglise [*au College*] sont encore de bas age'.

A loss of up to a quarter of the ministerial strength was an important weakening of the Calvinist Reformation in Béarn. It would have been more serious still had the principality not enjoyed the benefit of a distinctive order (separate from those of pastor, elder, deacon and doctor) of 'catechist'. Viret, following St Augustine, had advocated the benefits of establishing what he called 'catechumaines' in Béarn. In the 1560s, there were hopes that some former *curés* of the old church might consent to being catechists. It was seen as a role which might be fulfilled by students of theology at the college during vacation or by local schoolmasters. Their task was simple. They were to 'proposent les principaux pointz de la religion le plus simplement, clairement, familièrement que possible sera, sans entrer es questions ...'. They 'ont charge d'en trouver pour pourvoir aux Villages' and, along with the local deacons were the individuals who were principally involved in visiting the poor and the sick and saying prayers in rural locations. This was particularly important because of the number of 'annexed' rural churches in the principality. The difficulty was that some deacons and catechists, 'en faisant les prieres vouloyent passer les bornes & limites de leur charge en se meslant de faire de paraphrases sur le pseaume

---

[87] Bernard Casenove – Beza, Chastillon, 29 June 1584; 'Ce seroit un grand dommage si ceste ouvre assez heureusement commence par la grace de Dieu demeuroit sans estre continuee, car il y a esperance que ceste eglise qui est encore bien petite saugmente. Nous avons beaucoup de gens de principaulx qui sont bien instruictz, mais ilz sont si plein de chair quilz ne peuvent suivre Jesus Christ a descouvert. Il est vray quilz se pourront ranger pourveu que lannonciation de la parolle continue tousiours en ce lieu ...'. Cited from Bib. de Genève Lettres etc (Carton II) in *Bib. prote.* MS 548[1] p. 122.

[88] *Bib. prot.* MS 432 fol. 31 (30 September 1572) 'il étoit necessaire de prendre les deniers ecclésiastiques pour les employer suivant la nécessité urgente'.

qu'on auroit chanté'.[89] There were indissoluble problems, too, with annexed churches in the Calvinist ecclesiology. How were elders to be chosen, and how was the consistory to function, when it was supposed to reflect several distinctive communities?

The establishment of the royal college, later academy and university, of Orthez was perhaps the most important single institution of Calvinist Béarn. Founded by Jeanne d'Albret in 1566 in the substantial premises of the former Dominican convent there, it provided facilities second only to Geneva, upon whose academy its structure was modelled, in the French-speaking Protestant world before 1600.[90] An investigation of 1578–9 presented a glowing picture of its development.[91] By then it had a teaching staff of fifteen, including a rector to the Academy, a principal of the college and funded chairs in Hebrew, Greek, Philosophy and Theology.[92] Over 200 pensions were also funded.[93] Up to half of these were reserved for *protégés* of the *bénéficiers*, often lay abbots, and the rest were often occupied by the sons of Protestant ministers themselves. Here was a powerful stimulus to the self-perpetuating nature of the Béarn pastorate. By the time of the Revocation, a third of Béarn's ministers were themselves the sons of a minister in the province.[94] Among its first professors was Pierre Viret, part of whose library found its way to the Academy after his death, thus giving it one of the finest collections of theological texts in the south of France in the sixteenth century. Lambert Daneau was one of his successors and it was from there that he composed or completed several important works.[95]

One of Lambert Daneau's main concerns was with the question of superstition. Drawing on the writings of Tertullian and Augustine he attempted to delineate the boundary between right religion on the one hand and the variety of heresy, superstition and paganism on the other. In his

[89] *Bib. prot.* MS 433⁴ fol. 218.
[90] For the academy at Orthez, see M-M. Compère and D. Julia, *Les Collèges français, 16e–18e siècles* (Paris, 1984) pp. 511–13 and bibliography.
[91] In 1566–9 there were only a dozen or so boarders 'sinon depuis quelque nombre qui a été appelé par l'entretiennement procédant des deniers ecclésiastiques, combien qu'à Orthez il y en eut jusques à soixante et plus, tant des gentilshommes de Bayonne, Dax, St Saint-Sever, Agenois, de toute la Chalosse, de Béarn et basques que d'autres de moindre étoffe' (*ibid.*, p. 512).
[92] J. Lourde-Rocheblave, 'Les Anciennes Académies protestantes. Académie protestante d'Orthez (1566–1620)', *BSHPF*, 3 (1855), 280–92 and A. Planté, 'Documents pour servir à l'histoire de l'université protestante du Béarn' *Bull de la soc. des sciences, lettres et arts de Pau*, 2nd ser., 14 (1884–5), 186–333.
[93] See, e.g. the 'Escoliers pentionnaires sur les benefices de Bearn' listed in ADPA B 2368; 210 scholarships were available that year.
[94] Calculated from information in A. Sarrabère, 'Catalogue des ministres protestant béarnais à l'époque de la révocation de l'édit de Nantes', in *Revue de Pau et de Béarn*, 17 (1990) 59–78.
[95] C. Desplat, 'Lambert Daneau, l'Académie d'Orthez et les superstitions', in *Henri de Navarre et le royaume de France 1572–1589* (Pau, 1984) pp. 195–219.

Elenchi haereticorum, according to Olivier Fatio, he attempted to provide a universal science, a dialectic, which would identify and isolate all heresies, all superstitions, all satanism wherever and whenever they appeared.[96] Daneau provides us with a fascinating example of the intellectual presumptions of an intelligent Calvinist of his day. Society needs to be rationally ordered in a godly manner. This can only be done by a faithful and clear-thinking elite, for the people are corruptible and fickle. Amongst the people, the young and the female are particularly susceptible to being misled. They must be educated and corrected if necessary. Otherwise they will, like children, be naughty. Superstition is naughtiness and, whilst sometimes seemingly innocent, it contained within it, like all naughtiness, the seeds of sedition and subversion. One superstition would lead to another and to the abyss of sinfulness. The danger was ever-present and the battle would be never-ending. 'Tel est le désordre es Eglises réformées de ce Royaume' he reminded his audience with a reference which would have been taken to mean the invasion of 1568–9 in Béarn '[que le] danger d'un autre déluge est à craindre.' His treatise against dancing provides the intellectual case for the clause against dancing in the *Ecclesiastical Ordinances* which in turn refers back to an ordinance as early as 1565 which had also tried to outlaw the *plantats* (maypoles) and other carnival occasions, typical cultural manifestations of Pyrenean village life.[97] His other treatises on witchcraft and dicing are also, in a way, commentaries on clauses in the *Ordinances*. Yet the evidence from the seventeenth and eighteenth centuries suggests that neither the Protestant nor the Catholic Reformations were able to eliminate the *plantats* (maypoles), the *ségue* or nuptial rite or the *aurost* (formal keening over the dead in funeral ceremonies). And both religions had to adapt to local traditions and circumstance. Valley rivalries and suspicion of upland communities affected the implantation of Protestantism. In the Ossau, Protestantism found a fragile foothold; and from the syndic of the Aspe valley, comes a request as late as 1593 to be allowed to worship according to the old rite.[98] When the pastor Jean Touya was invited to serve in the Aspe valley in 1567, he refused, saying 'qu'il avait Entendu que cestoit un pays barbare & par ainsy n'iroit point'.[99]

Behind the enforcement of the *Ecclesiastical Ordinances* lay the 'honorable men' (*egregy mossen*) of the Sovereign Council. They held on to the Protestant ascendancy with a magisterial determination. When Henri de Navarre attempted rather half-heartedly to reintroduce a measure of

---

[96] Olivier Fatio, *L. Daneau et les débuts de la scolastique réformée* (Geneva, 1976) p. 44.

[97] Clause 74, *Ecclesiastical Ordinances. Ordonnance d'Antoine de Gramont* (10 November 1565); C. Desplat, 'Réforme et culture populaire en Béarn du XVIe siècle au XVIIIe siècle', *Histoire, économie et société*, 3 (1984) 183–202.

[98] A. Cadier, *Osse; histoire de l'eglise réformée de la vallée d'Aspe* (Pau and Paris, 1892).

[99] *Bib. prot.* MS 433⁴ fol. 110v. He was required to apologise before the National Synod.

Catholic toleration in the province during his period of enforced Catholic attendance at the French court from 1572–1576, the council (bolstered by the mythology created from the events of 1569–70) energetically defended the status quo.[100] In cooperation with the regent for Henri de Navarre, Catherine de Bourbon and some Protestant barons from the estates, the council did its best to exploit the perceived threats from France and Spain and to cement the Protestant hold on the principality.[101] At times of greatest danger, fast-days were ordered throughout the principality. *Jurats* were required to swear to uphold and abide by the Protestant faith. In the moments of crisis in the early 1590s they succeeded in raising sizeable amounts of revenue from the estates, despite their protests, sold more ecclesiastical property and protected the principality from the invasion planned by League supporters in France. But it would have been surprising had there been total unanimity of interests between the Calvinist establishment and the state and, in reality, there were significant differences of emphasis. The synod wanted more assistance to enforce the *Ecclesiastical Ordinances*, even to the extent of suggesting that the lieutenant general of the principality should ask to receive a report every two months from his *procureurs* on the degree to which it was being enforced through the jurisdiction.[102] The *jurats* jostled with members of the consistory over privileged seats in church, organised town meetings on Sundays and failed to enforce the ordinances against swearing, gaming and usury.

The real difficulties for the council of state, however, began when Henri de Navarre became king of France and converted back to Catholicism. The first demand of the papacy in return for his absolution was the readmittance of Catholicism in Béarn. Henri accepted the condition in 1595 and enacted it in the edict of Fontainebleau of April 1599.[103] The edict of Fontainebleau was like the edict of Nantes only the roles were reversed. The Catholics were the ones in Béarn to be granted a limited number (twelve) of guaranteed places of worship. Their clergy were given sums of money from the royal treasury whilst Protestant pastors continued to be maintained on the tithes and wealth of the Catholic church.

The Protestant councillors of state in Pau behaved very much like the Catholic *parlementaires* in France in trying to ensure that its clauses were put into practice only with the greatest of difficulty. They published the ordinance on 17 August 1599 but only accepted one of the clauses in its entirety, that which authorised the Catholic religion in thirteen specified

[100] See, for example, the letter from Bernard d'Arros, lieutenant-general of the principality to Henri de Navarre, 5 February 1573, printed in *BSHPF*, 77 (1928) 398–400.
[101] R. Ritter, *La Soeur d'Henri IV. Catherine de Bourbon* (2 vols., Paris, 1985).
[102] *Bib. prot.* MS 433⁴ fol. 174.
[103] C. Desplat, 'Edit de Fontainebleau du 15 avril 1599 en faveur des catholiques du Béarn', in *Réformes et révocation en Béarn* (Pau, 1986), pp. 223–46.

and small villages of the principality. This was followed by detailed remonstrances to Henri IV on 25 October 1599 although this did not prevent the king from forcing the registration of the original version of the edict through the council.

For the succeeding twenty years the Sovereign Council fought to preserve as many Protestant privileges as possible and identified that cause with its own authority and the province's privileges. In 1603, the two new bishops of Oloron and Lescar petitioned successfully for the right of Catholics to vet judges of the Sovereign Council. After stalling, the council eventually agreed to accept the two new bishops as *ex officio* members of the Sovereign Council too, although they did not initially exercise that right. The clause permitting the Catholic church to repurchase ecclesiastical estates, providing full compensation to the current owners, was particularly contentious. The Sovereign Council advised the king in 1599 that 'so many families of both religions had an interest in this repurchase that it could only provoke universal hatred towards the bishops and trouble and confusion in your state'. In reality, very little repurchase was undertaken by the Catholic church before 1617 and, if there was a Catholic revival in the principality before 1620, it was largely spontaneous since the bishops were without revenues to undertake any large-scale initiatives. They had to be subsidised even to attend the meetings of the Assembly of Clergy in France.

There was, however, a semi-autonomous revival of Catholicism in the years between 1599 and 1620. The few surviving Catholic baptismal registers of this period provide evidence for a patchy and non-institutional revival. The Catholic baptismal registers from Jurançon are one such example. Jurançon was a community on the *coteaux* just across the Gave from Pau. Its Protestant church was an annexe to Pau, and preachers came to it on a fortnightly basis. Its church had recently been burnt to the ground and needed rebuilding. It was here that Catholic baptisms from numerous communities in the Gave valley were recorded in a fashion which suggests that a Catholic parochial structure was not in place before 1620. The Catholic population was, however, not an insignificant minority. The baptisms for Pau suggest a community of some 500 or so inhabitants or 5–10 per cent of its population.

The remonstrances from the Sovereign Council in Pau to Louis XIII in the 1610s read like the complaints from a vulnerable elite. They were written by politicians in a province which prided itself on the mutuality of interest between governor and governed which the Reformation had, in a fundamental way, broken. When Louis XIII entered the church of St Martin in Pau in October 1620, sixty years after Jeanne d'Albret had proclaimed her Protestantism there, it was a signal both of the end of the Béarn Reformation experiment and of the independence of the principality

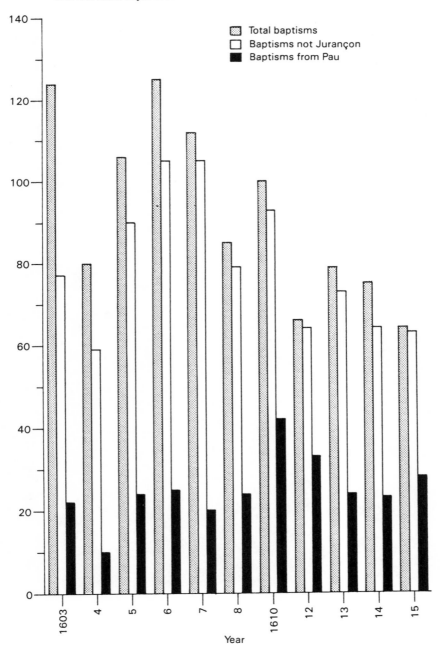

2 Catholic baptisms at Jurancon, 1603–1615
Source: Archives Communales Jurançon Series GG

of Béarn.[104] The decline in the Protestant congregations after 1620 would be dramatic.[105] By the 1660s there was little that was distinctive in the fidelity of Béarn's Protestants in comparison with their French coreligionists. Such was the 'striking failure of Béarn's magisterial Reformation to create an enduring Protestant community'.[106]

[104] C. Desplat, 'Louis XIII and the Union of Béarn to France', in Greengrass, *Conquest and Coalescence*, ch. 4.
[105] P. Benedict, 'The Huguenot Population of France, 1600–1685: The Demographic Fate and Customs of a Religious Minority', *Transactions of the American Philosophical Society*, 81 (1991), 71–5.
[106] *Ibid.*, p.74.

8   The changing face of Calvinism in Antwerp, 1550–1585

Guido Marnef

Not without some pride, the Calvinist minister, Jeronimus Bastingius, at the beginning of 1580 in a letter to the Italian theologian, Girolamo Zanchi, called the Calvinist church in Antwerp *celeberrima totius Europae Ecclesiae*.[1] A few years later, an English observer showed how impressed he was by the support for the Calvinist church when he declared 'that there are more persons professing the Reformed religion in Antwerp than in all Holland and Zeeland'.[2] The period of the Calvinist Republic (1577–85) indeed constituted an indisputable high point for the Calvinist church in metropolitan Antwerp. Already by about the middle of the sixteenth century a well-organised congregation had developed in Antwerp, which, however, had to face bitter persecution. Only the *annus mirabilis* or Wonderyear (April 1566–April 1567) provided a brief respite in the repression. It is just this alternation between religious persecution (1550–66 and 1567–77) and religious freedom (1566–7 and 1577–85) that makes Antwerp an interesting test-case for the study of the development of Calvinism. The capacity for adaptation, and the strength and weakness of a religion which profoundly agitated urban society, are thrown into so much sharper relief by reason of the markedly changing circumstances.[3]

Around the middle of the century Protestantism in Antwerp entered a new phase. Before 1550 it was a broad, somewhat eclectic evangelical movement which encompassed various reforming influences. At the same time, it was characteristic that – at least on the non-Anabaptist side – there was so far no mention of the formation of congregations in the strict sense. The new teaching was professed by individuals and small informal groups

---

[1] Letter of 18 January 1580 in *Operum theologicorum D. Hieronymi Zanchii* (8 vols., np, 1613), VIII, p. 409.

[2] Fremyn to Francis Walsingham, 24 February 1584, in *Calendar of State Papers. Foreign Series, July 1583–July 1584*, ed. S.C. Lomas (London, 1914), p. 354.

[3] For a detailed study of the events of the Reformation during the period of religious persecution in Antwerp, see Guido Marnef, 'Antwerpen in Reformatietijd. Ondergronds Protestantisme in een internationale handelsmetropool, 1550–1577 (2 vols., Louvain University Ph.D. thesis, 1991), to be published in English by Johns Hopkins University Press.

who saw no need to make a break with the Roman Catholic church.[4] Not till 1554–55 was a full-blown counter-church formed in Antwerp when a clandestine French and Dutch-speaking Reformed congregation was set up.

On 16 October 1551 the tapestry-weaver Jan van Ostende was tried in Antwerp. Van Ostende was acting as the minister of a group of believers. From his contacts with the Dutch refugee church in London, with Martin Micronius amongst others, and from his understanding of the Lord's Supper, it seems that he must be placed in the context of Reformed Protestantism.[5] Jan van Ostende's work was certainly not ineffectual. An Antwerp Lutheran complained of the growth of *secta haec sacramentariorum* and asked that orthodox Lutherans such as Joachim Westphal and Matthias Flacius Illyricus should write against the works of Micronius and van Ostende.[6] There is, however, no evidence to show that van Ostende was in charge of an organised Reformed congregation. After the martyrdom of van Ostende, the shoemaker Gaspar van der Heyden became the minister of the Antwerp Reformed. Apparently a structured church society came into being during 1555, for on 17 December that year van der Heyden wrote to the consistory of Emden 'that we have begun in Christ the Lord through the Holy Spirit to gather a small tender bride or congregation'. At the same time he had drawn up ordinances which laid down amongst other things that members of the congregation should meet together each Sunday. He had also found it advisable 'to require from each a confession of his faith so that consciences may be strengthened, all false teaching refuted and excluded and the Scriptures searched'. Gaspar van der Heyden clearly took his stand on a very strict attitude and wished everyone to be excluded 'who yet sometimes partake of the Roman abominations and superstitions',[7] an exclusivism that is certainly reminiscent of Calvin.

Alongside the Dutch-speaking congregation, a French-speaking or Walloon Reformed congregation also came into being in the fifties. A decisive move was made in that respect about 1554, when Jacques de Lo preached for some time, and at the end of 1553 and beginning of 1554 the ministers Juan Morillo and François Perussel stayed a while in the city before going on to Wesel.[8] The importance of the Walloon church of

---

[4] See Alastair Duke, 'Nonconformity among the *Kleyne Luyden* in the Low Countries before the Revolt', in his *Reformation and Revolt in the Low Countries* (London, 1990), pp. 101–24.

[5] Adriaen van Haemstede, *Historie der Martelaren* (Dordrecht, 1659), fols. 139v–140v; *Antwerpsch Archievenblad*, VIII, 392–405.

[6] *Briefsammlung des Hamburgischen Superintendenten Joachim Westphal aus den Jahren 1530 bis 1575*, ed. C.H.W. Sillem (2 vols., Hamburg, 1903), II, pp. 127–8.

[7] The letter is in *Calvinism in Europe 1540–1610. A collection of documents*, ed. Alastair Duke, Gillian Lewis and Andrew Pettegree (Manchester, 1992), pp. 133–6.

[8] Philippe Denis, *Les Eglises d'étrangers en Pays Rhénans (1538–1564)* (Paris, 1984), pp. 181–9. For Jacques de Lo, see Marnef, Antwerpen in Reformatietijd, II, p. 82, no. 32. For

Antwerp can also be seen from the substantial part it played in the re-establishment of the French-language church in Wesel, also in 1554.[9] The first permanent minister of the Walloon congregation of Antwerp was Evrard Erail, who was sent to that city from Geneva at the request of the Antwerp church.[10]

From the beginning, the French church of Antwerp was linked up with an international network. Close ties were constantly maintained with the French churches of Wesel and Frankfurt, and the Antwerp brethren acted as mediators when disputes or problems arose in these refugee communities.[11] A special relationship was also enjoyed with the French-speaking refugee church in Emden, established in 1554.[12] Genevan influence was not limited to the minister Erail only, as Calvin himself also expressed his concern for the lot of the Antwerp brethren.[13] After Queen Elizabeth's accession to the throne of England, both the French and the Dutch church of Antwerp had many contacts with the strangers' churches set up in London in 1559. From the very first years of its existence, the Dutch church maintained especially useful contacts with the church in Emden, which functioned as a kind of mother-church for the Antwerp brethren.[14] The widening international network was built up by the displacements brought about by persecution. Moreover, contacts were facilitated by the position occupied by Antwerp as a centre of international trade. Letters between Reformers in Switzerland, the German Empire, and England often reached their destination via Antwerp. Various ministers or theologians travelled to different parts in England or the Continent by way of the city, in which they often spent a short while.[15]

The young Calvinist communities which had to organise themselves clandestinely did not find life in Antwerp easy. Apart from the ministers, leadership resided in the hands of elders and deacons who were respectively

Morillo, see A.G. Kinder, 'A hitherto unknown group of Protestants in sixteenth-century Aragon', *Cuadernos de Historia de Jerónimo Zurita*, 51–2 (1985), 131–60. Perussel was a minister of the French church in London (1550–3), Wesel (1554–7), and Frankfurt (1557–61). The Spaniard Morillo was later in 1554 minister in Wesel, then in Frankfurt.

[9] Denis, *Eglises d'étrangers*, p. 189, note 2.

[10] *RCP*, II, p. 74. Erail served the Antwerp congregation till perhaps the end of 1559.

[11] Denis, *Eglises d'étrangers*, passim, and especially pp. 608–9. See also letter of François Perussel to Pierre de Val, Antwerp, 29 September 1554, in A.A. Van Schelven, *De Nederduitsche vluchtelingenkerken der XVIe eeuw in Engeland en Duitschland in hunne beteekenis voor de Reformatie in de Nederlanden* (The Hague, 1909), pp. 422–30.

[12] See letter of the French church of Antwerp to the French church of Emden, 13 February 1556, in Amsterdam, Gemeentearchief, *Archief Waalse gemeente*, 150, and the French church to that of Antwerp, undated [1556], in CO, XVI, col. 243–5.

[13] Calvin to the French church of Antwerp, 21 December 1556, in *ibid.*, col. 336–9.

[14] Andrew Pettegree, *Emden and the Dutch Revolt. Exile and Development of Reformed Protestantism* (Oxford, 1992), pp. 57–86.

[15] Many examples in *Original Letters relative to the English Reformation: chiefly from the archives of Zürich*, ed. H. Robinson (3 vols., Cambridge, 1846–8).

responsible for upholding church discipline and the support of the poor and the sick. In addition, repression had prompted the creation of a supplementary office, that of *weetdoener*. These *weetdoeners* – a kind of messenger – had to inform the members of the congregation where the church meetings would take place. At the same time, the difficult circumstances made it necessary to organise congregational life in a decentralised manner, in small groups. In 1558 the Dutch church was made up of sixteen or eighteen sections, each consisting of eight to twelve people. For preaching services two or three sections joined together.[16] The interrogation of the minister Jan Cornelissen in 1571 reveals that the city was divided into four districts, each with four elders, deacons and *weetdoeners*.[17]

The repression imposed a high mobility amongst the ministers. For the period 1550–66, it has been possible to identify twenty-nine persons who exercised their ministry in Antwerp.[18] The vast majority of them, seventeen in fact, were active for less than one year in Antwerp. They belonged to the large number of itinerant preachers who shuttled repeatedly between the congregations under the cross in the Southern Netherlands and the refugee centres abroad. Only seven ministers found steady employment in the city for more than two years. It was possible to trace the previous occupational activity of twenty-two ministers. Former priests, ten in number, were by far the strongest category represented. The situation in Antwerp thus confirms a pattern that was typical for Lutherans and Calvinists of the first generation.[19] Besides these, there were three schoolmasters, one lawyer, two merchants and six craftsmen. We have information about the level of education of fifteen of the Antwerp ministers. This shows that an academic education is much more characteristic of ministers connected with the French church than amongst their colleagues in the Dutch congregation. The Academy of Geneva very rapidly produced fruit for Antwerp Calvinism.[20] Six ministers of the Walloon church had benefited from an education there, while the older Academy of Lausanne appears in three cases, of which two are in combination with Geneva. Nine French-speaking ministers had received an academic education, against only three on the Dutch-speaking side. The need to set up their own training institutions was

---

[16] Dutch church of Antwerp to the consistory of Emden, 17 February 1558, in *Brieven uit onderscheidene Kerkelijke Archieven* (*WMV*, III–2), ed. H.Q. Jansen and J.J. Van Toorenbergen (Utrecht, 1878), p. 77.   [17] Van Haemstede, *Historie*, fol. 467v°.

[18] The following analysis is taken from the prosopographical material in Marnef, *Antwerpen*, II, 75–87. Jan van Ostende was also included in the data.

[19] Compare E.M. Braekman, 'Theological training of reformed ministers of the Low Countries', in H. De Ridder-Symoens and J.M. Fletcher (eds.), *Academic relations between the Low Countries and the British Isles 1450–1700* (Ghent, 1989), pp. 68–70, and R.W. Scribner, 'Preachers and People in the German Towns', in his *Popular Culture and Popular Movements in Reformation German* (London, 1987), pp. 123–43.

[20] Compare P. Mack Crew, *Calvinist Preaching and Iconoclasm in the Netherlands, 1544–1569* (Cambridge, 1978), pp. 86–7, 104–5.

clearly felt amongst the Dutch-speaking Calvinists of the first generation.

Before the Wonderyear at least sixty elders, deacons or *weetdoeners* were active in the Dutch or Walloon congregations.[21] The occupational activity of twenty-five of them can be traced, which demonstrates that merchants/ traders and people engaged in the textile sector were most strongly represented, with nine and twelve respectively. Twenty-five elders, deacons or *weetdoeners* were found to have been in a refugee church before or after their stint in Antwerp, most of them (eighteen) in London. The close contacts which existed between the churches of Antwerp and London, especially after 1559, were thereby further affirmed.

It has already been mentioned that from the start Gaspar van der Heyden understood the Calvinist church to be an exclusive gathering of believers who made a clean break with the Roman Catholic church and subjected themselves to strict rules. Van der Heyden and the Antwerp consistory made a distinction between the children of God and the children of the World, according to which the former category consisted of those who made confession of their faith and accepted ecclesiastical discipline.[22] In the eyes of the leaders of the Antwerp church ecclesiastical discipline certainly belonged to the *notae ecclesiae*.[23] When the minister Adriaen van Haemstede did not restrict himself to the narrow limits of the congregation, matters came to a serious dispute in the Dutch church. Van Haemstede, who served as second minister alongside van der Heyden, wished to address himself also to those members who from principle or for the sake of their social position did not yet desire to make a radical break with the Catholic church. On the other hand, the members of the consistory found it difficult to reconcile themselves with the open *salonpredikaties* – more informal services for the well-to-do – of van Haemstede which threatened the safety of their clandestine congregations.[24] The dispute with van Haemstede reveals one of the basic features of early Calvinism that had to tread a careful path in difficult circumstances, that is, the area of tension between the limited nucleus of church members and the wider circle of sympathisers who wished to have a less far-reaching commitment.

Calvin gave the sobriquet of Nicodemites to those who out of fear dared not take part wholeheartedly in the life of the church.[25] The powerful encouragement that he addressed to the brethren in Antwerp at the end of

---

[21] Prosopographical data in Marnef, *Antwerpen*, II, pp. 89–92, and passim.

[22] Consistory of the Dutch church of Antwerp to the consistory of Emden, 17 February 1558, in *Brieven uit onderscheidene Archieven*, p. 77.

[23] See also Alastair Duke, 'The Ambivalent Face of Calvinism in the Netherlands, 1561–1618', in his *Reformation and Revolt*, pp. 284–6.

[24] A detailed survey of the conflict in A.J. Jelsma, *Adriaan van Haemstede en zijn martelaars-boek* (The Hague, 1970), pp. 28–77.

[25] Carlos M.N. Eire, *War against the Idols. The Reformation of Worship from Erasmus to Calvin* (Cambridge, 1986), pp. 234–75.

1556 must be seen in this light.[26] Nicodemism remained however a constant factor in a community suffering under religious repression.[27] Even after the Wonderyear there were regular complaints in the Antwerp church about people who allowed their children to be baptised or who married 'in the papist fashion'.[28] In this respect it is significant that Calvin's well-known *Institutes* were not translated into Dutch before 1560, whilst his *Excuse à messieurs les Nicodemites* had already been printed in a Dutch version in 1554. From their beginnings in this year, the presses operated by Dutch refugees in Emden published a considerable number of anti-Nicodemite works, amongst which were translations of Calvin's treatises.[29]

The lack of reliable information makes it difficult to decide how many adherents early Calvinism in Antwerp could count. In interpreting the scanty figures, a distinction has to be made between church members in the strict sense and the wider circle of interested people who now and then came to hear sermons. Everything points to the fact that the number of members of the combined Dutch and French-speaking churches in the 1550s and early 1560s must be estimated at several hundred. Adriaen van Haemstede succeeded in increasing the Calvinist following considerably with the sermons he preached outside the congregation, especially when he preached openly at the end of 1558. At the beginning of December two clandestine sermons had attracted 200 and 400 hearers respectively. About 10 December a public meeting drew as many as 2,000 hearers.[30]

In spreading their beliefs, the Antwerp Calvinists did not restrict themselves to the narrow limits of their city. From the beginning Antwerp functioned as a mother church for small Reformed groups all over the Duchy of Brabant. The Antwerp congregation, moreover, developed into a church with a sort of supervisory capacity over a large part of Flanders, Holland and Zeeland.[31] The widespread network of commercial links possessed by Antwerp as an important centre of trade promoted to no small extent the central position of Antwerp Calvinism. Amongst other things, the city could thereby act as a central link between the refugee churches and their brethren who remained in the Low Countries. Additionally, the anonmity of a heavily populated metropolis of 100,000 inhabitants

[26] Letter of 21 December 1556, in *CO*, XVI, col. 336–9.
[27] Compare Barbara B. Diefendorf, *Beneath the Cross. Catholics and Huguenots in Sixteenth-Century Paris* (New York and Oxford, 1991), pp. 117, 121–3.
[28] Marnef, *Antwerpen*, I, pp. 290–2.
[29] Eire, *War against the Idols*, pp. 240–3, 273; Pettegree, *Emden*, pp. 66, 229–30, and Appendix, nos. 1, 2, 23, 63.
[30] W.G. Goeters, 'Dokumenten van Adriaan van Haemstede, waaronder eene gereformeerde geloofsbelijdenis van 1559', *NAK*, 5 (1908), 12, 60–1; report of Jan Gillis, City Pensionary of Antwerp, 13 December 1558, in Antwerp, Stadsarchief, *Privilegiekamer*, 478, No. 140.
[31] Marnef, *Antwerpen*, I, pp. 148–52; Johan Decavele, *De dageraad van de reformatie in Vlaanderen, 1520–1565* (2 vols., Brussels, 1975), passim.

provided an effective place of refuge for prosecuted coreligionists from other provinces and cities. It is no surprise that all but one of the synodal gatherings organised in the Low Countries before 1571 took place in Antwerp.[32]

In propagating their faith, the leaders of the Calvinist church had to take into account the competition from the Anabaptists, who could look back over a longer tradition in the Low Countries.[33] In Antwerp, where both religious movements had a strong presence, this confrontation found especially acute expression. The correspondence of certain Antwerp Lutherans reveals that at least some of the Lutherans who stayed in the city had orthodox Gnesio-Lutheran tendencies. Evidently the dispute with the Antwerp Calvinists in their very midst led to an increasingly definite confessional profile.[34]

Between 1550 and 1566 in Antwerp 302 Protestants were prosecuted, amongst whom were 196 Anabaptists (65 per cent), 86 Calvinists and 20 other 'heretics'. The fact that 117 of the 130 executions concerned Anabaptists, whereas proportionately more of the Calvinists were punished by banishment, indicates that the city authorities' target in the repression was Anabaptism. The prosecution of adherents of Calvinism was principally concentrated in the years between 1558 and 1564.[35] During the Wonderyear, however, the changed political situation provided the conditions for a rapid expansion of Calvinism.[36] A large number of exiles returned to Antwerp after the presentation of the Request (5 April 1566), in which the confederate lower nobility demanded the abolition of the Inquisition and the suspension of the placards against heresy. The 'hedge-preaching' organised by the Calvinists outside the city walls was increasingly successful. On 24 June a crowd of between 4,000 and 5,000 interested people gathered to hear a sermon, and the number leapt in the following month to between 20,000 and 25,000.[37]

That the open-air preaching of the Calvinists as well as that of the Lutherans was able to gain such a massive following within a relatively short space of time can only be explained by taking into account the complex and mobile character of the religious scene in sixteenth-century

---

[32] Gérard Moreau, 'Les Synodes des églises wallonnes des Pays-Bas en 1563', *NAK*, 47 (1965), 1–11.

[33] See Andrew Pettegree, 'The Struggle for an Orthodox Church: Calvinists and Anabaptists in East Friesland, 1554–1578', *Bulletin of the John Rylands University Library*, 70 (1988), 45–59.

[34] See letters in *Briefsammlung Westphal*, 2 vols., passim. On the Gnesiolutherans, see *TRE*, XIII, pp. 512–19.   [35] Marnef, *Antwerpen*, I, pp. 170–8.

[36] For the political situation, see Geoffrey Parker, *The Dutch Revolt* (Harmondsworth, 1990), pp. 68–99.

[37] R. Van Roosbroeck, *Het Wonderjaar te Antwerpen 1566–1567* (Antwerp, 1930), pp. 8–11, 16; F. Prims, *Het Wonderjaar (1566–1567)* (Antwerp, 1941), pp. 93, 99–109.

Antwerp. Between the adherents of an orthodox Catholicism, soon to be characterised by the Council of Trent, and the resolute followers of Luther, Calvin or the Radical Reformation there existed a wide, religiously heterogeneous middle group. Amongst these were to be found the 'protestantising Catholics', individuals who could no longer reconcile themselves with a number of doctrinal points or practices of the Catholic church, and could find points of contact in the Reformers' ideas, but had not – or not yet – let things go so far as making a break with the established church. The middle ground was also occupied by the hangers-on and the indifferent.[38] The Nicodemites were undoubtedly found on the interface between this middle group and organised Protestantism. A sudden shift in the political conditions could put pressure on those who belonged to this wide middle group to choose one of the two extremes, and that was exactly what happened in the Wonderyear. However, that does not mean in any sense that the thousands who attended the open-air preaching were suddenly and definitively converted into convinced Calvinists or Lutherans.

The Wonderyear brought fundamental changes for the Calvinist church of Antwerp at the organisational level. Emboldened by the political developments, in August 1566 the Calvinist leaders claimed the right to preach within the city walls. Members of consistories certainly had a hand in the 'iconoclastic fury' which was unleashed on Antwerp on 20 August. The destruction of images in churches and convents did not only have a religio-ideological aim,[39] at the same time it constituted an *acte de présence* by which the Calvinists wished to emphasise their real strength. Under pressure from William of Orange, who had been installed as superintendent of the city by the governor, Margaret of Parma, an agreement was reached which conceded three preaching places within the walls to the Calvinists and the Lutherans.[40] For the first time in the history of Antwerp their religion was recognised by the city authorities. In the course of the negotiations with Orange, within the fold of the Calvinist community a commission of eight deputies was set up which during the Wonderyear would look after the (mainly political) interests of the Calvinist church in relation to local, Dutch and foreign authorities. The consistory of the Dutch and Walloon congregation kept on functioning subsequently and concerned itself with the religious aspects of congregational life.[41] It is a

---

[38] J.J. Woltjer, 'De politieke betekenis van de Emdense synode', in D. Nauta *et al.*, *De synode van Emden, oktober 1571* (Kampen, 1971), pp. 22–49, and *Kleine oorzaken, grote gevolgen* (Leiden, 1975).

[39] See Eire, *War against the Idols*, p. 279: 'Iconoclasm was an inevitable outcome of reformed ideology'; David Freedberg, *Iconoclasts and their Motives* (Maarssen, 1985).

[40] The text of the agreement is in *Antwerpsch Archievenblad*, XI, 48–51, 56–8.

[41] This can be clearly seen in the extant correspondence of the commission and the consistories, given in Marnef, Antwerpen, I, p. 183, notes 29–30.

sign of Antwerp's great importance that often the commission of deputies acted on behalf of all the Reformed churches in the Low Countries.[42] Andrew Pettegree rightly stresses that during the Wonderyear the Calvinist church of Antwerp took over the leading role from the refugee churches.[43]

The socio-occupational recruitment of the Calvinist congregations was likewise drastically modified during the Wonderyear.[44] Of the 172 Antwerp Calvinists who were prosecuted after the Wonderyear for their part in the troubles we could identify an occupation in 103 cases. This indicates that we must place 54 per cent of those prosecuted in the merchant class, whilst the legal, medical, and teaching professions together made up 26 per cent. The relative overrepresentation of the commercial and the intellectual occupations means of course an underrepresentation of all other sectors. A study of the position regarding property reveals that 66 per cent of the 67 Calvinists that we were able to assess in this respect had property worth over 1,000 guilders, a situation that is in sharp contrast with that obtaining before 1566. The commission of deputies and the consistories were dominated by rich merchants and other people of consequence. In other cities, too, such as Bruges, Ghent, Valenciennes and Middelburg, merchants and well-placed citizens took their places in the consistories, whereas before it was particularly *gens de petite qualité* who had served in this capacity.[45]

An examination of the data shows that account must be taken of the fact that the civil authorities principally prosecuted those who had played a leading part in the Wonderyear. It goes without saying that prominent and well-situated people were strongly represented. Even though a marked selectivity lurks behind the repression, it is nevertheless true that a considerable advance took place in social recruiting by Antwerp Calvinism. Possibly a number of Calvinist leaders hoped to gain a seat on the city council or in the course of time to take over control of political power. The commission of Calvinist deputies functioned *de facto* as an alternative power circuit in the city. Yet we must not underestimate the religious

---

[42] See for example, the letter of the deputies to Augustus, elector of Saxony, 4 December 1566, signed as 'Antwerpiae Ecclesiae iuxta Evangelium Christi reformatae deputati et procuratores nomine et rogatu omnium Ecclesiarum Belgicarum', in Dresden, Staatsarchiv, Locat 9819, fol. 199.

[43] A. Pettegree, 'The Exile Churches during the *Wonderjaar*', in J. Van den Berg and P. Hoftijzer (eds.), *Church Change and Revolution. The Fourth Anglo-Dutch Church History Colloquium* (Leiden, 1991), pp. 80–99.

[44] Based on a thorough prosopographical investigation, of which the data is in Marnef, *Antwerpen*, II, pp. 149–294, and their interpretation in vol. I, pp. 184–99. See also Table 1 below.

[45] L. Vandamme, 'Calvinisme in het Brugse koopmansmilieu: het consistorielid Godefroot Slabbaert', in *Brugge in de Geuzentijd* (Bruges, 1982), pp. 123–34; L.A. Van Langeraad, *Guido de Bray. Zijn leven en zijn werken* (Zierikzee, 1884), pp. xliii–xliv; M. Delmotte, 'Het Calvinisme in de verschillende bevolkingslagen te Gent (1566–1567)', *Tijdschrift voor Geschiedenis*, 76 (1963), 145–76.

motives of those who committed themselves to the Calvinist religion. The risks of being a member of an underground church under the cross, forbidden by the authorities, had disappeared because of the great change in the circumstances of the time. Apparently, before this people had to a large extent hesitated to engage themselves fully in the Calvinist church because they were afraid of endangering their wealth and social position. It is surely no coincidence that before 1566 we do not encounter in consistories those people who during the Wonderyear functioned as Calvinist deputies or consistory members. Doubtless some of them had conformed outwardly with the official church and had made a pretence of having Catholic convictions. Many times in spies' dispatches to Margaret of Parma the conduct of dissembling Catholics was exposed. Substantial merchants who wished to make their commercial property secure were explicitly indicated in these reports.[46] Although Calvin never concealed his disdain for such Nicodemites, there is every sign that in time they represented a support for the Calvinist community that should not be underrated.[47] The merchants and established citizens who went over to the Calvinists in 1566 were not only of crucial importance for their financial support in building up the congregation. They also lent great power and prestige to Calvinism on account of the regard by which they were held in society.

In the spring of 1567 it was clear that the struggle for power which slackened during the Wonderyear developed to the disadvantage of the Calvinists and insurgents. The fall of Valenciennes to government troops on 23 March augured little good for the Antwerp Calvinists. On 9 April Lutherans and Calvinists held their last services in the city. Two days later William of Orange left the city, as did many Protestants. Under pressure from the duke of Alva, the new governor, and from the Council of Troubles set up by him, a severe repression was put in motion. In Antwerp 370 Calvinists were tried during the years 1567–76, of whom 22 were executed and 316 – most of them *in absentia* – banished.[48]

In spite of the fierce persecution, a well-organised Calvinist congregation continued to function in Antwerp. Between 1567 and 1577 at least twenty ministers were at work in the city. In addition to them we can identify forty-two elders, deacons and *weetdoeners*. Even at that time a fruitful exchange went on with the refugee churches. The important part played by the church of Antwerp in propagating the Reformed faith within the Low Countries

---

[46] For these reports, see Marnef, Antwerpen, I, p. 193, notes 71–2.

[47] A re-evaluation of the Nicodemites also in Andrew Pettegree, 'The Stranger Community in Marian London', *Proceedings of the Huguenot Society*, 24 (1987), 400–1.

[48] For a detailed analysis of the changed balance of power, the organisation of the repression and its results, see Marnef, Antwerpen, I, Ch. 8.

even before the Wonderyear was reduced during Alva's governorship because the severe repression had extinguished organised congregational life in most places. Yet it is significant that the first synodal gathering organised in the Low Countries after the Wonderyear again took place in Antwerp.[49] Moreover, the great trading centre of Antwerp continued to function as a point of contact between co religionists in the places of exile and in the Low Countries.[50] The exile churches proved indispensable to the Antwerp church under the cross: they served as places of refuge, as places of training and supply of ministers, and as sources of financial support.

The Calvinists, perhaps as many as several thousand, who left Antwerp following the end of the Wonderyear, formed in their turn a considerable reinforcement for the exiled churches. They found shelter above all in England, with a strong concentration in London, in the lower Rhineland, the Palatinate and Emden, and after 1572 also in the towns of Holland and Zeeland under the control of Orange.[51] On account of their commercial relations across Europe and their contacts with coreligionists in other countries and language areas, the fugitive merchants contributed greatly towards the formation of an international Calvinism. The same is true for students from Antwerp who spent time at Reformed universities and academies. When W. Brulez in a well-known contribution declared that the emigration of many Antwerp merchants, particularly after the fall of Antwerp in 1585, was a loss for that city but from a European perspective signified a great advance for commercial development,[52] the same was true also, *mutatis mutandis*, for the mass exodus of Calvinists.

The occupational situation of the Antwerp Calvinists of 1567–77 deserves a closer analysis. To provide a better understanding, we have brought together in Table 8.1 the data relating to prosecuted Calvinists from the years 1560–6, the Wonderyear and 1567–77.[53] We have added to them the data referring to the overall occupational situation in Antwerp in 1585.[54] These provide indeed an indispensable frame of reference if we are to reach valid interpretations.

[49] The decisions of this synod, held on 8 September 1570, in *Livre synodal contenant les articles résolus dans les Synodes des Eglises Wallonnes des Pays-Bas* (The Hague, 1896), pp. 13–14.

[50] See for example, Andrew Pettegree, *Foreign Protestant Communities in Sixteenth Century London* (Oxford, 1986), especially p. 223.

[51] For a survey of these, see Marnef, Antwerpen, I, pp. 304–24.

[52] W. Brulez, 'De diaspora der Antwerpse kooplui op het einde van de 16e eeuw', *Bijdragen voor de Geschiedenis der Nederlanden*, 15 (1960), 279–306.

[53] Based on the prosopographical details in Marnef, Antwerpen, II.

[54] The data on the global structure of occupations refer to approximately 10,000 adult men. See J. Van Roey, 'De sociale structuur en de godsdienstige gezindheid van de Antwerpse bevolking op de vooravond van de Reconciliatie met Farnèse' (17 augustus 1585) (Ghent University Ph.D. thesis, 1963, and 'De correlatie tussen het sociale-beroepsmilieu en de godsdienstkeuze te Antwerpen op het einde der XVIde eeuw', in *Bronnen voor de religieuze geschiedenis van België. Middeleeuwen en Moderne Tijden* (Louvain, 1968), pp. 239–57.

Table 8.1. *Occupational structure of Antwerp Calvinism, 1550–1577.*
Relative proportions

Number in sample	1550–66 68	Wonderyear 103	1567–77 99	1584–85 global
crafts	48.5	11.6	50.2	47.8
applied arts	16.1	2.9	9.0	3.6
professions	4.4	26.2	5.0	3.0
trade/transport	22.0	54.3	23.2	38.6
government/administration	1.4	0.9	—	3.1
church officials	7.3	—	8.0	0.3
military	—	0.9	—	0.8
others	—	2.9	4.0	1.2

These figures show that there are close agreements between the occupational situations in both periods of religious persecution. Craftsmen made up 48 to 50 per cent, which came very close to the occupational structure of the city as a whole. The trade and transport sector scored 23 per cent, approximately 15 per cent lower than was the case for the total. On the other hand, the applied arts and the professions were overrepresented. Within the broad category of crafts, the textile sector was significantly overrepresented and the more refined branches such as the silk industry and lace-making scored particularly highly.[55] No simple mono-causal scheme of explanation suffices to account for the relationship between occupational milieu and the choice of religious confession. The level of literacy, the industrial structure, and the concomitant level of mobility, certainly provided an explanation for specific occupational groups, but for others were of no use at all. In fact, different factors affected each one. Those who practised a more intellectually oriented occupation, who possessed a certain nobility of the spirit, and those who had trades which assumed specific skills and new techniques, displayed a greater openness to Reformed teaching. A strong territorial mobility and a weak integration into the traditional corporated framework promoted acquaintance with the Reformed message. In this respect, the situation in Antwerp offered similarities with that in French cities, such as Paris, Lyons and Rouen.[56]

An analysis of recruitment amongst the occupations reveals that Calvinism in Antwerp reached more or less every occupational group, although

[55] An analysis by occupational categories in Marnef, Antwerpen, I, 357–63.
[56] See Diefendorf, *Beneath the Cross*, pp. 108–10; Natalie Zemon Davis, 'Strikes and Salvation at Lyon', in her *Society and Culture in Early Modern France* (Cambridge, 1987), pp. 1–16; Philip Benedict, *Rouen during the Wars of Religion* (Cambridge, 1981), pp. 71–81.

not all to the same extent. The fact that amongst the Anabaptists the crafts were completely dominant – and particularly those trades which required simple manual work – also points to the likelihood that the occupation itself was exerting an important influence on the choice of a specific religion. Yet this does not really explain the underlying motives that prompted the choice. For that reason it is of interest to make a thorough investigation into the cultural life of the Calvinists prosecuted in Antwerp in 1567–77. In the small-scale gatherings organised in the clandestine church the central place was always taken by the reading and discussion of Holy Scripture. In the midst of the persecuted Calvinists there had developed a strong active and passive reading culture.[57] Consequently, the question arises as to whether a distinct cultural identity had developed amongst the Calvinists. Because of the lack of basic preliminary studies of the socio-cultural life of people in Antwerp as a whole, this question is difficult to answer. None the less, we have tried to explore the cultural background of the prosecuted Calvinists looking at the books and paintings they possessed and the Christian names they gave to their children.

Detailed research into the ownership of books seems impossible, because complete and systematic information about books was only provided exceptionally. Yet from the few book titles recorded, it seems that Bibles, New Testaments and books of Psalms were often found amongst book-owning Calvinists. This confirms Emden's pre-eminent position as a centre of printing.[58] We were able to chart the ownership of paintings of forty-eight Calvinists (13 per cent) tried in 1567–77. They possessed a total of 249 paintings of which the subject matter of 202 were reported.[59] Of all the paintings, 29 per cent had representations of subjects taken from the New Testament, and 19 per cent were from the Old Testament. We can deduce from this that the Calvinists' familiarity with the Bible was given a pictorial expression. Additionally, the names which parents gave to their children at birth can be a reflection of specific religious convictions. Because the baptismal registers of the Antwerp Calvinist church are not extant, we had recourse to the Christian names given by Antwerp Calvinists who were members of the strangers' churches in London. For the period 1567–77 we found the names of 168 children, 92 boys and 76 girls.[60] For the sake of comparison, we took a sample of the same size from the baptismal registers of the church of Our Lady in Antwerp.[61] This reveals that the practice of bestowing biblical names was much stronger amongst the Calvinists: 70 per

[57] Marnef, Antwerpen, I, especially pp. 112–4.   [58] Ibid., pp. 382–4.
[59] Based on the inventories of the confiscations conserved mainly in Brussels, Algemeen Rijksarchief, Rekenkamer. Acquiten, 2917, 2919, 2919bis, 3614, 3617, 3620.
[60] Based principally on Returns of Aliens Dwelling in the City and Suburbs of London, eds. R.E.G. Kirk and E.F. Kirk (4 vols., London, 1900–8).
[61] Antwerp, Stadsarchief, Parochieregisters, 6, fol. 155r°–157r° (January–March 1569).

cent of the boys and 64 per cent of the girls received biblical names as against respectively 36 and 37 per cent of the Catholics. The contrast lay particularly in the widespread use of Old Testament names amongst the Calvinists. Some of these names gave undoubted expression to well-known biblical patterns of expectation. The Antwerp Calvinists, who in their home town formed an oppressed minority, and abroad, in this case in London, lived in exile, possibly identified themselves with the ancient Hebrews who looked forward to their Promised Land.[62]

As a conclusion we can state that the ownership of books and pictures and the bestowal of names are certainly reliable indications of a particular consciousness. The Bible gave a specific expression to the religious and cultural life of the persecuted Calvinists. Such an assessment indicates that we ought not to underestimate the religious element in the process of choice, certainly not in those who were prepared to face the dangers that were inherent in life in a clandestine church.

The Pacification of Ghent which was concluded on 8 November 1576 laid down that the placards against heresy should be suspended in anticipation of the States General's taking a decision about the religious question. In January 1577 the last Protestants, six Anabaptists, were executed in Antwerp. In the years following the Pacification, Calvinism in Brabant and Flanders experienced a rapid expansion. In Antwerp and in other towns in Brabant the Calvinists gradually managed to take political control.[63] Official recognition of the Calvinist church was imposed by the religious peace settlement of 29 August 1578 which awarded four church buildings to the Antwerp Calvinists. After the promulgation of this settlement, Calvinism experienced a rapid growth, as is apparent in the correspondence of the ministers of the Dutch church. On 19 December 1578 Thomas Tilius announced:

As far as this congregation goes, by God's grace the hearers and members increase daily. 560 new members have been registered, of which many are rich people and the like. Yesterday the Lord's Supper was celebrated at St Andrew's and the Dominicans' Church. The total number of communicants was 1240.[64]

On 12 April 1579 Johannes Cubus declared that 'the church is increasing not only among the common people, but also among the prominent . . . so that we already have 12,000 hearers and more than 3000 incorporated members'.[65] A letter of the Antwerp consistory, dated 3 September 1579,

[62] A similar reflection in Benedict, *Rouen*, p. 106.

[63] Guido Marnef, 'Brabants calvinisme in opmars: de weg naar de calvinistische republieken te Antwerpen, Brussel en Mechelen, 1577–1580', *Bijdragen tot de Geschiedenis*, 70 (1987), 7–21.

[64] 'Briefwisseling van Thomas Tilius', ed. A.A. Van Schelven, *Bijdragen en mededeelingen van het Historisch Genootschap*, 55 (1934), 148–9.

[65] *Ecclesiae Londino-Batavae*, III–1, p. 551.

tells us that by then 4,000 members were attending the Lord's Supper. The number of those who came to hear the sermons could not be estimated. In any case, a much smaller number was attending the Lutheran sermons. According to this letter, the proportion of Calvinists to Lutherans was four to one.[66] This correspondence makes it clear that a systematic difference was made between the incorporated, officially registered members who were admitted to the Lord's Supper, and the wider circle of *toehoorders* or *liefhebbers* (sympathisers) who merely attended the sermons. It is noteworthy that the richer people only took the decisive step once the position of the Calvinist church was more or less consolidated. The classis of Brabant put the matter in a nutshell in a letter of 25 April 1579, stating 'that at the beginning mostly poor people came to the church, and the rich mainly afterwards when everything was in good order and security'.[67]

On 12 June 1579 a 'perpetual' religious peace was promulgated in Antwerp, which put still more church buildings at the disposal of the Calvinists. The latter were making capital out of the radicalisation of the Revolt in the Netherlands, as a result of which the Catholics came to be regarded to an increasing degree as supporters of Spain and consequently untrustworthy. On 1 July 1581 the public practice of the Catholic religion in Antwerp was forbidden. Henceforth only the Calvinists and Lutherans might organise themselves with the permission and support of the authorities. The city council had meanwhile fallen solidly into the hands of the Calvinists. The Calvinist ministers gave an exhortation at the annual renewal of the magistracy in which they reminded the aldermen of their Christian duties.[68] At this conjuncture the Calvinist community in Antwerp expanded to become a church which reflected the cosmopolitan character of the trading metropolis. Besides the Dutch and French-speaking congregations there was also an Italian congregation, to serve which in 1580 the city magistrate and some of the leading ministers tried in vain to attract the well-known theologian Girolamo Zanchi.[69] The congregation that was active in the English nation and was directed by sturdy English Puritans such as Walter Travers and Thomas Cartwright was closely identified with the Reformed tendency.[70] We can gain an idea of the numerical strength of the different religious movements in Antwerp at the end of the Calvinist Republic from the lists of the citizens' guard which were drawn up immediately after the capitulation of the city. In these lists the religious persuasions of the people concerned (10,788 adult men) were

---

[66] *Ibid.*, p. 561.   [67] *Ibid.*, III–1, pp. 552–3.

[68] *Antwerpsch Archievenblad*, V, 255–6; XVIII, 451–2; XXIV, 248–9.

[69] *Operum Zanchii*, VIII, passim. See also H. de Vries de Heekelingen, *Genève, pépinière du Calvinisme hollandais* (2 vols., Fribourg and The Hague, 1918–24), II, 305–10.

[70] S.J. Knox, *Walter Travers: Paragon of Elizabethan Puritanism* (London, 1962), pp. 42–53; A.F. Scott Pearson, *Thomas Cartwright and Elizabethan Puritanism 1535–1603* (Cambridge, 1925), pp. 180–7.

indicated;[71] 45 per cent were classified as Catholic, 26 per cent as Calvinist, 15 per cent as Lutheran, 2 per cent as Anabaptist, and for about 12 per cent there was no religion noted (unclassified or doubtful). If from these figures we extrapolate a total number of population of c. 82,000, then there were approximately 37,000 Catholics, 21,000 Calvinists, 12,000 Lutherans and 1600 Anabaptists.[72] After the fall of Antwerp on 17 August 1585 many Protestants left the city. Four years later, in 1589, the total number of inhabitants had fallen to 42,000, a reduction of nearly one half. Amongst the emigrants however there were also a number of Catholics who left Antwerp for economic reasons.[73]

The process of confessionalisation that occurred in Europe in the second half of the sixteenth century, did not by-pass Antwerp.[74] Around 1550 things got as far as fully developed alternative churches. The increasing tendency to set up distinct organisations went hand in hand with a stricter definition of doctrine. The lively rivalry that existed in Antwerp between Calvinists, Anabaptists and Lutherans sharpened this confessional differentiation. Not only did this growing confessionalisation differentiate the evangelical movement more strongly from the Roman Catholic church, it also drew more distinct boundaries and caused a growing rivalry within the broad Protestant family.

It is clear that the Calvinist movement was the best equipped to take up the cudgels with inimical authorities. Calvinism possessed a much greater versatility and dynamism than its Anabaptist and Lutheran competitors. To begin with, the Calvinist church had a very sound organisation at its disposal. Additionally, the Antwerp church occupied a central position in a network with international ramifications. Its contacts with the refugee churches were of essential importance for a community groaning under religious persecution. Calvinism was evidently an international movement with a solidarity that crossed national and regional boundaries. From the point of view of organisation the Lutherans were much weaker. Without the agreement of secular authorities they could not develop an organised church. Secret churches were strictly forbidden, and religious activities had to be restricted to the level of the family and private dwellings.[75] The Anabaptists it is true disposed of a good, small-scale congregational

---

[71] René Boumans, 'De getalsterkte van katholieken en protestanten te Antwerpen in 1585', *Belgisch Tijdschrift voor Filologie en Geschiedenis*, 30 (1952), 741–98.

[72] These figures must naturally be increased if we do not take into account the 12 per cent of unidentified men.

[73] Jan Van Roey, 'De bevolking', in *Antwerpen in de XVIde eeuw* (Antwerpen, 1975), pp. 95–108.

[74] See Heinz Schilling, 'Konfessionsbildung und Konfessionalisierung', *Geschichte in Wissenschaft und Unterricht*, 42 (1991), 447–63, with references to recent works.

[75] See 'F.J. Domela Nieuwenhuis (ed.), 'Bijdragen tot de geschiedenis der huijskercken', *Godgeleerde bijdragen*, 29 (1855), 401–18.

organisation, but these people who shunned the world put themselves on the margin of the urban community by their own teaching. A study of the topographical spread of the prosecuted Protestants reveals that this was quite literally the case.[76]

Moreover there was a dynamic element tied up in the recruitment of Calvinism. From the very beginning there was a tension between full members and more cautious people. When the political conditions altered, however, the same people contributed greatly to the strength of the Calvinist church. Developments during the Wonderyear and the Calvinist Republic indeed indicate unequivocally how Calvinism reached its indisputable zenith when it managed to identify itself with the political power. The political situation could however have a negative effect on the Calvinists' patterns of expectation as well. When a royal and papal Pardon was promulgated on 16 July 1570, at a moment when Alva and his Spanish troops had a tight grip on the city, no fewer than 14,128 persons were reconciled in Antwerp alone.[77] The way in which political conditions could have a real impact on religious mentality comes to the fore also in France, torn by religious wars. Explosions of Catholic violence and repression produced in that land a dampening of the spirits in Protestant ranks on a grand scale and induced many people to reconcile themselves with the Catholic church.[78] In Antwerp it was particularly the broad middle groups of church people who provided the massive shifts in the religious landscape. When the political conjuncture was favourable thousands were persuaded to go over to Calvinism. It is, however, important to recognise that there remained at such a time also a difference between the restricted circle of members and the wider group of sympathisers with a reduced commitment. In fact, in times of religious persecution as well as religious freedom the Calvinist church can be compared to a system of concentric circles in which the relationship to the ecclesiastical organisation became looser as the distance from the centre increased.[79]

---

[76] Marnef, Antwerpen, I, pp. 380–1.
[77] Brussels, Algemeen Rijksarchief, Papieren van Staat en Audiëntie, 271, fol. 257r°.
[78] Benedict, Rouen, 243–4; Denis Richet, 'Aspects socio-culturels des conflits religieux à Paris dans la seconde moitié du XVIe siècle', Annales E.S.C., 32 (1977), 776–7; David Rosenberg, 'Les Régistres paroissiaux et les incidences de la réaction à la Saint-Barthélemy à Amiens', Revue du Nord, 70 (1988), 501–10.
[79] Compare Duke, 'Ambivalent Face', 290–3.

9   Coming to terms with victory: the upbuilding of a Calvinist church in Holland, 1572–1590

Andrew Pettegree

It was characteristic of the new Reformed churches of the sixteenth century in France, The Netherlands and Scotland, that they first established their godly congregations in an extremely hostile environment. The first 'churches under the cross' were formed in the face of fierce persecution by the state, and at a severe cost in lives to the first generation of pioneers.[1] It has often been argued that Calvinism was, temperamentally and theologically, particularly well-suited to this condition of struggle and adversity. Calvin, in his letters to imprisoned friends and in his *Institutes*, urged with particular force the sanctity of suffering, and the necessity to witness to Christ through fortitude in tribulation. 'To suffer persecution for righteousness' sake is a singular comfort', he wrote in the *Institutes*, 'For it ought to occur to us how much honour God bestows on us in thus furnishing us with the special badge of his soldiery.'[2] In this context suffering becomes a vindication of faith.

How then must Calvinists react when the wheel of fortune turns in their favour? This question may legitimately be posed in considering the growth of Dutch Calvinist churches in the years after 1572, the period when Dutch Reformed churches first established their position in the emerging free Netherlandish state. In the space of a remarkably short time Calvinism in Holland was transformed from a proscribed sect to the dominant church, enjoying monopoly rights to open public worship. This was a situation of prosperity seldom equalled by, for instance, the numerically far more powerful French Huguenot churches.[3]

This was success, but of a very imperfect nature. For it was gradually borne in on the ministers labouring to establish their churches that the new

---

[1] Nicola Sutherland, *The Huguenot Struggle for Recognition* (New Haven, 1980). Alastair Duke, 'Building Heaven in Hell's Despite: The Early History of the Reformation in the Towns of the Low Countries', in his *Reformation and Revolt in the Low Countries* (London, 1990), pp. 71–100.

[2] John Calvin, *Institutes of the Christian Religion*, ed. John T. McNeill (Library of the Christian Classics, XIX–XX, 1960), I, 707.

[3] The solitary exception to this was Béarn, the domain of the kings of Navarre. See here Mark Greengrass, above, ch. 6.

freedoms would be hedged in by a variety of irksome restrictions. On a whole range of issues where the ministers had been used in their first churches (and particularly in the exile churches abroad) to the exercise of a largely unfettered responsibility, such as poor relief, the appointment of ministers, and controlling access to their own sacraments, the new situation and new responsibilities of the church in Holland called for difficult compromises, and brought sharp differences of opinion between ministers and town magistrates. In most cases the ministers were forced to give ground in order to maintain the support of the state power for their privileged position within the new state.

The whole process of building a church in the new free state thus required some painful psychological adjustments, which brought home to many a minister that there were disadvantages in exchanging the noble purity of exile for the opportunities and responsibilities of a new civic church. To a large extent it is possible to reconstruct this process of adaptation from the surviving records, the consistorial minutes, classical records and ministerial correspondence which for the Dutch church at least have been preserved in a generous profusion.[4] As the ministers' writings make clear, these were years of conflicting emotions, as their initial sense of triumph was increasingly tempered by an uneasy sense of opportunities lost and good intentions thwarted. Yet it is possible to see this experience, this coming to terms with the limitations of victory, as in many respects the formative experience of Dutch Calvinism. Certainly if we are seeking the key to understanding the individuality of Dutch Reformed tradition, and how it differed from the other European Calvinisms treated in this volume, then these initial years of church-forming in Holland take on a special importance.

In 1572, as the rebel forces under William of Orange established their fragile bridgehead in Holland, the contribution of Calvinists from the exile churches abroad was certainly crucial to the military effort. But the ministers extracted a heavy price for their cooperation. As each of the Holland towns went over to the rebels the ministers demanded and received the best and most prominent churches to re-establish their worship.[5] The ministers' correspondence with their friends abroad celebrated with wonderment and enthusiasm this transformation in their prospects. For the committed Calvinist these providential developments were a certain manifestation of God's gracious favour. 'The Lord works wonderfully', wrote the Enkhuizen church to London in June. 'We can never thank the Lord

---

4 For surveys of the available sources see *De Archieven van de Nederlandse Hervormde Kerk* (2 vols., Leiden, 1960–74); *Kerkelijke archieven. Gids voor kerkhistorisch Onderzoek. Deel 1*, ed. J.P. van Dooren and M.G. Spiertz (The Hague, 1982). A short introduction in English in *Calvinism in Europe. A Collection of Documents*, ed. Alastair Duke, Gillian Lewis and Andrew Pettegree (Manchester, 1992), pp. 5–6.

5 These events are described in my *Emden and the Dutch Revolt* (Oxford, 1992), pp. 194 ff.

sufficiently for opening so large a door to his Holy Word everywhere, and especially in Holland', reported the minister Gallinaceus from Delft in September. 'The Lord through his boundless mercy spreads out his light over our Fatherland more from day to day; the citizens of this town take such delight in the word of God'; this from Dordrecht in January 1573.[6]

In attributing victory to the Lord's goodness the ministerial letters largely ignore the fact that the Calvinist triumph was not achieved without considerable violence and the determined exercise of *force majeur*. In towns which had only reluctantly joined the Revolt, and which initially attempted to retain a certain balance between the competing faiths, the Reformed secured use of the best churches by a ruthless use of political power and, where necessary, a new wave of iconoclastic attacks.[7] The ministerial correspondence makes no mention of this, reporting simply that the churches had been cleared and worship begun. Nor do the letters reflect the fact that in striking out so hard for monopoly status the actions of the Calvinists cut across the preferred policy of William of Orange, who desired above all things to prevent the Revolt becoming a religious crusade. The letters of these years are in fact full of admiration for the political leadership of the Revolt, and especially Orange, their principal protector.[8] But then Orange gave the Calvinists good reason for satisfaction. Swiftly abandoning his hopes of a functioning religious peace within the rebelling towns, in the spring of 1573 Orange and the town magistracies bowed to Reformed demands for a ban on the mass. Later that same year Orange recognised the extent of his dependence on Calvinist help in the war effort by formally joining the congregation and taking communion at Delft. This milestone event was duly noted and celebrated in the ministerial correspondence.[9]

Reading through these letters from the first months and years of the Holland revolt, one is struck most of all by their confidence, and the expectation of continued good relations with the lay power. 'I see that we have a more godly government than ever France or Germany have had', wrote Jan van der Beke from Delft in February 1573.[10] The Reformed having swiftly secured the most prominent churches in the cities, now expected the continued cooperation of the magistrate in building their congregations. The first meetings of the classis of Dordrecht had no qualms about referring any point of difficulty in the establishment of their

---

[6] *Ecclesiae Londino-Batavae Archivum*, ed. J.H. Hessels (3 vols. in 4, Cambridge, 1889–97) (hereafter Hessels), III, nos. 201, 207, 220.

[7] As for instance at Delft, Leiden and Gouda. Pettegree, *Emden*, p. 197. C. C. Hibben, *Gouda in Revolt* (Utrecht, 1983), pp. 84–93. Cf. Wingius to London, December 1572, reporting the 'cleansing' of the churches of Delft and elsewhere: 'the people are for the most part longing for the true religion'. Hessels, III, no. 211.

[8] Hessels, III, nos. 213, 225: please pray for the Prince.

[9] Hessels, III, nos. 265, 270.   [10] Hessels, III, no. 226.

ministry to Orange: clearly they expected him to play a sympathetic and active role in their affairs.[11]

In return the ministers were themselves prepared to have some regard for magisterial sensibilities. On some matters where the town councils might expect to exercise authority, the church gave ground with an almost demonstrative properness. Thus an early meeting of the Dordrecht classis agreed that ministers were obliged to conduct marriages irrespective of whether the couple were members of their community, since marriage was 'a political matter', a formula repeated many times when the classis referred to the magistrates difficult cases relating to marital matters.[12] These were often matters in which the church would have acted themselves in the different circumstances of the exile churches or churches under the cross.[13] But, even with this degree of give and take, strains inevitably arose. The first and most pressing problem was that the demand for experienced ministers to lead the newly established churches greatly exceeded the numbers available. 'The harvest is great but the labourers few': this was a constant, almost monotonous refrain in appeals despatched to the exile churches to send over their best men.[14] But the churches abroad were soon swept bare, and it would take time before a new generation of ministers could be trained up. Those who accepted the call soon discovered that the ministry could not be sustained by faith alone. Practical problems such as accommodation and pay became pressing. In theory this should have presented no difficulties, since one of the first acts of the new regime in Holland had been to appropriate the goods of the former Catholic church, and this should have provided more than an ample income for the new ministers. But the town governments and the States had their own priorities, notably sustaining the war effort, and this skimmed off a large part of the available funds. Ministers even of the well-endowed town churches soon found the expected financial provision delayed and their pay badly in arrears, while often no funds were made available to establish ministerial posts in the surrounding towns and villages. There was no alternative but a wearisome series of direct appeals, first to the magistracy, and when this achieved little, to Orange. Even the establishment in 1574 of a common ministerial stipend, from 1577 administered in South Holland by a central institution, the *Geestelijk*

---

[11] *Classicale Acta, 1573–1620. Particuliere synode Zuid-Holland. I: Classis Dordrecht 1573–1600*, ed. J.P. van Dooren (The Hague, 1980), pp. 3, 5, 9, 22, 23, 31, 37 etc.

[12] *Classicale Acta*, ed. van Dooren, 7, 26, 52, 83. Cf. RV, I, p.4: decision of the synod of North Holland (August 1572) that it would be preferable if the churches 'could be relieved of these matters of weddings by political authority'.

[13] Such as marriage within the prohibited degrees, or potential cases of breach or promise. Sometimes the classis added as a rider a note of what their opinion *would* be if the authorities asked their advice! *Classicale Acta*, ed. van Dooren, 30.

[14] Hessels, II, no. 120; III, nos. 205, 206, 210.

Kantoor, did not end the problems.[15] Securing prompt payment of salaries and funding for new positions remained an enduring preoccupation of ministerial correspondence for many years to come.[16]

The problems over pay brought home to the ministers that they were not free agents: that the upbuilding of the church in Holland would inevitably depend on forging a successful relationship with the lay power. In the first years after the Revolt the ministers' letters reflect a generally optimistic view that this relationship would be a harmonious one. The ministers expected the cooperation of the magistrate in realising their goal of a thoroughly evangelised society. However, as the years went by, incidents proliferated which served to shake this early optimism, and give the ministers an altogether less sanguine view of magisterial priorities.

A first and enduring point of friction was the issue of authority over ministerial appointments. According to the first Dutch church orders drafted in exile, this should remain an exclusively church matter, under the authority of the church in question and the classis.[17] In practice, during the period 1572–4, the churches were happy to enlist the aid of sympathetic town councils in their attempts to secure the best qualified candidates for their new churches, so long as this did not compromise their theoretical control.[18] But what if the magistrates were less well disposed, and favoured a man unacceptable to the local congregation? The first notorious case of this sort occurred at Rotterdam in 1574.

Recent monograph surveys of a number of the towns of Holland have brought home with how little enthusiasm many of them joined the Revolt.[19] Although conservative towns like Gouda grudgingly admitted the rebel forces, they changed neither their governing class nor their essential outlook. Their policies over the next years were characterised by a grudging approach to Orange and the war effort and an absolute determination to prevent the new Reformed church disturbing the social fabric of the town.

---

[15] W. van Beuningen, *Het Geestlijk Kantoor van Delft* (Arnhem, 1870). The establishment of a common stipend did not prevent the better endowed churches from offering supplementary payments to attract the best men. Joke Spaans, *Haarlem na de Reformatie* (The Hague, 1989), p. 84. *Classicale Acta*, ed. van Dooren, 116–17. Cf. Rotterdam to London, January 1575: remember that our ministers are the best paid in Holland. Hessels, III, no 312.

[16] Van der Heyden to Cornelisz, August 1574, M.F. van Lennep, *Gaspar van der Heyden, 1530–1586* (Amsterdam, 1884), pp. 217–18. Polyander to Cornelisz, December 1574, Gemeentearchief Delft, 112, Collectie Cornelisz. Corput to Cornelisz, December 1578, September 1579. *Brieven*, ed. Toorenenbergen, *WMV*, 3, 2, 94–8, 111–12. The classis also lobbied for improvement of ministerial salaries, usually at the prompting of the less well-paid rural ministers. *Classicale Acta*, ed. van Dooren, 23, 31, 48, 109, 144, 145, 147, 156.

[17] *Acta van de Nederlandsche Synode der zestiende eeuw*, ed. F.L. Rutgers (*WMV*, 1, 4, 1889), 61–2 (Synod of Emden, 1571).   [18] Hessels, II, no. 119, III, no. 221.

[19] Most importantly Hibben, *Gouda*; Spaans, *Haarlem*; H. ten Boom, *De Reformatie in Rotterdam* (Amsterdam, 1987).

Rotterdam was in this respect similar to Gouda. Although Rotterdam joined the Revolt in 1572 this was essentially a pragmatic political decision, and the magistrates had no intention of allowing the ministers to exercise a controlling influence in the life of the city. The opportunity to underscore this determination came with the proposal to appoint Pieter Hyperphragmus to a second ministerial position in 1574.[20] Hyperphragmus was a maverick figure, undoubtedly committed to the Gospel, but a contentious and unorthodox thinker whose views had already caused considerable controversy during his time as an exile in Emden. Inevitably he was completely unacceptable to the orthodox Reformed, who reacted violently when the town council attempted to impose him. Faced with an apparent *fait accompli*, the consistory threatened an appeal to Orange, a manoeuvre which secured an adjournment during which the Reformed were able to gather evidence of Hyperphragmus's unsuitability. His nomination was then withdrawn, though the Council reinforced their claim to final authority by also dismissing the orthodox Calvinist minister, Hyperphragmus's chief opponent, Aegidius Johannes Frisius.[21]

It was a bruising encounter, and one with more general implications. For, as the consistory of Rotterdam emphasised in a letter to the church in Emden, if the Lords of Rotterdam, 'who have little love for the Gospel' were allowed to prevail, this could be a poison to all the Reformed churches in places in Holland where the authorities were not yet truly Godly.[22] And that might apply in quite a number of places. Rotterdam and Gouda have already been mentioned, but a similar political constellation was evident in Leiden, where in 1574 the magistrates appointed Caspar Coolhaes to a ministerial post without consultation with the church, a move which stored up considerable problems for the future.[23]

How would the Calvinist hierarchy react to a challenge of this sort? Certainly there were those in the ministerial body who favoured seeking a maximum of consensus, even if this meant accepting painful compromises. This line of argument was laid out with great clarity in a letter written towards the end of the Rotterdam dispute by Pieter de Bert, the man appointed to replace ministers Hyperphragmus and Frisius. In December 1574 de Bert wrote to explain to Arnold Cornelisz why evening prayers, condemned at the Provincial Synod of Dordrecht earlier that year, had in fact been introduced at Rotterdam. This was at the wish of the civil authorities, and de Bert preferred to accede in order to retain their friendship. 'We could indeed wish', he wrote, 'that the authorities would be

[20] On the Hyperphragmus affair see ten Boom, *Rotterdam*, pp. 158–65.
[21] *Ibid.*, p. 163.   [22] *Brieven*, ed. Toorenenbergen, *WMV*, 3, 2, 14–18.
[23] And see also the comment of the Enkhuizen church on the magistrates at Delft who 'have conducted themselves from the beginning as papists'. Hessels, III, no. 215.

satisfied with the ordinances of the church, but since they are Lords and we their subjects, we cannot prevent them showing their authority. We also believe that we should obey them in all things not against Christ's law, and not fall into their indignation over indifferent matters.' Such a conciliatory policy might ultimately bear fruit. 'We hope with our good will and friendship to move them so that they bend to the Gospel ... I hope that through our efforts a firm love will grow between the church and the authorities.'[24]

It was a coherent philosophy, but not apparently the majority view.[25] It was relatively easy for a man like Johannes Polyander, minister of the French church in Emden, to fulminate against the iniquities of the magistracy in Holland from the security of exile.[26] But the deliberations of successive provincial and national synods show that the leading ministers in Holland were every bit as reluctant to give ground. The first major synodal gathering after the establishment of the Holland churches, the provincial synod of Dordrecht in 1574, proposed no compromise over the matter of ministerial elections. This would remain an exclusively church matter, under the supervision of the consistory and classis.[27] Meeting at the height of the Hyperphragmus controversy this determination is not surprising, nor that it should be unacceptable to the town authorities. The Church Order drafted by the States of Holland in 1576, on the initiative of the Prince of Orange, thus proposed an entirely different relationship. Here it was suggested that the ministers should be chosen by the magistrates of the towns in question, albeit with the advice of their ministers, and with provision for an examination by the church of their doctrinal suitability before they were confirmed in office. The States accompanied their proposal with a long justification of lay influence over appointments to church office, not scrupling to cite against the ministers the example of Geneva itself.[28] This was even less acceptable to the church leadership, who returned to the charge at the synod of Dordrecht in 1578. This gathering reaffirmed that the appointment of ministers should be an exclusively church affair, albeit with the faint concession that the 'Reformed civil

[24] L. Knappert, 'Stukken uit den stichtingstijd der Nederlandsche Hervormde Kerk, III', *NAK*, 7 (1910), 365–9. Evening prayers were also maintained in Haarlem. Spaans, *Haarlem*, p. 84; A.A. van Schelven, 'Briefwisseling van Thomas Tilius', *BMHG*, 55 (1934), 128. For the Dordrecht decision, *Acta*, ed. Rutgers, 141.
[25] Although de Bert's stand did find support among the more politically aware of the minsters. See Taffin to Cornelisz, January 1575. *Brieven*, ed. Toorenenbergen, *WMV*, 3, 5, 147–9.
[26] See the letter of Polyander to Cornelisz of 10 December 1574 in Gemeentearchief Delft, 112, Collectie Cornelisz.   [27] *Acta*, ed. Rutgers, 136.
[28] C. Hooijer, *Oude Kerkordeningen der Nederlandsche Hervormde Gemeenten (1563–1638)* (Zaltbommel, 1865), pp. 121, 126–31. Selections translated from these documents in *Calvinism in Europe Documents*, nos. 46–50.

authorities' should be permitted fourteen days to enter an objection to the man appointed.[29]

By this time a new *cause célèbre* had emerged to trouble the church. In 1578 the town council at Leiden refused to ratify the recent elections to the consistory, on the grounds that one of those nominated was unsuitable. Invited by both parties to clarify the situation, the minister Caspar Coolhaes produced an opinion which essentially supported the right of the lay power to exercise final authority in appointments to church office. This apostasy appalled the orthodox ministers. Swiftly repudiated by his consistory, Coolhaes was summoned to recant, but all attempts to end the rift failed. The degree to which this long running dispute dominates ministerial correspondence during the year which followed is testimony to its importance, and the dire consequences it was believed would follow for the church should Coolhaes' view prevail.[30] The town council at Leiden showed no wish to abandon their champion, to the evident frustration of the more intemperate ministers. Menso Alting, who from the security of Emden took every bit as hard a line as his colleague Polyander, thundered in a letter to Cornelisz in 1580 that 'the daily vomiting forth of poison by Caspar of Leiden wounds me to my very soul ... If the magistrate were not such an enemy to all religion he would never permit the man such freedom.'[31] This was a far cry from the genial and optimistic assessments of magisterial motives from a few years before.

A second striking feature of this letter from Menso is the hostility he shows towards the new Leiden Academy. The publication of a disapproved text by Jacob Brokard was to Menso sufficient proof 'that the Leiden Academy is constituted for spreading errors and hiding the truth rather than spreading it'. This scepticism was widely shared, a measure of the ministers' frustration at the calibre of teachers that had been appointed. In 1581 the Antwerp minister Pieter de Bert doubted whether the Academy was yet in a condition to be entrusted with the education of his son, preferring to send him to the newly established school at Ghent. Other leading Dutch Calvinists continued to look abroad for training, to Geneva and particularly Heidelberg, for much of the 1580s.[32]

The disagreements over ministerial elections smouldered on to 1581,

[29] *Acta*, ed. Rutgers, 235.
[30] See the numerous letters in the Cornelisz correspondence from van der Corput, Kuchlinus and Taffin published in *Brieven*, ed. Toorenbergen, *WMV*, 3, 2, and 3, 5.
[31] Alting to Cornelisz, 24 March 1580. Unpublished letter in Gemeentearchief Delft, 112, Collectie Cornelisz.
[32] De Bert to Cornelisz, 11 March 1581, Knappert, 'Stukken, III', 378–9. Cf. Kuchlinus to Cornelisz, 29 March 1580: there is every cause for concern regarding the school at Leiden; van der Corput to Cornelisz, 17 August 1586: the Academy at Heidelberg is now good; I expect no immediate improvement at Leiden. *Brieven*, ed. Toorenbergen, *WMV*, 3, 5, 248, 3, 2, 263.

when the Synod of Middelburg confronted the issue once again, and for good measure summoned Coolhaes to answer to his heretical views. The Leiden authorities were not prepared to give ground and stood by their man; it was, in any case, by this time clear that Coolhaes was not alone in his readiness to champion the rights of the civil authorities to play their part in the selection of ministers. In 1582 new controversies erupted over the Gouda minister Herbert Herbertsz, whom the town authorities were determined to sustain against the condemnation of the local classis.[33] The issue at the core of these controversies was never in fact wholly resolved. In 1583 the States of Holland proposed an apparently sensible compromise, whereby the appointment of ministers would be entrusted to a joint commission of burgomasters and church delegates. This was a system which in fact was successfully adopted in some towns, such as Dordrecht, where relations between town and church were good.[34] But the hardline towns opposed this on the grounds that it gave too much ground, and the synod too preferred to stick to the principle of autonomy, even if this was never fully reflected in practice. The draft Church Order of 1583 was therefore never instituted, and the procedures followed for ministerial elections continued to follow a wide diversity of practices.

One is, on the whole, inclined to marvel at the persistent militancy of the ministers on this question, given their dependence on the magistrates not only for their salaries and living, but also for cooperation in achieving their goals in a number of other areas they believed to be crucial to the creation of a godly society. Some of these, such as the regulation of schools, super-vision of poor relief, and the elimination of competition from rival religious groups, provided further potential points of conflict between the two. How these issues were resolved depended very much on the climate of relations in the various Holland cities. They could become the subject of apparently tension-free cooperation or, where the authorities were less well disposed, near constant guerrilla warfare.

This variety is immediately apparent when one considers the first of these issues, the regulation of schools. Given the importance that the Reformed attached to members of the church being able to make a coherent, informed profession of faith, it is no surprise that the ministers regarded it as a high priority to establish their influence over educational institutions in the towns and villages where churches were established. The first meeting of the

---

[33] Hibben, *Gouda*, pp. 120–30. On Herbertsz see J.P. de Bie and J. Loosjes (eds.), *Biographisch Woordenboek van Protestantsche Godgeleerden in Nederland* (5 vols., The Hague, 1907–43), III, 701–15. D. Nauta, A. de Groot, O.J. de Jong, S. van der Linde, G.H.M. Posthumus Meyjes (eds.), *Biografisch Lexicon voor de Geschiedenis van het Nederlandse Protestantisme* (3 vols., Kampen, 1978–88), III, 178–81.

[34] Hooijer, *Oude Kerkordeningen*, 232–3. John P. Elliott, 'Protestantisation in the Northern Netherlands, a case study: the classis of Dordrecht, 1572–1640' (Columbia University Ph.D. thesis, 1990), p. 196.

classis of Dordrecht conducted a general enquiry into the state of schools in the region, and it was a theme to which the ministers returned repeatedly over the following years.[35] The classical acta reveal two main priorities in this campaign: to ensure that all schools used the Heidelberg catechism as their main text,[36] and to secure ministerial control over the appointment and examination of schoolmasters.

A survey of the regulations enacted suggests that in this last goal in particular the churches enjoyed only indifferent success. In a town like Dordrecht, where the ministers could rely on close cooperation from the urban patriciate, the church succeeded in establishing a high degree of control. Having staked their claim to oversight over the appointment of schoolmasters almost as soon as the church was established,[37] by the time local regulations were codified into a new school ordinance in 1591 the ministers had achieved everything they could have wished. The ordinance laid down that the directors of the Latin school were to exercise oversight over primary education, and all potential schoolteachers were to submit to examination by the consistory. These regulations enabled the Dordrecht church to establish a closely knit cadre of well-motivated educators, in which refugees from the southern Netherlands were strongly represented.[38]

In other towns, however, the town council was more reluctant to cede to the church so important an aspect of municipal patronage. In Rotterdam the Latin school remained firmly under the control of the town authorities, and the Reformed consistory failed to establish any real influence over schoolmastering appointments. Establishing a primary school in Rotterdam remained essentially a matter of private enterprise.[39] In Haarlem too the town council granted permission to open schools to schoolmasters of all religious persuasions, ignoring the pleas of the consistory that they should exercise stricter supervision. Here also the Latin school remained firmly under municipal control, and the Reformed exercised no influence over appointments.[40]

Disputes over the control of poor relief provided further points of tension. This was an important issue, not least because of the interpretative weight placed on the manipulation of poor relief in historical debates regarding the 'protestantisation' of the northern Netherlands after 1572. The role institutions of social relief might play in this process was first highlighted in a landmark article by Pieter Geyl. By controlling access to poor relief funds, it was suggested, the Reformed church was able to exercise a particularly potent weapon in influencing the behaviour of the

---

[35] *Classicale Acta*, ed. van Dooren, 5, 21, 26, 31, etc.   [36] *Ibid.*, 21, 35, 44.
[37] See consistory minutes for 10 October 1974. *Uw Rijk Kome. Acta van de kerkeraad van de nederduitse gereformeerde gemeente te Dordrecht 1573–1579*, ed. T.W. Jensma (Dordrecht, 1981), 21.   [38] Elliott, 'Classis Dordrecht', pp. 424–6.
[39] Ten Boom, *Rotterdam*, pp. 195–6.   [40] Spaans, *Haarlem*, pp. 151–3.

poor, ultimately forcing them into membership of the church in return for support.[41] Certainly this had been a material consideration in the exile churches, where the church leadership exercised a wide measure of control over who received support. In the exile context this became a formidable inducement to indigent newcomers to submit themselves to the discipline.[42]

The ministers returning to Holland in 1572 might well have expected to continue to exercise wide responsibilites in this area. Most of the new Holland churches swiftly moved to elect deacons to administer their poor chests.[43] But there was a long step between this and a Reformed takeover of municipal institutions. The magistrates often had rather different priorities. For them, after all, the Reformation represented an opportunity to eliminate competing institutions of poor relief, for instance the guild and monastic foundation which, proliferating in the later Middle Ages, had often disposed of much more considerable resources than the municipal poor masters.[44] Having taken their chance to bring these under town control, the town magistracies were understandably reluctant to cede all influence to the Reformed diaconate.

These conflicting claims were, as with the schools, differently resolved, depending on the state of relations locally between church and state. In Dordrecht the town magistrates were quite content to allow the Reformed diaconate a leading role in the provision of municipal charity. The magistrates took appropriate steps to see that the deacons disposed of sufficient funds to fulfil these obligations, even providing occasional supplements from municipal taxation. In return the consistory made no attempt to limit its duty of care to full members of the church.[45] This was a compromise which could recommend itself also to towns such as Rotterdam, in other respects less well disposed to the creeping influence of the church in town affairs.[46] And it was a compromise with which the

---

[41] Pieter Geyl, 'De protestantisering van Noord-Nederland', in *Verzamelde Opstellen* (4 vols., Utrecht, 1978–88), I, 214 (first published 1930). Interestingly this argument is very similar to that employed by contemporary Catholic observers in explaining the success of the Reformed in recruiting among the poor in 1566.

[42] As I have argued in my study of London: A. Pettegree, *Foreign Protestant Communities in Sixteenth-Century London* (Oxford, 1986), ch. 7. In Emden the *Vreemdelingendiaconie* was one of a number of institutions of poor relief, but its considerable resources made it a powerful force. *Stukken betreffende de diaconie der vreemdelingen te Emden, 1560–1576*, ed. J.J. van Toorenenbergen (*WMV*, 1, 2, 1876). On the various Emden diaconates see Marion Weber, 'Emden – Kirche und Gesellschaft in einer Stadt der Frühneuzeit', *Jahrbuch der Gesellschaft für bildende Kunst und Vaterländische Altertümer zu Emden*, 68 (1988), 78–107, 69 (1989), 39–81.

[43] *Uw Rijk Kome*, ed. Jensma, 10. The provincial synod of Dordrecht determined that deacons would not generally be members of the consistory, clearing up a point of ambiguity from the first phase of churchbuilding in 1566. *Acta*, ed. Rutgers, 139.

[44] A point made by Elliott, 'Classis Dordrecht', pp. 354–6.

[45] *Ibid.*, pp. 358–65.   [46] Ten Boom, *Rotterdam*, pp. 193–4.

Reformed seemed reasonably happy. The provincial synod of Dordrecht of 1574 seemed to anticipate arrangements of this sort when it made specific provision for cases where the deacons would be allowed a role in the management of municipal charity, in which case the magistrates were to be permitted the final choice of deacons from a double list proposed by the church.[47] But this recommendation was not repeated in the decrees of the national synod of 1578, and it is clear the Reformed often faced a hard struggle to exercise the influence they sought, particularly in towns which like Haarlem preferred to adopt a strict separation between religious and municipal charity. Here church members were assisted by the deacons, and non-members by the municipal almoners. A small subsidy from town funds was little consolation for the church leadership, entirely excluded from influence over communal institutions for the poor.[48] A similar situation pertained in many of the smaller towns and villages where the local poor overseers, often called the Masters of the Holy Spirit, remained well entrenched.[49] In many places it was the middle of the seventeenth century before the Reformed exercised any measure of control over local charitable institutions.[50]

The control of poor relief and regulation of schools both represented areas of mixed competence, issues on which the church could legimately give some ground since both involved care for the whole community, rather than just their own membership. But it was a different matter when the state intruded into matters which the ministers regarded as entirely a church affair. While recognising that their obligation to the wider community extended to preaching, marriage, even baptism, ministers regarded control over access to communion, the central institution of the confessing community, as exclusively a matter for the church. Access to communion, and if necessary denial of the sacrament, was the core of church discipline, which the ministers regarded as the very sinews of the church. The first Dutch Reformed church order, the London order of 1550, had made discipline a third mark of the true church alongside preaching and the sacraments, and this example was followed in all subsequent church orders and synodical acts.[51] But it was possible for the magistrates to take a different view. A church enjoying all the privileges of a public church might be expected to make its sacraments generally available, and this was the view propounded by the Holland States in their draft church order of 1576,

[47] *Acta*, ed. Rutgers, 149–50.   [48] Spaans, *Haarlem*, pp. 172–89.
[49] See the two surveys of rural parishes undertaken by the classis of Dordrecht in 1582 and 1589. *Classicale Acta*, ed. van Dooren, 112–13, 265–9.
[50] See H. ten Boom, 'De Diaconie der Gereformeerde Kerk te Tiel vanaf 1578 tot 1795', *NAK*, 55 (1974–5), 32–69.
[51] Marten Micron, *De Christlicke Ordinancien der Nederlantscher Ghemeinten te Londen (1554)*, ed. W.F. Dankbaar (The Hague, 1956), pp. 37, 105 ff.

when they suggested that all resident adults should be able to take the sacrament at the four annual communion services: what would in effect be an open communion.[52]

This viewpoint was strenuously opposed by most persons of influence within the church, who manifested throughout a fierce determination to preserve the integrity of the church and to establish its full institutional framework. On the question of the communion service the synod of Dordrecht in 1578 gave no ground, reiterating the church view that the sacrament should be limited to persons who had made a profession of faith.[53] The church seems to have been reasonably successful in maintaining this position. Although some towns continued to hanker after an open communion – Rotterdam for instance, which recommended reviving the States formula of 1576 in its reaction to the synod of Middelburg in 1582[54] – there is no evidence that this laxer practice was ever introduced. The communion service continued to be the preserve of the professed members of the church.[55]

The churches were equally resolute in their defence of consistorial discipline. One of the first acts of the Dordrecht classis had been to survey the state of the churches in their area in order to establish whether a consistory had been elected. Although this revealed that some of the churches had not yet proceeded to an election, the ministers recorded their unanimous agreement that discipine, and hence a consistory, was a necessity in every church (indeed it was a *sine qua non* for holding of the Lord's Supper).[56] The correspondence between ministers reveals their acute sensitivity to any suggestion that the discipline might be under attack. Thus in May 1575 Jean Taffin reported to Arnold Cornelisz the alarming suggestion that the States of Holland were proposing to include in their draft Church Order a clause that would ban consistories altogether. Government of the church would instead be vested in the hands of four lay commissioners.[57] In the event Taffin was able to avert this danger by enlisting the support of the Prince of Orange, who was reluctant to see the balance tipped so far against the churches at this time. But the ministers were not able to relax their vigilance throughout the abortive negotiations over the Church Order, carefully marshalling their arguments against any who would propose a purely Erastian church settlement.[58]

[52] Hooijer, *Oude Kerkordeningen*, 129–30.
[53] *Acta*, ed. Rutgers, 250.   [54] Ten Boom, *Rotterdam*, pp. 175–6.
[55] Although it was usual for non-communicants to attend the services and leave after the sermons. H. Roodenburg, *Onder Censuur. De kerkelijke tucht in de gereformeerde gemeente van Amsterdam, 1578–1700* (Hilversum, 1990), p. 101.
[56] *Classicale Acta*, ed. van Dooren, 2, 4.
[57] Taffin to Cornelisz, 21 May 1575. *Brieven*, ed. Toorenenbergen, *WMV*, 3, 5, 155–6.
[58] See van der Heyden to Cornelisz, 8 July 1575: 'there are those who spread the views of Erastus so as better to oppose the discipline. Therefore I would be like to have the response of D. Beza, if you have a copy.' Van Lennep, *Van der Heyden*, p. 224.

A second potential crisis blew up in 1583, again at a time of negotiations around the church order. By this time, ominously, the ministers seemed to have lost the sympathy of Orange, visibly irritated by the constant quarrelling of the ministers and by the disastrous consequences of Calvinist radicalism for his policies of reconciliation in the south.[59] In April Taffin reported that the Prince seemed now to incline to their opponents on the matter of the Church Order.[60] In the event the court preachers were able to talk him round, with the result that the States' concept was once again shelved. No Church Order was adopted, and nowhere was the consistory actually banned. But its influence on the life of the community as a whole varied very considerably. In a town like Dordrecht, where the city magistracy supported the work of the consistory closely (indeed, many of the city elite served a term as elder or deacon), the church council became an influential institution, increasingly valued for the role it might play in reinforcing social stability.[61]

But the influence of the consistory was definitely limited by the fact that its authority extended only to communicant members of the church. Here there is a clear contrast between the Dutch experience and that of other Calvinistic societies such as Scotland or indeed Geneva. The size of the community varied from town to town, but it was never in these years more than a small fraction of the population: certainly a much smaller number than the wider group who gave the Reformed church their general support and attended their services, sometimes known as 'liefhebbers' or in other contemporary documents, 'toehoerders'.[62] This disparity between a small core membership and a broader band of sympathetic but less committed citizens presented the churches with another problem, since it made clear the ease with which citizens could participate in most of the church's activities, if not the communion, without undergoing the rigours of full membership. In these circumstances the church's final sanction, excommunication, was much less of a threat than in the exile churches abroad, where separation from the church implied exclusion also from its society and

[59] On events in Flanders see especially Johan Decavele, *Het Eind van een Rebelse Droom* (Ghent, 1984); T. Ruys, *Petrus Dathenus* (Utrecht, 1919). Cf. Tilius to Delft ministers, November 1578: 15,000 men have been alienated from the Gospel according to the Prince. Van Schelven, 'Briefwisseling van Thomas Tilius', 147–8. Even in 1577 Marnix was expressing his concern at the attitude of the Prince. See G. Brandt, *Historie der Reformatie en andere kerkelijke geschiedenissen* (4 vols., Amsterdam and Rotterdam, 1677–1704), I, pp. 586–90.

[60] Two letters of Taffin to Cornelisz, 7 March, 17 April 1583. *Brieven*, ed. Toorenenbergen, *WMV*, 3, 5, 208–11.   [61] Elliott, 'Classis Dordrecht', pp. 156–61.

[62] For estimates of the size of the congregations see information collected in Alastair Duke, 'The Ambivalent Face of Calvinism in the Low Countries', in Menna Prestwich (ed.), *International Calvinism, 1541–1715* (Oxford, 1985), p. 110. On the *liefhebbers* see A. Th. van Deursen, *Bavianen en slijkgeuzen* (Assen, 1974), pp. 128ff. The term 'toehoerders' comes from a letter of Thomas Tilius in Antwerp of December 1578. Van Schelven, 'Tilius', 148–8.

caring institutions. In the Holland towns, as we have seen, non-members generally enjoyed equal rights to social care when they fell on hard times, and might attend church quite freely. The solemn denunciations of sinners which they witnessed when they did so, as defaulting members were arraigned before the congregation, would hardly have been an incentive to commit themselves to the community. There is evidence that the ministers sensed this; certainly they exercised considerable restraint in the application of the discipline. Even in a town like Dordrecht, where the church was well-organised and entrenched, excommunication was used very sparingly, with only two cases being recorded in the church's first six years of operation. Over a longer period, 1578–1640, the Amsterdam church excommunicated an average of only one member every two years, almost exclusively in cases when members had left the church for another confessional group.[63]

Thus if most churches soon proceeded to the election of a consistory, and attempts to abolish the institution had been fought off, its effectiveness was strictly circumscribed. If the discipline was to be strictly limited to communicant members of the church, a self-selecting elite, how much influence could the church hope to exercise over the morals of the community as a whole? The ministers in their correspondence were not slow to voice their frustrations that the establishment of the Lord's true church had not brought any perceptible improvement in the way people conducted themselves in their daily lives. These frustrations were focused on two issues in particular: firstly, the widespread evidence of disorderly conduct, drunkenness and the like, particularly when this was in direct competition with their own services, on fast days and the sabbath. Secondly, the persistent and apparently growing competition from other sectarians groups, such as the Anabaptists. These issues were not in fact unconnected, since the Anabaptist congregations made some play of their greater rigour in behavioural matters, to the intense irritation of the Reformed ministers. Thus in 1575 the church at London reacted with stony disapproval to a request for advice from some members of the Antwerp church, who wished to enforce a more restrictive dress code. The suspicion that this rigour sprang from Anabaptist sympathies is clear in London's answer: we are surprised, they said, that these men wish to be so strict in this, when they are so lenient to Anabaptists.[64]

The various Anabaptist groups had won a considerable popular following in the Northern Netherlands as standard-bearers of dissent since the 1530s, and they remained well-entrenched after 1572. Although they enjoyed none of the privileges of the Reformed, they clearly flourished in the new climate of religious freedom. To the alarmed Calvinist ministers the

---

[63] *Uw Rijk Kome*, ed. Jensma; Roodenburg, *Onder Censuur*, pp. 148, 423.
[64] Hessels, II, 523–38 (nos. 142, 143).

sectaries appeared to be growing ever more numerous and truculent.[65] They flourished especially in the islands and remote country areas of Holland, such as Voorne, Putten and in Waterland, but there were also substantial communities in most of the major towns.[66] The ministers looked to the local authorities for help in restricting the freedom of action of these competing churches.[67] But here they faced a particular problem, for it was clear that on this issue they did not enjoy the support of the Prince. This was brought home to them very clearly by an incident in 1577, when the magistracy of Middelburg, who on this issue shared the prejudices of the ministers, took punitive action against Anabaptists who had refused an oath demanded of all inhabitants. The Mennonites appealed directly to Orange, who then wrote to the Council asking that they be released from the oath: he had no wish to alienate a group who had contributed greatly to the struggle against Spain.[68] Both van der Heyden, the local minister, and Taffin, the Court preacher, were appalled, and enlisted the support of Marnix van St Aldegonde to change Orange's mind. But on this occasion he was not to be moved: Taffin and Marnix therefore found themselves obliged to appeal over Orange's head to the States of Holland in an attempt to neutralise the effect of Orange's concession, a curious reversal of their usual practice and expectations.[69]

Generally, however, the ministers met with little sympathy from the town councils, who had no more interest than Orange in restricting Mennonite freedoms. The ministers were ultimately forced back on their own resources: the ministerial correspondence and synodical minutes record their constant concern to keep up the pressure by polemicising against Anabaptist beliefs.[70] Over the longer term these efforts bore fruit. Helped no doubt by their privileged position in society, their control of the pulpit and the greater social respectability attached to the Reformed church, by

[65] See for instance Regius to Cornelisz, 20 October 1573; van der Heyden to Cornelisz, 22 August 1575. Knappert, 'Stukken', *NAK*, 7 (1910), 19–20, van Lennep, *Van der Heyden*, 217–18. Classis Dordrecht, March 1578: the sects increase daily. *Classicale Acta*, ed. van Dooren, 51. Cf. *Acta*, ed. Rutgers, 196.

[66] Ten Boom, *Rotterdam*, p. 181. Spaans, *Haarlem*, pp. 97–101. R.B. Evenhuis, *Ook dat was Amsterdam* (4 vols., Amsterdam, 1965–7), II, pp. 209–13. N. van der Zijpp, *Geschiedenis der doopsgezinde in Nederland* (Arnhem, 1952).   [67] *Acta*, ed. Rutgers, 213.

[68] Orange's letter is printed in J.P. Scholte, 'Bijdrage tot de kennis van de Godsdienstige verdraagzaamheid van Prins Willem I', *NAK*, 4 (1907), 46–8. F. Nagtglas, 'De Kerkeraad der Nederduitsche Hervormde Gemeente te Middelburg, tegenover de Doopsgezinden', *Bijdragen tot de Oudheidkunde en Geschiedenis, inzonderheid van Zeeuwsch-Vlaanderen*, 6 (1863), 237–61.

[69] Taffin to Cornelisz, two letters of March 1577. *Brieven*, ed. Toorenenbergen, *WMV*, 3, 5, 182–5. Marnix to van der Heyden, March 1577. *Oeuvres de Ph. de Marnix. Correspondance et Mélanges*, ed. A. Lacroix (Paris, 1860), pp. 226–33.

[70] *Acta*, ed., Rutgers, 160–1, 269, 432. F.S. Knipscheer, 'De Nederlandsche Gereformeerde Synoden tegenover der Doopgezinden (1563–1620)', *Doopsgezinde Bijdragen*, 50 (1910), 1–40, 51 (1911), 17–49. For cooperation over polemical works see the letters of Gaspar van

the mid-seventeenth century the challenge from the sects had much receded; Anabaptism had become a passive and much diminished force.[71] But this would have been little consolation to the first generation of ministers, struggling against an apparently omnipresent threat to their hopes of building a pure church.

The same sense of unremitting and apparently hopeless toil may be seen in the ministers' comments on their attempts to improve the moral climate in their towns and villages. This was important work, for it was clear to the ministers that the creation of a godly society demanded some general improvement in the moral climate in which the churches' members led their lives; for Calvinists (as distinct from the sectarian groups) it was impossible to conceive of a pure church within a hopelessly immoral society.[72] The difficulties of this situation were brought forcibly home by a significant conversation between the Dordrecht minister van der Corput and one of the local burgomasters, van der Mijle. Van der Corput had approached van der Mijle in the hope that the local authorities would support their campaign for new moral legislation, only to be told that the remedy lay in their own hands: they should do their duty in punishing and exercising discipline. But as van der Corput rightly insisted, the discipline could only be applied to communicants, the 'smallest group'; wider remedies lay outside their powers.[73]

The churches therefore looked to the civil power for help in combating licentiousness and abuse of the sabbath.[74] These problems appeared particularly acute in the rural areas, where the Reformed generally found it more difficult to assert their authority in the face of stubborn resistance from a rural population wedded to their traditional way of life. These difficulties are tellingly evoked in a series of letters to Cornelisz from his friend, the minister Winandus Beeck. Beeck was from 1582 minister in the two communities of Zoetermeer and Zegwaard, from where he directed a steady stream of lamentation and complaint to his colleague in Delft. In the villages, according to Beeck, days of fasting were ignored, drunkenness endemic and Sundays held in total contempt.[75]

der Heyden concerning his own pamphlet, *On the Covenant against the Anabaptists*, and Regius's thoughtful remarks on the need for these works to be written at a popular level. Van Lennep, *Van der Heyden*, pp. 226–31, Knappert, 'Stukken', 40–1. The two best known disputations with the Anabaptists were those at Frankenthal in 1571 and Emden in 1578, but in fact the Reformed promoted these debates almost continuously: six times in Amsterdam between 1586 and 1597. Roodenburg, *Onder Censuur*, p. 171.

[71] Roodenburg, *Onder Censuur*, p. 166.
[72] T.H.L. Parker, *Calvin's Preaching* (Edinburgh, 1992).
[73] Van der Corput to Cornelisz, 10 December 1578. *Brieven*, ed. Toorenbergen, *WMV*, 3, 2, 94–7.
[74] *Classicale Acta*, ed. van Dooren, 40, 47, 51, 59 etc. *Acta*, ed. Rutgers, 144, 213.
[75] L. Knappert, 'Stukken uit den stichtingstijd der Nederlandsche Hervormde Kerk: II. Eene plattelandsgemeente anno 1582', *NAK*, 7 (1910), 246–61. On Beeck see *Nieuw Nederlandsch biografisch woordenboeck*, III, 76.

Beeck was by no means a weak or inadequate man. In 1585 he served a turn as minister to the church which continued in secret in Antwerp after the city's capitulation to Parma, an exceptionally dangerous and demanding post.[76] But he seems simply to have been overwhelmed by the sheer godlessness of country life. His outbursts of frustration were directed particularly at the local officials who should have supported his efforts, but instead were obstructive, often demonstratively so: even to the point of inciting parishioners to misbehaviour during the sermons. This was a common complaint in the villages, where many figures of authority remained decidedly hostile to the new church. In consequence congregations remained small and the old Catholic customs were openly maintained.[77]

In the cities problems of this nature were less acute. The magistrates, for all that they might resent ministerial pretensions, could generally see that their interests coincided over most aspects of moral regulation, particularly in the larger cities with their migratory populations and growing numbers of poor. The ministers and the magistrates were at one over the need to combat drunkenness and illicit sex. In 1580 the States of Holland acceded to ministerial pressure for a new political ordinance to establish firmer controls over marital relations and illicit sexuality. Three years later the States of Zeeland instituted a far more comprehensive moral ordinance, along lines anticipated by the synod of Middelburg in 1581.[78] But the magistrates' compliance did not extend to humouring the ministers in their desire to eliminate all competition to the Sunday sermon, or in their hostility to most sorts of popular sociability. Thus although the ministers continued to fulminate from the pulpit against gaming, dancing and fairs – the ubiquitous *kermis* – they generally did so in vain.

This was never more the case than in the ministers' efforts to limit two forms of sociability dear to the urban middle classes, dancing and the theatre. Hostility to dancing was not universal among the Reformed, but seems to have increased as the sixteenth century wore on. The Amsterdam consistory dealt with a steady flow of cases, reaching a peak early in the seventeenth century. But the fact that the consistory used a rather gentler procedure that usual – visiting members in their homes to express displeasure privately – suggests some understanding of the fact that here they

[76] Knappert, 'Stukken, II', 256–8. Beeck also served as one of the classis Delft's two nominated moderators of a dispute in the Dordrecht church, so he was clearly a man of some reputation. *Classicale Acta*, ed. van Dooren, 180.

[77] Knappert, 'Stukken, II', 259–60. Even in the comparatively model classis of Dordrecht, a rural minister had to be relieved of his preaching obligations on the grounds that his church was deserted, and that his parishioners abused him as he walked through the streets. *Classicale Acta*, ed. van Dooren, 174.

[78] *Groot Placaet-Boeck*, I, 330–42, 349–60. P. Scherft, 'De generale synode van Middelburg en de Zeeuwse Statenordonnanties van 8 februari 1583', in J.P. van Dooren (ed.), *De Nationale Synode te Middelburg in 1581* (Middelburg, 1981), pp. 140–3.

were dealing with a class of offender not so easily bullied into submission.[79]

The church faced a similarly uphill struggle in its campaign against the theatre. Plays and dramatic festivals were an important part of Netherlandish culture; indeed, in the first half of the century the productions of the Chambers of Rhetoric, the *Rederijkerkamers*, had proved an effective means of disseminating unorthodox ideas. This notwithstanding, the Reformed in Holland had little time for theatricals. The idea that they could lead the unlettered away from popery was denounced by Taffin in 1575 as a mere pretext: they served only for profit and ostentation on the part of the players, time-wasting and voluptuousness for the audience.[80] This austere view generally prevailed. The national synods of 1578 and 1581 both denounced theatricals and called upon the city councils to take action.[81]

The magistrates, however, were not easy to persuade. As before the hardest struggle was with the recalcitrant Leiden council, who refused to disband their Chamber of Rhetoric in the face of strong synodical pressure. In attempting to persuade Leiden the synod advanced the bold claim that other towns such as Dordrecht and Delft had fallen into line, but this may have been over-optimistic. The city fathers in Dordrecht did withdraw financial support from their theatricals, but plays continued to be performed.[82] And the Rotterdam chamber, *De blauwe acoleyten*, appeared regularly at *rederijker* festivals, carrying off prizes at Delft in 1581, and at the major Leiden festival of 1596.[83] In Amsterdam lobbying against the theatre continued throughout the seventeenth century, with equal lack of success.[84]

The fact that the ministers made so little progress on this issue is not perhaps surprising, since the magistrates were here defending the favoured recreations of their own social class. But in fact town councils were little more accommodating with respect to the ministers' assaults on what might be called popular amusement culture. Notwithstanding frequent protests from synods, and from the classis, there is no sign that even in Dordrecht any magistrate or state official did anything to enforce Sunday observance in the period before 1590; abuse of the sabbath remained a running sore until well into the seventeenth century.[85] Perhaps here the magistrates were

---

[79] Roodenburg, *Onder Censuur*, pp. 321–9. The Dutch passion for dancing is evocatively treated in A. Th. van Deursen, *Plain Lives in a Golden Age* (Cambridge, 1991), pp. 85–7.
[80] Taffin to Cornelisz, April 1575. *Brieven*, ed. Toorenenbergen, 153–5. J. Wille, 'De Gereformeerden en het Toneel tot omstreeks 1620', *Christendom en Historie. Lustrumbundel* (Kampen, 1931), pp. 96–169.   [81] *Acta*, ed. Rutgers, 269–70, 449.
[82] RV, II, 456. Wille, 'Toneel', 152.   [83] Ten Boom, *Rotterdam*, pp. 196–8.
[84] Roodenburg, *Onder Censuur*, pp. 336–8. For an indication of the enduring popularity of *rederijker* drama, and its influence on Dutch art, see A. Heppner, 'The Popular Theatre of the Rederijkers in the Work of Jan Steen and his Contemporaries', *Journal of the Warburg and Courtauld Institutes*, 3 (1939–40), 22–48.
[85] *Acta*, ed. Rutgers, 144. *Classicale Acta*, ed. van Dooren, 40, 47, 51, 59 etc. English travellers in the Netherlands frequently remarked on the paradox of the disorderly Dutch Sunday.

wiser than the ministers realised, since by refusing to endorse the austere standards demanded they at least protected the ministers from the popular backlash that might have followed too radical an assault on popular sociability.[86] The magistrates might reasonably have judged that by sweeping away almost all of the old church year, to be replaced by the unchanging routine of the sermon service, the Reformed had already introduced sufficiently fundamental, and disconcerting, changes into the life of the community.[87]

But the ministers could hardly have been expected to have appreciated this at the time, and the frustrations they felt at the magistrates' lack of cooperation frequently boiled over in their letters. Thus in 1579, from the comfortable security of Emden, Jean Polyander fulminated against the use of organs in church, which despite the disapproval of the majority of the Reformed the synod of Dordrecht had asked might be retained for a time, presumably as a concession to the lay power.[88] 'I really marvel', thundered Polyander, 'that when other idols were removed, this noisy idol was retained.' But the protest was in vain, for the synod of Middelburg merely reiterated the formula of three years previously, with the pious hope of rapid improvement.[89]

Disagreements of this sort were probably no more than a simple manifestation of the fact that the ministers were not as much in control of their own destiny as they might have wished. It would be wrong, of course, to imply that the issues discussed here were the ministers' constant concern in these years. The vagaries of the political situation, and the ebb and flow of the war, provided other pressing preoccupations, not least when the change of fortunes of the Revolt in 1576–8 brought a new opportunity to revive Calvinist churches in the southern provinces. The ministers in Holland responded with a new burst of celebratory rhetoric, and concerted efforts to provide ministers sufficent to man the new churches.[90] Then came the reverses of the early 1580s, the loss of the South, and a new refugee

---

Thus Fynes Moryson noted in 1593 that the churches were 'seldom full, for very many Sectaryes, and more marchants proeffering gayne to the dutyes of Religion, seldom came to Church, so as in Leyden a populous Citty, I often observed at tymes of divine service, much more people to be in the markett place than in the Church'. Cf. Marvin A. Breslow, *A Mirror of England. English Puritan Views of Foreign Nations, 1618–1640* (Cambridge, MA, 1970), pp. 92–3.

[86] A point made by Elliott, 'Classis Dordrecht', pp. 487–8.

[87] The first synods of the Dutch church decided to retain only Easter, Whitsun and Christmas of the old Catholic festivals: later meetings reaffirmed the decision not to celebrate Good Friday or Ascension Day. *Classicale Acta*, ed. van Dooren, 14, 147, 227. *Acta*, ed. Rutgers, 142, 252–3.

[88] Polyander to Cornelisz, 27 February 1579. Gemeentearchief Delft, 112, Collectie Cornelisz. *Acta*, ed. Rutgers, 174, 253. Organs belonged to the municipality or parish, and thus presumably could not be removed without permission.

[89] *Ibid.*, 409.

[90] Pettegree, *Emden and the Dutch Revolt*, pp. 211–18.

influx to the Holland towns.[91] It was only in the last decade of the century, when the war settled to a rough equilibrium behind increasingly static frontiers, that the church in the Netherlands approached a settled state.

The 1590s was in many respects a watershed decade, since these political events were accompanied by a pronounced shift towards a more academically trained ministry, and the beginnings of the theological controversies which would preoccupy the church in the early seventeenth century.[92] But already by this time the fundamental relationship between church and state – the key determinant in my view, of the nature of Dutch Calvinism – had been fixed. For although no formal Church Order had ever been adopted by both church and state, the disputes and skirmishes of the first twenty years had effectively established the parameters within which both would operate.

How well did the Dutch church come to terms with this very partial victory? For all the ministers' gloomy reflections in the privacy of their correspondence, it is possible to detect a general desire to rub along with the lay power in practice. On any objective assessment Dutch Calvinism had achieved a considerable transformation in the religious culture of the nation, a change which would have been immediately apparent to any visitor to the austere, cleansed Dutch churches.[93] To the ministers themselves, facing the continuing challenges of competing religious groups, a passive magistracy and widespread indifference among the population, what was achieved was less obvious than what was still to do. But perhaps one should not take their gloomy reflections too much at face value. For all the limitations on their freedom of action, the Calvinist churches enjoyed a status which many other Reformed churches might have envied, privileged and protected, and guaranteed through their part in the emergence of the new state a unique role in its culture and civic life. This was a considerable achievement, even if it was far from the total conversion of society which many of the ministers might have anticipated in the first heady days of church-building in Holland.

[91] Data and literature on this emigration surveyed in J.G.C.A. Briels, 'De emigratie uit de Zuidelijke Nederlanden omstreeks 1540–1621/30', in *Opstand en Pacificatie in de Lage Landen* (Ghent, 1976), pp. 184–220.

[92] Van Deursen, *Bavianen en Slijkgeuzen*, pp. 227 ff. Elliott, 'Classis Dordrecht', pp. 182–8. Carl Bangs, *Arminius. A Study in the Dutch Reformation* (Abingdon, 1971).

[93] Gary Schwarz and Marten Jan Bok, *Pieter Saenredam* (The Hague, 1990).

10 Confessionalism and Absolutism: the case of Brandenburg

Bodo Nischan

1 The socio-political setting

'Calvinists are the Holy Roman Empire's worst enemies for they seek to overthrow its current constitution and ... turn Germany either into a "tyrannical oligarchy" or a "revolutionary democracy"', declared the Catholic publicist Kaspar Schoppe shortly after Elector John Sigismund of Brandenburg had made public his conversion to the Reformed creed.[1] Schoppe had good reason to be concerned: the defection to Calvinism of yet another major German prince was portentous and pointed to the growing confessional polarisation in the Empire. The Reformed communion in the Berlin cathedral on Christmas Day 1613 at which John Sigismund had announced his conversion marked the beginning of what, for lack of a better label, in the more recent scholarly literature generally has been referred to as Brandenburg's 'Second Reformation'.[2] The service itself, Stephen Lesieur, England's roving ambassador to the Empire, reported to King James I, was 'performed without anie opposition or tumult' but, he predicted, 'no doubt ... will occasion diversitie of discourses in Germanie and also here'.[3]

The elector insisted that he had converted 'not for secular gain but solely to give our heart and conscience peace'. While religious motives underlay his conversion, the timing was chosen for its political impact on his Palatine

Support for this study was provided by a grant from the East Carolina University Research Committee. I am also indebted to Catharine Randall Coats and Hans J. Hillerbrand for reading earlier versions of this article.

[1] Christian G. von Friedberg (Kasper Schoppe), *Newer Caluinischer Modell dess heiligen Römischen Reichs* ... (np, 1616), p. 115.

[2] See Heinz Schilling (ed.), *Die reformierte Konfessionalisierung in Deutschland – Das Problem der 'Zweiten Reformation'* (Gütersloh, 1986); and, 'Die Konfessionalisierung im Reich: Religiöser und Gesellschaftlicher Wandel in Deutschland zwischen 1555 und 1620', *Historische Zeitschrift*, 246 (1988), 1–45; Henry J. Cohn, 'The Territorial Princes in Germany's Second Reformation, 1559–1622', in Menna Prestwich (ed.), *International Calvinism 1541–1751* (Oxford, 1985), pp. 135–65; and Bodo Nischan, *Prince, People, and Confession: The Second Reformation in Brandenburg* (Philadelphia: University of Pennsylvania Press, 1994).

[3] 'Stephen Lesieur to King James I, Berlin, 29 December 1613', Public Record Office, London, SP 80/3, ff. 84f.

and Dutch allies whose support he needed in the Jülich-Cleves succession dispute.[4] But any advantages his new faith may have brought him in the Rhineland were more than offset by the many disadvantages it created at home and abroad. The Mark's population, notably the Lutheran clergy and aristocracy, strenuously resisted all calvinisation efforts. The 'Second Reformation' therefore remained an elitist movement, essentially limited to the elector's court and government and effectively realised only in those places and institutions which he controlled directly, notably at the University of Frankfurt on Oder and at the electoral grammar school in Joachimsthal.[5] The Reformed creed was equally unacceptable in nearby Prussia, not only to the duchy's powerful and independent-minded Lutheran estates, but also to king Sigismund III of Poland, Prussia's fiercely anti-Calvinist Catholic suzerain. In addition, John Sigismund's Calvinism greatly complicated relations with the emperor and Germany's Lutheran princes, particularly the ruler of Saxony. In fact, this alienation of Brandenburg's powerful and influential neighbour had been one of the chief arguments against confessional change in the months prior to the elector's public declaration.[6]

Significantly, none of the elector's many Lutheran critics initially mentioned the Rhenish inheritance. This fact is all the more astounding since literally dozens of treatises were produced that condemned the confessional changes at the Hohenzollern court. The Lutherans charged that John Sigismund's reasoning or theology was faulty, blamed unscrupulous and evil advisors, yet never once questioned his religious sincerity. Leonard Hutter of Wittenberg University, dubbed the *malleus calvinistarum*, even published a treatise auspiciously entitled *Calvinista Aulico-Politicus* (1614) in which he promised a complete *exposé* of 'the foremost and major political reasons why this damned Calvinism was introduced in Brandenburg'.[7] What he actually delivered was a lengthy catalogue of diverse metaphysical causes which, he claimed, explained the elector's step. Never once, however, did he mention a single political reason. Not until fifteen

---

4   John Sigismund to John George of Saxony, 10 February 1614, Zentrales Staatsarchiv Merseburg, Germany (hereafter cited as ZStA), Rep. 47.16, f. 47. For the impact of foreign policy on the timing of his conversion, see Alison D. Anderson, 'The Jülich-Kleve Succession Crises (1609–1620): A Study in International Relations' (Ph.D. Diss., University of Illinois, 1992), pp. 177–80. I wish to thank the author for very kindly sending me a copy of her dissertation.

5   For details, see Bodo Nischan, 'The Schools of Brandenburg and the "Second Reformation": Centers of Calvinist Learning and Propaganda', in Robert V. Schnucker (ed.), *Calviniana: Ideas and Influence of Jean Calvin* (Sixteenth Century Essays and Studies, X, 1988), pp. 215–33.

6   See Margrave John George to Simon Gedicke, Cölln a.d.Spree, 8 September 1613, ZStA, Rep.47.16.

7   Leonard Hutter, *Calvinista Aulico-Politicus Alter. Das ist: Christlicher und Nothwendiger Bericht/ von den fürnembsten Politischen Haupt Gründen/ durch welche man/ die verdampte Calvinisterey/ in die Hochlöbl. Chur und Marck Brandenburg einzuführen/ sich eben starck bemühet* (Wittenberg, 1614).

years after John Sigismund's public announcement, in 1628, did a Lutheran writer, Daniel Cramer of Pomerania, for the first time suggest a direct causal link between the Jülich-Cleves succession and the introduction of Calvinism in Brandenburg: 'In 1613 ... the Calvinist Reformation erupted in the Mark Brandenburg as a result of the inheritance quarrel over the Jülich lands. It started when several court councillors persuaded John Sigismund ... that he could gain the good will and support of the Dutch by conforming to the religion of their lands.'[8] Cramer's thesis stuck and has become the standard interpretation of the Hohenzollern conversion.[9]

Contrary to modern sensibilities as this may sound, John Sigismund, who claimed to have acted out of genuine religious conviction, and Cramer, who insisted that he was motivated by political interests, were both right. In that age of confessionalism, unlike in today's secular world, people's religious and political sentiments generally were so tightly and inextricably intertwined that it was virtually impossible to distinguish, not to mention separate, the two. In Brandenburg, as in other German states, religious and political issues converged in the early seventeenth century in what Heinz Schilling has termed 'a framework of confessionalisation and state building'.[10] This meant that the struggle for right doctrine – John Sigismund's attempt to turn the principality's Lutheran into a Reformed church – was simultaneously a conflict over the right political order. Thus, while religious conviction undoubtedly was a major motive for the elector's defection to Calvinism, the socio-political context within which this action occurred, was equally significant: by publicly converting to the Reformed creed, the elector in effect had aligned himself with the militant Calvinist action party in the Empire against his own conservative Lutheran estates at home and also against the Catholic Habsburg forces abroad.

In Brandenburg the landed aristocracy had become, by the end of the sixteenth century, the chief holder of economic power; it possessed the highest social status and wielded considerable political interest.[11] In

---

[8] Daniel Cramer, *Das Grosse Pomrische Kirchen Chronicon* (4 pts., Stettin, 1628), IV, p. 188.

[9] See, for instance, Hajo Holborn, *A History of Modern Germany: The Reformation* (New York, 1959), p. 301; Hans-Joachim Schoeps, *Preussen: Geschichte eines Staates* (Frankfurt/M, 1966), p. 28; and Gerd Heinrich, *Geschichte Preussens: Staat und Dynastie* (Frankfurt/M, 1981), p. 71.

[10] Heinz Schilling, 'The Reformation and the Rise of the Early Modern State', in James D. Tracy (ed.), *Luther and the Modern State in Germany*, (Sixteenth Century Essays and Studies, VII 1986), p. 21.

[11] On the Brandenburg Junker estates, see Gerd Heinrich, 'Der Adel in Brandenburg-Preussen', in Hellmuth Rössler (ed.), *Deutscher Adel 1555–1740* (Darmstadt, 1965), pp. 259–314; Peter-Michael Hahn, *Struktur und Funktion des Brandenburgischen Adels im 16. Jahrhundert* (Berlin, 1979); Hans Rosenberg, 'Die Ausprägung der Junkerherrschaft in Brandenburg-Preussen, 1410–1618', in Dirk Blasius (ed.), *Preussen in der deutschen Geschichte* (Königstein, 1980), pp. 95–142; and Peter Baumgart (ed.), *Ständetum und Staatsbildung in Brandenburg-Preussen* (Berlin, 1983). Note also William W. Hagen, 'Seventeenth-Century Crisis in Brandenburg: The Thirty Years War, the Destabilisation of Serfdom, and the Rise of Absolutism', *AHR*, 94 (1989), 302–35.

contrast, the ruler's position was weak. He was essentially a 'super Junker', a *'primus inter pares*, the largest landowner in a society dominated by landowners' interests', in F.L. Carsten's words.[12] The mainspring of Junker strength was the agrarian crisis of the late Middle Ages which had entailed a drastic redistribution of land and reorganisation of estate management.[13] The landed aristocracy had been able to take advantage of this social upheaval and, in the course of the sixteenth century, had emerged as the leading economic force in East Elbia. The growing demand for grain in western Europe and the general price inflation of the period further encouraged this development. As the Junkers' economic strength grew, so also did their political power. Simultaneously, however, the elector's position declined as he became increasingly dependent on the good will of the estates. As long as the economy continued to prosper the Junkers met, albeit grudgingly, his financial needs. But that changed dramatically when at the turn of the century grain prices plummeted and trade with western Europe experienced a momentary but sharp decline.[14] Many of the Junkers, heavily burdened with mortgages for land purchased during better times, now experienced serious financial difficulties themselves. They increasingly balked at the elector's monetary demands – demands which precisely at this point were escalating because of the Hohenzollerns' increasingly ambitious foreign policy.[15]

This greater involvement abroad was largely brought about by John Sigismund's marriage to Anna, daughter and heiress of the feeble-minded Duke Albrecht Frederick of Prussia and Marie Eleanore, sister of the duchess of Jülich-Cleves. The union not only strengthened the Hohenzollerns' inheritance rights in Prussia but also provided the basis for their dynastic claims in the Rhineland. And since the rulers of neither duchy had any direct descendants, John Sigismund found himself in an excellent position to assert his claims to both. While the Hohenzollern was casting his sights abroad, the Mark's landed aristocracy had become more preoccupied with local, regional affairs.[16] Ruler and Junkers increasingly seemed to

[12] Hans Rosenberg, *Bureaucracy, Aristocracy, and Autocracy: The Prussian Experience 1660–1815* (Boston, 1966), p. 31; and F.L. Carsten, *The Origins of Prussia* (Oxford, 1954), p. 174.

[13] For the following, see Rosenberg, 'Ausprägung der Junkerherrschaft', pp. 100–21; and Wilhelm Abel, *Agrarkrisen und Agrarkonjunkturen* (Hamburg, 1978), pp. 104–51.

[14] Abel, *Agrarkrisen*, pp. 152–61, and *Massenarmut und Hungerkrisen im vorindustriellen Europa* (Hamburg, 1974), pp. 130–8.

[15] See Eduard Clausnitzer, *Die märkischen Stände unter Johann Sigismund* (Halle, 1895), pp. 19–21, 49–72; and Helmuth Croon, *Die kurmärkischen Landstände 1571–1616* (Berlin, 1938), pp. 56–77, 131, 166–88.

[16] Baumgart speaks of an 'entscheidene Weichenstellung' in the estates' mentality in *Ständetum und Staatsbildung*, p. 8. Note also Otto Hintze's comment: 'Luthertum und Kalvinismus bedeuteten damals nicht bloss verschiedene religiöse Bekenntnisse, sondern gantz entgegengesetzte politische Weltanschauungen. Das Luthertum hängt damals in Deutschland untrennbar zusammen mit dem kleinstaatlichen Stilleben, mit dem landschaftlich beschränkten Partikularismus ..., mit der Abneigung gegen alles, was zur

approach politics from poles that were almost diametrically opposed, he viewing political issues in dynastic terms, they responding from a local, or at best regional, perspective. Given the elector's economic dependency, a conflict between the two was almost inevitable, particularly as he sought to bypass the estates' influence by relying more on new agencies, such as the privy council, and court officials – many of them foreigners and Calvinists – who were prepared to do his bidding.

The people with whom John Sigismund associated and whose advice he sought – his personal friends, Reformed councillors and court preachers – viewed the 'Second Reformation' as a necessary safeguard for both the Evangelical heritage which they saw imperilled by recent developments within Lutheranism, and Brandenburg's territorial interests abroad which, they felt, were threatened by the Catholic Counter-Reformation. They therefore backed the electoral court in its confrontation with the local Lutheran estates while, concomitantly, favouring a militant stance against the Habsburg Catholics. As Central Europe became more polarised along confessional lines and the cold war of ideological rhetoric finally issued in an armed conflict of unforeseen dimensions, the confrontation with Catholicism increasingly would take centre stage and become the dominant consideration.

It is within this socio-political matrix – defined by confrontation with the estates at home and the Vienna–Rome–Madrid axis abroad – that the political thinking of Brandenburg's Reformed needs to be analysed. Put simply, Calvinism – or better, its German cousin, the Reformed creed[17] – appealed to the Berlin court because it seemed to be the most dynamic, indeed the only viable means for coping with the myriad political and religious issues confronting it at home and abroad.

2   Calvinist apocalypticism

The new court Calvinism, as one can read in much of the modern literature, encouraged princely authoritarianism and thus prepared the way for the coming of political absolutism to Brandenburg–Prussia.[18] But how? And why?

Störung des Friedens führen könnte'; in 'Die Epochen des evangelischen Kirchenregiments in Preussen', in Gerhard Oestreich (ed.), *Gesammelte Abhandlungen* (Göttingen, 1967), III, p. 70.

[17] While there are subtle theological differences between the two, notably the stronger influence of Zwingli on Germany's Reformed, the terms 'Calvinist' and 'Reformed' are used interchangeably here as they were in early seventeenth-century Germany. For an excellent introduction to the Reformed theology of that period, see Richard A. Miller, *Post Reformation Reformed Dogmatics* (vols. 1–, Grand Rapids, 1987–), I, pp. 13–97.

[18] See for example, R. Mousnier, 'The Exponents and Critics of Absolutism', in J.P. Cooper (ed.), *The New Cambridge Modern History* (12 vols., Cambridge, 1957–79), IV, p. 115; Rudolf von Thadden, *Die Brandenburgisch-Preussischen Prediger im 17. und 18. Jahrhun-*

Most of what has been written about absolutism in Brandenburg unfortunately is based on generalisations derived from the reigns of Frederick William, the 'Great Elector', or Frederick III at the end of the century or, worse, Wilhelm I and II at the end of the nineteenth. More than a century ago Johann Gustav Droysen characterised John Sigismund's conversion as an epoch-making event that infused a new more ambitious spirit into Brandenburg–Prussian politics.[19] Otto Hintze, at the turn of the century, concurred but charged that Droysen had not paid sufficient attention to the spiritual values of Calvinism. Following the lead of his great contemporary Max Weber, Hintze concluded that 'Calvinism formed the bridge by which western European raison d'état made its entry into Brandenburg.'[20] More recently Gerhard Oestrich added yet another dimension to the debate by stressing the close association of Dutch Calvinist and late humanist neo-Stoic ideas.[21]

The problem with these and other similar interpretations is that they tend to project later views back into the early seventeenth century, endowing Hohenzollern court politics with teleological propensities that on closer inspection they did not possess. Since the 'Second Reformation' is viewed through the lens of early modern absolutism rather than post-Reformation confessionalism its unique characteristics are not sufficiently appreciated. The problem is compounded by an underlying Weberian assumption that sees Hohenzollern court politics mostly as a reflection of Reformed religious ideas, yet ignores the unique setting within which these views were formulated.

Because the confessional context has been disregarded – and this is the point to be argued here – the interpretative perspective which shaped Reformed political thinking at that time has been ignored as well: the generally shared conviction among Calvinists that they were living in a world polarised by the age-old struggle between the saints of Christ and the minions of antichrist. In this explanatory scheme the many local religious conflicts – in Brandenburg, the Palatinate, France, England, the Low Countries and elsewhere – were seen as manifestations of a much larger worldwide struggle between the forces of good and evil whose centres, in the

dert: Ein Beitrag zur Geschichte der Absolutischen Staatsgesellschaft in Brandenburg-Preussen (Berlin, 1959), esp. pp. 8, 84; Hartmut Lehmann, *Das Zeitalter des Absolutismus: Gottesgnadentum und Kriegsnot* (Berlin, 1980), pp. 84–6; and Cohn, 'Territorial Princes,' p. 155: 'Albeit with mixed success, Calvinism was thus partly instrumental in creating a more absolutist style of government in relations with the nobles and officials.'

[19] Johann Gustav Droysen, *Geschichte der preussischen Politik* (5 vols., Leipzig, 1868–86), II/2, p. 436.

[20] Otto Hintze, 'Calvinism and Raison d'Etat in Early Seventeenth Century Brandenburg', in Felix Gilbert (ed.), *The Historical Essays of Otto Hintze* (New York, 1975), p. 153.

[21] Gerhard Oestreich, 'Calvinismus, Neustoizismus und Preussentum', *Jahrbuch für die Geschichte Mittel-und Ostdeutschlands*, 5 (1956), 157–81. Note also Hans Thieme (ed.), *Humanismus und Naturrecht in Brandenburg-Preussen: Ein Tagungsbericht* (Berlin, 1979).

early seventeenth century, were Calvinist Republican Holland and Catholic Habsburg Spain.[22] The fight for right doctrine and political order thus took on an added urgency for Brandenburg's Reformed: for them it was part of the larger eschatological showdown with the forces of antichrist. In short, what students of German Reformed political thought generally have ignored is Calvinist apocalypticism.[23]

In Germany the Reformed tell people that 'the emperor is an abominable tyrant, a murderer and ruthless despot ... who wishes to exterminate the gospel and deprive the Evangelicals of their wives, children, welfare, and freedoms', complained Schoppe. They claim 'that the [Holy] Roman Empire is the beast which persecutes our Holy Lord'. Schoppe insinuated that much of the current turmoil was being caused by outside agitators from Geneva and the Low Countries. 'Of course the Catholic estates cannot sit by idly with folded hands but have to defend themselves and therefore look to Spain for help.'[24]

Abraham Scultetus from Heidelberg University, who spent much of 1614 in Berlin to help the 'Second Reformation' get started there, traced the origins of this eschatological confrontation back to the early days of the Reformation – 'about a hundred years ago when God began to reform and govern his church anew ... While Dr. Luther was the first to attack the pope publicly, he was not alone in exposing his fraud and deception', Scultetus added. 'For already there were many other pious and learned men in Switzerland and Upper Germany who proclaimed God's word loudly and clearly.' As the evangelical doctrine, further elucidated by Melanchthon, Oecolampadius and Calvin spread, 'the horror of the papal abomination was progressively revealed' while religious strife became more heated. 'In the German principalities, Elector Frederick II first introduced the Refor-

---

[22] On this international confrontation, see Claus-Peter Clasen, *The Palatinate in European History 1559–1660* (Oxford, 1966); Geoffrey Parker, 'The Dutch Revolt and the Polarisation of International Politics', *Tijdschrift voor Geschiedenis*, 89 (1976), 429–44; and Josef V. Polišensky, *The Thirty Years War*, trans. Robert Evans (Berkeley, 1971). Note also the more recent contributions by John R. Paas, *The German Political Broadsheet 1600–1700* (v. 1–, Wiesbaden, 1985–), I, pp. 55–63; Franz Bosbach, 'Die Habsburger und die Entstehung des Dreissigjährigen Krieges. Die "Monarchia Universalis"', in Konrad Repgen (ed.), *Krieg und Politik: Europäische Probleme und Perspektiven* (Munich, 1988), pp. 151–68, esp. p. 154 and 163; Andrew Pettegree, *Foreign Protestant Communities in Sixteenth-Century London* (Oxford, 1986), pp. 215–61; and Heinz Schilling, 'Nationale Identität und Konfession in der Europäischen Neuzeit', in Bernhard Giesen (ed.), *Nationale und Kulturelle Identität* (Frankfurt, 1991), pp. 218, 226 and 230.

[23] Significantly this subject has been widely explored for late sixteenth and seventeenth-century England: see, for instance, Michael Walzer, *The Revolution of Saints: A Study in the Origins of Radical Politics* (Cambridge, MA, 1966); Christopher Hill, *Antichrist in Seventeenth Century England* (Oxford, 1971); Bryan W. Ball, *A Great Expectation: Eschatological Thought in English Protestantism to 1660* (Leiden, 1975); and Paul Christianson, *Reformers and Babylon: English Apocalyptic Visions from the Reformation to the Eve of the Civil War* (Toronto, 1978).

[24] Schoppe, *Caluinischer Modell*, pp. 44, 74, 11.

mation in the Palatinate, Elector Otto Henry continued it, and Elector Frederick III honourably concluded it' when he converted from Lutheranism to Calvinism.[25] Calvinist preachers and teachers who had fled Catholic persecution in the Low Countries played a prominent role in carrying the Genevan creed to the Rhineland. After the passage of the Lutheran Formula of Concord in 1577 – the Reformed derisively called it the 'Formula of Discord'[26] – as Calvinists in the German lands found themselves pressed not only by Catholics but increasingly by Lutherans as well, the Helvetic doctrine continued to win more converts. In 1610 Margrave Ernst, the younger brother of Elector John Sigismund, who had 'fought in the army of Prince Maurice [of Orange] in Flanders',[27] 'became the first in the electoral house of Brandenburg to convert to the Reformed faith'.[28] Three years later, as we know, John Sigismund and his older brother, Margrave John George converted. These conversions, Schoppe was convinced, had greatly aggravated the Calvinist menace for now there were two electors – one in Heidelberg and the other at Berlin – who turned against the emperor. The Brandenburgers, he feared, were in a position to do immeasurable damage to the Habsburgs simply by opening their formidable fortresses and cities in the Rhineland to the Dutch.[29]

Of course, the Reformed did not leave such Catholic propaganda unanswered. The current persecution of 'God's people', remonstrated Scultetus, was reminiscent of the Roman persecutions of the first Christians. And as the blood of the early martyrs had become the seed of the church, so too, he was convinced, the blood of God's righteous would strengthen them in their struggle against the papal antichrist. The Spanish Catholics 'fielded entire legions in Germany, France, and the Netherlands to suppress the true faith'. But the harder they try, the more determined God's people will become in resisting them. Victory, Scultetus was convinced, ultimately would be theirs. 'Philip II, Spain's mighty king, has thrown all the resources he could amass ... against France, England, and the Netherlands to exterminate the true faith, but in the end has accomplished absolutely nothing. Instead he has lost vast treasures and accumulated huge debts ... yet the Reformed churches ... have continued to grow and prosper.' In this apocalyptic struggle between good and evil 'idols and superstitions have fallen and with them, the papacy's spooks and polter-

---

[25] Abraham Scultetus, *Historischer Bericht Wie die Kirchenreformation in Teutschlandt vor hundert jahren angefangen ... Hiebey sind zufinden ... Sculteti Newjahrs und Jubelfest Predigten im Jahr 1617 gehalten* (Heidelberg, 1618), pp. 266, 7, 272, 270.

[26] See Rudolph Hospinian, *Concordia discors: de origine et progressu formulae concordiae Bergensis liber unus: in quo eius errores et falsa dogmata ... demonstrantur et ob oculos ponuntur* (Zurich, 1607).

[27] Salomon Finck, *Christliche Leichpredigt ... Herrn Ernsten/ Marggraffen zu Brandenburg ...* (np, 1613), f. Div^v.

[28] Scultetus, *Historischer Bericht*, p. 366.   [29] Schoppe, *Caluinischer Modell*, p. 59.

geists'; but in their place has arisen 'the Reformed Evangelical doctrine'. This eschatological encounter between truth and falsehood, Scultetus was convinced, would reach its apogee 'when almighty God will reform his church completely, not through Luther, Zwingli or Oecolampadius, but through the one and only Christ, his Son'.[30]

Without taking due notice of this apocalyptic perspective in which contemporary events were seen, any discussion of Reformed political thought will fall short – hence the distortions created by projecting secular absolutistic notions forged in the eighteenth century back into the political landscape of the early seventeenth. The political thinking of the people at the Berlin court with whom John Sigismund consulted, was cast in confessional, not in modern secular, terms.

The road to this confessional perspective had been prepared long before John Sigismund succeeded to the electoral dignity or first communed in the Reformed manner. As Robin Barnes has shown, a strong apocalyptic heritage survived within Lutheranism. Significantly, it crested in the early seventeenth century just when Calvinism was beginning to exert its influence at the Hohenzollern court.[31] An equally important, albeit less noticed apocalyptic strand existed within the German Reformed movement. While these two traditions shared many characteristics, there also existed important differences. Lutheran eschatologists, very much like their Wittenberg mentor, were convinced that they could recognise a clear pattern of degeneration in history; they believed that this decline would continue and end only with the sudden and dramatic cosmic transformation in fulfilment of the scriptural prophecies about the end. Luther's Reformation, Barnes argued, 'actually heightened the tense expectation by declaring inane all hopes for the earthly future and by directing all hope to the imminent return of Christ'.[32] Calvinist apocalypticists, by contrast, tended to maintain a more militant and hopeful posture in the face of danger. Instead of expecting a sudden dramatic transformation of the world, they looked for gradual development. While seeing themselves as part of a larger world struggle against the forces of Satan, they were also convinced that in this struggle they would inevitably be victorious, even if

---

[30] Scultetus, *Historischer Bericht*, pp. 278, 290, 322, 326, 328.

[31] Robin B. Barnes, *Prophecy and Gnosis: Apocalypticism in the Wake of the Lutheran Reformation* (Stanford, 1988), p. 8, and Gottfried Seebass, 'Apokalyptik/Apokalypsen: VII. Reformation und Neuzeit', in *TRE*, 3: 280–89. Note also the important work by Jürgen Beyer who was kind enough to share with me two of this forthcoming articles: 'Lutheran Popular Prophets', in R.W. Scribner and T.R. Johnson (eds.), *Popular Religion in Germany and Central Europe 1400–1800* (London: Macmillan, forthcoming), and 'Lutherische Propheten in Deutschland und Skandinavien im 16. und 17. Jahrhundert', in Zentrum für Nordische Studien, Universität Kiel (ed.), *Europa in Scandinavia. Kulturelle Dialoge während der frühen Neuzeit, 1520–1720* (Frankfurt/M: Lang, forthcoming).

[32] *Ibid.*, pp. 52f.

progress at times was slow and setbacks were expected. Unlike the Lutherans therefore, the Reformed were eager to promote their victorious cause and, on the whole, tended to be more optimistic, more militant, and politically more engaged.

The news reaching Brandenburg in the waning decades of the sixteenth century – John George, a staunch Lutheran, ruled and Andrew Musculus, coauthor of the Formula of Concord, was superintendent – suggested that such optimism was needed. The Habsburg-supported papal religion was on the offensive everywhere and sending shudders throughout Protestant Europe. Robert Kingdon recently demonstrated how the murder of French Huguenots in the St Bartholomew's Massacre of 1572 was cleverly exploited by Calvinist propagandists to generate international support for the struggle against the Roman church and its allies. In Germany, one of the major regions where this battle for public opinion was being waged, Protestant pamphlets tended to be characterised by an almost 'single-minded concentration on the myth of the pious Coligny'.[33] The effects of this propaganda campaign were evident in Brandenburg and neighbouring regions. John Sigismund's predecessor, Joachim Frederick, then still administrator of Magdeburg, personally expressed to King Henry III his great dismay at the murder of thousands of Huguenots when the latter stopped briefly in Magdeburg on his way back from Poland to France in 1574.[34] And Andreas Werner, a Magdeburg publicist, described in great detail the horrors of the massacre, referring to it as 'an unprecedented Neronian and Herodian bloodbath in which the brave hero and French admiral Gaspard de Coligny and 12,000 of his most faithful followers were nefariously and ignominiously murdered in the fog of night'. Werner also noted the atrocities committed by the Spaniards against the Protestants in the Low Countries, where Parma's occupation of Maastricht in 1579 alone had caused 12,000 casualties.[35] Pamphlets, often with graphic depictions of the crimes committed by the Spanish, circulated widely in northern Germany and served as yet another grim reminder to Calvinists just how precarious their position had become.[36]

'Take pity on us as our enemies are oppressing us . . . Do not permit them

[33] Robert M. Kingdon, *Myths about the St Bartholomew's Massacres, 1572–1576* (Cambridge, MA, 1988), p. 118.

[34] Johann Christoph von Dreyhaupt, *Pagus Nelectici et Nuzici, oder Ausführliche diplomatisch-historische Beschreibung des zum ehemaligen Primat und Ertz-Stifft . . . Magdeburg gehörigen Saal-Kreyses* (2 vols., Halle, 1749–50), I, p. 305.

[35] Andreas Werner, 'Chronica Des Hochlöblichsten Keyserfreien Ertz und Primat Stiffts Magdeburg (1580)', in Heinrich Ammersbach (ed.), *Chur-Brandenburgische/ Märckische/ Magdeburgische und Halberstädtische Chronica* (Halberstadt, 1682), pp. 164, 172.

[36] See, for instance, *Kurtzer bericht/ dass jenigen was sich ihm Niderlandt in Religionssachen/ Und sunst von Anno MDLXVI . . . zugetragen hat/ mitt sampt dem Krich zwisschen Duca d. Alba und dem Printzen zu Oranien* (np, nd).

to exterminate your true faith; do not allow them to bring back the papal blasphemy', prayed Urban Pierius, superintendent at Cüstrin (Brandenburg).[37] Pierius welcomed the English victory over the Spanish Armada in 1588 with a lengthy thanksgiving oration:

England glorify the Lord and praise his name always and in eternity. Holland and Zeeland, place your hope in the Lord for he is our help and shield. Praise the Lord you princes in Germany . . . for he has done marvellous things and sunk the Spanish Armada . . .
'I will slay the [Spanish] blasphemers . . .', says the Lord. 'So that my glory will become manifest I have destroyed the wicked and smashed their mighty Armada. . . .
Thus all the Lord's enemies shall perish . . .!'[38]

The Cüstrin superintendent clearly was no hardline Lutheran for he also prayed: 'Help, give courage and sustenance to our brothers and sisters in the Palatinate, Hesse, Württemberg, France and the Netherlands, and wherever else they may need it!'[39] These were risky words in Gnesio-Lutheran Brandenburg – indeed, Pierius soon was accused of crypto-Calvinism and had to leave the principality shortly afterwards for Saxony, whence he made his way eventually to Bremen.

Similar sentiments were voiced by others who soon would emerge as leading advisors to John Sigismund. One of the more important of these was the Prussian Junker Fabian von Dohna, a Calvinist, who had served at the Palatinate court for over two decades.[40] Dohna explained later that he had gone to Heidelberg because that seemed to be the best place to defend the Reformed faith against the ever-growing threats of the Catholic Counter-Reformation: 'Spain was hostile to us . . . and the same was true for the emperor . . . Saxony and others hated us on account of our religion and because our theologians wrote so much against that wretched Book of Concord . . . In short, it seemed as if we were fighting everybody and everybody was fighting us.'[41] Fearing that the survival of Protestantism in his native Prussia was being jeopardised by the steady progress of the Counter-Reformation in neighbouring Poland, Dohna gradually had become convinced that the future of the duchy would best be served if the Brandenburg margraves also became the rulers of Prussia. From the early

---

[37] Urban Pierius, *Gemeine Beicht/ Absolution und Gebet/ wie dieselbe nach gethanen Predigten in der Kirchen zu Cüstrin der Newen Marckt Brandenburg gesprochen werden . . .* (Wittenberg, 1590), f. ciiiᵛ. On Urban Pierius (Birnbaum) (1546–1616), see his *Geschichte der Kursächsischen Kirchen- und Schulreformation*, ed. T. Klein (Marburg, 1970), pp. 14–54.

[38] Pierius, *Gemeine Beicht*, ff. Ciiiiᵛ–Diiᵛ.   [39] *Ibid.*, f. Ciiiᵛ.

[40] On Fabian von Dohna (1550–1621), see Adolf Jeroschewitz, 'Der Übertritt des Burggrafen zu Dohna zum reformierten Bekenntnis' (Diss., Königsberg, 1920) at the Staatsbibliothek Preussischer Kulturbesitz, Berlin.

[41] C. Krollmann (ed.), *Die Selbstbiographie des Burggrafen Fabian zu Dohna (1550–1621)* (Leipzig, 1905), p. 28.

1590s on, therefore, he devoted himself tirelessly to the promotion of the Hohenzollern succession. In this fight against 'the enemies of God's truth' and 'for the preservation of our dear fatherland', he told the Prussian estates, they must back the house of Brandenburg, not the Polish crown.[42] Fabian even 'visited ... the elector [Joachim Frederick] to explain the urgency of this matter to him ... so that we would not miss this opportunity and negotiate more seriously' for the Prussian succession.[43] Apparently Dohna was persuasive, for shortly afterwards Joachim Frederick dispatched him to Warsaw for talks with Sigismund III, who as king of Poland was also Prussia's overlord. Thanks to Fabian's efforts Sigismund granted Prussia first as a trust territory to Joachim Frederick (1605) and later as a Polish fief to John Sigismund (1611).

Fabian's nephew, Abraham von Dohna, played an equally prominent role. Abraham had held the post of quartermaster general in the Protestant Union army under Christian von Anhalt and had helped organise the siege of Jülich in 1610. In the fall of 1613 he represented Brandenburg at the ill-fated diet of Regensburg. A militant Calvinist and vocal supporter of the Heidelberg-centred Reformed action party, he blamed the Catholics for the failure of this diet. These 'disciples of the devil' and 'servants of the Roman antichrist' are 'so damn papal ... that they will even take the pontiff's piss for holy water', he growled.[44] Like his uncle Fabian, Abraham played a pivotal part in the events leading to Sigismund's public declaration of faith.[45] It was no coincidence that on the very same day on which he announced his conversion the elector named Abraham to his privy council which had been specifically organised a few years earlier to supervise the pending 'highly important and difficult matters, in particular those in Prussia and Jülich'.[46]

John Sigismund's relationship with the Dohnas then, suggests how inextricably intertwined religion and politics were in Brandenburg's 'Second Reformation'. By converting to the Reformed creed, the elector

---

[42] A. Seraphim, 'Eine politische Denkschrift des Burggrafen Fabian von Dohna (1606)', *Forschungen zur Brandenburgischen und Preussischen Geschichte*, 24 (1911), 143f.

[43] Krollmann, *Selbstbiographie Dohna*, p. 94. Note also the important essay by Christoph Römer, 'Der Beginn der Calvinistischen Politik des Hauses Brandenburg: Joachim Friedrich als Administrator', *Jahrbuch für die Geschichte Mittel- und Ost-Deutschlands*, 23 (1974), 99–112.

[44] Abraham von Dohna, 'Historische Reimen von den ungereimten Reichstag anno 1613', in Anton Chroust (ed.), *Abraham von Dohna* (Munich, 1896), pp. 205, 246, 292.

[45] Before announcing his conversion, John Sigismund also had sought Abraham's advice; see John Sigismund to Abraham von Dohna, Grimnitz, 15 December 1613, in Anton Chroust, 'Aktenstücke zur brandenburgischen Geschichte unter Kurfürst Johann Sigismund', *Forschungen zur Brandenburgischen und Preussischen Geschichte*, 9 (1897), 15f.

[46] Elector Joachim Frederick's instruction for the formation of a privy council, in Melle Klinkenborg (ed.), *Acta Brandenburgica. Brandenburgische Regierungsakten seit der Gründung des Geheimen Rates* (3 vols., Berlin, 1927–30), I, pp. 91–6.

aligned himself politically with the militant Calvinist action party in the Empire, centred at Heidelberg, against his conservative Lutheran estates at home and the Catholic counter-reformatory forces abroad.[47] Confessionally – or better, eschatologically – he joined the forces of light, the Dutch-led defenders of the pure gospel, against the forces of darkness, the Spanish power bloc of Catholic Europe.

The indifferent and even hostile reaction of the Mark's Lutheran populace to John Sigismund's calvinising efforts, but even more so international developments, specifically the coming of the Thirty Years War, reinforced this apocalyptic mood at the Hohenzollern court. Brandenburg became actively involved in the war in 1626 after Elector George William, who had succeeded John Sigismund, had tried in vain for eight years to dissociate himself from the conflict in Central Europe by pursuing a policy of unarmed neutrality. He and his Calvinist advisors would have much preferred an armed neutrality, but Brandenburg's powerful Lutheran estates, fearful that they might be drawn into the conflict, refused to grant the necessary financial backing. By the summer of 1626, however, it was obvious that neutrality had failed: with Danish and imperial troops crossing the electorate with impunity, George William increasingly lent his ear to Count Adam zu Schwarzenberg, a Catholic who had served him well while he was governor of the Rhenish provinces. The count's Catholicism initially seemed to be an asset rather than a handicap for it permitted him to stand above the interdenominational squabbles between the Reformed elector and his Lutheran subjects and, in addition, promised to facilitate negotiations with the imperial court. Not surprisingly, Schwarzenberg played upon the desire of the Lutheran estates for economy and security and quickly brought the elector into an alliance with the emperor (May 1627).

The alliance, however, was a total disaster and confirmed the Calvinists' worst nightmares. Imperial troops continued to stream into the country but, worse, the threat of the Catholic Counter-Reformation remained unabated, in fact escalated. Schwarzenberg's Catholicism, it quickly became clear, provided absolutely no protection against Ferdinand's confessional ambitions, and it certainly did not stop the Lutheran–Reformed quarrels. No wonder, then, that by the end of the decade the Reformed Räte in Berlin had pushed the count aside and seized the initiative again – with dramatic results, as we shall see.

The Habsburg emperor and his Catholic allies, it was becoming increas-

---

[47] I have explored the Palatinate's role in Brandenburg's Second Reformation in an essay entitled 'The Palatinate and Brandenburg's "Second Reformation"', in Derk Visser (ed.), *Controversy and Conciliation: The Reformation and the Palatinate 1559–1583* (Allison Park, PA, 1986), pp. 155–73.

ingly evident, were determined to use their military preponderance to restore the old faith by crushing the new. An imperial rescript, published on 16 February 1629, specifically singled out and condemned Calvinist rulers. It warned 'all and every elector, prince, and estate of the Empire ... to avoid the Reformed mobs and sects, to suppress the same, and to support both our true Catholic faith and the Augsburg Confession'.[48] Ferdinand demonstrated that he intended to carry out these threats when, only a few weeks later, on 25 March, he issued the Edict of Restitution, ordering the immediate recatholisation of all illegally secularised church properties and reaffirming the exclusion of Calvinists from the Peace of Augsburg.[49] This edict, Catholic hardliners were hoping, would eliminate Protestantism entirely from the German lands.[50]

To the small band of Reformed stalwarts at the Berlin court the forces of darkness, indeed, seemed to be triumphing everywhere. The goal of these 'Roman–Spanish birds of prey', proclaimed John Bergius, is to reduce all of Protestant Germany to 'Egyptian slavery'.[51] Bergius, an influential court preacher who served Brandenburg's first three Reformed electors, was convinced that the Catholics 'want to introduce the papal mass everywhere by force and abolish the religious peace' of 1555.[52] 'Their sole aim is to ruin all evangelical lands and to exterminate our churches.'[53] 'Let us,' he proclaimed elsewhere, 'take as our model the brave Dutch, who after pushing back the Romans [i.e. the Spanish Habsburgs] have been called champions of liberty.'[54]

The Lutherans' continued and unabated hostility only served to heighten this apocalyptic mood among John Sigismund's advisors. The former were incensed by the Reformed claim that 'in the church of the Brandenburg electorate horrible and crude papal superstitions remained ... that needed

---

[48] A copy of this rescript is found in ZStA, Rep.13.18–4, ff. 53–5.

[49] The edict is found in Michael C. Lundorp (ed.), *Der Römischen kayserlichen Majestät und Dess Heiligen Römischen Reichs ... Acta Publica und Schrifftliche Handlungen* (19 vols., Frankfurt/M, 1688–1721), III, pp. 1048–55.

[50] See Robert Bireley, SJ, 'The Origins of the *Pacis Compositio* (1629); A Text Of Paul Layman, S.J.', *Archivum Historicum Societas Jesu*, 42 (1973), 106–27; note also Geoffrey Parker, *The Thirty Years War* (London, 1984), pp. 83–8.

[51] Johannes Bergius, *39 Predigten/ über unterschiedliche schwere Sprüche Pauli/ vornehmlich aus seiner Epistel an die Römer*, ed. Conrad Bergius (Frankfurt/O, 1666), p. 772. This discussion of Bergius' political ideas incorporates material first published in my essay 'Calvinism, the Thirty Years War, and the Beginning of Absolutism in Brandenburg: The Political Thought of John Bergius', *Central European History*, 15 (1982), 203–23.

[52] Johannes Bergius, *Das die Wort Christi noch veste stehen ...* (Basel, 1624), p. 9. On Bergius (1587–1658) see my 'Johann Peter Bergius', in Gerd Heinrich (ed.), *Berlinische Lebensbilder: Theologen* (Berlin, 1990), pp. 35–60.

[53] Johannes Bergius, *Vier Trost-Predigten ... zum ... Ehrengedächtnis Des ... Herrn Levin von dem Knesebeck/ Churf. Brandenb. vornehmen Geheimbten Raths* (Berlin, 1640).

[54] Johannes Bergius, *Guter Bürger* (Danzig, 1656).

to be discarded'.[55] 'We do not need the dark lanterns of the Calvinists to reach perfection',[56] snorted Simon Gedicke. The Reformed speak of the need of another reformation, complained Matthias Hoe von Hoenegg of Saxony, but actually have initiated a 'dangerous deformation' by introducing the 'Calvinist soul poison'.[57] 'A simple idiot can see what they are up to', charged Leonard Hutter; the issue here is not 'the extermination of the papacy' but the 'introduction of Calvinism'.[58]

Yet for the Calvinists papal idolatry precisely was the issue. In the apocalyptic showdown with antichrist the supporters of the Formula of Concord were siding with the force of evil. By this treason of the Lutherans, the eschatological struggle had been extended to the very heart of Evangelical doctrine, justification by faith alone, which, the Reformed insisted, the Lutheran 'Formulists' had sacrificed again with their new and nefarious dogma of 'ubiquity'.[59] This doctrine, insisted Simon Pistoris, denies 'the very core of our Evangelical faith' and 'turns the sacrament into a miracle'.[60] It 'opens the doors and gates to old heresies', complained Martin Füssel.[61] 'Ubiquity' is like a *Sauerteig*, or poison, that destroys the gospel message, claimed Bergius. It is the first step toward Catholic transubstantiation and really amounts to a return to the 'magical consecration' of the 'papal mass'.[62] 'What superstitious papal ceremonies still survive in the Lutheran church derive largely from this faulty doctrine,' added Pistoris.[63] 'I really wonder about our brothers, the so-called Lutherans ...', mused Abraham Scultetus; 'I wonder because for years we have now preached loudly and written clearly about the Lord's Supper, yet they refuse to understand that the delusion of Christ's true physical presence remains the very cornerstone on which the entire papacy is founded.'[64]

---

[55] Hutter, *Calvinista Aulico-Politicus*, p. 3.
[56] Gedicke to Margrave John George, Berlin, 18 September 1613, Niedersächsische Staats – und Universitätsbibliothek Göttingen, Germany (hereafter cited as UBG), Cod.M-S.hist.189.I, f. 97.
[57] Matthias Hoe von Hoenegg, *Wolgegründete/ und zufördersit denen Evangelischen Christen in der Chur und Mark Brandenburg/ zu nothwendiger nachrichtung/ verfestigte Verantwortung* ... (Leipzig, 1614), Vorrede.   [58] Hutter, *Calvinista Aulico-Politicus*, p. 5.
[59] Technically, the Lutheran position after 1577 is more properly described by the terms 'ubivolipresence' or 'multivolipresence'; see Herman Sasse, *This is My Body* (Minneapolis, 1959), p. 341; and Theodor Mahlmann, *Das neue Dogma der lutherischen Christologie* (Gütersloh, 1969), pp. 222f.
[60] Simon U. Pistoris, *Zwölff vornehme wolgegründete Haubt-Ursachen/ Warum die Reformirte Evangelische Kirchen mit D. Luthers und seiner Nachfolger Auslegung der Worte Christi im H. Abendmahl ... nicht eins sein können* (Düsseldorf, 1613), p. 162.
[61] Martin Füssel, *Brutum Fulmen, Excommunicationis Apologiae Fuesselianae* ... (Berlin, 1617), p. 39.   [62] Bergius, *Dass die Wort Christi*, pp. 204–38.
[63] Pistoris, *Zwölff Haubt-Ursachen*, p. 294.
[64] Scultetus, *Historischer Bericht*, pp. 332f.

To the Reformed 'ubiquity' thus constituted the glue which sealed the Lutheran–papal bond. There are three major confessional groups in the Empire – Roman Catholics, Lutherans and Calvinists – allowed Hermann Fabronius of Hesse in 1612; but, he added, in reality there are only two 'for one party continues to side with the papists'.[65] 'Only those who either do not know or else do not want to know remain unaware of what the Spaniards' true ambitions are,' observed another Calvinist.[66] In the fall of 1614 – Spanish troops had just occupied Wesel and Duisburg in the Rhineland – elector John Sigismund ordered all pastors to offer special supplicatory prayers lest the cause of the gospel suffer even further setbacks. Instead of rejoicing at General Spinola's victories, he told the Lutherans, they should realise that 'we are all in this together and will all be oppressed, persecuted, and exiled' if the Spanish get their way.[67] The Mark's pastors refused, and they continued to balk whenever the court tried to order general prayers 'on behalf of his Electoral Highness' or his military efforts. John Sigismund was furious: the prayers were intended 'for the principality's benefit, not for our disgrace'. The pastors' behaviour, he complained, would have a most pernicious impact, 'for it breeds contempt ... for the sovereign, which in turn leads to disobedience, rebellion, tumult, and ultimately total ruin and destruction'.[68] And, we might add, to the Reformed it clearly demonstrated anew that in this struggle between good and evil, the Lutherans were siding with the enemies of God.   The coming of the Thirty Years War lent a special reality and urgency to apocalyptic visions and provided more evidence of the Ubiquitists' complicity. Early in the conflict, Elector John George of Saxony, the foremost Lutheran prince in the Empire, had joined Ferdinand II in suppressing the Bohemian revolt. Before Brandenburg became actively involved in the fighting, nearly a decade later, 'heaps' of anti-Reformed pamphlets appeared in Berlin and Frankfurt on Oder, site of the principality's famous university. None of these was more offensive to the Reformed – and more symptomatic of existing divisions! – than a tract entitled *Why it Is Better to Ally with Papists than with Calvinists* (1619). The pamphlet's anonymous authors stressed that they were dealing with a 'highly important and, for these dangerous times, most pertinent question'; their general objective, they explained, was to prove that Lutherans were better off 'trusting and keeping company with Papists than with Calvinists'. Elector George William and his advisors could not recall anything 'cruder, more abominable, and more pernicious'

---

[65] Hermann Fabronius, *Newe Summarische Welt Historia: unnd Beschreibung aller Keyser-thumb/ Königreiche/ Fürstenthumb/ unnd Völcker heutiges Tages auff Erden* (Schmalkalden, 1612), p. 56.
[66] *Politischer Discurs, Ob sich Franckreich der Protestirenden Chur unnd Fürsten wieder Spannien annehmen/ oder neutral erzeigen ... solle* (Berlin, 1615), f. Biʳ.
[67] Directive for penitential sermons and prayers, 22 October 1614, ZStA, Rep.47.20.
[68] John Sigismund to Privy Councillors, Königsberg, 5 January 1617, ZStA, Rep.47.17–18.

than this tract. They were convinced that it had been prepared specifically 'to confuse the common man, to inflame him against the small band of Reformed in this land, and to convince him that he was serving God by strangling and murdering Calvinists'; above all, it revealed anew the 'evil genius' that was animating Lutherans to choose the side of antichrist.[69]

3   Authoritarianism and constitutionalism

Given this apocalyptic perspective among Calvinists generally and Brandenburg's Reformed more specifically, how, then, did this shape their political views? It varied. It depended, to put it simply, on the historical, the socio-political, context in which Calvinists found themselves. 'In itself, apocalyptic thought displayed neither revolutionary nor conservative characteristics in its social and political thrust', Paul Christianson has noted.[70] Rather, it was a creed of action that reinforced existing attitudes.

In the Mark Brandenburg, where a powerful Lutheran aristocracy opposed both the faith and policies of the electoral court, the Reformed favoured the authority of the central government against that of the estates – but only at home. Abroad, that is on the imperial and international levels, where the Habsburg-Catholic power bloc was threatening their faith and dynastic interests, Brandenburg's court Calvinists sang a different tune: here they supported resistance against central, imperial authority. The common denominator uniting these seemingly disparate policies was the confessional factor, the conviction that they were engaged in a struggle which pitted them, champions of the true gospel, against the forces of darkness, the Catholics and their Ubiquitist accomplices.

In language not very different from that of Lutherans of the times or, for that matter, Martin Luther and John Calvin several generations earlier, the defenders of Brandenburg's 'Second Reformation' emphasised again and again that princes are 'God's regents' and 'anointed'. They 'represent God on earth and function as his vicars', noted John Bergius.[71] 'A sovereign basically has two obligations,' explained Pistoris: 'to protect the pious and to punish evil doers.'[72] In particular, he is responsible for maintaining true

---

[69] See George William's memorandum of 30 January 1620 on 'Warumb man lieber mit Papisten als Calvinisten gemeinschafft habe können', ZStA, Rep.47.19.

[70] Christianson, *Reformers and Babylon*, p. 7.

[71] Bergius, *39 Predigten*, p. 1185; cf. a sermon by the Lutheran court preacher Johann Fleck, *Idea Christianae Reipublicae, Oder Einfeltiger Abriß eines Christlichen Regiments/ Bey angehenden Brandenburgischen Landtage . . . 1602 . . . in der Thumbkirchen zu Cölln an der Sprew erkleret . . .* (Frankfurt/O, 1602). See also Heinz Duchardt, 'Das Protestantische Herrscherbild des 17. Jahrhunderts im Reich,' in Konrad Repgen (ed.), *Das Herrscherbild im 17. Jahrhundert* (Münster, 1991), pp. 26–42; and Harro Höpfl (ed.), *Luther and Calvin on Secular Authority* (Cambridge, 1991), esp. pp. vii–xxiii.

[72] Simon U. Pistoris, *Gründtliche/ lautere/ Richtige Ausslegung der Psalmen Davids von Anfang biss zum Ende*, ed. Martin Füssel (Frankfurt/O, 1618), p. 294.

faith and doctrine. If a ruler perceives the church in his realm to be in error, he is not only authorised, but obliged, to correct existing abuses, even if the majority of his subjects were to oppose him. This, John Sigismund explained, was precisely the reason why he had felt compelled to initiate his reforms: 'We decided to act because of the new, erroneous, and divisive teaching [of ubiquity] which, until recently, had been totally unknown in the church.'[73] Abraham Scultetus praised him for doing exactly what was expected of a good Christian ruler: 'he [had] swept the leftover papal dung out of Christ's stable'.[74] Similarly, Christoph Pelargus, the Mark's superintendent-general, lauded the elector 'for promoting the pure Christian religion free of all human addition and papal superstition'.[75]

In defending the elector's reforms, his Calvinist apologists often compared John Sigismund to such famous Old Testament heroes as Kings David, Solomon or Josiah. The frequent references to Josiah are particularly striking and revealing.[76] As was true for the Hohenzollern elector, desire for religious reform and intense dynastic ambition also motivated the Judean king. While he aimed at cleansing his land of idolatrous practices, notably the Canaanite Baal worship and Assyrian astral cult, his reforms also had profound political implications: they signified Josiah's claims to the old Davidic empire, specifically the former northern kingdom which had become a province of Assyria, the biblical equivalent to the contemporary Catholic-Habsburg scourge. The parallels to John Sigismund's religious reforms and his political ambitions in Prussia and in the Rhineland were unmistakable.

Because the ruler represents God on earth, subjects must obey him, the Reformed argued very much like their Lutheran contemporaries. 'May God keep good Christians from ever opposing their pious sovereigns', prayed the new Reformed court chaplain Martin Füssel.[77] Subjects may disagree with their ruler's faith, allowed Bergius and Knesebeck but, according to Christ's commandments, still must obey him.[78] And they must obey even 'tyrants who misuse the sword'. For 'they too derive their

---

[73] John Sigismund to Estates, Naumburg, 28 March 1614, UBG, Cod.MS.hist.189,I. f. 43.

[74] Abraham Scultetus (ed.), *Auff sonderbahren Befehl und Anordnung ... Johannis Sigismunds ... Glaubensbekenntnus der reformirten Evangelischen Kirchen in Deutschland* (Frankfurt/ O, 1614), Vorrede.

[75] Christoph Pelargus, *Josias, Imago Piorum Regnum Ac Principum ... Johann Sigismunds/ Marggraffen zu Brandenburg ... Leichbegangnuss* (Frankfurt/O, 1620), f. Hiiᵛ.

[76] See II Kings 22; Pelargus used this as the text for John Sigismund's funeral sermon (see *Josias, Imago Piorum*) and Scultetus for his '1617 Jubeljahrspredigt' (see *Historischer Bericht*, pp. 295–342).

[77] Martin Füssel, *Rettung dess Glaubens/ und Guten Nahmens D. Johannis Böhmens zu Königsberg in Preussen* (Frankfurt/O, 1616), f. Fiiiʳ.

[78] Thomas von Knesebeck, *Einfeltiger Bericht/ Wie sich ein jedes Christliches Hertz/ jetziger Zeit: Insonderheit aber Unterthanen gegen jhrer Obrigkeit/ Welche etwa verenderter religion beschuldigt wird/ verhalten sollen* (Frankfurt/O, 1614), 5th dialogue.

office and authority from God.... Only the tyrannical misuse of this authority is not from God, but stems from their sinfulness and from Satan,' thought Bergius. 'The worst tyranny is always better than a state without any sovereign at all.'[79] Insurrection against such a tyrannical regime surely will lead to divine retribution, observed Daniel Schaller, 'for God will not leave unpunished rebellious uprisings against the secular sovereignty'.[80]

Schaller commented on John Sigismund's authority at various times and, most interestingly, within different confessional contexts: first in 1609 as a crypto-Calvinist when he offered a series of dedicatory sermons to the young ruler who then, officially still a Lutheran, had just succeeded to the electoral dignity, and again several years later when Schaller, now an overt Calvinist himself, spoke in defence of Brandenburg's 'Second Reformation'.[81] The content of his arguments had not changed; their confessional label, however, had. The same was true for Frederick Pruckmann, chancellor of the privy council. He publicly converted together with the elector in 1613 but had established his reputation as an advocate of princely authority much earlier, in 1592 when he, then nominally still a good Lutheran, had published a treatise which he dedicated to Nicholas Crell, principal of Saxony's aborted 'Second Reformation'.[82] Pruckmann's high regard for princely authority had not diminished over the years; his denominational appellation had. Similarly Simon Gedicke, John Sigismund's erstwhile fiery Lutheran court chaplain, strongly defended the elector's sovereignty while the latter was publicly still a Lutheran; yet Gedicke violently condemned the Hohenzollern when he invoked those very same arguments to defend his new reformation.[83] Again, it was not disagreement over the specifics of the theory of sovereignty which created controversy, rather the confessional context in which these arguments were voiced.

While denying subjects the right to rebel against an unjust ruler, the Reformed – like the Lutherans – recognised one major exception that conceivably might justify disobedience. Noted Schaller, 'if your sovereign tries to coerce you to follow an order that would force you to act against God and your conscience, you have to resist ... for one must obey God

[79] Bergius, *39 Predigten*, pp. 1184, 1215, 1224.
[80] Daniel Schaller, *Homagium veteris Marchiae. Eine Huldigungspredigt/ gehalten bey versammlung der hohen Landes Obrigkeit/ und dero getrewen Unterthanen* ... (Magdeburg, 1609), f. Di.
[81] Significantly, in his 1609 homage sermon – delivered on St Bartholomew's Day! – Schaller pointedly omitted all references to the Formula of Concord while urging John Sigismund to promote God's pure doctrine.
[82] See Friedrich Pruckmann, *Paragraphus Soluta Potestas, Tractatus de Regalibus, in qua, quid princeps ratione legum, contractum* ... (Wittenberg, 1592).
[83] Simon Gedicke, *Drey Glückwunschungs Predigten/ zu unterschiedlichen Ehren ... Johanni Sigismundi/ Marggraffen zu Brandenburg* (Leipzig, 1612). Cf. idem, *Pelargus Apostata* ... (Leipzig, 1617); *Triumphus Calvinisticus* ... (Leipzig, 1615); or *Calviniana Religio/ Oder Calvinisterey* ... (Leipzig, 1615).

rather than man'.[84] Thomas von Knesebeck, privy councillor, concurred but noted that this principle could hardly be invoked in Brandenburg since John Sigismund, even though he had converted to Calvinism, had not forced his religion on anyone.[85] 'His Electoral Highness personally introduced the Reformation only at Berlin; it hasn't even happened at Frankfurt yet', noted Pelargus.[86]

Their point was well taken. Only John Sigismund had not imposed his creed on the principality, not because he did not want to, but rather because he was not able to. Faced with overwhelming opposition by the Lutheran populace, he had soon been forced to admit that the calvinisation of the principality's church, as initially envisioned, could not be realised, at least not yet.[87] Under pressure from the estates the court had to concede in 1615

that whosoever in the land wishes it may remain attached to the doctrine of Luther and the unchanged Augsburg Confession ... and also to the Book of Concord ... For His Electoral Highness in no way arrogates to Himself Dominion over consciences and therefore does not wish to impose any suspect of unwelcome preachers on anyone.[88]

Multi-confessionalism, the coexistence of a Calvinist court and popular Lutheran church, was thus the result. This, as John Sigismund's defenders noted repeatedly, hardly constituted the sort of religious tyranny that might justify dissent or opposition to the sovereign.

The situation, however, was very different on the imperial level where the Reformed, unlike the Lutherans, had no legal standing and hence every reason to feel very insecure. 'As the knife was put to the throat of the Lutherans, the Calvinists quickly realised how they would fare, especially since they knew very well who had started the war', noted one anonymous commentator.[89] Philip Nicolai at the turn of the century had predicted the beginning of a new but final persecution of the true church by the Pope in 1612.[90] And Christoph Kotter in 1620 had forecast the return of Frederick of the Palatinate to the Bohemian throne, the fall of the Habsburgs, and the

---

[84] Schaller, *Homagium*, f. Dii.

[85] Knesebeck, *Einfeltiger Bericht*, 5th dialogue.

[86] Christoph Pelargus, *Richtige kurtze Antwort ... Auff die zwey Fragen so jhm D. Daniel Cramerus, Pastor und Professor zu Stettin ... fürgelegt* (Frankfurt/O, 1615), f. Aiiiv.

[87] The plan for Brandenburg's Second Reformation was detailed in a privy council memorandum: Der Chfl. Bdbg. Stadthalter und Räte Bedenken wie die Reformation fortzuführen, 21 February 1614, ZStA, Rep.47.16.

[88] Revers des Churfürsten Johann Sigismunds, so bey derer Versammlung der Landstände disseits der Oder gegeben worden, Cölln a.d.Spree, 5 February 1615, in Christian O. Mylius (ed.), *Corpus Constitutionum Marchicarum* (11 vols., Berlin, 1737–51) VI, 1, No. 79.

[89] *Illuminirter Reichs- und Welt-Spiegel/ Darinnen vieler Potentaten/ Provintzen/ Städte/ und vornehmer Personen Zustand und Eigenschafft/ gleichsam in einer Quinta Essentia extrahiret gezeiget und fürgebildet wird* (np, 1631), p. 47.

[90] Philip Nicolai, *Historia des Reichs Christi/ Das ist: Gründliche Beschreibung der wundersamen Erweiterung ... der Kirchen Christi ...* (Frankfurt/M, 1659).

destruction of the papacy.[91] The same year also saw the first German edition of Tommaso Campanella's *Spanish Monarchy* which, Protestant readers believed, contained King Philip II's master plan for a universal Habsburg-Catholic monarchy.[92] Similar warnings were sounded by other contemporary broadsheets and pamphlets which circulated widely in northern Germany.[93] 'I prosecute my God-given victories until I have exterminated all my enemies', Ferdinand had allegedly declared.[94] No wonder Brandenburg's small, beleaguered coterie of Reformed loyalists had come to feel most insecure as the Catholic armies continued their victorious march north in the 1620s. With their very survival at stake, the eschatological struggle was beginning to acquire a special reality and urgency for them. Now more than ever, they realised, an all-out effort was required to stop the forces of antichrist.[95]

'While the common Christian may not actively oppose evil ... secular magistrates have received their swords and sceptres from God ... to protect their subjects against force and injustice', Bergius told the assembled Evangelical princes who had gathered at Leipzig in the spring of 1631.[96] He thought that they not only had the right but the duty to defend their political and religious freedoms against Emperor Ferdinand II. Accordingly, Bergius warned the assembled delegates that their subjects and God would never forgive them if they remained idle bystanders while Habsburg–Catholic armies devastated their lands and suppressed the true faith.

What Brandenburg's Reformed court chaplain was invoking here was essentially the 'constitutionalist theory of resistance' which German Lutherans had developed in the early sixteenth century to justify forcible resistance against emperor Charles V, and which German Calvinists,

---

[91] Barnes, *Prophecy*, p. 250.

[92] John M. Headley, "'Ehe Türckisch als Bäpstisch'": Lutheran Reflections on the Problem of Empire, 1623–28', *Central European History*, 20 (1987), 3–28, esp. 8–10.

[93] See, for instance, *Spanischer Wolffsmagen* (1625); *Das Teutsche Klopff Drauff* (1626); Levin Marschall, *Wilt du den Kayser sehen* ... (1629); and *Magna Horologii Campana* ... (1631). Note also the magnificent reproductions of contemporary broadsheets in William A. Coupe, *The German Illustrated Broadsheet in the Seventeenth Century* (2 vols., Baden-Baden, 1966/7), I, pp. 68f, 125, 129, 134, 156f; and Paas, *Political Broadsheet*, III, pp. 77–96.   [94] *Illuminirter Reichsspiegel*, p. 12.

[95] On the 'antichrist' as a tool of confessional propaganda, see Hans J. Hillerbrand, 'The Antichrist in the Early German Reformation: Reflections on Theology and Propaganda', in Andrew C. Fix and Susan C. Karant-Nunn (eds.), *Germania Illustrata*, Sixteenth Century Essays and Studies, 18 (Kirksville, 1992), pp. 3–18; and Klaus Aichele, *Das Antichristdrama des Mittelalters, der Reformation und Gegenreformation* (The Hague, 1974), pp. 84–6, 148–66. Significantly, early in the Thirty Years War the Heidelberg publisher Johann Lancelot produced a broadsheet, entitled *Parallela Christiana et Antichristiana* (1619), evidently an imitation of the immensely successful *Passional Christi und Antichristi* of 1521; see *WA* 9: 690–700, esp. 697.

[96] Johannes Bergius, *Brüderliche Eynträchtigkeit/ Auß dem 133. Psalm/ Bey der Protestiren-den/ Evangelischen Chur-Fürsten und Stände Zusammenkunfft zu Leipzig/ Anno 1631/ In Drey Predigten erkläret* (Frankfurt, 1635), p. 27.

notably David Pareus of Heidelberg, more recently had adapted to justify armed opposition against Ferdinand. This theory, as Quentin Skinner has noted, emphasised the duties of 'inferior magistrates as directly ordained by God'. It argued that electors and princes were responsible for the imperial constitution and therefore authorised to defend it, if necessary by offering armed resistance to the emperor.[97] Brandenburg and the Palatinate, complained the Catholics, now were misusing this theory to argue 'that whosoever elected and appointed him [the emperor] also may depose him'.[98]

Significantly, Brandenburg's court theologians did not recognise a similar right of resistance for the Junkers, the elector's own inferior magistrates.[99] This seemingly contradictory position, of course, makes sense only if viewed within the general confessional context of the period in which Calvinists believed themselves to be engaged in an eschatological struggle with the Habsburg-Catholics abroad and their Ubiquitist accomplices at home. The corollary of political resistance against the emperor therefore was resistance against the Junkers – in other words, princely authoritarianism in Brandenburg.

Bergius, himself an irenicist wont to emphasise Lutheran–Reformed agreements rather than disagreements, admonished the assembled Evangelical princes to join forces against the 'sinful brotherhood' of the 'Holy or Catholic League'. 'What Catholic holiness such leagues . . . have wrought, our own bitter experience now has fully taught us. Would that God made the children of light only half as eager and harmonious in the preservation of the Evangelical light and freedom as they are in the promotion of antichrist's darkness and bondage.'[100] Nothing, observed Bergius in another sermon at Leipzig, had prevented the collapse of the 'dilapidated Roman chair' more than the Protestants' disunity. 'The cunning of all cardinals, the sophistries of all monks and Jesuits, and even the League's [military] might could not have protected it, unless the Protestants had done it themselves by their constant squabbles.'[101] It is the princes' 'duty' to put

---

[97] See Quentin Skinner, *The Foundations of Modern Political Thought* (2 vols., New York, 1978), II, pp. 191–348. On the evolution of a Calvinist theory of resistance, which emphasised political rather than religious arguments, see Robert M. Kingdon, 'Calvinism and Resistance Theory, 1550–1580', in J. H. Burns (ed.), *The Cambridge History of Political Thought 1450–1700* (Cambridge, 1991), pp. 193–218, esp. pp. 206–18.

[98] Schoppe, *Caluinischer Modell*, p. 39.

[99] Note Winfried Schulze, 'Estates and the Problem of Resistance in Theory and Practice in the Sixteenth and Seventeenth Centuries', in R. J. W. Evans and T. W. Thomas (eds.), *Crown, Church and Estates* (New York, 1991), pp. 158–75, esp. p. 168.

[100] Bergius, *Brüderliche Eynträchtigkeit*, p. 11. Elsewhere I have tried to show how Bergius' theological orientation provided the intellectual rationale for a multiconfessional compromise; see 'John Bergius: Irenicism and the Beginning of Official Religious Toleration in Brandenburg-Prussia', *Church History*, 51 (1982), 389–404.

[101] Bergius, *Brüderliche Eynträchtigkeit*, p. 11.

an end to these divisions. 'If God's houses are to be properly protected against external force . . . good harmony must also exist within its walls.'[102]

Brandenburg's delegates to the Leipzig Conference – Sigismund von Götz, who had succeeded Pruckmann as chancellor of the privy council, and Levin von Knesebeck, a brother of the previously mentioned Thomas, all close friends of the influential John Bergius – clearly were addressing a common concern when they raised the question of military resistance. A Protestant defensive alliance, they suggested, could be organised without violating the imperial constitution. Their proposal was well received by most of the assembled estates and, after additional negotiations with the Saxons, resulted in what became known as the *Leipzig Manifesto*.[103] This final resolution, which was issued by the princes on 12 April 1631, created a defensive association, the *Leipziger Bund*, with an army of 40,000 troops to protect and 'uphold the basic laws, the imperial constitution, and the German liberties of the Protestant states'.[104] For Brandenburg's Calvinists the conference had been a major success. Simply put, the *Leipzig Manifesto* meant that their political programme – forged within the context of eschatological confrontation in which they believed themselves to be engaged – had been realised: at the height of the war when the Habsburg-Catholics seemed at the verge of total triumph, Brandenburg's Reformed had brought Germany's Protestants – even Ubiquitist Saxony – together against the forces of antichrist.[105]

The fact that Lutherans and Calvinists had joined forces, even though the Reformed had portrayed the 'Ubiquitists' as close allies of the papal antichrist and the Lutherans themselves had made no bones about their preference for Rome over Geneva, shows yet once more the malleability of political thought in this age of confessionalism. It reminds us anew of the futility of identifying any one political orientation – be it authoritarian or constitutional – with any one specific denominational tradition. And, last but not least, it also shows how by the early 1630s confessional tempers were beginning to cool as Lutherans and Calvinists, both facing extinction at the hands of Hispanic leviathan, finally had learned to think in more pan-Protestant terms.[106]

---

[102] *Ibid.*, p. 43.
[103] For details, see Bodo Nischan, 'Brandenburg's Reformed Räte and the Leipzig Manifesto of 1631', *Journal of Religious History*, 10 (1979), 365–80.
[104] The Leipzig Manifesto is found in Lundorp, *Acta Publica*, IV, pp. 144–6.
[105] This mood was well expressed in a contemporary pamphlet by Irenaeus Heiland (pseud), *Apocalyptisches, Doch Politisches Bedencken/ Was die Evangelischen und protestirenden Churfürsten und Stände . . . zugewarten* (np, 1631).
[106] Significantly, while the princes met, their theologians held a colloquy and displayed a similar harmony; here too the Reformed took the initiative. For details, see my 'Reformed Irenicism and the Leipzig Colloquy of 1631', *Central European History*, 9 (1976), 3–26.

4   Conclusion

How, then, did Calvinism prepare the way for political absolutism in Brandenburg-Prussia? I have tried to argue in this paper that the Reformed were as likely to support princely authority as estates' rights. Which side they chose depended largely on the socio-political conditions under which they had to assert themselves. In early seventeenth-century Brandenburg, as well as in Prussia, where John Sigismund's interests were opposed by the Lutheran Junkers at home and the Catholic emperor abroad, the Reformed supported the elector's authority against the estates while concurrently defending his constitutional rights against the emperor. Here the Lutherans were the defenders of constitutionalism and opponents of princely absolutism.

The roles were reversed in other socio-political settings. For instance in East Friesland, as Heinz Schilling has shown, the absolutist rulers were Lutherans, but their opponents, in the towns of Groningen and Emden, were Calvinists who identified with local civic and communal traditions.[107] The conceptual glue that united these diverse, seemingly contradictory political orientations – Brandenburg's autocratic aulic Calvinists and Emden's libertarian civic Calvinists – was their apocalypticism, the conviction that they, the defenders of Christ's true gospel, were fighting the force of evil, antichrist, made manifest anew in the early seventeenth century by the Vienna–Rome–Madrid axis. Whether this apocalyptic perspective encouraged them to advocate an authoritarian or a constitutional position depended mostly on the historical context in which they found themselves. One thing was certain, however: regardless of which side a particular Calvinist chose, his apocalypticism assured that he would do so with great fervour and optimism, convinced not only that the truth was his but also that he would ultimately triumph.

No wonder, then, that Kaspar Schoppe on the eve of the Thirty Years War declared Germany's Calvinists to be guilty of both 'tyrannical oligarchy' and 'revolutionary democracy'. To Brandenburg's Lutherans, especially the landed aristocracy, John Sigismund's 'aulic Calvinists' indeed must have appeared as 'tyrannical oligarchs', even though to the emperor they must have looked more like 'revolutionary democrats'.

[107] See Heinz Schilling, *Civic Calvinism in Northwestern Germany and the Netherlands*, Sixteenth Century Essays and Studies, XVII (Kirksville, MO, 1991), pp. 69–105; note also his seminal *Konfessionskonflikt und Staatsbildung* (Gütersloh, 1981).

11   Calvinism in Hungary: the theological and ecclesiastical transition to the Reformed faith

David P. Daniel

By 1620, Hungary, the south-eastern frontier of Latin Christianity, had turned Protestant. The majority of the population was either Lutheran or Reformed. The Lutheran movement had attracted Germans, Slovaks, south Slavs (Croatians and Slovenes) and about fifteen to twenty per cent of the Magyars who became Protestant. Most of the Magyars but very few south Slavs, Slovaks and Germans were members of Reformed churches. A small Anti-Trinitarian community was established and persevered in Transylvania and eastern Hungary whose members were mainly Szeklers and Magyars. The remainder of the population were Catholics, members of Orthodox communities, Jews or Muslims.[1]

This religious diversity was accentuated by the geographic distribution of Protestants in Hungary. Lutherans generally inhabited the peripheral lands of the kingdom where the variety of ethnic groups in the population was greatest. They occupied a crescent-shaped territory that stretched from Croatia in the south-west, northward through western Hungary (the Burgenland) towards Bratislava where it curved eastward to include most of upper Hungary (the Felvidék, roughly analagous to modern-day Slovakia) before it turned to the south-east and reached into Transylvania or Siebenbürgen (Erdélyi) where the borders between the various religious and ethnic communities became diffuse. Reformed communities were established in the heartland of Hungary, which included western Hungary, the territory along both banks of the southward flowing Danube and Tisza rivers but especially in the counties beyond the Tisza and in Transylvania.[2]

The transformation of the religious landscape in Hungary during the

---

[1] For the literature concerning the history of the Reformation in Hungary see especially: Mihály Bucsay, *Der Protestantismus in Ungarn, 1523–1978, Ungarns Reformationskirchen in Geschichte und Gegenwart, I. Im Zeitalter der Reformation, Gegenreformation und katholischen Reform* (Vienna, 1977); Monika Gletter, 'Probleme und Aspekte der Reformation in Ungarn', *Ungarn-Jahrbuch: Zeitschrift für die Kunde Ungarns und verwandte Gebiete*, 10 (1979), 225–239; and David P. Daniel, *The Historiography of the Reformation in Slovakia* (Sixteenth Century Bibliography, X, 1977).

[2] In order to make it possible to use modern maps, the place names provided in the text are those currently used since, during the sixteenth century a place might have a Hungarian, German, Latin and/or Slavic name (See the accompanying table, p. 207, for various forms

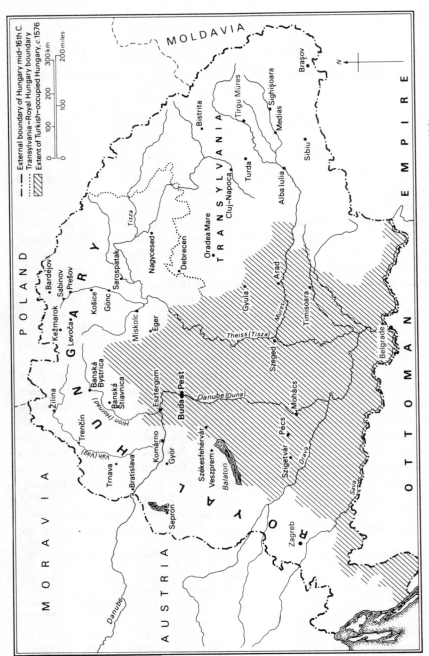

3 Sixteenth-century Hungary. *Source: The Early Reformation in Europe*, ed. A. Pettegree (Cambridge, 1992)

Table 11.1. *Comparative table of place names*

Contemporary	German	Hungarian	Slovak	Latin
Alba Iulia (R)	Weissenburg	Gyulafehérvár		Alba Iulia
Aiud (R)	Strassburg	Nagyenyed		
Ardud (R)	Erdöd	Erdöd	Erdöd	Erdöd
Banská Štiavnica (S)	Schemnitz	Selmecbánya	Banská Štiavnica	Schemnitzium
Banská Bystrica (S)	Neusohl	Besztercebánya	Banská Bystrica	Neosolium
Bardejov (S)	Bartfeld	Bártfa	Bardejov	Bartpha
Bistriţa (R)	Bistritz	Beszterce	Bystrica	Bistrice
Braşov (R)	Kronstadt	Brassó		Corona
Bratislava (S)	Pressburg	Pozsony	Bratislava	Posonium
Buda(pest) (H)	Ofen	Buda	Budín	Buda
Cluj-Napoca (R)	Klausenberg	Kolozsvár		Claudiopolis/Colosvarium
Csepreg (H)	Tschapring	Csepreg		
Eger (H)	Erlau	Eger	Jáger	Agriensis
Esztergom (H)	Gran	Esztergom	Ostrihom	Strigonium
Györ (H)	Raab	Györ	Ráb	Jaurinum
Kežmarok (S)	Käsmark	Késmárk	Kežmarok	Caesareopolis/Kesmarkium
Komjatice (S)		Komjathy	Komjatice	
Košice (S)	Kaschau	Kassa	Košice	Cassovia
Kremnica (S)	Kremnitz	Körmöcbánya	Kremnica	Cremnitzium
Levoča (S)	Leutschau	Lócse	Levoča	Leutschovia
Mediaş (R)	Mediasch	Megyes		Megyes
Oradea Mare (R)	Grosswardein	Nagyvárad	Várad	Varadinum
Poprad (S)	Deutschendorf	Poprád	Poprad	Villa Teutonicalis
Prešov (S)	Eperies	Eperjes	Prešov	Eperiessinum
Sabinov (S)	Szeben	Kisszeben	Savinov	Cibinium
Sárvár (H)		Sárvár		Sárvár
Satu Mare (R)	Sathmar	Szatmárnémeti	Szatmár	Szattmár-Német
Sibiu (R)	Hermannstadt	Nagyszeben		Cibinium
Siebenbürgen (R)	Siebenbürgen	Erdélyi	Sedmohradsko	Septemcastri (Transylvania)
Sighişoara (R)	Schässburg	Segesvár		Segesdvar
Spiš (S)	Zips	Szepesség	Spiš	Scepusia
Sopron (H)	Ödenburg	Sopron		Sopronium
Spišská Nová Ves (S)	Zipser Neudorf	Igló	Spišská Nová Ves	Nova Villa
Stražky (S)	Neere	Straska	Strazy	Neerensis
Székesfehérvár (H)	Stuhlweissenberg	Székesfehérvár		Alba Regalis
Tăşnad (R)	Tschanad	Tasnád		
Timişoara (R)	Temeschburg	Temesvár		
Tîrgu Müres (R)	Neumarkt	Marosvásárhely		Vasarhely
Trenčin (S)	Trentschin	Trencsény	Trenčin	Trenchinium
Turda (R)	Thorenburg	Torda		Torda
Zvolen (S)	Altsohl	Zólyom	Zvolen	Veterosolium
Žilina (S)	Sillein	Zsolna	Žilina	Zolna

Note:
(R)umania, (H)ungary, (S)lovakia (Czecho-Slovakia)

sixteenth century by the emergence of two large, independent Protestant communities, divided by confessional allegiance, their geographic distribution and, to a large extent, by the ethnic composition of their membership took place within a politically partitioned Hungary. After the defeat of the Hungarian army at Mohács (29 August 1526), the first siege of Vienna (1529) and a decade of military skirmishes, greater Hungary was *de facto* divided among three powers. The central core of the Danubian–Tisza basin and its largely Magyar population was governed by the Turks. Transylvania and the *partium* – the counties between the Tisza river and Transylvania, with a mixed population of Magyars and Szeklers, Germans and Wallachians – were administered by John Zápolyai, his son, John Sigismund, and finally by the Báthorys. The remnant, royal or Habsburg Hungary, included most of Croatia and Slovenia with their south-Slavic population, the western counties of the Burgenland, where the number of Germans and Slavs equalled or even exceeded the number of Magyars, and upper Hungary, populated by Slovaks, Germans and some Magyar magnates and townspeople as well as Poles, Ruthenians and Jews. The number of Magyar magnates and lesser nobles in royal Hungary increased during the early sixteenth century as they fled their residences in the Turkish occupied region.[3]

The formation of two major Protestant communities in Hungary and their interaction with one another and with other religious movements in the region makes difficult an elaboration of the peculiarities of each without reference to the Reformation in Hungary as a whole. Moreover, since the preserved documentary evidence is quite limited, scattered and sketchy, it is

of the names of the most important places in the regions with a mixed population.) Modern scholars have generally utilised the version of the place name corresponding to the language in which they are writing. It seems most logical, when writing in English, to use the current name. Personal names, which likewise varied according to language, have been Anglicised.

[3] For English language works concerning the general political history of Hungary within the context of the Austrian Habsburg Empire see: Robert A. Kann, *A History of the Habsburg Empire, 1526–1918* (Berkeley, 1974); Victor S. Mamatey, *Rise of the Habsburg Empire, 1526–1815* (New York, 1971); R. J. W. Evans, *The Making of the Habsburg Monarchy, 1550–1700* (Oxford, 1979); Denis Sinor, *History of Hungary* (London, 1959); C.A. Macartney, *Hungary: A Short History* (Edinburgh, 1962); Ervin Pamlényi (ed.), *Die Geschichte Ungarns* (Budapest, 1971); Janos M. Bak, *Königtum und Stände in Ungarn im 14.–15. Jahrhundert* (Wiesbaden, 1973); and Heinrich Marczali, *Ungarische Verfassungsgeschichte* (Tübingen, 1910) offer an introduction to the political context of the Reformation of the sixteenth century in Hungary. The importance of the Turks for the spread of the Reformation and in the early modern history of Hungary has been treated ably by Stephen A. Fischer-Galati, *Ottoman Imperialism and German Protestantism, 1521–1555* (Cambridge, 1959) and Vojtech Kopčan, *Turecké nebezpečenstvo a Slovensko* (Bratislava, 1988). For the economic impact of the Turkish occupation of central Hungary, which was not as devastating as hitherto supposed, see: Vera Zimányi, *Economy and Society in Sixteenth and Seventeenth Century Hungary (1526–1650)* (Budapest, 1987).

not surprising that Reformation scholars still consider as unresolved three basic questions. First, why did the Helvetic Reformed movement spread so quickly after 1550? Second, why were the overwhelming number of its adherents Magyar? Third, what was the theological orientation of the Reformed movement in Hungary?[4] The historical evidence available, however, does suggest some reasonable hypotheses. An examination of the course, content, contacts and context of the Reformation in Hungary as a whole does indicate some reason why the Magyar Protestants 'turned Swiss'.[5]

In no other region of eastern Europe was the Reformation of the sixteenth century so broadly established or so diversely expressed as in Hungary. Reports of Luther's activities as well as copies of his publications circulated among the intelligentsia in Hungary as early as 1521. A small, influential humanist circle in Buda – including Simon Grynaeus, Viet Winsheim, John Kressling, Conrad Cordatus, who briefly served as Mary Habsburg's court chaplain, and the military tutor of king Louis II, George of Brandenburg – early expressed support for the movement emanating from Wittenberg. Support for Luther also appeared, about the same time, among the largely German population in the royal free and mining cities of upper Hungary and in the cities and towns of Transylvania whose

---

[4] R. J. W. Evans, 'Calvinism in East Central Europe: Hungary and Her Neighbours', in Menna Prestwich (ed.), *International Calvinism, 1541–1715* (Oxford, 1985), pp. 167–96. See also the review of Bucsay's *Der Protestantismus in Ungarn* by Pál I. Fónyad, *Ungarn-Jahrbuch* 10 (1979), 324–35.

[5] Despite a wealth of information available on the Reformation in Hungary, the results of the older and more recent scholarship has not received much attention by Reformation historians in general. Useful general introductions to the topic and the literature include, in addition to the items cited in note 1: Johann Borbis, *Die evangelisch-lutherische Kirche Ungarns in ihrer geschichtlichen Entwicklung* (Nördlingen, 1861); Stephen Linberger, *Geschichte des Evangeliums in Ungarn sammt Siebenbürgen* (Budapest, 1880); Matthias Szlávik, *Die Reformation in Ungarn* (Halle, 1884); Georg Loesche, *Luther, Melanchthon und Calvin in Österreich-Ungarn. Zu Calvins vierter Jahrhundertfeier* (Tübingen, 1909); Jozef Szabó, *Der Protestantismus in Ungarn* (Berlin 1927); Imre Révész, *A magyar protestantizmus története* (Kolozsvár, 1923) with an English version by George A. Knight, *History of the Hungarian Reformed Church* (Washington, 1956); Jenő Zoványi, *A reformáció Magyarországon 1565-ig* (Budapest, 1922) and his *A magyarországi protestantizmus 1565-tol 1600-ig* (Humanizmus és reformáció, VI, 1981); William Toth, 'Highlights of the Hungarian Reformation', *CH*, 9 (1940), 141–56; Erich Roth, *Die Reformation in Siebenbürgen, Ihr Verhältnis zu Wittenberg und der Schweiz* (Siebenbürgsches Archiv, 2, 4, Cologne–Graz, 1962, 1964); Gábor Adriányi, 'Die Ausbreitung der Reformation in Ungarn', *Ungarn-Jahrbuch*, 5 (1973), 66–75; Kálmán Benda, 'La Réforme en Hongrie', *BSHPF*, 122 (1976), 1–53; Karl Reinerth, *Die Gründung der evangelischen Kirchen in Siebenbürgen* (Studia Transylvanica, V, 1979); Alexander S. Unghváry, *The Hungarian Protestant Reformation in the Sixteenth Century under the Ottoman Impact. Essays and Profiles* (Lewiston, 1989); and Katalin Péter, 'Die Reformation in Ungarn', in Ferenc Glatz (ed.), *Etudes Historiques Hongroises 1990, 4, European Intellectual Trends and Hungary* (Budapest, 1990), pp. 39–51. See also the encyclopedia by Jenö Zoványi, *Magyarországi Protestáns Egyháztörténeti Lexicon* (Budapest, 1977).

prosperity resulted from their privileged legal status and their extensive economic and cultural contacts with Poland and the Empire. Influenced by humanism and the modern devotion, urban leaders and nobles in Hungary had been seeking to exercise greater control over ecclesiastical institutions under their jurisdiction. They accepted the reforms advocated in Wittenberg because they seemed to sanction their aims and actions.[6]

The Roman Catholic hierarchy and the lesser Magyar nobility, however, considered the Wittenberg reform movement a significant threat. The papal legate, Cardinal Campeggio, the Bishop of Esztergom, Cardinal Ladislaus Szalkai and the jurist Stephen Werböczy railed against the 'German heresy'. The lesser Magyar nobles resented the influence of foreigners, especially Germans, at court and upon the economic life of the kingdom. In 1523, 1524 and 1525, Hungarian diets decreed that Lutherans and those favouring them shall have their property confiscated and be purged from the land or punished with death. Advocates of reform were forced to flee Buda and the court. However, it seems that only a few individuals openly supported the evangelical reform movement in Hungary before 1526. Most of these were German-speaking townspeople or younger members of the humanist intelligentsia who obtained works published by Luther from merchants who regularly visited the Empire. The publication in Augsburg in 1525 of a tract by Conrad Reyss from Buda expressing support for Zwingli is an anomaly and the provenance of this work is uncertain.[7] Zwingli's theology had little if any influence in Hungary prior to the battle at Mohács.

The defeat of the Hungarian army at Mohács in August 1526 by the Turks under Suleiman I, during which king Louis, six of the twelve bishops of the kingdom, 500 nobles and more than 16,000 soldiers perished, opened the way for the spread of the Reformation throughout Hungary. Many of the humanists viewed the victory of the Turks as a divine chastisement for the sins of the nation, political as well as religious.[8] Throughout Hungary, the number of magnate families who supported and enabled the spread of the Reformation among the non-German population grew steadily throughout the sixteenth century and included the Thurzós, Révays,

---

[6] David P. Daniel, 'Hungary', in Andrew Pettegree (ed.), *The Early Reformation in Europe* (Cambridge, 1992), pp. 49–69.

[7] György Székely, 'Gesellschaft, Kultur und Nationalität in der Lutherischen Reformation in Ungarn', in Leo Stern and Max Steinmetz (eds.), *450 Jahre Reformation* (Berlin, 1967), pp. 201–26; Gusztáv Heckenast, 'Uj adatok az elsö magyarországi reformátorok életrajzához', *Világtörténet*, 11 (1966), 138.

[8] Tibor Klaniczay (ed.), *Handbuch der Ungarischen Literatur* (Budapest, 1977), pp. 29–55; Marianna D. Birnbaum, 'Humanism in Hungary', in Albert Rabil, Jr, *Renaissance Humanism, Foundations, Forms, and Legacy*, (3 vols., Philadelphia, 1988), II, pp. 309–21; Gyula Farkas, *Ungarns Geschichte in Documenten* (Wiesbaden, 1955), pp. 45–48; Tibor Kardos, *A magyarországi humanizmus kora* (Budapest, 1955).

Balássas, Töröks, Nádasdys, the Perényis, Homonnai Drugeths and the Drágffys. The town councils or nobles reformed existing or established new schools, called evangelical preachers and provided financial assistance so that talented students could study at Wittenberg and other universities abroad. As they contended to secure their positions in Hungary and sought allies and money, neither Ferdinand Habsburg nor John Záployai could afford to act aggressively to stop the spread of the Reformation in the cities or among the nobility. Nor were they particularly eager to fill vacant church posts, the benefices of which were 'administered' by nobles. By mid-century most of the major cities and towns in royal Hungary and Siebenbürgen had turned Protestant as had some of the upper nobility or magnates.[9]

The first Magyars who sympathised with the cause of ecclesiastical reform were humanists such as Benedict Komjáthy, Gabriel Pesti Mizsér and John Sylvester (Erdösi).[10] While they supported the reform of the church in the spirit of other Christian humanists, the reforms they actually implemented were quite modest and in keeping with the ecclesiastical attitudes of the humanists. Moreover, even those first generation reformers who actively propagated and sought to implement significant ecclesiastical reform in Hungary and were greatly influenced by the movement emanating from Wittenberg seemed to have been eclectic in their theology. Thus, as these 'evangelical' humanist reformers initiated the Reformation in Hungary they also introduced variety in practice and formulations which laid the foundations for the confessional controversies and divisions which occurred after mid-century.

For example, Sylvester, who studied at both Krakow and Wittenberg, worked on the estates of Thomas Nádasdy. In 1541, he published a Hungarian translation of the New Testament at Sárvar and in 1554 became professor of Hebrew in Vienna. His friend and colleague, Matthias Biró Dévai,[11] was among the first Magyars openly to espouse the cause and engage in ecclesiastical reform. A humanist, whose *Orthographica Hungarica* (Krakow, 1549) contributed to the development of Hungarian as a literary language, Dévai was a popular preacher and an ardent if enigmatic reformer. Called the 'Hungarian Luther' he had more in common with the theology of Melanchthon and other humanist evangelicals than with the more uncompromising positions of Luther. Like several of the other first generation reformers in Hungary, Dévai was a former Franciscan, had studied at Krakow, visited Wittenberg – three times during his career – and

9 Tibor Fabiny, 'Luthers Beziehungen zu Ungarn und Siebenbürgen', in Helmut Junghans (ed.), *Leben und Werk Martin Luthers von 1526 bis 1546, Festgabe zu seinem 500 Geburtstag* (2 vols., Berlin, 1983), II, pp. 641–6.
10 Bucsay, *Der Protestantismus in Ungarn*, pp. 90–1.
11 István Botta, *Dévai Mátyás a Magyar Luther (Budapest, 1990); Bucsay, Der Protestantismus in Ungarn*, pp. 54–7.

acknowledged his debt to the Wittenberg reformers. At the same time, again like his Magyar evangelical contemporaries, he demonstrated an independence in his theology, especially concerning the real presence of Christ in the Lord's Supper and the soul-sleep of the saints.[12] He had no fixed abode and frequently changed his residence in the face of danger. Dévai preached in Buda, Košice and on the estates of Nádasdy, Péter Perényi, Caspar Serédi and Caspar Drágffy, and was arrested at least twice for his activities. His views were censured by the Franciscan Gregor Szegedi in the first published work of the Counter Reformation in Hungary, *Censurae in propositiones erroneas Mathiae Dévai Bíro* (Vienna, 1538).

During the 1540s, Dévai's views concerning the real presence were criticised by other evangelical reformers. Dévai opposed the liturgical and theological elements of the Roman mass and de-emphasised the physicality of the presence of Christ in the sacramental elements while affirming the reality of His presence, bound with and connected to the signs of the spirit. Michael Radaschinus and Leonhard Stöckel, the pastor and the rector of the humanist school in Bardejov, chastised Dévai for having forsaken Luther. The controversy was brought to the attention of Luther who was disturbed by the reports concerning Dévai. In 1544 he wrote to the city of Prešov, in north-eastern Hungary, to express his astonishment at the reports he had received indicating that Dévai had not learned such views at Wittenberg.[13] However, Dévai's position seems to have been held by many other early evangelical reformers in Hungary. In July 1544, a synod at Oradea in Siebenbürgen held that the spiritual body and blood of Christ is present, communicated and dispensed to the believer. Yet they still considered themselves Lutheran. In 1545, shortly after Dévai had died, a synod at Ardud accepted twelve articles on church discipline, the last of which stated that the Augsburg Confession was their doctrinal standard.[14]

Shortly after Dévai had returned to Hungary, Michael Sztárai began his career as a reformer. Like Dévai, Sztárai was influenced by Luther and Melanchthon and was more concerned with practical and moral reform than with theological definitions. Trained at Padua and a member of the Franciscan order until his conversion to the evangelical cause sometime during the 1530s, Sztárai worked in the western half of Hungary occupied by the Turks where, by his own account, he founded at least 120 congregations. He was elected Senior twice, first in Laskó and then in Tolna. Because of his conservative liturgical views and his imprecise

---

[12] *Disputatio de Statu in quo sint beatorim animae post hanc vitam, ante ultimi iudicii diem. Item de praecipuis articulis christianae doctrinae, per Matthiam Devay Hungarum. His addita est expositio examinis quomodo a Fabro in carcere sit examinatus.* (np, nd).

[13] *WA Br.* 10, no. 3984, pp. 55–556; Toth, 'Highlights of the Hungarian Reformation', 149.

[14] Iohannes Ribini, *Memorabilia augustanae confessionis in regno Hungariae* (2 vols., Posonii, 1787, 1789), I, p. 66.

formulations concerning the real presence, he was attacked by those favouring Helvetic theology as a Lutheran, and by the Lutherans as a Sacramentarian.[15]

Clearly Helvetic in his theological orientation was Stephen Szegedi Kis who studied at both Vienna and Krakow before matriculating at Wittenberg in 1543 where he received his doctorate in theology the following year. Upon his return to Hungary, he worked as a teacher in the Danubian basin and then on the estates of General Peter Petrovics in Timişoara. He was instrumental in helping to establish a district organisation for the Reformed churches in southern Hungary at the synods at Torony in 1549 and 1550. Matthias Gönci was elected Senior of the district since Szegedi Kis was ordained by Sztárai for the pastorate at Laskó only in 1554. After 1558 he served in Kálmáncsa where he was arrested as a suspected spy by the Turks and held for one and a half years until a ransom of 1,200 talers was paid. Upon his release he became pastor in Ráckeve for nine years and then served as the superintendent for the Danubian district. By his death in 1572 he had produced several works (published posthumously) including a doctrinal theology which exhibited his affinity for the theology of Heinrich Bullinger and a distaste for the 'ubiquitarianism' of Brenz and the 'memorialism' of Zwingli, an affinity shared by many second generation Magyar reformers.[16]

By 1550, the evangelical reformation had spread throughout Transylvania. In Sibiu and Braşov the Lutheran movement predominated. In Sibiu, Dominican monks were expelled from the city in 1529 but it was only in 1536 that Matthias Ramser, educated in Vienna and formerly pastor in Sabinov in upper Hungary, became the first Lutheran city pastor.[17] Political difficulties with Zápolyai postponed the formal organisation of the church there until the after the colloquy held at Sighişoara in 1538 and a diet held at Turda in 1542. The latter extended to each of the three 'nations' in Transylvania (Germans, Magyars and Szeklers) the right to govern themselves through their own national assemblies or 'universities'.

Representatives of several currents of religious thought met at Sighişoara in 1538. The Catholics were represented by bishop Utjesenovics-Martinuzzi of Oradea, bishop Statilius of Alba Iulia and bishop Frangepan of Eger. The humanist evangelicals who sought to reform the existing church

---

[15] Bucsay, *Der Protestantismus in Ungarn*, pp. 57–60.
[16] *Ibid.*, pp. 65–69; William Toth, 'Stephen Kis of Szeged, Hungarian Reformer', *ARG*, 44 (1953), 86–102.
[17] H. Pitters, 'Luther und die Anfänge der Reformation in der Siebenbürgisch-Sächsischen Kirche. Siebenbürgische Beziehungen zu Wittenberg in der 1. Hälfte des 16. Jahrhundert', in Hermann Pitters and Gerhard Schullerus (eds.), *Gefördet und Gesegnet: Die Kirche der Siebenbürger Sachsen und ihr lutherisches Erbe* (Beihefte der Kirchlichen Blätter, IV, 1983), pp. 37–57.

from within included Adrian Wolfhardt, Martin Kálmáncsehi Santa and Anton Verantius, all from Alba Iulia. The openly Protestant position was defended by Stephen Szántai who had been arrested in Košice and brought to Sighişoara to defend his views. Zápolyai's court physician, John Renezei, openly expressed his support for Szántai; Adrian Enyedi and Kálmáncsehi, appointed as judges by Zápolyai, did so secretly. After being publicly chastised, Szántai was allowed to return to his post in Košice. Shortly thereafter, five of the canons of the chapter in Alba Iulia joined the evangelical cause. Two of them, Sebastian Károlyi Boldi and Kálmáncsehi eventually became bishops in the Magyar Reformed church.[18]

In Braşov, John Honter emerged as a leading advocate of reform. In many ways he was the epitome of a humanist evangelical, magisterial reformer. He studied in Vienna and Krakow, sojourned in Basle and was familiar with the positions of both the German and Helvetic reformers. Upon his return to Transylvania, he established his own press in Braşov in 1539 and worked to reform the school and church in the city. As a member of the inner council, he was the effective leader of the reform party. In 1542 he issued a church order for the region. Two years later he succeeded Jeremias Jekel, who had disagreed with Honter's direct involvement in ecclesiastical matters, as the city pastor of Braşov. In 1547, the Saxon 'university' used Honter's *Formula reformationis Coronensis* to prepare a new church order to govern all the German Protestants in Siebenbürgen. However, the independent course being pursued by Cluj became more obvious when, in 1550, a confession by Martin Bucer was published there.[19]

Lutheranism spread relatively rapidly during the 1530s and 1540s in the cities of royal Hungary and representatives of the five royal free cities of north-eastern upper Hungary (Prešov, Sabinov, Bardejov, Kežmarok, Levoča and Košice) met in synod at Prešov in 1546 and accepted sixteen articles concerning liturgy and polity. The first article declared their allegiance to the Augsburg confession of 1530.[20] The seven mining cities of central upper Hungary, including Banská Bystrica, Zvolen and Kremnica, likewise adopted Lutheranism while in western Hungary, Simon Gerengel preached Lutheran doctrines to the Germans of Sopron.

---

[18] Bucsay, *Der Protestantismus in Ungarn*, pp. 83–4.

[19] Martin Bucer, *Confessio de Coena Domini recens scripta, Item epistola Joannis Bretii de verbis Domini, Hoc est Corpus Meum, opinionem hostium Sacramenti Coena refellens* (Colosvarini, 1550). For the situation in Siebenbürgen see: Ludwig Binder, 'Johannes Honterus und die Reformation im Süden Siebenbürgens mit besonderer Berücksichtigung der Schweizer und Wittenberger Einflüsse', *Zwingliana*, 13 (1973), 545–97; Erich Roth, *Die Reformation in Siebenbürgen. Ihr Verhältnis zu Wittenberg und der Schweiz* (Siebenbürigshes Archiv, 2, 4, 1962, 1964); Oskar Wittstock, *Johannes Honterus, Der Siebenbürger Humanist und Reformator* (Göttingen, 1970).

[20] Ribini, *Memorabilia*, pp. 67–70; Ludwig Binder, 'Die frühesten Synoden der evangelischen Kirche in Siebenbürgen', in Franklin Clark Fry (ed.), *Geschichtswirklichkeit und Glaubensbewährung. Festschrift für Bischof Friedrich Müller* (Stuttgart, 1967), pp. 220–44.

By mid-century, the advocates of reform had begun to gain effective control not only of individual congregations but also of pastoral fraternities throughout the kingdom, especially in northern Hungary and Transylvania. However, the theological differences among these 'evangelical' reformers had not yet led to major theological controversies or division. During the next half century, the evangelical reform movement fractured along theological, ecclesiastical and ethnic lines. This confessionalisation of the Reformation in Hungary culminated in the establishment of Lutheran and Reformed orthodoxy during the first quarter of the seventeenth century. This process was prepared by the experience of students from Hungary at Wittenberg and then at other German, Swiss and eventually Dutch universities. It was stimulated by the need to achieve legal toleration as the revitalised Catholic hierarchy and individual members of the Society of Jesus sought to halt and then reverse the spread of the Reformation throughout the kingdom and encouraged by the Peace of Augsburg (1555) which provided a precedent on how such toleration might be achieved. The defeat of the Lutheran forces of Hesse and Saxony at Mühlberg in 1547 also played its part.

From 1522, when George Baumheckel from Banská Bystrica and Martin Cyriacus of Levoča became the first students from Hungary to matriculate at Wittenberg, until the end of the century, more than 1,000 students from the kingdom followed in their footsteps. The number of Magyar students increased substantially after 1540 and declined quickly after the purge of Crypto-Calvinists and Philippists in 1574 and again in 1592. In 1546 some students from Hungary formed a loose national organisation to provide financial assistance to Magyar students and to govern their spiritual, social and academic life. Based upon the model of the Hungarian Bourse at Krakow it was refounded as the Hungarian Coetus in 1555 when its leaders prepared new rules for the organisation. After 1565 admission to the Coetus required subscription to the *Confessio Formula Juramenti* and its repudiation of Anti-Trinitarianism. Melanchthon showed special solicitude for the Coetus and many, if not most, of its members were Philippists who exhibited an affinity for Helvetic theology and Calvinism. From its founding until its closure and the removal of its funds and charter to Hungary in 1614, it remained a purely Magyar organisation; no German or Slav from Hungary joined it.[21] The members of the Coetus were Magyars who had been attracted to Wittenberg by its 'humanism' and not primarily by its 'Lutheranism'. They had been influenced as much by Italian, largely neo-Platonic humanism, which had spread widely through the kingdom during the late fifteenth century, as by the northern Christian humanism

---

[21] Géza Szabó, *Geschichte des ungarischen Coetus an der Unitersität Wittenberg, 1555–1613* (Halle, 1941).

which was introduced into Hungary at the dawn of the sixteenth century. Moreover, after 1560, they combined their visit to Wittenberg with sojourns at other universities and academies where Helvetic influences were in evidence. After returning home, they contributed to the confessionalisation of the Reformation in Hungary.

The catalyst for the confessionalisation of the evangelical Reformation in Hungary was the defeat of the Lutherans in the Empire at Mühlberg. One year later, in 1548, the Hungarian Diet ordered the expulsion of Zwinglians, Sacramentarians and Anabaptists from the kingdom. The Catholic hierarcy, seeking to re-establish its effective authority over the churches of the evangelicals, still legally under their jurisdiction, sought to apply this edict as well as those from the 1520s against all religious innovators in the kingdom. They employed visitations to ferret out reformers and lapsed Catholics. To defend themselves, to disassociate themselves from more radical religious movements and to seek toleration on the basis of the German precedent of Augsburg, the evangelical communities in Hungary prepared confessions of faith to define the content of the gospel they preached and taught as orthodox. The confessions which they prepared and presented to political or religious authorities in an attempt to secure toleration, or which they adopted, together with regulations concerning life and practice, to govern their pastoral fraternities or conferences, resulted in the fragmentation of the evangelical movement into distinct confessional communities. As each confessional community sought to establish what were orthodox formulations of its faith, and to legitimate liturgical practices and effective forms of ecclesiastical administration, intraconfessional disputes subsequently widened the divisions between the communities. At the same time, the ethnic differences and even economic differences between the communities became increasingly evident. It was the lesser Magyar nobility and citizens of the smaller market-towns who were particularly attracted to the Reformed movement[22] while the Germans, the upper nobility and the Slovaks became Lutheran.

In upper Hungary, three confessions of faith based upon the *Augustana* and the *Corpus Misnicum* or collected works of Melanchthon were prepared: the *Confessio Pentapolitana* of the five royal free cities of Saroš and Spiš counties, prepared by Leonhard Stöckel in 1548 for presentation to Bishop Stephen Bardala who initiated a visitation of the region; the *Confessio Montana* of 1558 compiled by Ulrich Cubicularius for the seven mining cities when Nicholaus Oláh, archbishop of Esztergom sought to implement the canons of the Council of Trent; and the *Confessio Scepusiana* of 1569 prepared by Cyriac Koch or Obsopaeus and Valentin Megander for the fraternity of the pastors of the twenty-four towns of Spiš

---

[22] Glettler, 'Reformation in Ungarn', 234–6.

county when bishop George Bornemissa of Oradea threatened a visitation to restore them to the Catholic fold. Succinct and moderate in expression these confessions contained no anathemas although they expressly repudiated Anabaptism. Concerning the Lord's Supper they held that 'the true substantial body and blood of Christ, born of the Virgin and which suffered on the cross, is received by the Church'. The confessions also maintained that all things which promote true piety and are consistent with good conscience and order may be practised by the church since, in these matters Christians enjoy evangelical freedom.[23]

In Transylvania and the *Partium*, German and Magyar ecclesiastics likewise prepared confessions of faith. While indicating their great respect for the teachings of Luther and Melanchthon, the leading Magyar reformers, among them Michael Sztárai, Gallus Huszár, Stephen Szegedi, Martin Kálmáncsehi, Stephen Kopási and Caspar Károlyi drew freely from various theologians, especially from Philip Melanchthon[24] and Heinrich Bullinger.[25]

The theological formulations of Melanchthon and Bullinger were diversely interpreted throughout the region and initially provided the means to overcome or cover over theological differences among the evangelical reformers. When Matthias Zabardy, bishop of Oradea sought to reimpose Catholicism in his diocese in 1554, a synod at Óvári resolved to reintroduce the use of the host, auricular confession and the old festivals while the removal of altars was placed in the hands of the magistrates. In its articles

[23] David P. Daniel, 'The Influence of the Augsburg Confession in South-East Central Europe', *SCJ*, 11 (1980), 109.

[24] For the relationship of Melanchthon to the Reformation in Hungary see especially: Adalbert Hudak, 'Melanchthon un die Slowakei', in Desider Alexy (ed.), *Ein Leben für Kirche und Volk. Zum 90. Geburtstages des Professors der Theologie, Dr. Roland Steinacker* (Stuttgart, 1960), pp. 33–7; Endre Kovács, 'Melanchthon und Ungarn', in *Philipp Melanchthon, Humanist, Reformer, Praeceptor Germaniae* (Berlin, 1963), pp. 261–9; István Borzsák, 'Zur Frage der Rezeption Melanchthons in Ungarn', in Leopold Magon (ed.), *Studien zur Geschichte der deutsch-ungarischen literarischen Beziehungen* (Berlin, 1969); Wilhelm Neuser, 'Melanchthons Abendmahlslehre und ihre Auswirkung im unteren Donauraum', *Zeitschrift für Kirchengeschichte*, 84 (1973), 49–59; Hans Scheible, 'Melanchthons Beziehungen zum Donau-Karpaten-Raum bis 1546', in Georg and Renate Weber (eds.), *Luther und die Siebenbürgen. Ausstrahlungen von Reformation und Humanismus nach Südosteuropa* (Siebenbürgisches Archiv, 19, Cologne–Vienna, 1985), pp. 36–67.

[25] For Bullinger's relationship to and contacts with Hungary see especially: István Schlegel, 'Die Beziehungen Heinrich Bullingers zu Ungarn', in Walther Hubatsch (ed.), *Wirkungen der Deutschen Reformation bis 1555* (Darmstadt, 1967), pp. 351–95; Endre Szindely, 'Bullinger und Ungarn', in Ulrich Gäbler and Erland Herkenrath (eds.), *Heinrich Bullinger, 1505–1575. Gesammelte Aufsätze zum 400 Todestag, 2. Beziehungen und Wirkungen* (Zürcher Beiträge zur Reformationsgeschichte, VIII, 1975), pp. 360–83, and his *Bullinger Henrik magyarországi kapcsolatai* (Studia et Acta Ecclesiastica, II 1967), 57–86; and Barnabas Nagy, 'Quellenforschungen zur ungarischen Reformationsliteratur unter besonderer Berücksichtigung der Beziehungen zu Bullinger', *Zwingliana*, 12 (1965), 191–206.

on the Lord's Supper, the formulations of the Wittenberg Concord with some modifications were employed. One year later, at a synod in Ardud, Demeter Tordai, elected superintendent at Óvári, was condemned for replacing the altar in his church with a communion table. But, just two years later, the clergy in Oradea and Tăşnad for which Kálmáncsehi served as bishop, accepted a confession concerning the Lord's Supper which was Helvetic in its formulations.[26]

Bullinger's correspondence with individuals in Hungary began in the 1540s. His correspondents included Martin Hentius, Joseph Makarius, Gallus Huszár, Lucas Szikszói, Matthias Thuri, Peter Horhi Mélius Juhász and Gergely Belényesi (the only Magyar to have had direct contact with John Calvin).[27] In 1551, at the request of the Secretary of the Hungarian State Chancellery in Vienna, John Fejérthoy, Bullinger prepared his *Libellus Epistolaris* for Hungary, published in 1559 by Gallus Huszár in Óvári and by Gaspar Heltai in Cluj. Even prior to its publication, manuscript copies were circulated among Magyar Reformed clerics.[28] It is indicative of the situation in Hungary that the irenic Huszár, who corresponded with Bullinger and was active as a reformer in northern and western Hungary before his death as pastor of Pápa in 1575, also published the *Postilla* and the hymnbook of the Magyar Lutheran Peter Bornemisza and worked together with Peter Horhi Mélius Juhász in Debrecen. His son David, one year after assuming the pastorate of Pápa in 1576, published a Hungarian translation of the Heidelberg Catechism.[29]

The influence of the theology of Bullinger and of the Second Helvetic Confession can be seen in several confessions adopted in eastern Hungary and Transylvania between 1559 and 1570: the Confession on the Lord's Supper of 1559 adopted at Tîrgu Mures, the *Confessio Catholica* of 1562, the confessions adopted by the synod of Debrecen in 1567, at Csenger in 1570 and the canons of Hércegszölös of 1576.

The confession on the Lord's Supper of Tîrgu Mures, the first confession written in Hungarian, drew upon the theological formulations of Zwingli and Bullinger when it stated that only believers receive by faith through the agency of the Holy Spirit the benefits of the Sacrament. Believers commune

---

[26] Bucsay, *Der Protestantismus in Ungarn*, pp. 104–11.

[27] Schlégel, 'Die Beziehungen Heinrich Bullingers zu Ungarn', pp. 359–72; Barnabas Nagy, 'Geschichte und Bedeutung des Zweiten Helvetischen Bekenntnisses in den osteuropäischen Ländern', in Joachim Staedtke (ed.), *Glauben und Bekennen, Vierhundert Jahre Confessio Helvetica Posterior, Beiträge zu ihrer Geschichte und Theologie* (Zürich, 1966), pp. 111–12.

[28] Issued in a bilingual Latin/German edition by Barnabas Nagy. Heinrychi Bullingeri, *Epistola ad Ecclesias Hungaricas earumque pastores scripta MDLI* (Budapest, 1968).

[29] Bucsay, *Der Protestantismus in Ungarn*, pp. 109–10; *A Kerestyen Hitről Valo Tudomannac Rövid Kerdesekben foglaltatott Sommaia, mellyet egesz esztendő altal minden Vr-napiara rend szerent magan valo reszekben rendöltünc* (Pápa, 1577). The publication was dedicated to Francis Nádasdy and Elizabeth Báthory from Somlyó.

with the whole Christ, but in a spiritual and not a physical manner. The means for this participation is the Holy Spirit through whom Christ Jesus bestows and shares all of his gifts.[30]

Two years later, when the bishop of Eger sought to force the predominantly Reformed inhabitants of the city to return to the Catholic faith, they adopted a confession of faith prepared by Peter Mélius and Gregor Szegedi of Debrecen, the *Confessio Catholica*, also known as the *Confessio Debrecinensis* or the *Confessio Agrovallensis* after the two places it appeared in print in 1562. In this lengthy document, doctrinal, moral, legal and even medical and scientific questions are discussed. Concerning the personal union of the two natures of Christ it stated that the human nature is accepted and absorbed, but not destroyed, by the divine Logos or Word, and is thus transformed and made spiritual.[31]

At the synod at Tarcal of 1562, attended by Peter Mélius, Helvetic formulations concerning questions of the Lord's Supper and predestination were accepted. Despite the opposition of the Magyar Lutheran minority party, the synod adopted the *Confessio Christianae Fidei et eiusdem collatio cum papisticis haeresibus* of Theodore Beza who regularly corresponded with individuals in Hungary and contributed to the strengthening of Calvinist influence in Hungary.[32] Gabriel Perényi, a Lutheran and the major landowner in the region, sought to expel the Reformed pastors from the region. He succeeded in removing Stephen Kopácsi from Sárospatak but, two years later, the pastors reiterated their acceptance of their confession and made obligatory the use of Calvin's catechism in their churches.[33]

After Perényi's death, the school at Sárospatak became a citadel of the Reformed movement in Hungary. Gaspar Károlyi, pastor at Gönc, became the senior of the district. In this capacity, he had to contend with the influence of Lukas Egri and the Anti-Trinitarian movement which emerged in eastern Hungary and Transylvania around mid-century. The growth of Anti-Trinitarianism was perceived by the Reformed to be as great a threat to their churches as was crypto-Calvinism for the Lutherans. It accentuated the emerging confessional divisions and the significance of christological questions in theological controversies among the evangelical reformers in Hungary.

The German Lutherans in Transylvania, led by Paul Wiener from

---

[30] *Beschluss und Form der Lehre vom Testament und Abendmahl.* See Bucsay, *Der Protestantismus in Ungarn,* note 4, pp. 108ff for excerpts of the German edition of the German translation of the confession published in Heidelberg in 1563.

[31] E.F. Karl Müller, *Die Bekenntnisschriften der reformierten Kirche* (Leipzig, 1903), pp. xxxvii–xxxviii and pp. 265–376 which provide some extracts from the confession.

[32] Leo Weisz, 'Zürich und der evangelische Glaube in Ungarn', *Reformatio, Zeitschrift für evangelische Kultur und Politik,* 5 (1956), 639–41.

[33] Ribini, *Memorabilia,* 1, pp. 166–70; Bucsay, *Der Protestantismus in Ungarn,* pp. 124–25.

Carniola and, after 1554, by Matthias Hebler from Upper Hungary, issued their own confession of faith based upon Melanchthon's Saxon Confession of 1551. Then, in 1562, in their brief confession on the Lord's Supper, they reiterated their Lutheran understanding of the 'real presence' of Christ in the Lord's Supper. The differences between the Lutheran and the Reformed parties was made even more obvious at a synod called by John Sigismund in 1564. Meeting under the presidency of George Blandrata, the synod of Aiud confirmed that the Reformed and Lutherans in Transylvania were not able to resolve their theological and liturgical differences.[34] Eleven years later, in 1572, after the irenic Hebler was succeeded by Lucas Unglarus, the Lutherans, at a synod in Mediaş, adopted the *Formula Pii Consensu Inter Pastores Ecclesiarum Saxonicarum* and the unaltered Augsburg Confession as their theological norms.[35]

The Magyar Reformed community asserted their disagreement with both the Lutheran view of the 'real presence' and with Anti-Trinitarian christology with which they had to contend especially in the *Partium* and Transylvania. Mélius and Kálmáncsehi emerged as the leading polemicists of the Reformed, especially in their struggle with Anti-Trinitarianism. Their opponents included the Saxon, Francis David (Herter) and the Italian physician George Blandrata (Biandrata).

Francis David was from Cluj, studied in Alba Iulia, Wittenberg and Frankfurt on the Oder before returning to Transylvania. He became, in rapid succession, rector of the school at Bistriţa and then at Cluj, then pastor of the city, then superintendent of the Magyar-speaking Lutherans in Transylvania. Within three years David, who ardently defended Lutheran christology against Francis Stancarus and Lutheran sacramental theology against Kálmáncsehi, was persuaded by Mélius to accept the Reformed position on the Lord's Supper. In 1560 he had to relinquish his post as superintendent but not his pastorate. Four years later he was elected bishop of the Magyar Reformed in Transylvania and forced to give up his position in the 'Saxon Nation'. His friendship with George Blandrata, the physician and confident of John Sigismund, led to his appointment as court preacher. By 1570 David was the leading Anti-Trinitarian cleric in Transylvania. Eventually, he split with Blandrata and adopted anti-adorationist

[34] Peter F. Barton and László Makkai, *Ostmitteleuropas Bekenntnisschriften der evangelischen Kirchen A. und H.B., Des Reformationszeitalters III/1 (1564–1576)* (Budapest, 1987), pp. 23–34 (the only volume in the series published); Bucsay, *Der Protestantismus in Ungarn*, p. 126.

[35] Ludwig Binder, 'Die Konkordienformel und die evangelisch-lutherische Kirche in Siebenbürgen', in Jobst Schöne (ed.), *Bekenntnis zur Wahrheit, Aufsätze über die Konkordienformel* (Erlangen, 1978), pp. 141–60; Samuel Piringer, 'Die Reformatorische Erkenntniss Martin Luthers und das Bekenntnis der siebenbürgisch-sächsischen Kirche aus dem Jahr 1572', in Pitters and Schullerus, *Gefördet und Gesegnet*, pp. 117–30.

and even Judaizing views. This resulted in his arrest and imprisonment in Deva castle where he died.[36]

His earlier friend and later theological opponent, Peter Mélius Juhász was born in Somogyi county in southern Hungary in 1536, studied at Tolna under two Lutheran teachers and then, from 1552 to 1554 under Stephen Szegedi Kis. He attended Wittenberg where he became the Senior of the Hungarian Coetus. Upon returning to Hungary he became pastor in Debrecen in 1558 and subsequently superintendent or bishop of the Reformed in the region. He was influenced by the works of Luther, Melanchthon, Beza, Calvin but especially those of Bullinger. Yet, like many of the other leaders of the Magyar Reformed, he preserved his theological independence.[37]

Martin Kálmáncsehi Sánta, after leaving his position as canon at the chapter in Alba Iulia, worked briefly in Mezótúr and by 1551 was in Debrecen. He became involved in a dispute over the Lord's Supper with the Lutherans of Oradea when they accused him of Sacramentarianism because, according to a report of George Draskovics, he held that the body and blood of Christ were present in the Lord's Supper neither through transubstantiation nor in any other physical manner but only as a sign or symbol and also because he rendered the elements no special adoration and celebrated the sacrament without vestments or special vessels. While this bespeaks an affinity for the theology of Zwingli other sources indicate that Kálmáncsehi's theological stance was much closer to that of Beza and Bullinger. He was excommunicated in 1552 at a synod of conservative clerics and he responded in kind. With the support of the guardian of Johann Sigismund Zápolyai, Peter Petrovics, he was able to effect cultic reforms at two synods in northern Hungary in 1552 and one the following year in Siebenbürgen. Forced to flee when Matthias Zabardy, Bishop of Oradea, sought to enforce the edict of 1548 against Sacramentarians, Kálmáncsehi took refuge on the estates of Petrovics until 1556 when, due to another change in the political climate, he was able to return to Debrecen. After debates with David and Heltai over the Lord's Supper in Cluj he moved to Óvári where he died in 1557.[38]

The christological debates which affected all of the major evangelical parties in Hungary including the conflict between the Reformed and the Anti-Trinitarians, were presaged by the Stancarian controversy. Francis

[36] Unghváry, *Hungarian Protestant Reformation*, pp. 323–69; Béla Varga, *Dávid Ferenc és az Unitárius vallás* (Budapest, 1979).
[37] Bucsay, *Der Protestantismus in Ungarn*, pp. 113–20; Unghváry, *Hungarian Protestant Reformation*, pp. 275–313; Mihály Bucsay, 'Leitgedanken der Theologie Bullingers bei Petrus Melius. Ein Beitrag zur Ausstrahlung des Zuercher Reformators nach Ungarn', in Gäbler and Herkenrath, *Heinrich Bullinger, 1504–1575*, II, pp. 197–214.
[38] Bucsay, *Der Protestantismus in Ungarn*, pp. 104–6.

Stancarus, like Blandrata, was an Italian physician and had become embroiled in the Osiandrian controversy in Königsberg (Prussia) in 1551. Returning to Hungary in 1553 to serve Peter Petrovics he participated in a debate with Leonard Stöckel of Bardejov at which Francis David was present. Shortly after, Melanchthon's repudiation of the works of Stancarus was published by Caspar Heltai in Cluj and the views of Stancarus were condemned at several synods. In 1555 David took up his pen against Stancarus.

Stancarus held that Christ can be considered the mediator between God and man only according to his human nature. In a series of syllogisms he held that since the mediator had to die and the divine is not capable of death, Christ is not able to be the mediator according to his divine nature. Moreover, since no one is able to be a mediator to himself, if Christ were a mediator according to his divine nature, he would be a mediator to himself who is one God, Father and Holy Spirit.[39]

David countered with six arguments, each of which defended Chalcedonian christology of an inseparable hypostatic union of two natures in Christ so that the work of reconciliation must be considered the work of the whole Christ, of both the divine as well as of the human nature. In 1558 the pastors of Cluj also published a condemnation of Stancarus. Stancarus left Transylvania the following year for Poland. But the christological debates raging in Hungary, which focused on the real presence in the Lord's Supper, took a more radical turn in the 1560s to include the nature of the Trinity.

David, who earlier had joined with Peter Melius, Kálmáncsehi's successor in Debrecen to refute Stancarus, was drawn more and more towards the Anti-Trinitarianism by Lucas Egri of Eger, a former colleague of David's in Cluj, and by George Blandrata. Egri taught that the eternal Logos was not to be identified with Christ as the Son of God. His views were condemned by the Reformed at a synod at Gönc in January 1566 and by Lutherans in Košice in 1568 after which he recanted. In the meantime, David openly questioned the doctrine of the Trinity from his pulpit. He was chastised by Melius and charged with heresy by Peter Károlyi, rector of the city school. Melius and Károlyi also urged John Sigismund Zápolyai to call a national synod after a work by David and Blandrata, *The False and True Knowledge of God* was published in Alba Iulia. This general synod of the Magyar Reformed churches in eastern Hungary and Transylvania adjourned with the issue unresolved.[40] Blandrata and David then issued an Anti-Trinitarian version of the Heidelberg Catechism which infuriated and insulted the

---

[39] George Huntston Williams, *The Radical Reformation* (Philadelphia, 1962), pp. 714–15.

[40] Williams, *Radical Reformation*, pp. 715–32; Bucsay, *Der Protestantismus in Ungarn*, pp. 134–9; Robert Dán, *Humanizmus, reformáció, antitrinitárizmus és a héber nyelv Magyarországon* (Budapest, 1972);

Reformed.[41] At the synod of Turda in 1567 the Anti-Trinitarians maintained that there was but one God, that the Son was subordinate to the Father and the Holy Spirit was nothing more than the power of God at work.

The spread of these Anti-Trinitarian views led Melius to convene a synod at Debrecen which accepted three confessions of faith. Two of them were by Melius, one in Latin, the other in Hungarian, both directed against David and the Anti-Trinitarians. The third confession of faith adopted as the theological norm for the Magyar Reformed church, was the Second Helvetic Confession.[42] After further debates and synods, the Anti-Trinitarians formally separated from the Reformed community on 28 January 1568.

Two years later, Melius sought to distance the Reformed from the Anti-Trinitarians further at a synod of the Reformed at Csenger for which he prepared a tract. It served as the basis for the *Confessio Csengerina* adopted by the synod.[43] The article on the Lord's Supper specifically repudiated transubstantiation and those who hold 'that the natural body of Christ, born of the Virgin, is received by the corporeal mouth'. It further denied that 'the body of Christ is contained in the bread, [which is] against the rule of faith and of nature, nor is it received in the sacrament by the physical mouth at all, since the confession of faith and the Scriptures teach that the body of Christ has ascended into heaven'. The confession goes on to state that 'it is impossible and contrary to nature that that which is contained is greater than that which contains or that which is laid down in a place can be greater than the place itself'. The confession considers the sacrament a 'sign of the covenant' and denies it is merely a sign or a remembrance of an absent Christ since, as the following article indicates, 'Christ is everywhere present with his elect'.[44]

By 1570, the evangelical reform movement in Hungary had fractured into three distinct groups, the Lutherans, the Reformed and the Anti-Trinitarians, the latter drawing support primarily from the Szeklers and Magyars. Having distanced themselves from the Anti-Trinitarians, the Reformed were attacked vigorously by the Lutherans of upper Hungary. From 1570 until the end of the century the Lutherans debated among

[41] Géza Kathona, 'Die Deformation des Heidelberger Katechismus in den Kämpfen gegen den Antitrinitarismus', in Tibor Bartha *et al.*, *Der Heidelberger Katechismus in Ungarn* (Budapest, 1967), pp. 85–121.

[42] László Makkai, 'Zwei Bekenntnisse der Synode in Debrecen, 1567', in Barton and Makkai (eds.), *Ostmitteleuropas Bekenntnisschriften der evangelischen Kirchen*, pp. 127–32; Barnabas Nagy, 'Geschichte und Bedeutung des Zweiten Helvetischen Bekenntnisses', pp. 108–41.

[43] József Barcza, 'Confessio Csengerina, 1570', in Barton and Makkai (eds.), *Ostmitteleuropas Bekenntnisschriften der evangelischen Kirchen*, pp. 261–2.   [44] *Ibid.*, pp. 266–7.

themselves the acceptance of the Book of Concord as their doctrinal standard. This led also to an increase in tensions with the Reformed as, to the christological debates over the real presence, were added conflicts over liturgical practices, the use of instrumental music and religious art in public and private worship. In the Lutheran intraconfessional disputes, 'crypto-Calvinist' became the normal pejorative used by the 'concordists'.

A striking feature of these intra-Lutheran confessional controversies is that the most ardent and effective defenders of the Formula of Concord and 'ubiquitarian' or 'concordist' theology were Germans from the Empire who had assumed pastorates or teaching positions in Hungary, the Croatian nobleman, founder and rector of a private academy in Strážky, Gregor Horváth Stančič, and two Slovaks who had received all of their theological training in Hungary, Eliáš Láni and Severinus Scultéty. The Philippists or crypto-Calvinists included Magyars and some Germans from Hungary who had studied at Wittenberg after 1555.[45]

The controversy began when Thomas Froehlich attacked Flacianism at a synod in Košice in 1574. When, shortly after he moved to the mining cities, he was attacked as a 'crypto-Calvinist' by Gregory Meltzer. The battle moved eastward, to Spiš and Šaroš counties, just north of the Reformed citadels of Sarospatak and Debrecen. Mentho Gogreff published a treatise on the Lord's Supper in which he set forth the views of Luther, Brenz and Melanchthon on the sacrament so that his readers might 'recognise the malicious and murderous Calvinists as one learns to know a bird by its song'. Matthias Thorakonymous or Kabat responded with a now lost work in which he called Gogreff a heretic of the worst sort, a Flacian. In 1586, Gaspar Creutzer joined the fracas with his first polemical work, *A Warning Concerning the teachings of the Sacramentarians, Zwinglians and Calvinists* (Bardejov, 1586) which set the agenda and parameters of the debate for the next decade and a half. He listed five questions which could unmask suspected false teachers, that is crypto-Calvinists. To this Caspar Pilcz responded with a work, *Signs by which a little Lamb of Christ can be recognised*[46] in which he cautioned true Christians against idolatry and held that the presence of Christ in the sacrament cannot be physical or earthly since 'to be fleshly is to be an enemy of God'. After a further exchange of tracts by Creutzer and Pilcz, Sebastian Ambrosius, John Mylius and Thomas Fabricius Tolnai entered the debate, the first two attacking the views of the 'ubiquitists' as being against reason, Scripture

---

[45] David P. Daniel, 'The Reformation and Eastern Slovakia', *Human Affairs* 1, 2 (1991), 180–2.

[46] Although this work has been lost its contents can be reconstructed from the response of Creutzer published in Kežmarok, *Proba, Der Calvinischen Merckzeichen, Caspari Pilcii Kirchdorffers, dabey er vermeint, ein Scheflein Christi zu erkennen sein.*

and the teaching of Melanchthon, the latter justifying the removal of images from the churches. Severinus Scultéty, Horváth Stančič and Albert Grawer responded to Ambrosius and Mylius while Eliáš Láni defended, against Fabricius, the principle of Christian liberty in the devotional and didactic use of images in worship. This debate between the 'concordists' on the one hand and the Philippists and 'crypto-Calvinists' on the other continued for the next decade and effected the definitive split between Lutherans and the Reformed in eastern Hungary and Transylvania.[47]

An attempt was made to bridge the gap between the Lutherans and the Reformed at the colloquy of Csepreg in western Hungary. The Reformation had spread throughout the region under the patronage of the Lutheran Nádasdys, whose residence was at Sárvar and the Reformed Batthyánys who resided at Güssing castle. The first Protestant superintendent in the region was Matthias Szegedi who had been elected in 1576. But, in 1585, he was succeeded by Stephan Beythe at Güssing. Beythe was a persuasive preacher and a botanist of international repute. In a synod a Csepreg he introduced twenty-seven articles to regularise the life of the district. These, however, precipitated a controversy between the majority of the pastors, who were German and Lutheran and the Reformed, most of who were Magyar, and between the two magnate families. In 1591 an attempt was made to resolve the conflict and heal the breach at another synod held at Csepreg at which the doctrine of the Lord's Supper was discussed. Beythe represented the Reformed; the Lutherans were represented by Severinus Scultéty from upper Hungary, who was on his way home from his ordination in Graz by its orthodox Lutheran superintendent, Jeremias Homberger. Neither side was interested in reconciliation. When Beythe refused to continue the discussions after the first day's meeting, Nádasdy declared the colloquy over. He made the Augsburg Confession the doctrinal standard for the pastors working on his lands while Beythe stood firmly for Calvinism. Two years later he prepared the introduction for a tract presenting the Reformed view of the Lord's Supper by Stefan Patay while in 1595 Nádasdy held a consultation at which a 'Formula Concordiae' was accepted by the German Lutheran pastors. Beythe continued to serve as the superintendent of both confessions until his death when Stephen Klaszenkovics was elected superintendent for the Lutherans. An independent Reformed district was established on the lands of the Batthyánys in 1614.

---

[47] David P. Daniel, 'The Acceptance of the Formula of Concord in Slovakia', *ARG*, 70 (1979), 260–77 provides an introduction to these controversies. See also the following works by György Ráth, 'A felsomagyarországi kryptokálvinisták hitvitázó-irodalmáról', *Irodalomtörtéte Közlemények*, 2 (1892), 310–24; 'Gradeczi Horváth Gergely és Lám (Ambrosius) Sebestyén Hitvitája', *Irodalomtörténete Közlemények*, 4 (1894), 150–67, 299–319, 412–27; and 'Pilcz Gáspár és ellenfelei', *Magyar Könyvszemle* (1892/3), 28–86.

During the 1630s Adam Batthyány and Francis Nádasdy finally resolved the dispute and accepted the same religion; they converted to Roman Catholicism.[48]

By the dawn of the seventeenth century, the division of the Protestant Reformation into two distinct communities, one Lutheran the other Reformed, was complete. However, they still were not legally recognised or tolerated in the kingdom except in Transylvania. Rather, as they grew and gained control of the pastoral conferences of the established church, the Roman Catholic hierarchy and members of the Society of Jesus attempted to implement the reforms mandated by the Council of Trent and to reverse the spread of Protestantism. They had been impeded during the sixteenth century by the lack of enthusiastic support from the Habsburgs, by an insufficient number of trained clergy, by the opposition of the magnates and the towns, by political discord and, during the first half of the seventeenth century, by the determined resistance of three Hungarian nobles from Transylvania, Stephen Bocskai, Gabriel Bethlen and George Rákóczi I.

Bocskai, Bethlen and Rákóczi were staunch members of the Reformed community in Hungary, magnates and shrewd military commanders. In Transylvania they enjoyed the religious toleration which had been established by the diet in Turda (June 1557). By armed resistance they were able to secure for the Protestants in Hungary legal toleration and the right to establish their own separate ecclesiastical organisations: Bocskai in the Peace of Vienna (1606), Bethlen in the Peace of Mikulov (1621) and Rákóczi in the Treaty of Linz (1645).

During the fifteen years' war with the Turks Bocskai became increasingly discouraged by Habsburg policies towards Hungary. He had hoped that the Habsburgs would free central Hungary from the Turkish yoke and extend to the Protestants throughout the kingdom the toleration established in the Empire by the Peace of Augsburg (1555). Bocskai was disappointed on both issues. The Habsburgs, Rudolph II and archduke Matthias, were unwilling or unable to mount a concerted campaign against the Turks. They were equally unwilling to extend toleration to the Protestants in Bohemia and Hungary.

On 7 January 1604, Francis Forgách, bishop of Nitra, supported by General Barbiano seized the church of St Elizabeth in Košice and ordered the expulsion of Protestant clerics, the seizure of other churches in the hands of the Protestants and forbade Protestant worship even in private homes. Shortly thereafter, Martin Pethe, archbishop of Kalocsa and

---

[48] Imre Gyenge, 'Zwei Feudalherren und zwei Konfessionen, Glaubensstreitigkeiten der Lutheraner und Calvinisten Westungarns im 16. Jahrhundert', *Jahrbuch für die Geschichte des Protestantismus in Österreich*, 96 (1980), 214–23.

provost of the Spiš chapter, ordered a visitation of the cities of the largely Lutheran Spiš counties and the implementation of the decrees of the Council of Trent. When the Hungarian Diet met in the spring of 1604 it agreed to provide financial support for the war against the Turks on the condition that it would then take up religious-political questions created by the events in upper Hungary. However, on 6 March, Matthias unexpectedly adjourned the diet. To the twenty-one articles approved by the Diet he added a twenty-second which confirmed all previous laws favouring the Catholic church, including those ordering the expulsion of religious innovators. He also forbade the discussion of religious issues at future diets. Any attempt to initiate such discussions would be considered treason. Bocskai was persuaded by Gabriel Bethlen and other Magyar nobles in Transylvania and eastern Hungary to accept the leadership of the anti-Habsburg forces. His defeat of Barbiano in October 1604 began the 'Bocskai Revolt'. He and his supporters justified their actions by appealing to the right of armed resistance, the *jus resistendi*, expressly recognised by the 'Golden Bull' of 1222.

Two years later, Matthias accepted the Peace of Vienna which recognised the constitutional right of the Hungarian Diet to approve all legislation pertaining to the nation. Article 22 of 1604 was declared null and void. The magnates, nobles and privileged royal cities as well as the troops in the military frontier were accorded the freedom to follow their own faith. No law interfering with or infringing upon this freedom was to be enacted and all public offices, civil and military, were open to all qualified candidates without respect to their religion. However, the clause that nothing in the treaty was to be interpreted as detrimental to the Roman Catholic church proved, despite the assurances of Matthias, the source of continued friction between Catholics and Protestants in Hungary. The Peace of Vienna was to be guaranteed by the emperor and archduke Ferdinand of Austria, the Estates of Bohemia, Moravia, Silesia and Upper and Lower Austria. In October, Sultan Ahmed I and the Habsburgs agreed to the Treaty of Szitvatörök which brought to an end the 'Fifteen Years War' with the Turks and inaugurated a truce which endured for half a century.

Two years later, the Hungarian Diet meeting in Bratislava incorporated the Peace of Vienna without the troublesome clause 'without detriment to the Roman Catholic Religion' into the corpus of Hungarian law. Matthias, eager to secure his election as the king of Hungary, reluctantly agreed to accept this and the right of the Protestants to form their own ecclesiastical organisations and elect their own administrators. The existence of separate Protestant churches in Hungary was finally recognised in law and in accordance with this the Synods of Žilina (1610) and Spišská Podhradie

(1614) established separate ecclesiastical organisations for the Lutherans in upper Hungary.[49]

However, the Catholic hierarchy and especially the Jesuit Peter Pázmany, the son of a Reformed Magyar lesser nobleman, sought to subvert the decisions of the Diet of 1608 by polemic, politics and military force. Gabriel Bethlen replaced Bocskai, who had died in 1606, as the leader of the opposition to the Habsburg policy of Counter-Reformation and consolidation of royal authority. As the Thirty-Years War erupted after the Defenestration of Prague (1618), Bethlen took to arms to defend the Protestants and, after occupying most of royal Hungary, forced archduke Ferdinand of Austria to accept a truce. Shortly thereafter, he declined to accept his election as king of Hungary by the Diet of Banská Bystrica which also enacted several articles designed to reassert the legal status of Protestants in Hungary. The Reformed subsequently regularised their own ecclesiastical districts and superintendencies or bishoprics and in 1621, the Reformed churches which gathered at Komjatice in Nitra county adopted canons which described them as an Orthodox Church accepting the Helvetic Confession (*Ecclesia orthodoxa Helveticam confessionem amplectens*) and in June 1630 the seniorat of Zemplen county became the first Reformed church in Hungary to required subscription to both the Helvetic Confession and the Heidelberg Catechism in the pastoral oath of office.[50]

However, it was not until two decades later, as the Thirty Years War drew to a close and George Rákóczy had inherited the mantel of Bocskai and Bethlen as the defender of religious toleration for the Protestants and the political rights of the Hungarian nation that the Peace of Linz (1645) reaffirmed and enlarged the legal rights extended to the Protestants in Hungary. Freedom of worship was extended to the serfs and churches were no longer considered to be the 'property' of either secular or ecclesiastical landowners. At a national synod of the Reformed churches, held at Satu Mare in July 1646 they officially adopted as their normative doctrinal standards the Second Helvetic Confession and the Heidelberg Catechism. The Magyar Reformed church, one of the four major Calvinist churches established in Europe, had finally established its legal existence and its theological norms almost 125 years after the Reformation began in Hungary and a century after the first evangelical synods were held.

[49] Géza Lencz, *Der Aufstand Bocskays und der Wiener Friede. Eine kirchenhistorische Studie* (Debrecen, 1917); David P. Daniel, 'The Fifteen Years War and the Protestant Response to Habsburg Absolutism in Hungary', *East Central Europe/L'Europe du Centre-est*, 8 (1981), 38–51.

[50] Nagy, 'Geschichte und Bedeutung des Zweiten Helvetischen Bekenntnisses', pp. 118–22. For the development of Calvinist orthodoxy in Hungary and the peculiar theological influences at work in seventeenth-century Hungary see Géza Szabó, *A Magyar Református Orthodoxia a XVII. század teológiai irodalma* (Budapest, 1943).

Why did the Helvetic or Reformed movement spread so rapidly after 1550 and why did it find its supporters primarily among the Magyars? It is clear that the Reformed movement established itself most quickly and firmly in those regions not directly under Habsburg control and where the Catholic hierarchy was not able to exercise its legal authority over the churches effectively. In these territories, moreover, contacts with Italy had been particularly lively during the fifteenth century. At the dawn of the sixteenth century, the influence of Italian humanism, strongly neo-Platonic in orientation, was joined with Erasmian or Christian humanism. The students from the region sought out humanist institutions abroad, including the university of Wittenberg where large numbers of Magyar students enrolled after the death of Luther and before expulsions of the 'crypto-Calvinists' in 1574 and 1592. During this period, the Hungarian Coetus and the Philippism at Wittenberg shaped their theological development. Most of the evangelical literature available in Hungarian emanated from the Reformed community. The substantially different ethnic composition of the Reformed and Lutheran communities and extant documentary evidence reveals that ethnic tensions did exist between the lesser Magyar nobility and free peasants and the largely German municipalities in Hungary as well as between the German and Slovak intelligentsia on the one hand and the Magyar on the other. While this ethnic rivalry was far less evident among the approximately two-score magnate families, they were divided into pro-Habsburg and anti-Habsburg parties, the former generally opting for Lutheranism if they became Protestant, the latter tending to accept the Reformed faith. The patronage of the nobles, the royal free cities and the market towns was usually decisive in determining the religion of those on their lands.[51]

What was the content of that Reformed faith? Certainly it was Helvetic. But even as it was Melanchthon more than Luther who provided the theological formulations employed by the Lutherans until the introduction of the Book of Concord, it was Bullinger and Beza, rather than Calvin who were the most influential Helvetic theologians among the Magyars until the dawn of the seventeenth century. Calvin's works began to circulate more widely and Calvinist orthodoxy began to take root only after 1575 when Magyar students began to visit universities in the Rhineland and in the Netherlands in increasing numbers. The struggle to obtain legal recognition and toleration for the Protestant confessions in Hungary finally led them to

[51] For the decisive role played by the nobility in establishing the religious allegiance of specific communities and, in particular, the question of ethnicity and confessional allegiance see the study of the emergence of the small Calvinist community in Slovakia by Branislav Varsik, 'Vznik and vývin slovenských Kalvánov na východnom Slovensku', Historický časopis, 39 (1991), 129–148.

define their faith more clearly in harmony with the reigning theology of their coreligionists abroad.

Finally, the debates with the Lutherans concerning the presence of the human nature in the sacrament, the reception of the body and blood of Christ by the impenitent, the related christological issue of the communication of attributes and the propriety of utilising pictures, statues and instrumental music in the Christian worship indicates that there was a fundamental disagreement among the two communities concerning the relationship between the spiritual and the material. The Reformed and the Philippist Lutherans tended to utilise a polar understanding of the relationships between the spiritual and the material, between the signs and the things signified, between the vehicle and the means of communication and the essential spiritual reality which was communicated. For them, the spiritual, divine nature of Christ was the essential source and agent of reconciliation while the human nature of Jesus was the material vessel which was made spiritual by the indwelling of the divine Logos yet remained spatially circumscribed. The Lutherans, on the other hand, maintained that the communication of the divine and human natures meant that both spatial and temporal terms were inadequate to discuss the person of Christ. The perceived polarities between matter and spirit were not essential but accidental. Neither space nor time can limit Christ, His person, His work or His presence. This fundamental difference in attitude among the reformers towards the relationship between matter and spirit was the larger context which fuelled their theological debates and inexorably led them along separate paths as they wrestled with the ultimate question of Christianity, the question put to St Peter by Jesus himself, 'Who do you say that I am?' (Luke 9:20).

12   Calvinism and the Gaidhealtachd in Scotland

Jane Dawson

In the early modern period Scotland was divided by language into two separate regions. The Gaidhealtachd, the Gaelic-speaking area, had receded during the later middle ages. By the start of the sixteenth century, except for a pocket in the south-west of Scotland, it was largely confined to the region beyond the Highland Fault Line covering the Highlands and the Western Isles (see Figure 4). In the Lowlands, Scots was spoken and was the language of the Court, its government and administration. This linguistic divide reflected a growing polarisation between distinct Highland and Lowland cultures. An increasingly hostile view of Gaelic society developed in Scotland from the later sixteenth century. This process was accelerated by the union of the crowns of Scotland, England and Ireland in 1603 and the subsequent removal of the Court to London. In the new British state the Gaelic language in both its Irish and its Scottish homelands would be subjected to the cultural imperialism of the dominant Anglo-Scots vernacular.[1]

The existence of two distinct languages and cultures in Scotland faced the new Protestant Kirk with a problem. In common with other European Protestants, the Kirk was committed to abandoning the Latin of the Catholic church and using the local vernacular. But Scots and Gaelic were not simply two dialects; they were separate languages with completely different linguistic roots. The Kirk had to cope with two vernaculars and, of even greater importance, two diverging cultures and societies. Misunderstandings could easily arise, as in 1624 when some Lowland ministers instructed their clerical brethren from the Highlands to stop attending presbytery meetings in 'unsemly habits'. The Lowlanders, who had been carrying out a visitation of the presbytery of Inverness, were shocked by the sight of ministers dressed in bonnets and plaids.[2] To Lowland eyes they

I am most grateful to Dr Donald Meek for all his assistance, particularly with the intricacies of the Gaelic language in the early modern period, and also to Professor Bruce Lenman and Drs Ronald Cant, John Bannerman and Terence McCaughey for their helpful comments.

[1] C.J. Withers, *Gaelic in Scotland, 1698–1981* (Edinburgh, 1984); *Gaelic Scotland* (London, 1988).

[2] *Extracts from the Records of the Synod of Moray*, ed. W.M. Cramond (Elgin, 1906), p. 7.

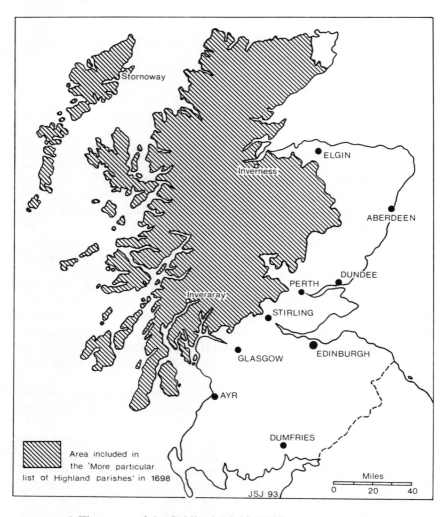

4 The extent of the Gaidhealtachd in 1698
Source: C.W.J. Withers, *Gaelic in Scotland 1698–1981* (Edinburgh, 1984), p. 47

must have appeared to be barbaric men who did not belong in the Scottish Kirk at all. Although the Gaelic clergy looked completely alien to their Lowland counterparts, they were wearing the normal dress of a Highlander. These ministers were good Calvinists but they were also good Gaels. They had evolved a distinctively Gaelic form of Calvinism by taking the ideas and institutions of the Kirk and fitting them into a Highland context.

The characteristic feature of the type of Calvinism found in Scotland's Gaelic-speaking areas was the willingness to adopt set forms and practices and adapt them to suit the local situation. This was demonstrated in the adoption of the traditional methods and personnel of the 'Gaelic learned orders' to communicate the Protestant message and spread it throughout the Highlands and Islands. It can also be viewed in the flexible approach to the institutional structures of the Scottish Kirk which strove for maximum effectiveness on minimal resources. In these ways the Gaelic clergy had the self-confidence and assurance both to fit Calvinism into their own culture and to change that culture to accommodate the new demands of the Protestant message.

The creation of a Gaelic Calvinism in the first century of the Scottish Reformation has gone largely unnoticed. As in the case of the Lowland attitude towards clerical tartan, appearances can be deceptive. It was perfectly true that the kind of reformation achieved by the Scottish Kirk in the Lowlands between 1560 and 1660 was not replicated in the Highlands and Islands. However, this did not mean that James VI was correct when he asserted that his Gaelic subjects were 'wilde savaiges voide of Godis fear and our obedience'.[3]

I

The strong Protestantism which spread into the Highlands and Islands between 1560 and 1660 was of a very different nature to that practised in the Lowlands of Scotland. It was a Gaelic version of Calvinism not only in the sense that it employed the Gaelic language in its worship but also because it had been adapted to fit Gaelic society and culture. In early modern Scotland the Gaelic language itself took two different forms: Scottish Vernacular and Classical Common Gaelic. The literary language of Classical Common Gaelic was shared with Gaelic Ireland and was the vehicle for the high culture of a single pan-Gaelic world. Traditional learning in law, medicine and literature was composed and then transmitted in this common tongue. In particular, it was the language of the professional poets with their complex and rigid rules of composition and versification. This literary tradition was transmitted in manuscript form using the specialist corra-litir script by the Gaelic learned orders.[4]

By the sixteenth century Classical Common Gaelic survived in both

---

[3] James VI's Instructions to the Commission to Improve the Isles, 8 December 1608, in *Collectanea de Rebus Albanicis* (Iona Club, 1847), p. 115.

[4] D.S. Thomson, *Introduction to Gaelic Poetry* (Edinburgh, 1990 edn), ch. 1; R. Black, 'The Gaelic Manuscripts of Scotland', in *Gaelic and Scotland*, ed. W. Gillies (Edinburgh, 1989), pp. 146–74.

manuscript and oral form. Its orthography and typography remained in an experimental state and it had not yet made the transition to a printed language with the consequent standardising effect. The classical language was not in everyday use but was primarily employed by an elite to perform certain specific tasks.

It is a matter of learned debate precisely how much the common people understood of the compositions in Classical Common Gaelic. Over time the spoken language in Scotland had diverged from the more archaic literary language and was also moving away from the corresponding Irish vernacular. In the sixteenth and seventeenth centuries Scottish Vernacular Gaelic was becoming more self-confident and developing its own freer forms of poetry. However, Classical Common Gaelic remained the prime vehicle for literary culture.[5]

To some extent the products of this literary culture needed to be interpreted to make them fully comprehensible in the vernacular of the day. The Gaelic learned orders, and to a lesser extent the aristocracy, acted as bridges between the two forms of the language. This was made much easier because of the great emphasis upon the oral performance and transmission of the literary culture and produced what Professor Thomson has styled 'the culture of oral literacy'.[6] The normal skills acquired by a member of the learned orders made them the natural interpreters into the vernacular.

The Gaelic learned orders, with their carefully graded hierarchies, provided the professional skills for the rest of their society in the fields of literature, music, law, medicine and some of the specialist crafts such as armourer. They were drawn from hereditary families who were given special status and privileges within Gaelic society. The orders placed great emphasis upon oral transmission and memorisation. These skills were taught by the tradition-bearers in the long and extremely rigorous training of the special schools, most of which were located in Ireland. The professional poets learned to compose their poems entirely in the mind, working out the complicated metrical structures whilst, it is claimed, they were lying on their backs in a darkened hut with a boulder on their chests. They also developed literary skills but these were regarded as subordinate to the traditional methods of non-literate learning.[7]

The setting for the oral transmission of this literary culture in Classical Common Gaelic was provided by the regional courts of the major magnates of Gaelic Scotland. As well as acting as patrons to the learned orders, the

[5] Thomson, *Introduction*, ch. 3.
[6] *Ibid.*, p. 99; J. Bannerman, 'Literacy in the Highlands', in *The Renaissance and Reformation in Scotland*, ed. I.B. Cowan and D. Shaw (Edinburgh, 1983), pp. 214–35.
[7] D.S. Thomson, 'The Gaelic Learned Orders and Literati in Medieval Scotland', *Scottish Studies*, 12 (1968), 57–78.

Gaelic chiefs and their households were conversant with the literary culture
and language of the orders. Some, such as the first earl of Argyll and his
countess, were themselves able to compose poems in the special metres.[8]

During the later medieval period both the learned orders and the native
aristocracy had employed their communication skills to increase contact
with the rest of Scotland and Europe. They had provided the linguistic and
cultural links between vernacular Gaelic and Latin and Scots, the languages of the church, international scholarship, government, law and
administration. The contributors to the Book of the Dean of Lismore
demonstrated that they were literate in three languages, Gaelic, Scots and
Latin and moved easily between the three cultural worlds. Located in the
communications corridor between Perthshire and Argyll which linked the
east and west of Scotland, these men were fully in touch with the
developments in Lowland Scotland and the rest of Europe.[9]

By the time of the Reformation both the learned orders and the
aristocracy had considerable experience as the key points of contact
between the relatively enclosed world of the Gaidhealtachd and the wider
world of European culture. The members of the orders, in particular, had
developed the fascinating combination of skills as literate tri-lingual
scholars and as oral transmitters. It was this unique expertise which was to
prove of crucial importance to the spread of Protestantism in the
Gaidhealtachd.

A direct translation of the Protestant message from Scots into Gaelic was
not possible because neither Scottish Vernacular nor Classical Common
Gaelic were ideally suited to act as the sole medium of transmission. In
order to convey new theological and philosophical concepts in a manner
which could be readily understood by non-literate Gaels, different aspects
of the two varieties of Gaelic needed to be combined. A printed, literary
language had to be linked to a totally comprehensible vernacular and
transmitted to a predominantly non-literate population. This required
complete familiarity with both varieties of Gaelic and of the Scots and Latin
of the Calvinist texts. The learned orders and the aristocracy possessed the
necessary expertise to translate Calvinism properly and comfortably into
the Gaelic language.

This oral literate culture made it possible for the Protestant message to be
disseminated through the traditional channels of communication within
Gaelic society. The Protestant faith was novel and it challenged many of the

[8] W. Gillies, 'Courtly and Satiric Poems in the Book of the Dean of Lismore', *Scottish Studies*, 21 (1977), 35–53.
[9] D.E. Meek, 'The Scots-Gaelic Scribes of Late Medieval Perthshire: An Overview of the Orthography and Contents of the Book of the Dean of Lismore', in *Bryght Lanternis*, ed. J.D. Maclure and M. Spiller (Aberdeen, 1989), pp. 387–404.

old ways of life and thought but it could become the basis for a new set of traditions which would themselves harness older concepts and be handed down in the established way. This was clearly recognised by John Carswell, the most important champion of the Reformed faith in the early years of the Reformation.

Carswell provided the perfect example of a man who combined the skills of the learned orders with those of the conventional university training of a late medieval cleric. It is not known whether Carswell, like some of his contemporaries, acquired his Protestant convictions whilst studying at St Andrews University. By 1560, the time of the Scottish Reformation, Carswell had become the clerical leader of the campaign to evangelise the Western Highlands. He was made superintendent of Argyll in the new Kirk and also held the office of bishop of the Isles until his death in 1572.[10] He was the head of a group of Protestant ministers based in Argyll which was fully supported by the large and extremely powerful Clan Campbell led by the Calvinist fifth earl of Argyll, who was Carswell's personal patron. This backing gave that group the self-confidence to develop their own brand of Calvinism.[11]

The confidence and clarity of vision of the Argyll Protestants can be seen in Carswell's greatest achievement, his translation of the Book of Common Order, the 'Foirm na n-Urrnuidheadh', published in Edinburgh in 1567.[12] Carswell saw this liturgical translation as part of a wider programme which would have included the Scriptures if he had had the opportunity to complete them. He wanted to provide a new corpus of Protestant material to replace Catholic doctrine and ideas in Gaelic culture.

Although he wished to change the subject matter taught by the learned orders, Carswell did not want to alter the traditional methods of transmission. In the Introduction to his 'Foirm', he berated the professional poets who preferred to 'maintain and improve vain hurtful lying worldly tales composed about ... the sons of Milesius and about the heroes and Fionn mac Cumhaill and his warriors', instead of teaching the Word of God. Carswell was not attacking the poets themselves but wanted them to employ Biblical stories in their poetry instead of the ancient epics. He wanted them to stop praising the warrior honour code of pre-Christian Ireland and start writing about religious values and virtues.[13]

Carswell had clearly encountered some opposition in the 1560s from professional poets within Gaelic society and certain families such as the MacMhuirichs, the learned orders of South Uist. Despite his modest

[10] D.E. Meek and J. Kirk, 'John Carswell', revised version in J. Kirk, *Patterns of Reform* (Edinburgh, 1989), pp. 280–304.

[11] J. Dawson, 'Clan Campbell and the Scottish Reformation', unpublished paper given to the Scottish Reformation Conference, 1990.

[12] *John Carswell's Foirm na n-Urrnuidheadh*, ed. R.L. Thomson (Scottish Gaelic Text Society, XI, Edinburgh, 1970).   [13] *Foirm*, pp. 179–80.

disclaimers, Carswell had some professional training in the composition of classical poetry and made every effort to ensure that his 'Foirm' would reach the exacting literary standards which would satisfy some of his critics. The 'Foirm' was the first book ever printed in Gaelic and was a landmark of literary prose in Classical Common Gaelic. The very fact that Carswell was able to undertake the translation and to employ words and concepts which would be acceptable and comprehensible in a certain sector of Highland society, suggest that he was working within a milieu which was already familiar with the language of Gaelic Protestantism.[14]

Through his work as a translator and as a superintendent, Carswell sought to capture the expertise of other members of the learned orders for the Protestant cause. In the medieval period one major section of the Gaelic orders had pursued their careers within the church. They had taken clerical orders and held benefices or acted as notaries. During the first century of the Reformation, most of these professional clerics remained at their posts and provided the personnel for the new Kirk in the Highlands.[15] The MacPhails of Muckairn were one well-documented family who provided a succession of Protestant ministers to carry on the clerical tradition of their Catholic ancestors.[16] The familiar names of the clerical families such as the Omeys, the MacLachlans, the MacEwans, the MacKinnons and the MacQueens, reappear in an early seventeenth-century list of ministers serving in the church in the Islands.[17] A generation later the detailed records for the Synod of Argyll show that the majority of the ministers who attended the synod came from the families of the old learned orders with a few more recently established clerical dynasties, particularly the specialised cadet branches of leading clans such as the Campbells, Macgregors and the MacLeans, providing nearly all of the rest.[18] Serving the church was exclusively a family affair in the Highlands and Islands until the severe dislocation caused in 1690 by the Presbyterian/Episcopalian split after the Glorious Revolution.[19]

The importance of gaining this professional clerical group and turning it

[14] I am grateful to Dr Meek for this observation.
[15] *Originales Parochiales Scoticae*, ed. C. Innes (Edinburgh, 1854); *Records of the Dioceses of Argyll and the Isles, 1560–1860*, ed. J.B. Craven (Kirkwall, 1907); *Fasti Ecclesiae Scoticanae*, ed. D.E.R. Watt (Scottish Record Society, Edinburgh, 1969); C. Haws, *Scottish Parish Clergy at the Reformation* (Scottish Record Society, Edinburgh, 1972); Kirk, *Patterns*, pp. 285–6.
[16] J. Bannerman, *The Beatons* (Edinburgh, 1986), pp. 150–1.
[17] Report of the diocese of the Isles, 1626 in *Collecteana*, pp. 122–5; J. Bannerman, 'The MacLachlans of Kilbride', *Scottish Studies*, 21 (1977), 5, 12.
[18] *Minutes of the Synod of Argyll*, 1639–61 (2 vols., Scottish History Society, 3rd ser. 37 & 38, 1943–4).
[19] J. Macinnes, *The Evangelical Movement in the Highlands of Scotland* (Aberdeen, 1951). For the post-1690 difficulties see W. Ferguson, 'The Problems of the Established Church in the West Highlands and Islands in the Eighteenth Century', *Records of the Scottish Church History Society*, 17 (1969–72), 15–31.

into the spearhead of the Reformation in the Highlands cannot be overestimated. These men provided the personnel to staff the Kirk and the expertise to mediate the Protestant message to the rest of Gaelic society and to give Calvinism its Gaelic voice and dress. The policy of translation employed by the Gaelic scholars demonstrated that they sought something more than the transferance of the Scots version of Calvinism into another tongue. They were consciously striving to create their own brand of the Reformed faith. Carswell used the Book of Common Order promulgated by the Scottish General Assembly but also returned to the original Latin version of the 'Form of Prayers' (1556) of the English-speaking congregation of Geneva, on which it was based. He was prepared to make major textual changes when he deemed them necessary. He included an entirely new blessing for a boat with set responses, which was of obvious relevance to the sea-faring society of the Highlands and Islands. He also created a new Catechism which, while based on Calvin's Little Catechism, was a free adaptation designed to suit his needs.[20] Following the same pattern the later Gaelic translators of the Bible and the longer Catechisms went directly to the texts in Latin or the Biblical languages rather than working from the Scottish versions.[21]

The culture of oral literacy helps to explain why the delay in securing a printed Gaelic Bible did not prevent the spread of Protestantism within the Gaidhealtachd. Although biblical translation was part of Carswell's original plan, the complete Bible in Scottish Gaelic was not produced until 1801 though a Classical Gaelic version had been available a century earlier and a New Testament from 1603 in Classical Gaelic and one in Vernacular Scottish Gaelic by 1767.[22]

Evidence from elsewhere in Europe would suggest that without a printed vernacular Bible the spread of Protestantism would be seriously inhibited. However, in the Highlands, despite the lack of a Scottish Gaelic Bible the Biblical message was conveyed to the people. Rob Donn, the non-literate poet, who was active in the first half of the eighteenth century before there was a printed version in the Scottish vernacular, possessed a profound knowledge of the Bible. His poetry was full of allusions to Biblical characters and stories and he employed the main tenets of Reformed theology without difficulty. He could have achieved this easy familiarity with Scripture only through listening to the local minister.[23]

---

[20]   *Foirm*, pp. lxxv–vi.
[21]   *Adtimchiol an Chreidimh: The Gaelic Version of John Calvin's Catechismus Ecclesiae Genevensis*, ed. R.L. Thomson (Scottish Gaelic Text Society, Edinburgh, 1962), p. xvi.
[22]   D.E. Meek, 'The Gaelic Bible', in *The Bible in Scottish Life and Literature*, ed. D.F. Wright (Edinburgh, 1988), pp. 9–23; 'Language and Style in the Scottish Gaelic Bible, (1767–1807)', *Scottish Language*, 9 (1990), 1–16.
[23]   T. McCaughey, 'Protestantism and Scottish Highland Culture', in *An Introduction to Celtic Christianity*, ed. J.P. Mackey (Edinburgh, 1989), pp. 180–1.

Rob Donn and many others before him would have attended weekly worship which started with the reader's service. This was an hour-long reading of the Bible which the Reader would translate directly from the English printed version in his hand.[24] Further instruction would be given in the exegetical sermon which followed. There were numerous personal translations of parts of the Bible which had been made by the ministers in their sermon preparation. In 1657 a search was made for 'sundrie parcells translated allreadie' by the ministers of the Synod of Argyll to provide the basis for their proposed translation of the Scriptures.[25] The advantage of these informal systems of translation was that the Biblical content could be conveyed in the vernacular and even in the particular local dialect so that it was completely comprehensible to the listeners. When Dr Samuel Johnson was travelling in the Hebrides in 1773 he was informed by Mr MacLean, a minister in Coll, that even though there was a printed New Testament in Scottish Vernacular the minister still preferred to use his own translation as he could then adapt the language to local needs.[26]

This highlights the problem which an earlier translation would have encountered. Until the 1653 translation of the Shorter Catechism the other religious literature, such as Carswell's liturgy and Calvin's Catechism, had been rendered into Classical Common Gaelic. A printed version of the Bible in this literary language needed some interpretation to be entirely comprehensible to the ordinary people. A similar problem arose over the typography and orthography of the Classical Gaelic Bible. Before it could be circulated in Scotland it had to be reprinted in Roman type and the language modified to suit Scottish requirements. When these technical problems were combined with the much lower levels of literacy in the Highlands, the delays over the production of a vernacular Bible became more explicable. It must be stressed that the absence of such a Bible in the first century after the Reformation did not cripple the evangelical effort.[27]

In addition to teaching them the Biblical narrative, the Calvinist ministers had two further methods of conveying their Protestant message. The first and most important was the sermon. In 1583 when he was rigorously examined by the Presbytery of Stirling, John Campbell, bishop of the Isles, could prove that he had preached regularly at Iona and Ardchattan. He had stopped preaching only when he had travelled into the

24 J. Macinnes, 'The Christian Church', in *The Hub of the Highlands: The Book of Inverness and District* (Edinburgh, 1975), p. 159.   25 *Synod of Argyll*, II, p. 146.
26 *The Companion to Gaelic Scotland*, ed. D.S. Thomson (Oxford, 1983), p. 23.
27 Meek, 'Gaelic Bible', and 'Gaidhlig is Gaylick anns na Meadhon Aoisean', in *Gaelic and Scotland*, pp. 131–45 (English abstract 233–5); C.J. Withers 'The Highland Parishes in 1698', *Scottish Studies*, 24 (1980), 63–88. Similar problems arose later in Ireland, N. O'Ciosain, 'Printed Popular Literacy in Irish, 1750–1850: Presence and Absence', in *The Origins of Popular Literacy in Ireland*, eds. M. Daly and D. Dickson (Dublin, 1990), 45–57. I am grateful to Dr Houston for drawing this article to my attention.

Lowlands. The Presbytery, who also insisted upon a trial sermon, were satisfied with the doctrine of the sermon but felt that he had not sufficiently opened up the sense and meaning of the text. Campbell accepted the criticism, apologising for having to rush his sermon preparation on that particular occasion as he had to go to Glasgow to reconcile two of his friends who had been feuding.[28]

By the middle of the seventeenth century two sermons and two lectures every Sunday were regarded as normal. The Presbytery of Skye was severely rebuked by the Synod of Argyll for providing preaching only once on the Lord's Day.[29] In a 'mixed' parish with both Highlanders and Lowlanders the minister was expected to preach one diet (a sermon and lecture) in Gaelic and the other in Scots. This burden was sufficiently onerous for Donald McCloy the old minister at Kilmodan (Cowal) to resign his charge because he was unable to preach twice 'for want of breath to make out ane hours speaking'.[30]

In 1623 the Irish Franciscan friars, who had been sent to recover the Highlands for Catholicism, were in no doubt that Protestant preaching was the major obstacle to the success of their mission. They dismissed the significance of the communion services remarking, somewhat surprisingly, that it was the same as the mass anyway so not doing as much harm as the sermons! The friars felt that they needed to be able to refute the arguments which were presented by the Protestant preachers. To do this they requested formal permission from their superiors to listen to the morning sermons incognito so that they could produce counter arguments in the afternoon.[31]

The primacy of preaching within the Highland Kirk was demonstrated by the system of priorities for a vacant parish. The minister with his sermons came to the parish but the parishioners had to travel to the nearest minister themselves for the services of baptism and marriage. In fact the excellent cover provided by the preachers in one vacant parish was given as the main reason why the parishioners were so slow to fill the vacancy.[32]

As well as the formal sermons on the Lord's Day and during the week in those places where there were mid-week services, there were the 'exercises' of the presbytery and synod. This were primarily in-service training for the clergy but the lay elders who also attended these meetings of the higher church courts would have heard a sermon or lecture a day from the participating ministers. At these occasions 'expectant' or prospective ministers gave trial sermons. The Synod of Argyll was particularly diligent in testing preaching ability in Gaelic as well as knowledge of the Biblical

---

[28] *Stirling Presbytery Records*, ed. J. Kirk (Scottish History Society, XIX, 1981), pp. 79–80, 82–4, 103–4, 146–9, 164–6.
[29] *Synod of Argyll*, II, pp. 103, 119.   [30] *Ibid.*, I. pp. 147–8, 207.
[31] *Irish Franciscan Mission to Scotland, 1619–46*, ed. C. Giblin (Dublin, 1964), pp. 30, 69.
[32] *Synod of Argyll*, I, p. 210; II, pp. 52–3, 101, 129–30.

languages and Reformed doctrine. In the more linguistically mixed area under the jurisdiction of the Synod of Moray ministers who could preach only in English were permitted to remain in post. In the Western Highlands the synod of Argyll was considerably tougher and told the extremely competent James Garner who had no Gaelic to resign his 'Highland' parish in Kintyre and move to a 'Lowland' one.[33]

Alongside the sermon the other major method of introducing Calvinist tenets into Gaelic society was through the Catechism. In an oral culture learning by rote was the normal manner in which knowledge was acquired and stored in the memory. In 1567 Carswell had included his own version of Calvin's Catechism in the 'Foirm'. This was followed by the translation at the start of the seventeenth century of Calvin's Catechism which was printed c. 1630. The two initial catechisms were composed in Classical Common Gaelic but in 1653 the Shorter Catechism was translated by a team of ministers into Scottish Vernacular. It was so popular that within six years it had to be reprinted. A shorter and simpler version with only twenty or thirty questions for use by the very young and the very old was planned but not completed.[34]

Every Sunday the minister was expected to explain two of the questions from the Catechism during the lecture immediately after the sermon. Just before the blessing two different members of the congregation were called upon to repeat two of the questions. These exercises were in addition to the weekly catechising which the minister was expected to undertake in some part of his parish and to the religious instruction he provided on his domestic visits.[35] The careful exposition of the Classical Common Gaelic phrases of the catechism by the minister helped this Calvinist text to become the 'theological classical poetry' of the early modern period in the High-lands. A skilful minister could explain the words and concepts in his sermons and play 'tunes' with them in the same way as the professional poets had manipulated the traditional metres and images in their compositions.[36]

Within the Highlands and Islands boys were used to teach the catechism to individual households. In return for their board and lodging and some help from the church's poor box, the boys stayed with a household until all its members had mastered their catechism by heart. A rather more ambitious scheme, also using poor boys, was tried which attempted to teach more people to read in English so that they could read the Scriptures directly themselves. Not surprisingly in view of the complexities of the task, this was less successful. Knowledge of the catechism was required by parishioners before they could avail themselves of any of the services

---

[33] *Ibid.*, I, p. 6; II. pp. 94, 135, 212–3.   [34] *Ibid.*, II, pp. viii–ix, 131.
[35] *Ibid.*, II, pp. 40–1, 55, 103.   [36] I am grateful to Dr Meek for this observation.

offered by the Kirk, whether communion, baptism or marriage. Anyone who refused to learn the catechism by heart or at least to 'use diligence' to memorise it was to be cited before their presbytery.[37]

The singing of metrical psalms was one method employed by Calvinist communities throughout Europe to spread the Protestant message among the non-literate. Translating the psalms into Gaelic presented a whole range of technical problems. Neither the musical tradition nor the normal forms of versification in Gaelic culture fitted the requirement of regularly stressed syllables necessary for the metrical psalms. Although the first fifty psalms in Gaelic, the 'Caogad', were produced in 1659 the complete Psalm Book did not appear until 1694.[38] With little popular poetry in Gaelic surviving from the Reformation period, it is difficult to know whether many Protestant poems and songs were composed or used. Several of the exponents of the emerging vernacular poetry were clergymen, such as Hector MacLean of Coll (An Cleirach Beag), John Stewart of Appin and MacCulloch of Park. They did employ religious themes in their work as did the poets the Mac Mhurchaidhs, the father and son who were Mackenzies of Achilty. Where clear doctrinal viewpoints emerged in this poetry, they were Protestant and sometimes recognisably Calvinist.[39]

The Gaelic ministers used the conventional Protestant tools of the Biblical narrative, explained and reinforced by the sermon and catechism, to evangelise the Highlands and Islands of Scotland. They were far more effective in spreading Calvinism through a remote rural area than their struggling counterparts in comparable regions of Europe.[40] They were able to utilise to the full the existing culture of oral literacy. Although there was a linguistic barrier between Classical Common Gaelic and Scottish Vernacular, this did not produce a horizontal split between elite and popular cultures. The traditional role of the learned orders in bridging the language-gap was taken over by the Gaelic ministers. This ensured that, despite the lack of printed material in Gaelic, Calvinist precepts could be brought to the non-literate in forms which they could understand.

---

[37] *Synod of Argyll*, I, pp. 192–4; II, pp. 35, 40–1, 84–5.
[38] *The Gaelic Psalms*, 1694, ed. D.C. MacTavish (Lochgilphead, 1934).
[39] Thomson, *Introduction*, pp. 107–39; McCaughey, 'Protestantism', 182–3.
[40] For example in the Netherlands, A. Duke, 'The Reformation of the Backwoods', in *Reformation and Revolt in the Low Countries* (London, 1990), pp. 227–68. Nearer to home, there was also the important contrast with the situation in Gaelic Ireland, which had an almost identical culture to the Scottish Gaidhealtachd but where neither the Gaelic learned orders nor the native aristocracy were favourable to Calvinism. The type of Protestantism which flourished in Ireland was associated with the English Conquest and was extremely hostile to Gaelic language and culture. After the Ulster Plantation, it was reinforced by the radical elements of Scottish Lowland Calvinism, see A. Ford, *The Protestant Reformation in Ireland* (Frankfurt-am-Main, 1987).

II

Traditional communication skills were the key element in the spread of Calvinism within the Gaidhealtachd, but the formal framework of the Kirk was also important (see Figure 5). It was one of the few institutions which functioned properly in both the Highlands and Lowlands of Scotland. In theory it was organised in exactly the same way in both regions. However, there were three main practical problems in extending the tight Lowland organisation to the Highlands and Islands. Within the Highland region itself, with the minor exceptions of Inveraray and later Stornoway and Campbeltown, there were no urban centres.[41] The small, 'frontier' burghs on the eastern fringe of the Highlands, such as Inverness, Chanonry or Dingwall, could provide a meeting place for the church courts but they were not large enough to act as a religious powerhouse for their rural hinterlands, as some burghs had done in the Lowlands.

By far the greatest obstacle was the parish structure itself which the Kirk had inherited from its medieval predecessor. This legacy combined the old problem of size with a new Protestant difficulty over accessibility. The parishes within the Gaidhealtachd were very large, some of them stretching twenty miles across. In addition to the geographical extent and inhospitable terrain of the parishes, many of the church buildings in the Highlands were placed in peculiarly difficult locations. They had been built on the holy sites associated with the intrepid Celtic church saints who had preferred isolation to comfort. Frequently the saints had chosen small islands off the coast or in the middle of a loch to withdraw from the world. In the medieval period the location of these churches did not present too many problems because they were primarily used for special religious festivals or as pilgrimage centres.

The Reformation brought about an even more dramatic change to the pattern of worship within the Highlands than elsewhere in Scotland. Under the Protestant regime all parishioners were expected to attend worship at their parish church every Sunday. For the first time this created serious difficulties within the Highlands and Islands over access to those buildings which were in such awkward locations. The necessity of ferrying the whole congregation to Inishail church, on an island at the top of Loch Awe, for a set time every Sunday morning, brought severe logistical complications. This situation left regular worship open to disruption by the weather or occasionally by human agency. In the middle of a dispute about a new church at Appin, the ferryman simply refused to carry the minister across

---

[41] These were burghs in the legal sense of having a formal charter and being permitted to trade, but they remained small communities with only Inveraray developing into a proper communications centre.

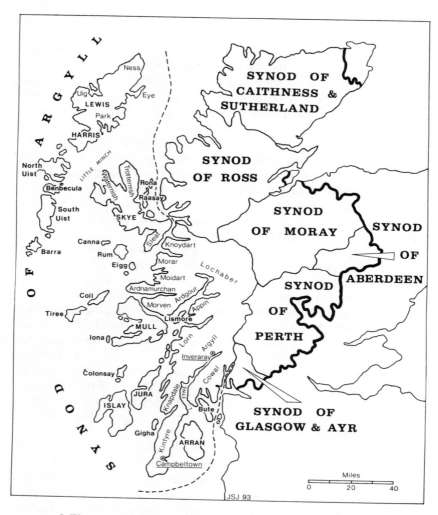

5 The synod of Argyll and the other synods in the Highlands in the
1640s

Source: D. Stevenson, *Revolution and Counter-revolution in Scotland
1644–51* (London, 1977), p. 260

the narrow stretch of water from the island of Lismore and so no services could take place in Appin.[42]

The obvious solution of building new churches in suitable locations was not possible because of the immense cost. Sufficent resources were not found for the Highlands and Islands until the 'parliamentary' churches of the early nineteenth century and the massive church-building programme undertaken after the Disruption of 1843. There were ambitious plans in the seventeenth century for a complete rationalisation of the existing parish system. Some useful adjustments to parish boundaries were made but only a handful of new churches were built.[43] As a cheaper compromise other buildings were used for worship. There was a 'preaching-house' at Camp-beltown in Kintyre in addition to the parish church. Some of the medieval chapels were also utilised and this became the source of a dispute in Mull.[44]

Many religious services were held in the open air, just as local courts continued to be convened outside on traditional sites, such as moot hills. It would have been natural to gather in the open to listen to a preacher in the warmer summer months, when so much of Highland life was lived out of doors or in the temporary shelters of the shielings in the summer pastures. Even when there was a local church close by as at Kilmalieu, the people of Inveraray came to the Parson's Pulpit under a rock on the banks of Loch Fyne to hear Ninian MacVicar.[45]

When viewed from the outside or through the eyes of contemporary Lowlanders the huge parishes and the paucity of churches and clergy appeared to leave the Highlands and Islands very badly provided and almost incapable of producing a truly reformed community. Although the difficulties could not be entirely overcome, they could be circumvented. In the Lowlands the organisation and efficency of the Kirk were regarded as essential to the creation of the godly society. In the less formal society of Gaelic Scotland the structures of the church were not given such a prominent place. The difference in attitude can be seen in the modification of the parish ministry to suit the conditions of the Highlands and Islands.

Although the Highlands and Islands had exactly the same set of institutions, they did not operate in the same way as those in the Lowlands. The ministers were still called to particular charges and their main task was to serve their parishes. To a far greater extent than in the Lowlands, a

[42] J. Dawson, 'The Origin of the "Road to the Isles": Trade, Communications and Campbell Power in Early Modern Scotland', in *People and Power in Scotland: Essays in Honour of T.C. Smout* (Edinburgh, 1992), pp. 74–103.

[43] *Synod of Argyll*, I, pp. 49–59, 227–54; II, pp. 68–73.

[44] *Ibid.*, II, p. 72; *Collecteana*, pp. 126–7.

[45] *Records of Argyll*, ed. Lord Archibald Campbell (Edinburgh, 1885), pp. 50–1. I am grateful to the late Mr Mackechnie of Bridge of Douglas (Argyll) for sharing his great knowledge of Inveraray and its environs with me.

Highland minister was an itinerant, working as a member of a team moving on circuit through his district.[46] The clergy had to travel to different locations within their parishes which could be uncomfortably large and preach by turn in each district. The parish at Inveraray (Kilmalieu), which covered a relatively small area, had four named preaching stations.[47] In addition the ministers shared the burden of preaching in those parishes which were vacant. Every opportunity was used to increase the number of sermons and to turn any journey into a preaching tour. One minister from Arran was instructed to stop and preach both on his outward and on his return journeys to the presbytery. Special efforts were made by the clergy to provide extra sermons at the fishing grounds for the seasonal influx of fishing folk. These itinerant practices reflected the peripatetic nature of Gaelic society and had similarities to the traditional bardic circuits.[48]

The parish was not treated as the primary unit of organisation within the Highlands and Islands because it did not correspond to the social, political or geographical divisions within the Gaidhealtachd. The ministers were forced to work together in a team at the district level. This usually corresponded with the presbytery but, as in the division of the presbytery of Lorn, were sometimes smaller areas which made greater geographical sense.[49] Particularly in the remoter areas where, if the local clan chief were uncooperative, the kirk session was weak or non-existent, cases of church discipline tended to be passed up to the presbytery or even the synod. These higher courts were constantly trying to tighten the institutional structure and chivvied recalcitrant kirk sessions or presbyteries, inspecting their books and demanding improvements. But they did realise the practical limitations imposed upon them by the communications system of the Highlands. As the ruling elders who attended the Synod of Argyll complained, no-one else in Scotland had to travel so far or so long to attend meetings. As a consequence the number of meetings was reduced, particularly for the winter months, and a more lenient standard of attendance enforced on those who came from the Isles.[50] It was remarkable that both the clergy and the eldership were prepared to spend so much time and effort travelling to ensure that the presbyteries and synods functioned as efficiently as they did. The Gaelic ministers wanted to retain the institutional framework of the Scottish Presbyterian system, though they were quite prepared to modify it to suit the practicalities of their region.

---

[46] Cf. similar practices in the nineteenth century, D.E. Meek, 'Dugald Sinclair: The Life and Work of a Highland Itinerant Missionary', *Scottish Studies*, 30 (1991), 59–91.

[47] *Records of Argyll*, 50.   [48] *Synod of Argyll*, I, pp. 91–2; II, pp. 145–6, 156.

[49] A.E. Anderson, 'Notes from the Presbytery Records of Lorne', *Transactions of the Gaelic Society of Inverness*, 36 (1931–3), 112–38.

[50] *Synod of Argyll*, I, pp. 5, 27, 73, 172.

III

The long-term success of Protestantism and its ability to put down roots depended upon the conversion of the Gaelic aristocracy. The dominant position of the chiefs and their massive influence within the kin-based society of Gaelic Scotland was recognised by the Protestant ministers. Throughout the first century of the Reformation the clergy looked to the lay magnates for support. In return they praised their aristocratic patrons almost as fulsomely as the professional poets. They were far more willing than their Lowland counterparts to give a dominant role in the running of church affairs to such 'godly nobles'. This appreciation of the importance of the regional princes was clearly set out by Carswell in his Epistle addressed to his own patron, the fifth earl of Argyll. He compared the Campbell chief to the kings of the Old Testament such as David and Hezekiah who had brought the true religion into their territories and had destroyed idolatry.[51]

Such praise for the nobility reflected the social and political realities of Gaelic Scotland where even royal authority was exclusively exercised through the regional magnates. Protestantism would not have made any real impact without the support of the earls of Argyll and their Campbell kin. Clan Campbell was the most powerful kin group in the Western Highlands and the earl of Argyll's influence extended over the whole region. Throughout the early modern period the Campbells remained totally committed to the Calvinist and later Covenanting Kirks. In the northern Highlands Protestantism was encouraged by the earls of Seaforth with their MacKenzies. In addition, the Kirk could rely upon the active cooperation of many of the lesser kindreds, such as the Rosses of Balnagown and the Munros of Fowlis in the north and the MacLeans of Duart and MacLeods of Harris and Skye in the Western Isles.[52]

In its crudest form the support of the powerful Gaelic chiefs gave the Kirk access to military muscle and enabled it to coerce its enemies. In 1562 the fifth earl of Argyll had travelled through the south-western Highlands 'destroying idolatry' and 'cleansing' the churches. Carswell praised his patron and chief as a great protector of ministers in those difficult and dangerous early days of the Reformation.[53] The legal authority of the chiefs, who held extensive heritable jurisdictions and gave the law to the Highlands, was also employed to reinforce church discipline through civil penalties imposed in their courts.

More important than coercion was the example which a Protestant chief set for his kin, friends and allies. In matters of religion, as in war and peace, it was assumed that clansmen would normally follow their chief's lead. An

---

[51] *Foirm*, pp. 173–9.   [52] Macinnes, *Evangelical Movement*, ch. 1.   [53] *Foirm*, pp. 176–7.

interesting exception to this occured in Clan Campbell when the seventh earl was converted to Roman Catholicism. He was virtually disowned by his strongly Protestant clan and the leadership passed to the earl's son, the future covenanter marquis of Argyll.[54] Alliances between Protestant kin groups were frequently consolidated by marriage ties or by fostering children from other clans. In the strongly Protestant atmosphere of the fifth earl of Argyll's household, his foster son, Lachlan MacLean of Duart, the future chief of the main branch of the MacLeans, became a convinced Protestant.[55] In the Gaidhealtachd, as elsewhere in Europe, women also had an important part to play in the spread of Protestantism. The network of Perthshire chiefs who were prepared to give military support to the Protestant Lords of the Congregation in 1559–60 were all linked by marriage alliances to women from Protestant families. One of those women, Katherine Ruthven, the sister of Patrick, Lord Ruthven and the wife of Colin Campbell of Glenorchy, was a close friend of John Carswell.[56]

The Franciscan friars of Antrim knew to their cost the great importance of the local chief and the extent of Protestant success in winning over the native aristocracy in the Highlands and Islands of Scotland. During the first half of the seventeenth century they had embarked upon a series of evangelising missions to Gaelic Scotland. They were under no illusions about the difficulty of their task. Despite the advantage of being native Gaelic speakers who, unlike any Lowland Scottish missionary, could fit easily into Scottish Highland society they still had to operate under cover. One priest assumed the identity of a Gaelic poet to explain his presence and journey throughout the region. In this disguise he penetrated a chief's household and attempted to convert the chief. This ploy achieved one notable success when Campbell of Cawdor was converted to Roman Catholicism.[57]

In their reports to Rome the missionaries explained that it was impossible to establish a permanent base in Scotland because they were always operating in hostile, Protestant territory. Although they had the support of a few Catholic chiefs, the friars were constantly on the move and frequently had to escape from danger by sailing back to northern Ireland. The mission

[54] E.J. Cowan, 'Fishers in Drumlie Waters: Clanship and Campbell Expansion in the Time of Gilleasbuig Grumach', *Transactions of the Gaelic Society of Inverness*, 54 (1984–6), 269–312.

[55] N. Maclean-Bristol, 'The Macleans from 1560–1707', in *The Seventeenth Century in the Highlands* (Inverness Field Club, 1986), p. 79.

[56] J. Dawson, 'The Ties That Bind: Clan Campbell and Marriage Alliances', unpublished paper given to the Conference of Scottish Medievalists, 1990. Letters from John Carswell to Katherine Ruthven, Scottish Record Office, GD 112/39 at 8/15 and 11/3.

[57] Giblin, *Irish Franciscan Mission*, pp. 26, 53–4.

achieved its greatest success in the southern Hebrides because it was assisted by the Catholicism of the major proprietors, the MacNeills and the Macdonalds of Clanranald, who held the Uists and Barra.[58]

Much of Protestant activity was also focused upon the chief's court or household which provided the key point of contact between Gaelic society and the outside world. Here, new ideas, people and habits were first encountered and, from this secure bastion, spread out into the rest of Gaelic society. This process can be seen at work in the changes in personnel and ideology which transformed the household of the Campbells of Glenorchy when Grey Colin and his son Black Duncan ruled Breadalbane.[59]

In Gaelic society a regional magnate maintained a large retinue and moved with it throughout his 'country'. His peripatetic court would lodge with his clansmen and tenants consuming the rents in kind. On these periodic progresses the chief would bring his Protestantism along with his household.[60] The religious component of the visit would include Protestant services conducted either by the local minister or the chaplain who accompanied the chief. More informally there would be Bible readings at the end of the meal before the guests had left the table.[61] As lavish hospitality for large numbers of guests was regarded as one of the most important attributes of a good chief, these readings would reach many of the people in the area. In these settings the Protestantism of the elite could spread naturally throughout society.

In the early years of the Reformation the chief's visit to the remoter regions of the Highlands and Islands might provide the first encounter with the new religious ideas. This would offer an opportunity to experience Protestant worship and hear sermons and Scriptural readings within the chief's household. It would also be the occasion for settling the new religion into the locality. In this way the normal chief's circuit through his territories could easily assume the attributes of an ecclesiastical visitation. This happened in 1574 when Colin, sixth earl of Argyll, ensured that all the churches were properly 'planted' in his region and each was supplied with either a minister or a reader supported by an adequate stipend. All the parishes visited on the progress possessed and were using for worship and discipline copies of Carswell's 'Foirm'.[62]

[58] *Ibid.*, pp. 33, 51, 55, 59, 106, 108, 174, 178.
[59] G. Macgregor, 'The Macgregors', (unpublished Ph.D. thesis, University of Edinburgh, 1989).
[60] J. Dawson, 'The Fifth Earl of Argyle, Gaelic Lordship and Political Power in Sixteenth-Century Scotland', *Scottish Historical Review*, 67 (1988), 1–27.
[61] Description of the household of Sir Lachlan MacLean of Duart (d.1648) in poem cited in Thomson, *Introduction*, p. 132.
[62] *Calendar of State Papers Relating to Scotland*, eds. J. Bain *et al.* (Edinburgh, 1898–1969), V, p. 34.

If regular attendance at church can provide a reliable guide, Protestantism was spread from the chief and his household to large sections of the population in the Highlands. Some unexpected evidence for church attendance can be found in the account of a vicious feud. The MacLeods of the Waternish peninsula on Skye were all in a building at Trumpan which they used for worship though their parish church was several miles away at Kilmuir, Dunvegan. One Sunday the Macdonalds of Uist sailed across the Little Minch and, knowing that the whole community was at worship and there would be no lookouts, were able to sneak up and lock the door of the building. In revenge for the previous massacre of their clansmen on Eigg, the Macdonalds then set fire to the thatched roof killing everyone inside except one girl who raised the alarm.[63] In 1603 the same fate is alleged to have befallen the congregation of the church in Kilchrist, Easter Ross when the Glengarry Macdonalds burnt the building.[64]

The new Protestant requirement that the whole parish attend worship at a set time each week left that community vulnerable to its enemies. The Sunday service provided all too tempting an opportunity if those enemies were intending to massacre the entire population including the women and children rather than fight a clan battle between the two groups of warriors. An effective defence was made more difficult by the practice of not carrying weapons into church buildings. One Protestant clan, the Macfarlanes of Arrochar, who feared a Sunday attack, left a few men with all the weapons on guard watching the 'String Road', the route to the church at Luss, whilst the rest of the clan listened to the Calvinist sermon.[65] This unexpected hazard for those clans who fully embraced Calvinism does provide the historian with some indications of church attendance!

IV

The willingness of the Gaelic clergy and aristocracy to mould Calvinism and Presbyterian structures to fit their own culture was most strikingly displayed in their acceptance of certain aspects of local belief, which other Calvinist ministers found it all too easy to condemn. Unlike their Lowland brethren, the Gaelic clergy did not regard all forms of witchcraft as inherently evil. During the scares which afflicted the rest of Scotland in the

---

[63] This incident is known as the Battle of the Spoiling of the Dyke after the subsequent mass burial when the MacLeods caught up with the MacDonalds and killed them, C. Bingham, *Beyond the Highland Line* (London, 1991), p. 107.

[64] By tradition this massacre was the setting for the clan piobaireachd, Cill Chriosd or Glengarry's March, I.F. Grant and H. Cheape, *Periods of Highland History* (London, 1987), p. 115. However, a case for dismissing the whole tale has been made, D.J. Macdonald, *Clan Donald* (Edinburgh, 1978), pp. 340–1.

[65] *The Dewar Manuscripts*, ed J. Mackechnie (1964), pp. 107f.

sixteenth and seventeenth centuries there was no witch-hunting in the Highlands.[66] The Gaelic language had a rich vocabulary to distinguish the different varieties of supernatural activity and the particular contexts in which they were employed. This enabled the Gaelic clergy to be much more discerning and to condemn black magic and sorcery but tolerate other supernatural beliefs. In particular they made a sharp distinction between witchcraft and the hereditary gift (or curse) of second sight.[67]

The tradition of the seer was an integral part of Highland life.[68] The Gaelic clergy saw no reason to condemn it nor to associate it in any way with the Devil. They regarded the foretellings as a natural phenomenon and linked them with some of the forms of prophecy found in the Old Testament. Ninian MacVicar, the minister at Inveraray, was renowned for his prophecies including the accurate prediction of the circumstances of his own death by drowning.[69] The Gaelic clergy took a similar relaxed attitude towards the fairy culture of Gaeldom.[70] Within the Highlands and Islands belief in the fairies had remained distinct from the world of Catholic saints and miracles. The clergy could therefore accept the fairies and yet attack all those practices associated with Catholic worship and reverence for the saints.[71]

The willingness of the Gaelic ministers to judge for themselves what they felt to be appropriate within their own culture was demonstrated by their attitude towards the rituals of death. This was an area of immense significance within Gaelic society where the bonds of blood and kin were seen to embrace all generations whether living or dead. It was important to be buried with one's kin in the clan burial ground even if this were not the local parish church. This freqently involved carrying the coffin considerable distances along one of the network of coffin routes to bring it to the right graveyard.[72] Most of the customs associated with these large funeral

---

[66] C. Larner, *Enemies of God: The Witch-hunt in Scotland* (Edinburgh, 1981).

[67] J.G. Campbell, *Witchcraft in the Highlands* (Wakefield, 1974 edn); evidence concerning the use of witchcraft at the end of the sixteenth century came to light during the investigations over the murder of Campbell of Cawdor, *Highland Papers*, ed. J. Macphail (Scottish History Society), I, pp. 165–9; also see, W. Matheson, 'The Historical Coinneach Odhar and Some Prophecies Attributed to Him', *Transactions of the Gaelic Society of Inverness*, 46 (1969–70), 66–88.

[68] *The Seer in Celtic and Other Traditions*, ed. H.E. Davidson (Edinburgh, 1989).

[69] *Records of Argyll*, p. 53.

[70] The learned Episcopalian minister Robert Kirk of Aberfoyle, as well as his work as a Biblical translator and advocate of the Gaelic language, collected the fairy lore and wrote his account in *The Secret Commonwealth of Elves, Faunes and Fairies* (1691), D. Maclean, 'The Life and Literary Labours of the Rev. Robert Kirk of Aberfoyle', *Transactions of the Gaelic Society of Inverness*, 31 (1922–4), 328–66.

[71] For example *Synod of Argyll*, I, p. 67. For a wide-ranging discussion of the relationship between Christianity, Celtic culture and the supernatural see, J.P. Mackey, 'Magic and Celtic Primal Religion', *Zeitschrift für Celtische Philologie*, 45 (1992), 66–83.

[72] Dawson, 'Road to the Isles'.

processions and the wakes which preceded them had not been explicitly connected with Catholic worship. They could be left intact by the Protestant Gaelic ministers who, at the same time, had no compunction about changing the funeral service itself. The one element of the funeral rituals which the Protestant clergy did try to suppress was the 'corronach' or wailing by the mourning women. This practice was thought to be 'unseemly to be used in any true Christian kirk, where there is preaching and true profession of the comfortable resurrection of the dead'. It was recommended that the local minister explain why it should not be used when he preached or taught the catechism. Those subsequently offending were to be punished.[73]

In the sixteenth and seventeenth centuries the Gaelic ministers demonstrated remarkable assurance in their willingness to accept Calvinism whilst adapting its structures to suit their own cultural heritage. They seemed confident that they could be true to both aspects of their identity as learned Gaels and Calvinist ministers. In the same way the Gaelic magnates who became Protestant saw no major conflict between this and their traditional role as clan chiefs. But it became increasingly difficult to live successfully in the two worlds of the Highlands and the Lowlands and this put a tremendous strain upon Gaelic Calvinism.

The Scottish Kirk, dominated by Lowland preconceptions, found it almost impossible to recognise the merits of the adaptations which the Gaelic ministers had made. It interpreted the religious situation in the Gaidhealtachd as a failure to implement the full presbyterian system and so strove to extend the Lowland model to the Highlands and Islands. In particular, the use of the Gaelic language as the main medium for the Protestant faith was viewed with increasing suspicion. It was felt that in Scotland 'true' religion and 'civilised' behaviour could be found only in an Anglo-Scottish cultural setting. The whole of Gaelic society, its language and culture were steadily eroded by the unrelenting pressures towards uniformity and centralisation placed upon it by the British state. Together Kirk and state ensured that, although some aspects did survive into the eighteenth century, in its early modern form, Gaelic Calvinism was a relatively short-lived plant.

In the century after the Scottish Reformation, men such as John Carswell had been able to create a Calvinist church in one of the most unpromising environments in Europe. By exploiting the unusually strong culture of oral literacy, they produced a rural Calvinism which worked. Their success provides a healthy reminder that Calvinism could flourish in communities with the scattered settlement patterns of upland pastoral areas. It also

---

[73] *Synod of Argyll*, I, p. 61; II, p. 175.

demonstrates that it was possible for Calvinism to survive with little help from the printing press and without a popular literate culture based on the printed word. The partial assimilation of Calvinism to Gaelic culture achieved in the Scottish Gaidhealtachd can help to provide an explanation for Calvinism's overall success within Europe. The evidence from this peripheral and unusual region points to the flexibility of the Calvinist movement during the early modern period. It suggests that Calvinism was able to adapt to the various indigenous cultures of Europe whilst retaining a sufficiently coherent core for it to remain a recognisable international movement. Despite the ridicule of their Lowland contemporaries and the neglect of historians, the Highland ministers in their bonnets and plaids had no doubts about their own double identity. They were both good Gaels and members of the brotherhood of international Calvinism.

13   Merchants and ministers: the foundations of international Calvinism

Ole Peter Grell

The importance of godly merchants and ministers for the success and propagation of Calvinism in the second half of the sixteenth century is generally recognised. Together, these two groups came to dominate the growing number of Reformed communities, exercising considerable social and moral control over the congregations they served as ministers and elders. Their role and significance for the creation and maintenance of contacts between Calvinist individuals and communities across Europe, i.e. international Calvinism, has, however, received less attention. In what follows, I shall try to demonstrate how this international network of Reformed ministers and merchants came about and provide some examples of how it operated.

Retrospectively, it can be argued that Calvin's flight in 1536 from France to Basle in Switzerland, and his later move to Geneva, was to set the scene for what became a Reformed diaspora of considerable proportions later in the sixteenth century. What began as a relatively small-scale exodus of primarily Protestant ministers, eventually turned into mass emigration later in the century. However, as opposed to the later mass movement of Reformed emigrants, the early emigration was not unique to Calvinism, but was shared with other Protestants.

Even if the diaspora of the 1530s, 1540s and 1550s was characterised by the part played by the Reformed clergy it has to be emphasised that it also included an important lay and broadly evangelical element. This early emigration was largely a consequence of the growing confessionalisation of European states and societies, such as the Habsburg Netherlands ruled by Charles V and France under Francis I, and was primarily targeted on Switzerland, England and Germany.[1]

Among the famous Reformed ministers who like Calvin left France in the 1530s and 1540s and sought refuge in Geneva were Pierre Viret, Nicholas

---

[1] For the early emigration from the Netherlands, see A. Pettegree, *Emden and the Dutch Revolt. Exile and the Development of Reformed Protestantism* (Oxford 1992), pp. 1–25. For France, see M. Greengrass, *The French Reformation* (Oxford 1987), pp. 24ff.

des Gallars and Theodore Beza, while Reformed Italians, such as Bernardino Ochino and Peter Martyr fled to Strasburg via Basle in the 1540s. A few years later Ochino and Martyr found their way to England on the invitation of archbishop Thomas Cranmer. Here they were joined in 1549 by Martin Bucer and Paul Fagius who made England their new home as a consequence of Strasburg's acceptance of the Augsburg Interim. Their arrival in England at the beginning of the reign of Edward VI was complemented by the return from exile of a number of English Protestants such as John Hooper, who had sought refuge in Bullinger's Zurich. During the short reign of Edward VI England became a safe haven for Reformed Protestants on a par with the Swiss cities of Zurich, Basle and Geneva, harbouring several leading Reformation theologians such as the Pole Johannes a Lasco.[2] Within popular Reformed mythology England, as a place of refuge, was perceived to be second only to Geneva, which was gradually coming to represent the new Jerusalem for the embryonic Reformed movement.

Consequently, Geneva, a city of around 10,000, more than doubled its size because of the arrival of religious refugees of mainly French and Italian origin, from Calvin's recall in 1541 to his death in 1564,[3] while the foundation of the stranger churches in London under the superintendency of Johannes a Lasco demonstrates the importance of England for the Reformed exodus. Whereas the prominence of Geneva within international Calvinism began to fade rapidly less than a decade after Calvin's death, England retained its significance for the Reformed diaspora, in spite of the brief Catholic interlude under Mary (1553–8). It can be argued that without the Marian exile, which saw such leading English Protestants as Christopher Goodman, William Whittingham and Anthony Gilby seek shelter in Geneva, John Jewel in Zurich, John Foxe in Basle and Edmund Grindal in Strasburg, English Protestantism may not have become an integral part of European Calvinism. But by having acquired a stake in the Reformed diaspora these exiles, on their return to England at the accession of Elizabeth, played a prominent part in guaranteeing that the Elizabethan government extended its hospitality to Dutch/Walloon and French Reformed emigrants throughout the sixteenth century. That the Elizabethan government's rationale for welcoming such a substantial influx of Reformed immigrants might have been economically motivated is of little significance in this context. There were, on the other hand, important

[2] See A. Pettegree, *Foreign Protestant Communities in Sixteenth-Century London* (Oxford 1986), pp. 133–81.
[3] See W. Monter, *Calvin's Geneva* (New York 1967), pp. 165–6 and W. Monter, 'Historical Demography and Religious History in Sixteenth-Century Geneva', *The Journal of Interdisciplinary History*, 9 (1979), 435–51, especially 402–4.

economic reasons why London especially remained an attractive option for Calvinist merchants fleeing France and the Netherlands in the sixteenth century. As opposed to Geneva which had been a prosperous entrepôt for German and Italian merchants in the fifteenth century, but which by the mid-sixteenth century had witnessed considerable economic and financial stagnation, England, and especially London, had gained constantly in economic importance.

The mass exodus which followed this first stage of the diaspora began in the late 1560s and continued over the next thirty years. It differed from the earlier and religiously diffuse emigration by being predominantly Reformed in character. It consisted of a small but important number of refugees from northern Italy, especially from the city of Lucca, where Peter Martyr had last been active shortly before his flight to Basle/Strasburg, of a considerably greater number of exiles from France following the outbreak of the Wars of Religion (1562), and last but not least of huge numbers of refugees from the Southern Netherlands as a result of Alva's repression.

It was a mass exodus of Reformed merchants and highly skilled craftsmen which was primarily brought about by the aggressive Counter-Reformation policies of the governments in these areas, even if it should be born in mind that economic considerations, especially among the merchant-elite, may have played a considerable part in the timing of the emigration. It has been estimated that the Spanish reconquest and re-Catholisation of the Southern Netherlands under the Duke of Alva and Alexander Farnese caused around 100,000 people to flee these areas, especially Flanders, Liège, Tournai and Valanciennes, between 1567 and 1590.[4] In the wake of the St Bartholomew Massacre (1572) they were joined by French coreligionists, some of whom had already helped reinforce Calvinism in Flanders by seeking shelter there from the Wars of Religion in the 1560s.

They settled primarily in Germany where they sought refuge in most of the important trading centres such as Frankfurt, Nuremberg, Cologne, Hamburg/Stade, Aachen, Wesel and Frankenthal, and in England, where they demonstrated a clear preference for London, and other towns and cities of south-east England, such as Colchester and Norwich where they constituted between a fifth and a third of the population around 1600; and, of course, especially in the case of the craftsmen, in the United Provinces, where the towns and cities of Holland and Zeeland, such as Leiden and

---

[4] J.G.C.A. Briels, *De zuidnederlandse immigratie, 1572–1630* (Haarlem 1978). It should be borne in mind that the mobility of the refugees makes any accurate estimate of the size of the emigration difficult. See also H. Schilling, 'Innovation through Migration: The Settlements of Calvinistic Netherlanders in Sixteenth- and Seventeenth-Century Central and Western Europe', *Social History*, 16: 31 (1983), 7–33, especially 9–10.

Haarlem became their preferred destination.[5] It should be emphasised, however, that this diaspora was made up of a series of emigrations and hardly ever constituted a simple migration from one place to another. It was a complex affair and would often continue for a couple of generations, not coming to an end until the first decades of the seventeenth century.

The motives and character of this emigration – whether it was mainly religious or predominantly economic in origin – has been a bone of contention among a generation of Dutch and Belgian historians.[6] No doubt motives were mixed, but economic reasons do not necessarily exclude religion or vice versa. There is, after all, nothing contrary to good Calvinism in making a sound choice of where and when to emigrate. As long as one did not compromise one's faith, a sound choice of time and place, making the best use of the resources God had put at the disposal of Man, can, in fact, be interpreted as an obligation for the Godly. Accordingly, the claim by many economic historians that the significance of economic motives grew when the emigration of wealthy Reformed merchants and entrepreneurs accelerated in the 1580s does not necessarily undermine the religious commitment of this group. In fact, the whole-hearted commitment to Calvinism of the merchant elite is underlined by the prominent role it played, serving as elders and deacons, within the exiled Reformed churches which the refugee communties established in nearly all the places where they settled.

Even if questions may be raised about the initial religious commitment of some of the wealthier emigrants the effect of joining the diaspora cannot but have reinforced their sense of belonging. In other words, emigration however diffuse its reasons and causes was a major social experience which can only have served to reinforce the Reformed faith of those who undertook it. When reading the Old Testament these refugees would construe their experience as a direct consequence of God's Providence and see it as evidence of the New Covenant. As these refugees settled in most of the major cities in northern Europe they came to form an international movement, perhaps less through their Calvinism, which often differed in points of doctrine, and their conviction of being God's chosen people, than through their shared experience of displacement and minority existence in

---

[5] For England, see O. P. Grell, *Dutch Calvinists in early Stuart London* (Leiden 1989), pp. 7–32 and O.P Grell, 'A Friendship Turned Sour: Puritans and Dutch Calvinists in East Anglia', in E. S. Leedham-Green (ed.), *Religious Dissent in East Anglia* (Cambridge 1991), pp. 45–67. For Germany, see H. Schilling, *Niederländische Exulanten im 16. Jahrhundert* (Gütersloh 1972), and H. Schilling, 'Innovation'. For craftsmen settling in the United provinces, see J. I. Israel, *Dutch Primacy in World Trade 1585–1740* (Oxford 1989), pp. 35–7.

[6] See especially the works by J. A. van Houtte and H. van der Wee. For a summary of this debate, see H. Schilling, 'Innovation', 10–11.

foreign and occasionally hostile environments. This social and, in my opinion, most prominent aspect of international Calvinism was reinforced by the tendency of these merchants to intermarry and their reliance on each other for business.[7]

This international dimension of the Second Reformation was further enhanced by the foundation of Reformed academies and universities, starting with the Academy in Geneva in 1559. For the Reformed ministers this development acquired a special significance. Thus Calvin's Academy, which was intended to provide a centre for the education of Reformed ministers, proved a resounding success, attracting more than 300 students from all over Europe in 1560.[8] By the 1570s the Genevan Academy's paramount position in the education of Reformed ministers had been taken over by the University of Heidelberg and a number of newly founded academies, such as Ghent (1578–83) and Herborn (1584). They were later supplemented by the new universities in the United Provinces, of which Leiden (1575) became the most famous, and at the turn of the century by the French Reformed Academies of Sedan and Saumur. By then the *peregrinatio academica*, visiting the most famous Reformed seats of learning, was gradually gaining ground among the more privileged, Reformed students of theology. Significantly, however, all these academies and universities continued the Genevan tradition of attracting large numbers of international students, adding another important international aspect to Calvinism, through contacts and friendships between individual ministers and their teachers.

Accordingly it is my contention that the social experience of exodus and diaspora, which Reformed merchant endured to an even greater extent than most of their coreligionists, was of paramount importance in providing Calvinism with an international character. This was especially the case since these merchants provided the lay leadership, of elders and deacons, of most of the Reformed churches. A further and significant manifestation of this Reformed internationalism was generated by the common experience of a considerable number of their consistorial colleagues, the ministers,

---

[7] Undoubtedly Calvin's and other Reformed leaders' refusal to tolerate 'nicodemism' among their followers served to reinforce emigration. For 'nicodemism', see R. Stauffer, 'Calvin', and A. Duke, 'The Ambivalent Face of Calvinism in the Netherlands 1561–1618', in M. Prestwich (ed.), *International Calvinism 1541–1715* (Oxford, 1985), pp. 15–37, especially pp. 23–4 and pp. 109–33, especially pp. 117–8. For Johannes a Lasco's writings against 'nicodemism', see Pettegree, *Foreign Protestants*, pp. 124–5. See also H. A. Oberman, 'The Impact of the Reformation; Problems and Persepctives', in E. I. Kouri and T. Scott (eds.), *Politics and Society in Reformation Europe* (London, 1987), pp. 3–31, especially 15–20.

[8] G. Lewis, 'Calvinism in Geneva in the Time of Calvin and Beza, 1541–1608', in Prestwich (ed.), *International Calvinism*, pp. 39–69, especially p. 64.

especially through their educational background in an international academic environment.[9]

In order to illustrate how this operated in practice, I shall focus on London, one of the major centres for the Reformed diaspora, and on some of the leading members of the stranger churches in particular.

Undoubtedly, Cesar Calandrini, who became a minister to the Dutch Reformed church in London in 1639, was an archetypal product of international Calvinism. Cesar's family history is closely linked to the Reformed diaspora which began in the 1560s. He belonged to one of three closely connected aristocratic merchant families who had fled the repression of the Counter-Reformation in Lucca. Well in advance of their conversion to Protestantism, which according to family tradition should have been inspired by the preaching of Peter Martyr in the 1540s while he was Prior of the St Frediano monastery, the three families of Diodati, Burlamachi and Calandrini were firmly ensconced among the mercantile oligarchy in Lucca. Considering both the timing of their flight, twenty years after the departure of Peter Martyr, and their trade contacts with French commercial centres, such as Lyon, which were strongly Calvinist, it is, however, highly likely that members of these families did not fully convert to Reformed Protestantism until they encountered Calvinism in France. This was certainly the case of Pompeo Diodati who, while in Lyon, decided to free himself 'from the yoke of Antichrist and to dedicate myself wholly to the pure service of God' and consequently decided to emigrate to Geneva.[10]

Having converted to Calvinism in 1562, Pompeo Diodati had to wait another four years before those of his family who shared his religious belief were ready to leave Lucca. Obviously, considerable time was needed for these merchant/financiers to dispose of their real estate and disengage from business involvements before emigration could be contemplated. When that was achieved, most of the Diodatis, Calandrinis and Burlamachis who were already related, but later used the opportunity to reaffirm their family alliances through further marriages, left Lucca between September 1566 and March 1567. They appear to have faced no problems in leaving the city and travelled in style via Lyon, where Pompeo joined them, not to Geneva as originally intended, but to Paris. Here they acquired a country house, Luzarches, seven miles outside the city and Pompeo married Laura Calandrini, sister to Giovanni. This purchase of a considerable estate, near

---

[9] For the Calvinist academies, see R. Stauffer, 'Calvinism and the Universities', in L. Grane (ed.), *University and Reformation* (Leiden, 1981), pp. 76–98. For an example of the *perigrinatio academica*, see Grell, *Dutch Calvinists*, pp. 139–44.

[10] Quoted from 'Narrative of Pompeo Deodati' printed in A. F. W. Papillon, *Memoirs of Thomas Papillon of London, Merchant, 1623–1702* (Reading, 1887), p. 412.

Paris, is a clear indication that the families must have been able to dispose of, or transfer, considerable parts of their property before leaving Lucca. Thus in June 1567 when they were officially banished and the Lucchese government confiscated their remaining property, the damage must have been limited.

However, the renewal of the French Wars of Religion in the autumn of 1567 meant renewed exile. Initially, in November 1567, they were forced to flee before the advancing Catholic armies, but were fortunate to find another French refuge in Montargis where they were offered protection by the widow of the duke of Ferrara, Renée de France, daughter of Louis XII, who had played host to John Calvin when he was in Italy in 1536. They were unable to return to Luzarches and Paris on a permanent basis until 1570. There they remained until the St Bartholomew Massacre in August 1572, when most of them fled to Sedan. By then the families had begun to split up, some settling in Antwerp, others in Frankfurt, Nuremberg and Stade/ Hamburg. Pompeo Diodati, on the other hand, 'resolved to go thence to Geneva, which I had all along desired, and feeling that God had afflicted us in France because we had not gone thither in the first instance, as I purposed'. Still, it took Pompeo and his immediate family another three years before they reached Geneva and one is left with the distinct impression that their arrival was eventually caused more by accident than intent.[11]

Giuliano, the most senior member of the Calandrini family to leave Lucca, died in Sedan shortly after the St Bartholomew Massacre. His two sons, Cesare and Giovanni (the latter was the father of Cesar Calandrini who became a minister to the Dutch Church in London), left France in the years immediately after the massacre and established a merchant-house in Antwerp. Here Giovanni married Marie, daughter of the wealthy Antwerp merchant Jean de Maistres, while his brother Cesare married her sister Esther three years later in Frankfurt. The brothers must have moved on shortly before the Spanish siege and recapture of Antwerp in 1584–5 and settled in Frankfurt. Two children were born to Giovanni Calandrini during his family's residence here. Gian Luigi, born in 1585, eventually settled in Geneva where he became a shareholder and codirector with his father-in-law, Francesco Turrettini, of the city's most prominent banking/ merchant organisation, The Grand Boutique.[12] He also became closely involved with one of the leading European financial establishments of the

---

[11] 'Narrative of Pompeo Deodati', pp. 411–21. See also W. Monter, 'The Italians in Geneva: A New Look', *Genève et l'Italie: Etudes publiées a l'occasion du 50e anniversaire de la Société genevoise d'études italiennes par Luc Monnier* (Geneva, 1969), pp. 53–77, especially p. 69, 71–3.

[12] For The Grand Boutique, see W. Bodmer, *Der Einfluss der Refugianteneinwanderung von 1550–1700 auf die schweizerische Wirtschaft* (Zurich, 1946), pp. 41–9, 82–3, 151.

early modern period, the merchant/banking-house set up in Amsterdam/ London by his father Giovanni and another brother-in-law, the famous London banker of the Stuart period, Philip Burlamachi. His financial contacts were extensive and he became the Genevan Republic's leading banker until he was ruined by Philip Burlamachi's spectacular bankruptcy in England in 1634.[13] His brother Philip, born two years later, looked after the interests of the Calandrini/Burlamachi firm in Amsterdam after his father and brother-in-law had moved to London at the start of James I's reign. In 1622 Philip collaborated with Sir Henry Wotton in Venice in a Calvinist attempt to raise funds for the recapture of Bohemia.[14]

Shortly after Philip's birth Giovanni Calandrini moved to Stade near Hamburg. In 1589 he became an elder to the Reformed church in Stade and by 1597 he was heavily involved in the English cloth trade exporting over a thousand pieces to Hamburg in late 1597. The Dutch Republic's increasing dominance over world trade must by the 1590s have encouraged Giovanni to move his business to Amsterdam, where he arrived in 1599.[15] In Amsterdam, eight years later, in his mid-sixties, he remarried. The bride, Catherina Pietraviva, was the widow of Assuerus Regemorter, who had been a minister to the Dutch Church in London from 1585 to 1604. Most likely the couple's acquaintance went back to the period 1582–5, when Assuerus Regemorter had served the Reformed Church in Antwerp as a minister. Giovanni and his family would have been likely members of Regemorter's congregation.[16] The marriage appear to have been the Calandrini family's first contact with the stranger churches in London with whom they were to be so closely associated by the second decade of the seventeenth century.

Within a year of his marriage, Giovanni had moved to London together with his son-in-law, Philip Burlamachi, who had married his eldest daughter Elizabeth in February 1608. Apart from the already mentioned

---

[13] A. Pascal, 'Da Lucca a Ginevra', *Revista Storica Italiana*, 2 (1935), 253–315, especially 262–3. For Philip Burlamachi, see R. Ashton, 'The Disbursing Official under the Early Stuarts: The Cases of William Russell and Philip Burlamachi', *Bulletin of the Institute of Historical Research*, 30 (1957), 162–74. See also R. Ashton, *The Crown and the Money market 1603–1640* (Oxford, 1960), pp. 20–2.

[14] D. C. Dorian, *The English Diodatis* (New Brunswick, 1950), pp. 312–13; for Wotton's contacts to Jean Diodati, see p. 99.

[15] For Giovanni Calandrini, see W. Baumann, *The Merchant Adventurers and the Continental Cloth-trade (1560s–1620s)* (Berlin, 1990), p. 262, 271–2 and Dorian, *English Diodatis*, p. 310. For Dutch Republic, see Israel, *Dutch Primacy*, p. 42.

[16] For the marriage, see Grell, *Dutch Calvinists*, p. 124. From the late 1570s until the fall of Antwerp in 1585 several members of the Calandrini/Burlamachi/Diodati/Turrettini clan settled in Antwerp, among them the later founder of The Grand Boutique, Francesco Turrettini, who served the French Reformed church in the city as an elder for a couple of years between 1579 and 1585, see Bibliotheque publique et universitaire de Geneve, MS Suppl. 438, f. 66r.

sons, who settled in Geneva and Amsterdam, another of Giovanni's sons, Marco, remained on the Continent. He conveniently continued the family enterprise in Stade/Hamburg where by 1633 he was among some of the major lenders to the Danish Crown.[17] With one exception all the other children settled in England. Giuliano and Pompeo joined the merchant house of Calandrini/Burlamachi, Cesar became a minister while Anna-Maria, the other daughter, married the Huguenot military architect and engineer, David Papillon, who together with his mother had fled to London in 1588.[18]

Meanwhile, Giovanni's brother, Cesare Calandrini, had moved from Frankfurt to Nuremberg. Here he was active in the cloth trade from 1597 and established a partnership with another Reformed refugee from Lucca, Ludovico Perez, who was already among the wealthiest merchants in Nuremberg. Cesare also continued his collaboration with Giovanni and between 1602 and 1609 their operations in Nuremberg received considerable investments from the influential Frankfurt banker, Johann von Bodeck, who was a Reformed refugee from the Southern Netherlands. Cesare's standing within Nuremberg must have been considerable since the city council made him a member of the commission for the improvement of the coinage in 1620.[19] In 1626 Cesare's son, Jeremia Calandrini, was among the originators of the European collections for Calvinist refugee ministers from the Upper Palatinate. This was a relief work which was to continue for the next twenty years and see the close involvement of the Dutch church in London and Jeremia's cousin, Cesar Calandrini.[20]

By the early seventeenth century the prominent financial and commercial position held by Cesare in Nuremberg and Giovanni Calandrini/Philip Burlamachi in London/Amsterdam helped reinforce the family network. Younger members of the Geneva-based branch of the family, such as Nicolao Diodati, Pompeo's son, and Vincent Burlamachi, Fabrizio's son, came to live with their relations in these mercantile centres in order to learn the trade and the necessary languages.[21]

Cesar, who was born at Stade in 1595, appears to have been the first member of the Calvinist wing of the Calandrini family to have been destined for a scholarly or ecclesiastical career. He commenced his univer-

---

[17] See Dorian, *English Diodatis*, p. 310 and J. T. Lauridsen, *Marselis Konsortiet* (Århus, 1987), pp. 32–3.

[18] For Papillon, see *Dictionary of National Biography*.

[19] For Cesare Calandrini in Nuremberg, see G. Siebold, 'Zur Situation der italienischen Kaufleute in Nürnberg während der zweiten Hälfte des 17. und der ersten Hälfte des 18. Jahrhunderts', *Mitteilungen des Vereins für Geschichte der Stadt Nürnberg*, 71 (1984), 186–207; L. Bauer, 'Die italienischen Kaufleute und ihre Stellung im protestantischen Nürnberg am Ende des 16. Jahrhunderts', *Jahrbuch für Fränkische Landesforschung*, 22 (1962), 1–18 and W. Baumann, *The Merchant Adventurers*, 271–2.

[20] Grell, *Dutch Calvinists*, pp. 176–9.   [21] MS Suppl. 438, f. 58r, 74r.

sity education when he matriculated at the Academy in Geneva in May 1612. The choice of Geneva for the 17-year-old was undoubtedly influenced by family rather than academic reasons. The presence in Geneva of several influential family members who could provide guidance for the young man, not to mention his relation, Jean Diodati, at the Academy, must have been decisive. Jean Diodati, who had become professor of Hebrew at the early age of 21, had by 1609 been given a Chair in Theology and had served as Rector of the Genevan Academy. When Cesar Calandrini matriculated in 1612, Jean Diodati was already renowned internationally as a leading Calvinist theologian.[22] Thus a tutor of the highest quality was available in Geneva from within the family.

Before he returned to England, where he continued his studies in Oxford, Cesar Calandrini also studied for a while at the newly founded Academy at Saumur (1599). The presence in Saumur of such leading orthodox, Calvinist theologians, as Franciscus Gomarus and Louis Cappel would have been an obvious attraction. Initially, Calandrini's stay in Oxford was short, in November 1616, six months after he had been admitted as a reader to the Bodleian Library he matriculated in theology at the university of Leiden where only a year later he concluded his studies. During his stay in Leiden Calandrini renewed his acquaintance with the Huygens family, with whom the Calandrinis had been close while living in Amsterdam, and he developed his friendship with Constantine Huygens, the Dutch poet and diplomat, with whom he shared lodgings in Leiden and kept up a correspondance after his return to England.[23]

Back in London in late 1617 Cesar Calandrini became a 'proponent' or trainee minister in the French church. He was an obvious choice, bearing in mind that this was the community where his brothers-in-law, Philip Burlamachi and David Papillon, had already served as elder and deacon.[24] These early contacts to the French church probably also account for Cesar's marriage in August 1621 to Elizabeth Harderet, a grand-daughter of the minister to the French community in London, Robert le Macon, sieur de la Fontaine, who had died in 1611.[25] Only a few months after his return, in March 1618, Cesar was examined and ordained by the joint body of ministers of the Dutch and French churches.[26] Their support and the

22 Grell, *Dutch Calvinists*, p. 63 and Dorian, *English Diodatis*, 98–9, 248.
23 For Saumur, see Stauffer, 'Calvinism & Universities', 87–8; for Calandrini, see A.G.H. Bachrach, *Sir Constantine Huygens and Britain 1596–1687* (Leiden, 1962), pp. 58–62 and Grell, *Dutch Calvinism*, pp. 62–5.
24 French church, Soho Square, London, MS 4, consistory book 1588–1615, f. 483r, 503v and MS 5, consistory book 1615–1680, f. 10r, f. 46r, f. 74v,77r.
25 Grell, *Dutch Calvinists*, p. 63. Elizabeth was also the daughter of a leading elder of the French church in London, see P. R. Sellin, 'Caesar Calandrini, the London Dutch, and Milton's Quarrels in Holland', *Huntington Library Quaterly*, 31 (1968), 239–49, especially 245, n. 25.   26 French church MS 5, f. 26r.

backing of the apostate archbishop of Spalato, Marco Anthonio De Dominis, who had become dean of Windsor and preached occasionally to the small Italian congregation at Mercer's Chapel in 1617, secured Calandrini the appointment of minister to the Italian Reformed church in London. Consequently, the Italian church was reconstituted, elders and deacons once more elected, and the church re-admitted as a member of the Coetus of the stranger churches.[27]

Initially, Cesar Calandrini aquired an influential mentor in De Dominis and lodged with him at the Savoy Hospital. Later, he found it increasingly difficult to reconcile his Calvinism with De Dominis's Catholic syncretism. In this respect Calandrini's personal experience of the synod of Dordrecht may have played a considerable part. He arrived in Dordrecht on 13 January 1619, exactly two months after the start of the synod, in the company of archbishop Abbott's chaplain, Dr Thomas Goad, who replaced Joseph Hall in the British delegation. This journey may well have provided the foundations for the continued contacts between the two men in the years to come.[28] Cesar, who for a period at least stayed with his relation and teacher, Jean Diodati, a member of the Genevan delegation, at the house of the headmaster of the French school in Dordrecht, Jean de Grave, appears to have attended the remaining sessions of the synod.[29]

Jean Diodati, a strong supporter of the Counter-Remonstrant position, was eventually elected as one of the deputies of the synod entrusted with drawing up the canons. Upon the adjournment of the synod Diodati appears to have visited Cesar Calandrini in London, after having attended 'a meeting in Cambridge'. Considering that two of the four English delegates to Dort were resident Cambridge academics, namely John Davenant, Lady Margaret Professor of Divinity and Master of Queen's College, and Samuel Ward, Master of Sidney Sussex College, not to mention the single Scottish delegate, Walter Balanqual, who was a fellow of Pembroke College, a briefing of the British delegation by one of the synod's deputies in Cambridge seems an obvious explanation for this visit.[30]

During the synod Cesar Calandrini appears to have become increasingly

[27] J. J. van Toorenenbergen (ed.), *Gheschiedenissen ende Handelingen die voornemelick aengaen de nederduytsche Natie ende gemeynten wonende in Engeland ende in bysonder tot Londen* (*WMV*, 3, 1, 1873), pp. 416–17.

[28] J. A. Worp, *Constantijn Huygens Briefwisseling 1608–1687* (6 vols., The Hague, 1911–17, RGP vols. 15, 19, 21, 24, 28, 32), Letter no. 60. See also Guildhall Library MS 7424, f. 49ff. and C. R. Elrington (ed.) *The Whole Works of James Ussher* (17 vols., Dublin, 1847–64), vol. 16, p. 214. For the English delegation, see N. Tyacke, *Anti-Calvinists. The Rise of English Arminianism c. 1590–1640* (Oxford, 1987), pp. 99–100.

[29] *Huygens Briefwisseling*, nos. 60, 64. Vincent Burlamachi, another member of the family, also stayed with Jean Diodati at the same lodgings in Dordrecht at this time, see MS Suppl. 438, f. 75v.

[30] *Huygens Briefwisseling*, no. 66; Dorian, *English Diodatis*, pp. 100–1; Tyacke, *English Arminianism*, pp. 44–5.

hostile towards the Remonstrants. On 24 April 1618 he informed Constantine Huygens that 'the Remonstrants seem to have appropriated all the tricks of the Jesuits, especially Episcopius' and in another letter of 17 July 1619 Calandrini concluded by stating that 'you must cast out the Remonstrants'.[31]

On his return Cesar Calandrini finished his studies in theology at Exeter College, Oxford under the guidance of its Rector and newly appointed Regius Professor of Divinity, John Prideaux. Prideaux's orthodox Calvinism and negative attitude to the Remonstrants would have proved attractive to Calandrini who appears to have stayed in contact with his teacher after his student days.[32] Shortly after he had acquired his BD, on 20 June 1620, Calandrini was instituted to the well-endowed rectory of Stableford Abbots in Essex. Since this was a benefice held by Prince Charles we can safely asume that this was one of the last favours De Dominis, with his excellent Court contacts, was able and willing to bestow on his *protégé*. By then, De Dominis appears to have developed doubts about Calvinism in general and the validity of Calandrini's Reformed ordination by the stranger churches in particular. His attempt to get Bishop Thomas Morton of Lichfield, a solid Calvinist who had already condemned Arminianism as early as 1609, to reordain Calandrini, was, not surprisingly, unsuccessful.[33] Clearly, De Dominis had little or no concept of the theological position of at least one of the leading Jacobean bishops, and when shortly before his departure to Rome he denounced Calandrini as a Genevan and a Puritan he also took the opportunity to include Thomas Morton. This incident may well have inspired the two leading English Arminians, Richard Montagu and John Cosin, to try to have Calandrini ousted from his rectory and replaced with an Arminian candidate of their own in 1624, a scheme which eventually came to nothing.[34]

Calandrini's extensive list of English correspondents confirms his theological position as similar to that of the stricter Calvinists or Puritans within the Church of England. It includes names such as the ministers Herbert Palmer, John Davenport, Stephen Marshall, Thomas Gataker, Thomas Edward, Dr Thomas Goad, Dr Walter Balanqual, James Ussher and John Prideaux. Likewise, the great majority of his continental correspondents belonged to the orthodox, Counter-Remonstrant wing of European Calvinism, including such leading figures as Festus Hommius, Henrich Alting,

---

[31] *Huygens Briefwissling*, nos. 64, 66; compare with the neutral letter of August 1617, no. 35.

[32] See J. Foster, *Alumni Oxoniensis* (4 vols., Oxford, 1891–92), I, p. 230; Guildhall Library MS 7424, f. 49ff and Tyacke, *English Arminianism*, pp. 72–4.

[33] Grell, *Dutch Calvinists*, pp. 63–6; see also Tyacke, *English Arminianism*, p. 71 (for Thomas Morton) and p. 122 (for Bishop Neale's interview with De Dominis).

[34] *The Correspondence of John Cosin, D. D. Lord Bishop of Durham*, Part 1 (Pub. of the Surtees Society, L11, 1869), pp. 27–30.

Johannes Polyander, Andreas Rivet, Maximilian Teellinck and Johannes de Laet in the United Provinces, Benedict Turrettini and Jean Diodati in Geneva and Pierre du Moulin in France.[35]

For some years Calandrini continued to serve the Italian church in London as its minister while simultaneously looking after his parish in Stableford Abbotts. This was made possible through Stapleford Abbotts geographical position *vis-à-vis* London, being only 'some 3 hours riding' away.[36] Cesar Calandrini resided in the City until 1626, becoming closely involved in James Ussher's great Protestant scheme, the *Bibliotheca Theologica*, an elaborate attempt to write a providential history of the True Church based on the best available sources. This was an enterprise where Calandrini's many international contacts in the world of trade and Reformed religion must have been useful.[37]

When nearly twenty years later Cesar Calandrini was elected minister to the Dutch church in London the guidance he had received from Ussher in providential history must have proved beneficial. He took over the responsibility for writing the history of the Dutch exile community begun by his predecessor, Simon Ruytinck, who had served the church from 1601 to 1621.[38] Apart from Calandrini's personal interest in providential history which he shared with a number of Reformed Protestants, who held the study of time and history second only in importance to that of the Bible, his family appears to have been deeply concerned with its own history. Several members of the Burlamachis, Diodatis and Calandrinis wrote detailed histories of the exodus from Lucca and their subsequent tribulations in exile, such as Renée/Renata Burlamachi, a sister-in-law of Cesar and his uncle, Pompeo Diodati, just to mention a few. Copies of these manuscripts seem to have circulated within the wider family where, in some cases, they were translated for the use of later generations.[39] The aim of these family histories, as well as most Reformed works of history from this period was, of course, to work out and understand God's will and plan for the world in general and for the elect in particular.[40]

[35] Guildhall Library MS 7424, f. 49ff.
[36] See Guildhall Library MS 7397/7, f.102v and *Cosin Correspondance*, p. 27.
[37] See H. Trevor-Roper, *Catholics, Anglicans and Puritans* (London, 1987), pp. 124–39.
[38] For Calandrini's contribution, see *Gheschiedenissen*, pp. 389–483; see also his draft in MS, Guildhall MSS 9622/1 and 2.
[39] See MS Suppl. 438 (in Italian); 3 copies in English of Pompeo Diodati's Memoirs in Papillon of Acrise Place MSS U1015, F 8, Kent County Archives; 1 copy in French of Pompeo Diodati's Memoirs and 1 copy in French of Renata Burlamachi's Memoirs in Trinity College, Dublin, see T. K. Abbott (ed.), *Catalogue of the Manuscripts in the Library of Trinity College, Dublin* (London, 1900), no. 1152, VIII.
[40] There is a considerable literature on Protestant providential and apocalyptic history, see among others J. W. Thompson, *The History of Historical Writing* (2 vols., New York, 1942), especially I, pp. 520–645; K. R. Firth, *The Apocalyptic Tradition in Reformation Britain 1530–1645* (Oxford, 1979), pp. 1–31, and A. Zakai, *Exile and Kingdom. History and Apocalypse in the Puritan migration to America* (Cambridge, 1992), pp. 12–55.

This preoccupation with providential history which came to characterise late sixteenth and early seventeenth century Calvinism was not only reinforced by, but, in my opinion, closely linked to the experience of exodus and diaspora. Thus, it is no coincidence that the three major martyrologies of Reformed Protestantism, and the first Reformed works to promote providentialism to a wide audience, those of Jean Crespin, Adriaan van Haemstede and John Foxe, all grew out of their authors' personal experiences of persecution, flight and exile.[41]

The history of the Dutch community in London by Simon Ruytinck and Cesar Calandrini, fits neatly into this category of Calvinist historical works. The authors wrote a providential history of the community which thanks to God's Grace and Mercy had survived all the tribulations and tests to which it has been exposed. It is a history, which together with the Bible, would have served to confirm members of the Dutch Reformed church in the belief that they belonged to the elect. Thus, when Ruytinck recorded how the Dutch/Walloon exiles, who had fled London at the start of Mary's reign, arrived in Copenhagen, and how they were expelled, he added 'that they had trusted in God who had preserved them in Copenhagen, where several thousand people had died from the plague while none of the exiles had even been ill'. Similarly, when Calandrini described the aftermath of the trial in 1619 of several of the most prominent members of the Dutch/Walloon merchant community in London for illegal export of bullion, he emphasised how most of the witnesses against the foreign merchants had later fallen on hard times and had been seen begging at their victims' doors. 'Likewise, shortly afterwards several of the judges had lost the King's favour and their offices and been imprisoned in the Tower', where many had later died. King James himself, who was considered heavily involved in the case by the Dutch/Walloon communities, 'had only managed to survive in bad health for a few years'.[42] Clearly, if God did not always protect the elect he could, at least, be counted on to punished their enemies.

Cesar Calandrini may also have had personal reasons for continuing Ruytinck's history. He had been one of Ruytinck's close friends and contributed a poem to the volume of poetry, *Epicedia in Orbitum*, comme-

---

41 Exile has been recognised as being of paramount importance for the development of the apocalyptic tradition in Britain, see Firth, *Apocalyptic Tradition*, p. 69; for the general significance of migration within ecclesiastical history and the way Puritan emigrants to America viewed their own situation, see Zakai, *Exile*, p. 8 and passim. For Adriaan van Haemstede, see A. J. Jelsma, *Adriaan van Haemstede en zijn martelaarsboek* (The Hague, 1970); for *Jean Crespin*, see J. Gilmont, *Jean Crespin* (Geneva, 1981); for John Foxe, see Firth, *Apocalyptic Tradition*, pp. 69–110.

42 *Gheschiedenissen*, p. 23, 393. Ruytinck wrote two accounts of his history: Guildhall MS 9621 which was used by Toorenenbergen for *Gheschiedenissen*; and Guildhall MS 9620, which differs on a number of points and is divided into headed chapters, often of a providential nature. Further historical notes by Ruytinck can be found in Guildhall MS 10,055.

morating Ruytinck's death.[43] Later, when Calandrini was continuing Ruytinck's history, he described his predecessor's death as a colossal loss to the community, 'because he was extremely energetic and active in all good services. He deserves to be given the ornaments of the most outstanding pastors of the soul, whom he truly followed: For zeal for thy house has consumed me (Psal 69:9) and the love of your members (Church) has exhausted me.'[44]

Simon Ruytinck had a lot in common with his younger friend. Like him he belonged to the Reformed diaspora and like the Calandrinis Ruytinck's family had been influential in their place of origin. His father, Jan, had been secretary of Ghent before the family fled to Norwich in 1573.[45] Like Calandrini, Ruytinck had studied at two of the major Reformed seats of learning, Leiden and Geneva, and like his friend he appears to have mastered a number of languages.[46] Ruytinck's manuscripts and published books show us a man, who in spite of his orthodox Calvinism was characterised by a tolerant, learned and humanist outlook.[47]

Ruytinck may well have introduced Calandrini to the small but influential community of historically inclined merchant/scholars within the Dutch church in London. They were all close to Ruytinck and are probably best described as belonging to the more 'liberal', humanist, strand within the Reformed tradition. Three prominent members of this circle, Emanuel van Meteren, Jacob Cool (Ortelianus), and Johan Radermacher/ Rotarius are likely to have befriended Cesar Calandrini. Jacob Cool contributed together with Calandrini, to the *Epicedia* in commemoration of Ruytinck , having already dedicated his *Paraphrasis ... vanden CIIII Psalm* to Simon Ruytinck in 1617, while Cesar Calandrini's father, Giovanni wrote an entry in Van Meteren's *Album Amicorum*.[48] Simon Ruytinck wrote a biography of

[43] *Epidecia in Orbitum* (Elzevier, Leiden, 1622).   [44] *Gheschiedenissen*, 395.

[45] *Nieuw Nederlandsch Biografisch Woordenboeck* (hereafter NNBW), IV, 1181–2.

[46] See Simon Ruytinck's two theses, *Theses Physicae de Elementis*, Leiden 1597 and *Disputationum Theologicarum Repetitarum. Decima quinta de Creatione Homines, Leiden ad Imaginem Dei* (Leiden, 1598). Ruytinck received his first degree in Leiden under the auspices of the famous French Reformed theologian, Pierre du Moulin, who was then professor of philosophy at the University of Leiden. For Ruytinck's languages, see *Gheschiedenissen*, p. 395.

[47] For Ruytinck, see O. P. Grell, 'Calvinist Agape or Godly Dining Club?', *NAK*, 68 (1988), 36–45. In his extensive coverage of the Hampton Court Conference in 1604 Ruytinck's sympathy was evidently with those Puritan ministers who were dismissed, but it was tempered by the observation that a good cause had been damaged through the rashness of some of those ministers who, wanting to carry the Reformation further, had acted without common consent, *Gheschiedenissen*, pp. 187, 179.

[48] See Jacob Cool, *Paraphrasis vanden CIIII Psalm* (Middelburg, 1626), and J. A. van Dorsten, "I. C. O.': The Rediscovery of a Modest Dutchman in London', in J. A. van Dorsten, *The Anglo-Dutch Renaissance* (Leiden, 1988), pp. 8–20. For Giovanni Calandini's entry, see Emanuel van Meteren, *Album Amicorum*, Bodleian Library MS Douce 68, f.110 (signed as 'Lucensis', dated Leiden, 20 August 1607) and Bachrach, *Constantine Huygens*, p. 61.

Emanuel van Meteren, who died in April 1612, which was added to the 1614 edition of Van Meteren's famous history of the Dutch Revolt. According to Ruytinck, he had written it 'out of love and esteem' for Van Meteren.[49]

Recent scholarship which has been concerned with the merchant/ historian Emanuel van Meteren and his two friends and associates, his second cousin, Jacob Cool, named Ortelianus after his famous uncle, the cartographer Abraham Ortelius in Antwerp, and the merchant/scholar Johan Radermacher, have portrayed these men as strongly heterodox Calvinists and members of the freemasons of the late sixteenth and early seventeenth century, the Family of Love.[50] Considering that this view is based on circumstantial evidence it is surprising that it has been left unchallenged.

In the case of Emanuel van Meteren, the Antwerp born and apprenticed merchant, who in 1583 became Consul to the Dutch merchants in London, the perception of him as a heterodox and possible Familist owes much to his involvement in the bitter dispute within the Dutch church in London in 1561. Van Meteren was among the most prominent defenders of the minister Adriaan van Haemstede, who had argued for a tolerant approach to Anabaptists. This politically highly sensitive issue eventually led not only to van Haemstede's excommunication, but also to that of a number of his supporters in the Dutch church, including van Meteren, who did not make his peace with the church until a decade later.[51] Combined with van Meteren's friendship with Abraham Ortelius, who probably was a member of the Family of Love, and his often quoted introduction from 1599 to the first edition of his history of the Dutch Revolt, this has been taken as proof of his Familist leanings.

The fact that van Meteren became reconciled with the Dutch Reformed Church in London in 1571 and, according to Simon Ruytinck, that the ministers of the church attended him on his deathbed, appears to have been disregarded.[52] Furthermore, the minister Simon Ruytinck's friendship

[49] See *Gheschiedenissen*, p. 274 and L. Brummel, *Twee Ballingen's lands tijdens onze opstand tegen Spanje: Hugo Blotius (1534–1612), Emanuel van Meteren (1535–1612)* (The Hague, 1972), pp. 119, 125.

[50] This view was launched by J. A. van Dorsten, *The Radical Arts* (Leiden, 1972), pp. 32–7; it was accepted by Brummel, *Twee Ballingen*, pp. 127–8, N. Mout, 'The Family of Love (Huis der Liefde) and the Dutch Revolt', in A. C. Duke and C. A. Tamse (eds.), *Britain and the Netherlands, VII. Church and State since the Reformation* (The Hague, 1981), pp. 76–93, especially p. 84, and E. M. Janssen, 'A 'Trias Historica' on the Revolt of the Netherlands: Emanuel van Meteren. Pieter Bor and Everhard van Reyd as Exponents of Contemporary Historiography', in A. C. Duke and C. A. Tamse (eds.), *Britain and the Netherlands, VIII. Clio's Mirror. Historiography in Britain and the Netherlands* (Zutphen, 1985), pp. 9–30, especially p. 15.

[51] For a recent analysis of this episode, see Pettegree, *Foreign Protestant Communities*, pp. 173–5.

[52] See Simon Ruytinck's Levensbericht in the 1614 edition of Emanuel van Meteren's, *Commentarien Ofte Memorien Vanden Nederlandtschen Staet, handel, Oorloghen ende*

with and biography of Van Meteren seem to contradict the accepted view of van Meteren as a Familist.[53]

Similarly, much has been made of van Meteren's history as being unusually pragmatic and uninfluenced by religious prejudice. It is correct that van Meteren in his introduction to the 1599 edition appeals to both Catholics, strict Calvinists and *politiques*. The introduction clearly demonstrates his distaste for religious persecution and intolerance, but it also, and more importantly shows him as an orthodox, liberal Calvinist who belived in providential history, stating that he had written his history 'In order that such a History may serve as a mirror of insight for the Netherlanders, and all other nations, of the true knowledge of the wars described, and that they may understand God's just decisions and providential grace'.[54] And below, when recommending his history to the *politiques*, van Meteren stated his hope that they 'might recognize in the outcome of the various events the wise and righteous judgements of God, and moreover find that He does not give his commandments in vain but that he wants to be served and honoured in this world with body and soul'.[55] Van Meteren, in other words, wanted to write a Godly, providential work of history. This was a solidly Calvinist enterprise pursued, as we have seen, by his friends, the ministers Simon Ruytinck and Cesar Calandrini.

Like his relation Emanuel van Meteren, Jacob Cool was born in Antwerp, where his father had briefly returned from London in the early 1560s.[56] He was by trade a silk-merchant, but retained a strong scholarly interest throughout his life. In this, he was initially encouraged by his learned uncle in Antwerp, Abraham Ortelius, who expressed his satisfaction over Jacob's interest in history in 1587 and later himself taught his nephew in Antwerp.[57] Cool, who became a good classicist, a learned collector of Greek and Roman coins and medals, a herbalist and an author of a number of religious books, retained his interest in history in later life. Thus, when his *protégé* and nephew, Abraham vanden Bossche informed him about his educational progress in 1623, he stressed that 'Theology attracts me, and after that I long for the study of History.'[58]

Cool's devotional authorship confirms him as a staunch Calvinist.

Gheschiedenissen van onsen tyden .., f. 672ff and Brummel, *Twee Ballingen*, p. 125; for the reconciliation, see Pettegree, *Foreign Protestant Communities*, p. 180.

[53] Furthermore, Emanuel van Meteren's son-in-law, Abraham der Kinderen, served the Dutch church in London as a deacon, see Grell, *Dutch Calvinists*, pp. 263, 274. See also J. H. Hessels (ed.), *Ecclesiae Londino-Batavae Archivum*, I–III (1–2) (Cambridge, 1887–97), I, no. 224.

[54] The introduction to the 1599 edition is quoted in Brummel, *Twee Ballingen*, p. 123

[55] Cited in Janssen, 'Trias Historica', p. 17.

[56] His father might well have belonged to the pro-Haemstede wing within the Dutch church in London, since his first wife was a sister of Adriaan van Haemstede, see Hessels, I, no. 47; see also Van Dorsten, *Radical Arts*, p. 23.

[57] Hessels, I, nos. 149, 161.   [58] *Ibid.*, no. 364.

Before printing his works, he often circulated them among friends within the Reformed churches in England and the Netherlands. His tract, *Of Death, a true Description*, which was published in Dutch in 1624 and in English in 1629, was forwarded to the minister of the Dutch community in Colchester, Jonas Proost, the minister in Grijpskerke near Middelburg, Wilhelm Thilenius, who was elected a minister to the Dutch community in London and Willem Teellinck in Middelburg, all of whom belonged to the Counter-Remonstrant wing of the Reformed churches. They all praised the godly qualities of Cool's tract and Proost replied:

I wish to pray unto God, and to imitate you in this respect, that in the serenity of prosperity and health, I may have like thoughts of death and a similar preparation of mind, as a splendid testimony of that spiritual life, which the Author of life, Jesus Christ, works in those that belong to him.[59]

Thirty years earlier, Cool's Reformed faith appears to have caused him some problems with his Familist/spiritualist uncle.[60] But in spite of his association with his uncle and a considerable number of scholars who did not belong to the Reformed faith Cool remained firmly anchored within the Reformed tradition. He eventually served the Dutch community in London as an elder from 1624 until his death in 1628. This was undoubtedly a capacity where his many international contacts would have proved useful.[61]

Cool and Van Meteren's friend and correspondent, Johan Radermacher, is yet another Reformed merchant/ scholar with a strong Antwerp connection. Born into a patrician family from Aachen in 1538, Radermacher spent some of his early years in London, where he lived with his parents when the Dutch Church in Austin Friars was established in 1550.[62] After his father's death in 1554 Radermacher was apprenticed to the wealthy Antwerp merchant Aegidius Hooftman and it is from this period that his friendship with Emanuel van Meteren dates.[63] Five years later Radermacher was back in London where he was actively involved in obtaining the church in Austin Friars for the use of the Dutch community.[64] In 1561 he was elected a deacon to the Dutch church.[65] A few years later Radermacher appears to have returned to Antwerp, from where he once more emigrated to London

---

[59] Hessels, I, nos. 366, 370, 371.   [60] *Ibid.*, nos. 228, 229
[61] See O. P. Grell, 'Plague in Elizabethan London: The Dutch Response', *Medical History*, 34 (1990), 424–39, especially 429–30.
[62] For Radermacher's birthplace and date of birth see H. Kellenbenz, *Unternehmerkräfte im Hamburger Portugal- und Spanienhandel 1590–1625* (Hamburg, 1954); for his presence in London, see Hessels, III, no. 1660. See also entry *s.v.* Radermacher in *Nationaal biografisch Woordenboek* 13 (Brussels, 1990) col. 674–80.
[63] Hessels, I, no. 330.   [64] *Ibid.*, III, no. 1657
[65] A. A. van Schelven (ed.), *Kerkeraads-Protocollen der Nederduitsche Vluchtelingen-Kerk te Londen 1560–1563* (Amsterdam, 1921), p. 202; like so many other Dutch/Walloon exiles he also had ties to the French Church in London, see Van Dorsten, *Radical Arts*, p. 37.

after the 'Wonderyear' (1566).[66] He took up membership of the small Italian church in London on his return, but cannot have remained a member for long.[67] By August 1571 he had been elected an elder of the Dutch church, a position he kept until he re-emigrated to Antwerp in December 1580.[68]

In Antwerp, Radermacher joined the Reformed community on his arrival and reported back to his consistorial colleague, the minister Gotfried van Winghen, that the Reformed church in Antwerp was prospering and the 'number of followers of Christ was increasing'.[69] At this stage Radermacher was seriously contemplating joining those of his lay consistorial colleagues in London who had decided to serve 'the churches under the cross' during the great apostolic age of the London community in the 1570s. Eventually, he decided against becoming a minister and settled for an eldership within the Antwerp community.[70]

Radermacher who was instrumental in recruiting the London community's student, Assuerus Regemorter, as a minister for the Reformed church in Antwerp, played an active role within the Antwerp community until the city's surrender to the Spaniards in 1585.[71] He then returned to Aachen, his birthplace, where he was elected an elder to the Dutch church in 1589. In 1598 he was made 'Weinmeister' of Aachen, but when shortly afterwards the city returned to Catholicism Radermacher moved via Hamburg, where he was actively importing cloth from England in 1599, to Middelburg. By 1602 he had become an elder in the Reformed church in Middelburg.[72]

Undoubtedly, Johan Radermacher had some unusual interests, not least in hermeticism and the philosophy of John Dee, but his life and career can hardly be described as heterodox. To make him a member of the Family of Love would make a mockery of the overwhelming evidence of his Calvinism.[73]

---

[66] Hessels, I, no. 331.

[67] See R. E. G. Kirk and E. F. Kirk (eds.), *Returns of Aliens Dwelling in the City and Suburbs of London under James I*, (4 vols., Publications of the Huguenot Society of London, X, London 1900–8), I, p. 388; see also K. Bostoen, 'Kaars en Bril: de oudste Nederlandse Grammatica', *Archief. Medelingen van het Koninklijk Zeeuwsch Genootschap der Wetenschappen* (1984), 2–49, especially 11. (I should like to thank Dr O. Boersma for drawing this article to my attention.)

[68] W. J. C. Moens, *The Marriage, Baptismal, and Burial Registers 1571 to 1874 and Monumental Inscriptions, Dutch Reformed Church, Austin Friars* (Lymington, 1884), pp. 146, 209; for Radermacher's continued activity as an elder, see Hessels, III, nos. 223, 231, 535, 675, and II, no. 185.   [69] Hessels, II, no. 185.

[70] See Hessels, II, nos. 188, 189, 190, 194, 197, and III, no. 722 (by 15 July 1581 Radermacher had become an elder in Antwerp); see also Grell, *Dutch Calvinists*, 120–8.

[71] Radermacher was given a gift by the city of Antwerp for negotiating the city's surrender, see *Nationaal biografisch Woordenboek* 13, col. 675.

[72] J. Reitsma and S. D. van Veen (eds.), *Acta der provinciale en particuliere synoden gehouden in de noordelijke Nederlanden gedurende de jaren 1572–1620* (8 vols., Groningen, 1892–9), V (Zeeland), p. 50.

[73] See Hessels, I, no. 334; see also Rademacher's entry in Abraham Ortelius's *Album*

Like his associates Radermacher had a strong interest in history as can be seen from his involvement in Philip Marnix's plans for a history of the Dutch Revolt which was promoted by the national synod which met in Dordrecht in 1578. The Colloquium of the Dutch exiled churches in England which met that year commissioned Radermacher to be responsible for all the relevant material about the English communites to be included in Marnix's history.[74]

Of far greater significance, however, was Radermacher's role in the world of international Calvinism. Together with his friends and colleagues within the Dutch community in London Radermacher constituted an important link in the chain of international Calvinism, which had been strung together in the Reformed diaspora and reinforced through its complex web of emigrations. It was merchants and ministers like him and his friends who through emigration, education and trade created a European Calvinist network, which incorporated most of the leading trading centres, such as Hamburg, Frankfurt, Nuremberg, Amsterdam, Middelburg, London, and briefly in the 1570s and 80s Antwerp. Their social experience of exodus and displacement served to reinforce their feeling of election and sense of belonging to the New Covenant. For such exiles providential history became the mortar which kept the 'faithful' together, providing them with both identity and purpose. It served to actualise biblical time, transporting it into the present, thus reinforcing their sense of election. Among the Reformed exiles gathered in London this is strongly in evidence in the community's long-term concern for providential history, starting with Emanuel van Meteren, Johan Radermacher and Jacob Cool and continued by Simon Ruytinck and Cesar Calandrini.

Amicorum, where he quotes Jeremiah 18, 6 and Paul's Letter to the Romans 8, 28, both places expressing strong providentialism, see Abraham Ortelius, *Album Amicorum*, f. 94, in Pembroke College, Cambridge.

74 See Brummel, *Twee Ballingen*, pp. 148–9 and J. J. van Toorenenbergen (ed.), *Acten van de Colloquia der Nederlandsche Gemeenten in Engeland 1575–1609* (*WMV*, 2, 1, 1872), pp. 49–50. Radermacher was the owner of a considerable library. It contained over 1500 volumes and was predominantly theological in orientation, comprising more than 560 works in Latin and many more in Spanish, Italian, French, English, German and Dutch. His taste appears to have been typically Reformed with the works of Calvin, Beza, Bullinger, Bucer, Zanchius, Ursinus and Oecolampadius especially well represented in several languages. It also comprised a considerable number of historical works which was only matched by his interest in medicine. Radermacher's interest in providential history is clearly indicated by his ownership of a copy of Bullinger's sermons on the Apocalypse and folio-copies of Crespin's and Foxe's martyrologies, not to mention a copy of John Bale's, *The Image of Both Churches*. See *Catalogus Miscellaneus Variorum Ac Insignium Imprimis Latinorum, Italicorum, Hispanicorum, Gallicorum, Anglicorum, Germanicorum, & Belgicorum Librorum Doctissimi viri D. Ioannis Radermacheri Senoris, Mercaturae & literarum studiosi, qui obijt Middelburgi Anno 1617* (Middelburg, 1634), J4r (Bullinger), G1v (Crespin), H2r and v (Foxe and Bale), and K. Bostoen, 'Kaars en Bril', 12.

Index